Governing Cities Through Regions

Governing Cities Through Regions
Canadian and European Perspectives

Roger Keil, Pierre Hamel, Julie-Anne Boudreau, and Stefan Kipfer
editors

WLU PRESS

**WILFRID LAURIER
UNIVERSITY PRESS**

LAURIER
Inspiring Lives.

Wilfrid Laurier University Press acknowledges the financial support of the Government of Canada through the Canada Book Fund for its publishing activities. This work was supported by the Research Support Fund.

Canada

Canada Council   Conseil des arts
for the Arts   du Canada

ONTARIO ARTS COUNCIL
CONSEIL DES ARTS DE L'ONTARIO
an Ontario government agency
un organisme du gouvernement de l'Ontario

Library and Archives Canada Cataloguing in Publication

Governing cities through regions : Canadian and European perspectives / Roger Keil, Pierre Hamel, Julie-Anne Boudreau, and Stefan Kipfer, editors.

Includes bibliographical references and index.
Issued in print and electronic formats.
ISBN 978-1-77112-277-1 (paperback).—ISBN 978-1-77112-261-0 (pdf).—ISBN 978-1-77112-262-7 (epub)

1. Metropolitan government—Canada—Case studies. 2. Metropolitan government—Europe—Case studies. 3. Regionalism—Canada—Case studies. 4. Regionalism—Europe—Case studies. I. Hamel, Pierre, 1947–, author, editor II. Keil, Roger, [date], author, editor III. Kipfer, Stefan, [date], author, editor IV. Boudreau, Julie-Anne, author, editor

JS1710.G65 2016   320.8'50971   C2016-903716-9
                                               C2016-903717-7

Front cover image by Roger Keil. Cover and text design by Angela Booth Malleau.

© 2017 Wilfrid Laurier University Press
Waterloo, Ontario, Canada
www.wlupress.wlu.ca

Contents

Section C: European Regions

Acknowledgements

THIS PROJECT STARTED when the financial crisis changed the world we live in. Urban regions have been the terrains, origins, and recipients of the fallout from this crisis all at once. The authors assembled in this volume have observed, researched, and analyzed "their" urban regions during the past decade as a collective enterprise. Initial meetings in Montreal, Toronto, and Paris set the stage for what turned out to be a longitudinal study of the governance of cities through regionalization in times of crisis. Those meetings and the investigations in various locales were assisted by many across a network of researchers from Vancouver to Katowice, from Manchester to Barcelona. We thank our European collaborators, Susanne Heeg at Goethe University in Frankfurt and Patrick Le Galès at Sciences Po, who hosted a memorable meeting of our group in Paris at the outset of our work.

Some of the researchers for the project and authors in this book began as graduate students and have since moved on. We thank them for their enormous contribution to the success of this enterprise and for their long-lasting interest in the matters of regional governance that underlie this publication: Teresa Abbruzzese, Jean-Paul Addie, Ahmed Allahwala, Antoine Noubouwo, and Christoph Siegl. Others accompanied the project along the way. Among them were Isabelle Bordeleau and Julie Hagan in Montreal and Robert Fiedler, Vera Hoffmann, Evan MacDonough, Sarah Martin, Christine Mettler, and Helen Thang in Toronto. We also owe a big thanks to those who helped edit the manuscript as it evolved: Anna Coté, Jenny Lugar, Claire Major, and Daniel Taylor.

The project was funded by a standard research grant from the Social Sciences and Humanities Research Council of Canada. We are grateful for their support.

Many thanks to the editors at Wilfrid Laurier University Press for their careful work on the manuscript.

Governing Cities Through Regions was, finally, one of the first projects under the roof of the City Institute at York University. CITY's coordinator, Sara Macdonald, deserves a big Thank-You for assisting this work in countless ways.

Roger Keil, Julie-Anne Boudreau, Pierre Hamel, Stefan Kipfer
Toronto, April 2016

Conceptual, Comparative, and General Considerations

CHAPTER 1
Regional Governance Revisited
Political Space, Collective Agency, and Identity

Roger Keil, Pierre Hamel, Julie-Anne Boudreau, Stefan Kipfer, Ahmed Allahwala

THE REGION is back in town. Galloping urbanization (and some shrink-age) has pushed beyond the old notions of historical metropolitanism. City-regions experience, in Edward Soja's terms, "an epochal shift in the nature of the city and the urbanization process, marking the beginning of the end of the modern metropolis as we knew it" (2015: 375). Territorial boundaries of the region are not hard and fast limits to the reach of regional actors; contradictory structures of regions are not territorially bound. These contradictions in real existing regionalism (Addie and Keil 2015) find their expression in new literatures and publication projects to which this book wants to make a contribution.

The flagship journal *Regional Studies*, for example, identified a number of new challenges for regions and regional studies alike that arose after the global financial crisis of 2008–9. Among them have been new urban and regional inequalities across restructured spaces, unsustainable conse-quences of financialization, climate change effects of regional economic growth, and accelerated urbanization itself (Turok et al. 2014). In the *International Journal of Urban and Regional Research*, a set of contribu-tions, some of them written by authors of chapters in this present volume, respond to the significance of the notion of the "regional" itself in the context of today's urban and regional studies. The editors of this debate on "what place for the region," Simon Parker and Michael Harloe, put forth the argument that the region had been a key element of the journal's early intellectual agenda but in quite different terms than it is today. To them, variegated regions and concepts of regions exist in the relevant critical debate: the administrative region, the functional economic region, the networked region, the cultural region, to which we might add the bioregion as a working concept (2015: 365). The contributors to the debate emphasize the region's relevance in North America (Addie and Keil 2015), Africa (Beall et al. 2015), and Europe (Tomàs 2015), and in the literatures that emerge from those variegated experiences. They agree that the city-region remains key to observing processes of urbanization today and analyzing how economic processes and everyday life are contested. One of the main issues raised in these publications is the varying scale and size of regions, which range from the upscaled metropolis and the megaregion (Harrison and Hoyler 2015), all the way to "multiscalar regionalism" in continental realignments (Soja 2015).

The objective of this book is to broaden and deepen our understanding of metropolitan governance through an innovative comparative project that crosses several political cultures, engages with Anglo-American, French, and German literatures on the subject of regional governance, expands the comparative angle from issues of economic competiveness and social cohesion to specific topical and relevant fields of policy, politics, and governance in metropolitan regions such as housing and transportation, and extends comparative work on municipal governance to regional governance. There are three methodological assumptions that anchor our thinking:

1) Uneven and contested economic and demographic growth has characterized many urban regions until the onset of the most recent global financial crisis and beyond.

2) This growth takes shape in a new morphological, spatial, scalar, and topological manner that Europeans have begun to recognize as *Zwischenstadt* or In-Between City (Sieverts 2003; Young, Wood, and Keil 2011).

3) The institutional changes triggered by these growth dynamics are characterized by intense social struggles over territorial, cultural, and political space.

The New Regionalism–Da Capo

The current enthusiasm for the topic builds already on two decades of a new regionalist debate that it is "multi-stranded, draws on diverse theoretical sources, and works with a wide range of different and sometimes incompatible definitions of the terms region and regionalism" (Painter 2008, 346). Following Painter (2008: 343–45), four kinds of new regionalism literatures can reasonably be distinguished: First, one based on economic geographies of industrial agglomeration, untraded interdependencies, and clustering; second, one that emphasizes "soft" institutional supports for regional development of the kind lumped together under this first category; third, one that stresses the "hard" institutions, particularly of the state; and fourth, a discourse Painter considers distinctive for North America: regional governance of expanding metropolitan regions.

In much of the literature on regionalism there is a tendency to rebind the (economically) unbound regions through political processes and institutions (Painter 2008). We see the distinction here between "regional spaces" and "spaces of regionalism," whereby the first is meant to denote the economic and the second the political attempts/realities of constructing regionalism (Jones and MacLeod 2004: 435). Regional spaces are claimed to be the heart of the new globalized economy (Soja 2015), and sometimes counter-hegemonic claims for political and citizenship rights are "bounded" territorially in regions. Generally, there is a distinction between economic flows as an unbounded, relational space, and the more territorialized space of political action (Painter 2008: 347; Jones and MacLeod 2004: 437; MacLeod and Jones 2007).

New uneven political geographies challenge existing schemes for both state intervention and activism at multiple scales. The extent to which one can speak of the emergence of a collective actor at the city-regional scale depends on the degree of consensus in each city-region about such diverging goals as economic competitiveness, cultural and "creative" strategies, and megaprojects on one hand, and social cohesion and environmental sustainability on the other. As citizens refuse to compromise their living environments, they cross traditional urban/suburban, ethnic, racial, and class divides (Young and Keil 2014). Ongoing social and technical infrastructure issues such as sprawl, transportation gridlock, and the provision of water and sewerage services stretch the regional imagination and policy-making capacities of politicians, experts, corporations, and activists across urban regions. Public health concerns are regionalized as cities become more vulnerable to global threats of pandemic disease and classical spatio-institutional arrangements for human security are tested. Resilience and sustainability fixes are being sought at the regional scale (Hudson 2008, 2009a, 2009b; Macdonald and Keil 2012; Keil and Macdonald 2016).

There are theoretical tensions between the various "territorial, scalar, networked, connected" approaches that have been advanced in the debate on regions (see MacLeod and Jones 2007 for an overview). In this respect, MacLeod and Jones (2007: 1186) have argued that "the degree to which one interprets cities or regions as territorial and scalar or topological and networked really ought to remain an open question: a matter to be resolved *ex post* and empirically rather than *a priori* and theoretically." Most critical theoretical concepts that have been advanced to understand urban and regional politics—regime, growth machine, regional regulation, structured coherence—have assumed some form of institutional and territorial overlap if not homology, and some form of regional boundedness of and for politics. This clearly stands in contrast with the predominantly topological understandings of regions as advanced, for example, by Amin (2004), who also proposes an alternative way of thinking of the region politically. Of course, any attempt at creating regional coherence "is always a political construction" (Allen and Cochrane 2007: 1163), as "[r]egions are continuously subjected to multiple spatial and scalar selectivities of state and other dominant organizations," the result of which "is enacted significance, but not coherence" (Langendijk 2007: 1205).

Regional politics is and must be to some degree territorially bounded. Participants in regional politics act both "in" the region (through competition and contestation) and "for" the region (in collective decision-making processes). In most cases, politics "in" and "for" the region presuppose, but also redefine, a territorial notion of the region. In some policy areas— such as in transportation and housing—this reflects the material character of these two infrastructures. Yet, multiple tensions remain between unbounded scaled and networked topologies and the need to get people moved around, housed, employed, cared for, and entertained with the help of material, social and institutional infrastructures and a political system built on some form of territorialized political accountability and legitimacy. We need to remind ourselves here of Harvey's argument that we can really only talk about a *tendency* toward "structured coherence" because regional class alliances are "always unstable," "and its spatial range in any case fuzzy and usually internally fragmented to some degree" (Harvey 1989a: 148). However, beyond this instability, defining the political sphere as an autonomous field helps understand the sustainability of interaction in a given regional territory. Different notions of power are crucial here: "power over" process, things, and people that technocrats and political elites continue to claim can be contested by civil society actors looking above all for "power to" accomplish change (Stone 2006: 23).

Politics "in" and "for" regions are always fundamentally concerned with the construction and deconstruction of identity at the centre of its purpose: "Narratives of regional identity lean on miscellaneous elements:

ideas on nature, landscape, the built environment, culture/ethnicity, dialects, economic success/recession, periphery/centre relations, marginalization, stereotypic images of a people/community, both of "us" and "them," actual/invented histories, utopias, and diverging arguments on the identification of people. These elements are used *contextually* in practices, rituals, and discourses to construct narratives of more or less closed, imagined identities" (Paasi 2003: 477; see also Rodríguez-Pose and Sandall 2008). In many cases, regional governing coalitions—growth machines or regimes—attempt to define *the* identity of a region and appropriate and deploy it for their purposes. In this sense, to quote Harvey, "capitalism builds a physical and social landscape in its own image" (1989a: 162). But each elite image is contested, as the politics of regionalism from below is a crucial if underexposed aspect of regionalism today (Jonas and Ward 2007). The creation of political institutions on the basis of a regional identity, for example, might create a state space to further capital accumulation at the expense of other purposes, but they also might open spaces for alternative designs to meet social welfare needs or goals of ecological sustainability (see Morgan quoted in MacLeod and Jones 2007: 1186–87).

Regional Governance

The concept of governance has enjoyed great popularity in political studies in the past twenty years. We need to further define the use of the term governance for this book and the main tenets of governance theory and its application to urban and regional studies. Jessop (1997: 111; cited in Rhodes 2000: 58) usefully defines governance as the "complex art of steering multiple agencies, institutions and systems which are both operationally autonomous from one another and structurally coupled through various forms of reciprocal interdependence." Much of the literature on governance (and "new governance theory" in particular) assumes the limited power of the state, including the central state, and a process of diminishing state power. Kooiman (2000, quoted in Stoker 2000: 93), for example, argues that "Governance becomes an interactive process because no single actor has the knowledge and resource capacity to tackle problems unilaterally." Similarly, Hirst (2000: 18–19) argues that "governance relates to the new practices of coordinating activities through networks, partnerships and deliberative forums that have grown up on the ruins of the more centralized and hierarchical corporatist representation of the period up to the 1970s. Such negotiated social governance is growing in salience; typically it is to be found at the micro and meso level in cities, regions and industrial sectors." One of the key, if questionable, assumptions of much of the literature on new governance is the limited ability of central government to steer. Our research thus interrogates the role of the state (at all levels) in the governance of metropolitan regions and the process of regional "scale making" (Keil and Mahon 2009).

The normative undertones of much "governance theory" need to be problematized. The focus on the social diversity of policy problems—in addition to their increasing specialization—often leads to a discrediting of traditional forms of political decision-making and state regulation. It naturalizes (post-political) networks of social regulation (see also the critical accounts of governance by Swyngedouw 2005; Walters 2004). Metropolitan regions are often described as socially and geographically difficult to discern, so there seems to be an affinity between the post-modern metropolis and new governance theory. William Walters (2004) articulates three useful points of critique. First, he suggests that governance literatures posit an "antipolitics of governance" by displacing conflict from research agendas (2004: 33). Governance is thus founded on a "liberal notion of consensus and mutual accommodation." Second, and treating "governance as political sociology," governance literatures often mis-state the state. It implies a "qualitative shift in the nature of power" and treats this shift one-sidedly, as a shift toward "diffuse, fragmented, networked, complex" forms of power (38). If governance theory presents contemporary rule as fragmented, decentred, and polyarchic, it does so in part by constructing a sort of golden age in the past when states were "whole." Third, governance literatures work with a "metanarrative of complexity." In this view, "governance represents a political response to growing social complexity," which is either left undefined or captured in vaguely system-theoretical terms.

It is equally important not to overstate the disappearing power of the state. What are the factors that explain the continuing power of the state? What explains the opening up of governance structures to non-state actors? How do we account for variation and divergence in terms of structures, processes, and institutions of regional governance? In this vein, Peters makes the important point that "one problem with some components of the "new governance" literature is that it virtually defines away some of the more interesting parts of the available variance. By appearing to argue that the state or the centre of government is largely incapable of ruling, it appears to refuse to consider that indeed there are cases in which the centre may be effective" (Peters 2000: 42).

The question is: How are regions governed if not along territorially integrated lines? What are the dominant social conflicts arising in this process? We argue that in this era of globalization and neo-liberalization, regional governance is co-constituted by crisis-induced institutional readjustment of regional governance (competitiveness-cohesion, and constantly changing alliances among actors) and social movement politics. While we acknowledge the leading role of state projects and strategies in the formulation of regional governance (Brenner 2004), we also recognize the non-state political projects related to regionalism. Those can include regional food alliances, watershed stewardship, greenbelt initiatives, industry and labour associations, regional labour market policies by private consortia, mobility sharing activities, and the like.

We hypothesize that, first, neo-liberal governmentality has been generalized to the point that it does not have to be established aggressively through explicit policy of rollback and rollout (as happened, for example during the Harris years in Ontario [Keil 2002]); and, second, that the far-reaching crises of regulation that have gripped the capitalist urban system in Canada and Europe *as a result of neo-liberal rollout* now demand new orientations in collective action that involve both "reformed" neo-liberal elite practices and elite reaction to widespread contestation of neo-liberal regulation. We are exploring through our empirical lenses whether we can discern the emergence of a post-neoliberal regional governance regime; i.e., whether urban and regional regulation that was widely seen as having included consecutive phases of rollback and rollout neo-liberalism (Peck and Tickell 2002) has now moved to a third phase, which could be described as "roll-with-it neoliberalization" (Keil 2009). While present in distinct stages or phases at times, especially when advanced with deliberately aggressive "revolutionizing" rhetoric, rollback, rollout, and roll-with-it are really rather "moments" of neo-liberalization that occur simultaneously or in overlapping and mutually re-enforcing fashion (Keil 2009).

The literature on governmentality has been useful in pointing toward new subject positions in a more diversified and unpredictable metropolitan world. This literature has linked considerations of policy and government to critical questions of everyday life (understood from the perspective of a Foucauldian approach to subject-formation). How these questions figure in a reaffirmation of capitalist hegemony in and during networked forms of governance remains critical to an understanding of governance theory in general and the governance of urban regions in particular, especially in the fields of housing and transportation (Addie and Keil 2015; Davies 2011).

Parker and Harloe note that "regionalization is a purposive multi-authored process, ... always prone to negotiation, calculation and the deployment or threat of force among and between its respective constituents" (2015: 365). Their comment points to governance as a central theme of the literature. Governance has been on the agenda of critical urban and regional studies for some time now. In a rapidly urbanizing world, metropolitan regions have become the terrain of conflict and cooperation. This relevance of the region is not to be confused with simple territoriality but must be seen as a product precisely of competing relationalities in global assemblages. Governance does not automatically congeal in regional government. This book concerns itself specifically with differences in regional governance responses to structural forces of globalization. These include state restructuring, continental economic and political integration, fiscal austerity and the demise of Keynesian-inspired national strategies of territorial redistribution and equalization, as well as de- and selective reindustrialization, the resulting disappearance of manufacturing jobs, and the rise in interurban competition. We ask whether there are new regional governance arrangements, what forms they take, and who the actors advocating for regional governance are. At the core of the empirical work from which this book draws is a comparative study of the Canadian cities of Montreal and Toronto and the European cities of Frankfurt and Paris. Work on these cities focused predominantly on housing and transportation. While these cases were investigated with different research intensities, the core comparability was ensured by a joint research protocol. In addition, we present case studies from other Canadian and European cities to highlight the combination of path-dependency and convergence in regional governance across the Atlantic.

Extant research on comparative urban governance has examined a variety of modalities of regional political regulation. We will apply the preliminary lessons of the urban governance debate to the metropolitan regions we see emerging. Urban regions have become an important scale for the governance of highly complex societies in North America and Europe (Brenner 2004; Le Galès 2002), in particular where urban regions serve as the scale and medium of societal differentiation in a competitive neo-liberalizing economy (Brenner 2004).

From Urban Politics to Regional Governance

In the late 1980s a series of important publications signaled the formation of a very productive period of work in urban political economy, urban political studies, and urban geography on the nature of power and politics in cities under the challenge of accelerated restructuring. The publication of Logan and Molotch's *Urban Fortunes* (1987), Clarence Stone's *Regime*

Politics (1989), Harvey's extended essay on the subject in his *The Urban Experience* (1989a; first published in 1985 under different cover), his work on the shift from managerialism to entrepreneurialism (1989b), and Stone and Sanders's (1989) *The Politics of Urban Development*, amounted to a strong starting point for a new generation of debate on the urban political question. This debate coincided, of course, with a fervent exploration of the crisis of Fordism and the after-Fordist restructuring that had begun to change most industrialized countries into a leopard skin of more or less successful, competing regions, some on the upswing, others on a downswing. At the same time, a new geography of global capitalism emerged, with a skeleton of global city-regions as the assumed structural basis (Acuto and Steele 2013; Keil, Ren, and Brenner 2016). The new urban politics and the restructuring literatures focused on cities (and their counterparts, suburbs), on urban economies and on the politics of centrality (for the most part). They asked about power, regimes, and growth-machines, and analyzed those at a scale that was predominantly local, and at best metropolitan (Jonas and Wilson 1999; Lauria 1997).

A departure from this framework toward a more regional set of problematics can be discerned in five areas:

1) We start from the assumption that, as Addie (2013: 209) has argued, "the functional networks of contemporary global urbanization increasingly transcend the jurisdictional, territorially defined boundaries of the metropolis." Any process of spatialization related to regionalization is inevitably tied up in techno-social networks through which they are enabled and constrained, as networks explode and bypass administrative containers (Addie 2013: 193; McFarlane and Rutherford 2008: 365). Accordingly, Addie adds, "the metropolitical relations between city and suburb no longer harness the development trajectories of city-regions." The governance of sub- and exurbanizing regions through three modalities—state, capital accumulation, and private authoritarian governance— provides both the institutional framework and the substance of the metropolitan system of governance (Ekers, Hamel, and Keil 2012; Hamel and Keil 2015). Appropriately, the question has been asked: "where is urban politics"? (Rodgers, Barnett, and Cochrane 2014). The response has recently been more often than not: in the region, in the topological relationalities of urban places, and in the in-between (Young and Keil 2014; Addie and Keil 2015).

2) A related departure points away from (just) territory toward a "relational metropolitics" (MacLeod and Jones 2011: 2460). MacLeod, seeing much metropolitan splintering now at work in

urban regions, adds: "The cumulative effect of such metropolitan splintering may well be over-extending our established interpretations of urban landscapes *and* city politics including the new urban politics. For ... the unfolding twenty-first century urban-regional geography—at times resolutely territorializing yet simultaneously relational, connecting places, material objects and communities trans-territorially—is rendering cities less discernible, prompting a reassessment of the maps, concepts and theories at our disposal to make cities legible" (2011: 2631). Whereas the shift from Fordism-Keynesianism to Post-Fordism-Neo-liberalism included a shift in scalar regulation from the national state to the urban region itself, and while difference among those regions in a global market place became more important than their equality in national urban systems (Brenner 2004), we now encounter an even more dramatic shift away from regionally bounded territoriality to more topologically constructed relationships of metropolitan spaces that are constituted regionally (Amin 2004). New urban governance forms must be viewed as products of complex struggles in networked and hierarchical interrelations among often entirely antagonistic actors.

3) Scale remains a critical concern of regional governance (Keil and Mahon 2009). This leads to the question whether it will be possible to apply literatures on urban power and politics, initiated and deployed for the analysis of *cities* in North America and Europe with variable success, to the scale of the metropolitan *region* and not just the urban core, for which much of this literature was meant to serve (Young and Keil 2014). This upscaling of urban to regional application originated perhaps in, and was influenced by, Harvey's notion of a "structured coherence" that spanned the urban region (defined as the commuter shed). Scholars and practitioners began to think in earnest about regional political growth machines, regional regimes, or, to use a "regulationist" term, a *regional* mode of regulation. The new regionalist literature and its critics have pushed the boundaries of this debate further.

4) This leads to the question of *regional collective agency*. City-regions don't act "naturally" as collective actors but "against a background of transformation of constraints and opportunities for cities, actors within them react by trying to organize a mode of governance that gives the city a status as actor" (Le Galès 2002: 273). Le Galès (2002:10) detects, at the city level in Europe, "a collective decision-making system, common interests—or those perceived as such—integration mechanisms, internal and external representation of the collective actor, and a capacity for innovation." By contrast, in North America, regime theory has explained collective agency of cities as the outcome of contested (development) politics of changing elite and popular groups (Jonas and

Wilson 1999; Lauria 1997; Parker 2004). In this book we propose to expand the traditional collective agency perspective in these approaches from the municipality to the urban region and the metropolitan scale (as others have similarly proposed: Boudreau et al. 2006; 2007; Gibbs et al. 2002; Gibbs and Jonas 2001; Jones 2004). In this view, the collective actor—a generic term subsuming in fact multiple actors converging occasionally and able to build transitory compromises—is always redefining and repositioning itself at the regional scale through new coalitions, territorial compromises (Schmid 1996) and contestations (Leitner, Peck, and Sheppard 2007).

5) While most of the rhetoric and discussion on the "bargaining position" (Savitch and Kantor 2002) of urban areas is linked to the imaginary of cities as places of centrality, the *focus* of this international comparative book, however, is not the urban *centre* but the *urban region*. We will ask, accordingly, to what extent do we see the emergence of a growing web of metropolitan governance? How do various actors conceive the region and what do they think are appropriate modes of governance? While competitiveness and economic success are often associated with the creative economy of urban cores, the focus of this book is the *urban region*, with its growing web of metropolitan governance.

This leads to the central questions this book wishes to address: *Does the globalized urban region get established as a political space* in which collective actors emerge, or does the region act collectively? How is the emergence of a city-regional political space affecting state restructuring processes? What are the impacts of this emergent political space on the political process? Does this new political space affect the political process beyond a simple reshuffling of intergovernmental relations because it is more than a set of institutions and involves (to various degrees) civil society?

What are the dominant *"modalities of governance"* in the respective city-regions? Do we see convergence or divergence in terms of the development of metropolitan governance? What explains divergence? What actors are pushing the creation of regions and for what political purposes? How do the state, the market, and private and civil society modalities of regional governance coincide (Ekers, Hamel, and Keil 2015)?

Are the city-regions predominantly *defined* economically, socially, politically, or bioregionally? How do inherited political cultures and institutional milieux shape the institutionalization and articulation of metropolitan governance structures and processes? What is the role of social conflict and collective action in the respective modalities of governance?

What levels of government promote the creation of city-regional governance? In what way do the specific intergovernmental relations and structures of multi-level governance shape (facilitate or hinder) the creation of regional/metropolitan governance structures?

Canada and Europe: The Comparative Gesture

Comparative perspectives are now at the centre of urban and regional research. Colin McFarlane (2010: 725) has recently noted that "Urbanism has always been conceived comparatively" and goes on to explain the many ways this has been done. It can be stated at the outset that comparative urban research—especially in the context of urban and regional governance—explains socio-spatial relationships in a world of expanded globalized horizons; it has at its disposal sophisticated methods available for comparative research across long distances over longer time frames. There is now a strong set of existing approaches to operationalize such comparisons (Boudreau et al. 2006; 2007; Brenner 2005; 2001; Brenner and Keil 2006; Elwood 2004; Heeg 2001; Heinelt and Kübler 2005; Hitz et al. 1995; Hoffmann-Martinot and Sellers 2005; Jouve and Booth 2004; Kantor and Savitch 2005; Kübler 2006; Langhagen-Rohrbach 2003; Mayer 2012; Newman and Thornley 2005; Pierre 2005; Robinson, 2004; Savitch and Kantor 2002; Savitch and Vogel 1996; 2004; Sellers 2002; 2005).

This book takes up this comparative challenge in a number of ways. At the centre of this project is a loose Canada–Europe comparison with a focus on four specific cities that were examined in depth: Toronto, Montreal, Paris, and Frankfurt. Insights and observations from these cities are complemented by conceptual chapters and individual case studies from regions and cities in Canada and Europe. In using this comparative angle, we are well aware of the fact that the notions of "Europe" and "Canada" are themselves constructed (Tomàs 2015; Phelps and Vento 2015; Keil et al. 2015).

The Canadian experience has many similarities with the European case (Boudreau et al. 2007). We assume for Canada what Brenner has found for Europe: metropolitanization has created "(a) high value added socioeconomic capacities, advanced infrastructures, industrial growth, inward investment, and labor flows [that] are increasingly concentrated within major metropolitan regions, and (b) territorial disparities between core urban regions and peripheral towns and regions [that] are significantly intensifying" (2004: 180). In Canada, urbanization has bifurcated into a pattern of globalized, successful, growing, dynamic city-regions (such as

Calgary, Edmonton, Montreal, Ottawa, Toronto, and Vancouver) and a large number of declining towns (mostly in the old industrial and resource economy belts of the East and the North [Bourne 2004; Simmons and Bourne 2003]). Like their European counterparts, Canadian metropolitan regions are adjusting to new realities of heightened interurban competition (Conference Board 2006; External Advisory Committee 2006). Although Canada and Europe rank among the most urbanized areas in the world, this high degree of urbanization leads to very different urban systems on the ground, with Europe having territorially balanced city systems for the most part and Canada being somewhat densely settled really only along the border with the United States. Due to the growing importance of city-regions in Canada and Europe, there are now increasing tensions between the demands of more complex urban societies and economies and the political constitutions (and institutions) of nation states, which have historically relegated municipalities and regional governments to dependent status (more in Canada and France than in Germany). As the rhetoric of a "regionalized" global economy has taken hold in academic and policy discourse, there is a need for a concerted comparison to understand the new governance frameworks.

Canada is situated between the urban experiences of more market-oriented urban development of the United States and the more state-led developments in European cities (for more on Canadian "in-betweenness," see Young and Keil 2014 and Charmes and Keil 2015). This afforded us excellent comparative perspectives. It is commonly assumed that municipalities in North America are weaker than their European counterparts. As actor and institution, city-regions do not necessarily succeed easily in coping with the challenge of urban governance at a metropolitan scale. To structure their interests and to plan ahead on the basis of shared values remains a real challenge for city-regions. Inequalities and conflicts of interests between the centre and the periphery—to take only one category of division between actors and institutions on the urban scene—are quite strong. On the other hand, the traditional focus on the classical city centre in Europe, in contrast to a comparatively stronger political weight of suburban politics (Walks 2004a; 2004b; 2005) in Canadian urban regions, has prioritized urban over metropolitan issues in Europe and increased the political urgency of regional solutions in Canadian urban regions. Both Canada and Europe have long histories of regional governance, especially structured around suburban expansion in the second half of the twentieth century, when variously interacting dynamics of state, capital, and private authoritarian governance molded territorial governance units at metropolitan and city-regional levels (Ekers, Hamel, and Keil 2015; Hamel and

Keil 2015; Hirt and Kovachev 2015; Keil, Hamel, Chou, and Williams 2015; Phelps and Vento 2015).

The four cities at the heart of this book's empirical chapters (Toronto, Montreal, Paris, and Frankfurt) are the financial centres of their respective countries (and province, in the case of Quebec); they are dynamic, expanding global cities, characterized by multicultural diversity and immigration, and have seen periods of heightened conflict across their urban regions. The cities provide a focus for much regional and national economic, cultural, and political development, but perhaps more importantly, they are the hubs through which their regional economies are articulated within the wider international system. The four city-regions (as well as the additional case study regions) are all in OECD countries. They are part of what some call the global North. Assuming variation in the response to globalization, we have chosen cities with resources that give them the capacity to build strategies in this competitive global era. At the same time: (1) these cities have followed different historical paths (due to their geographical location, but also to their economic and political role within their respective nation-states; (2) these cities do not have access to the same resources (public and private); (3) these cities seem to opt for different (particular) alternatives in response to market trends; (4) urban regimes (and thus strategies elaborated by actors) in these cities are built on different foundations and with different actor-constellations.

The four case city-regions perform comparable functions as first and second tier global cities, including (1) their rapid integration into newly globalized urban networks; (2) their explosive demographic growth; (3) their strongly altered built environment; (4) their constantly shape-shifting flexible economies; (5) their increasing social polarization; (6) their stressed urban natural environments; and (7) their vanguard cultural function in their respective countries. However, their place-specific path dependencies and contextual embedding within historically and geographically distinct political-economic and social networks has produced divergent and contested urban morphologies, administrative boundaries, and governance regimes (Brenner and Theodore 2002; Sancton 2005; Brenner and Keil 2006; Langhagen and Fischer 2005; Reiss-Schmidt 2003; Le Galès and Lorrain 2003).

Furthermore, combined with these overall growth trends, and reflecting their role as ports of entry and diverse sites of multiculturalism, the metropolitan populations of the four cities contain significant proportions of first generation immigrants and people of colour resulting from historically and geographically specific migration flows. These spatial data highlight the rapid, dynamic expansion of these city-regions beyond their spatial, political-administrative boundaries. In turn, this suggests the theoretical and methodological difficulties in treating metropolitan governance regimes as within spatially distinct, self-contained administrative units, thus reflecting the significance of conducting comparative urban governance research through analyzing the networks and processes engaged with by key actors beyond place-bounded conceptions of the contemporary city-region.

The additional Canadian cases—Vancouver, Winnipeg, and Calgary—share some of the characteristics of Toronto and Montreal, but they are also quite distinct in their path dependencies and current problem constellations. Vancouver and Calgary (the latter at least until the oil prices took a hit in 2014) are among the economic success stories in Canada. Based on real estate and oil, they replicate some of the land development and resource industrial histories for which the Canadian political economy has been known since the beginning of colonization (Keil and Kipfer 2003). Winnipeg, on the other hand, is a typical slow-growth city that shares some experiences with the otherwise very different post-socialist Katowice. The additional European cases, Manchester-London in the UK, the Katowice region in Poland, Barcelona in Spain, and the Italian regions, reflect various European traditions of urban governance—the Mediterranean, the Anglo-Saxon and the Eastern versions—and contrast well with the French and German cases. The British experience shows similarities with Frankfurt and Paris as well as with Toronto. Barcelona shares with Montreal the regional peculiarity of regional dissent from their respective Spanish and Canadian nation states.

Most existing comparative urban research focuses on intracontinental (Europe, Latin America) case studies or bilateral case studies in closely similar environments (New York–London; Toronto–Montreal; Toronto–Los Angeles). Our comparison, largely based on qualitative research methods, adds to this body of literature through a strong emphasis on transatlantic variances and similarities (Brenner 2001; Mills et al. 2006). This effort falls in line with existing research that has recently begun to recognize the transnational, multiscalar character of metropolitan governance and politics (Hoffmann-Martinot and Sellers 2005; Sellers and Hoffmann-Martinot 2006; (www.usc.edu/dept/polsci/sellers/IMO/IMO English.htm; see also a project called Métropolisation et Société [MéSo] funded by the Fonds québécois de recherche sur la société et la culture [FQRSC]; for an overview of the European case, see Kübler 2006). Our project builds on and takes further the transatlantic perspective chosen in these endeavours.

We believe that urban and regional research cannot simply transfer or extrapolate theories and concepts without considering the political, institutional, and cultural contexts in which city-regions are embedded. However, international comparative research allows us to creatively test emerging theoretical ideas and concepts that will help us to rethink and reevaluate—and possibly modify—old theoretical certainties. And it is international comparative research that is the most important source for this kind of theory building. What we have in mind here is the refinement of theoretical, methodological, and empirical thinking that reveals the productive dialectic of general tendencies and specific conditions found in today's thoroughly globalized policy environment (McCann and Ward 2010; on the benefits of comparative urban research and theory-building, see Häußermann et al. 2008). We particularly propose a new focus for comparative urban research. Building on the constructivist foundation of much of the scalar literature (Keil and Mahon, 2009; Brenner 2004), we do not invoke the comparison of self-contained places in this work. Although we recognize the spatial boundedness of certain policy and planning processes in all regional governance, we are not proposing to work with an areal representation of these city-regions. We are comparing processes, not areas. We are specifically examining the margin of manoeuvre that individual actors have in these processes. Terrains of resistance will reveal and help us identify the conflict lines of the governance system (Mayer 2006).

For the purpose of this book project, we have sought to analyze the influence of a multitude of political scales on structures and processes of regional governance. For Toronto and Montreal as well as the additional Canadian cases this would be the federal, provincial (quasi-national for Quebec), and municipal scales. For the European case studies, continental integration has also been assumed to have facilitated the increasing importance of regions (see also Tomàs 2015 on this question).

The emergence and characteristics of structures of urban governance are influenced by the inherited institutional milieu and dominant political culture. DiGaetano and Strom (2003: 363) define institutional milieux as "the complexes of formal and informal political and governmental arrangements that mediate the interactions among the structural context, political culture, and political actors." For our purposes, this leads to the following question: what role do metropolitan regions play in the national regime of territorial-economic regulation in the various countries? DiGaetano and Strom (2003: 365) argue that "political systems are not just the sum of their formal political structures, however. Political institutions in each city are linked together by informal arrangements we call modes of governance…. Comparing urban modes of governance requires distinguishing those informal political relationships that determine *how* cities are governed." They propose an integrated approach to comparative urban governance combining structural, cultural, and rational actor approaches to cross-national comparison, and claim that "different combinations of intergovernmental and cultural settings … furnish different environments for the development of local political institutions and modes of governance" (2003: 375).

We may propose, initially, that the political culture of English Canada and Great Britain is the least statist and most privatist, with those of post-communist Poland and (Mediterranean) Italy following closely. The political culture of France is the most statist, with those of Germany, Quebec, and Catalonia not too far removed. This would mean, for example, that the extent of institutional change toward partnerships is less pronounced in the Paris region than in Toronto. Based on this reasoning, we can pose the following questions and hypotheses. To what extent can we discern a process of convergence in the emergence of regional governance structures, practices, and arrangements? Can we see similar patterns emerging across the Atlantic and across the various national contexts? What accounts for different trajectories in the development (or lack thereof) of regional governance arrangements?

The structure of this book is as follows. We begin with Julie-Anne Boudreau and Pierre Hamel's introduction to the notions of social agency and collective action, which points beyond the more institutional and structural categories advanced in the opening chapter. Margit Mayer takes this perspective further in her chapter on movements and politics in an expanding (sub)urbanizing region. Susanne Heeg explores the governance role of the place entrepreneurs and investors who rule the built environment in European cities. Bernd Belina and Ute Lehrer, finally, deconstruct the monolithic idea of an urban region by introducing the notion of the constantly emerging scalar fix in large metropolitan regions which recognizes the sub-regional actors across a metropolitan area and their struggle for identity in a globally competing urban region.

In the next section, various contributors examine the diversity of urban and regional governance in Canada. Toronto receives the most attention here, as there is a chapter on the state of the art in the region (Roger Keil and Jean-Paul Addie) as well as on transportation (Addie) and housing (Teresa Abbruzzese) as special policy areas that were subject to specific empirical research. This Toronto subsection is followed by chapters by

Pierre Hamel on Montreal, Christopher Leo on Winnipeg, Byron Miller on Calgary, and Emmanuel Brunet-Jailly with Ève Arcand on Vancouver.

In the next section, we look at the European cases. Roger Keil and Christoph Siegl undertake a study of regional governance in Frankfurt, while Stefan Kipfer, Julie-Anne Boudreau, Pierre Hamel, and Antoine Noubouwo look closely at governance constellations in contemporary Paris. These cases are followed by Mark Whitehead's chapter on governance in the Katowice region, Mariona Tomàs's discussion of regional governance in Barcelona, and Simon Parker's explanation of the traditions and current state of urban and regional governance in Italy. Finally, Ian Gordon, Michael Harloe, and Alan Harding compare and contrast the London and Manchester city-regions in the context of urban and regional governance in the UK. A short conclusion with a few summary observations and lessons by the editors concludes the book.

References

Acuto, M. and W. Steele, eds. 2013. *Global city challenges*. Basingstoke: Palgrave Macmillan.

Addie, J.-P. D. 2013. "Metropolitics in motion: The dynamics of transportation and state re-territorialization in Greater Chicago and Toronto." *Urban Geography* 34(2): 188–217.

Addie, J.-P. D. and R. Keil. 2015. "Real existing regionalism: The region between talk, territory and technology." *International Journal of Urban and Regional Research* 39(2), March: 407–17. DOI: 10.1111/1468-2427.12179.

Allen, J. and A. Cochrane. 2007. "Beyond the territorial fix: Regional assemblages, politics and power." *Regional Studies* 41(9): 1161–75.

Amin, A. 2004. "Regions unbound: Towards a new politics of place." *Geografiska Annaler* 86B: 33–44.

Beall, J., S. Parnell, and C. Albertyn. 2015. "Elite compacts in Africa: The role of area-based management in the new governmentality of the Durban city-region." *International Journal of Urban and Regional Research* 39(2), March: 390–406. DOI: 10.1111/1468-2427.12178.

Boudreau, J-A., P. Hamel, B. Jouve, and R. Keil. 2006 "Comparing metropolitan governance: The cases of Montreal and Toronto." *Progress in Planning* 66(1): 7–59.

Boudreau, J.A., P. Hamel, B. Jouve, and R. Keil. 2007. "New state spaces in Canada: Metropolitanization in Montreal and Toronto compared." *Urban Geography* 28(1): 30–53.

Bourne, L. S. 2004. "Beyond the new deal for cities: Confronting the challenges or uneven urban growth." *Research Bulletin* (21). Toronto: Centre for Urban and Community Studies, University of Toronto.

Brenner, N. 2001. "World city theory, globalization and the comparative-historical method: Reflections on Janet Abu-Lughod's interpretation of contemporary urban restructuring." *Urban Affairs Review* 36(6): 124–47.

———. 2004. *New state spaces: Urban governance and the rescaling of statehood.* Oxford: Oxford University Press.

———. 2005. "Rethinking the logic of comparison in critical urban studies: Promises and pitfall of the globalization debates." Paper presented at the Association of American Geographers Annual Meeting, Denver, April 8.

Brenner, N. and R. Keil, eds. 2006. *The global cities reader.* London and New York: Routledge.

Brenner, N. and N. Theodore. 2002. "Cities and the geographies of 'actually existing neoliberalism.'" *Antipode* 34(3): 349–79.

Charmes, E. and R. Keil. 2015. "The politics of post-suburban densification in Canada and France." *International Journal of Urban and Regional Research.* Published online July 15, 2015. DOI: 10.1111/1468-2427.12194.

Conference Board of Canada. 2006. *Canada's hub cities: A driving force of the national economy.*

Davies, J. S. 2011. *Challenging governance theory.* Bristol: Policy Press.

DiGaetano, A. and E. Strom. 2003. "Comparative urban governance: An integrated approach." *Urban Affairs Review* 38: 356–95.

Ekers, M., P. Hamel, and R. Keil. 2015. "Governing suburbia: Modalities and mechanisms of suburban governance." In P. Hamel and R. Keil, eds., *Suburban governance: A global view* (19–48). Toronto: University of Toronto Press.

Elwood, S. 2004. "Partnerships and participation: Reconfiguring urban governance in different state contexts." *Urban Geography* 25(8): 755–70.

External Advisory Committee on Cities and Communities. 2006. *From restless communities to resilient places.* Ottawa: Infrastructure Canada.

Gibbs, D. C. and A. E. G. Jonas. 2001. "Rescaling and regional governance: The English regional development agencies and the environment." *Environment and Planning C: Government and Policy* 19: 269–88.

Gibbs, D. C., A. E. G. Jonas, and A. While. 2002. "Changing governance structures and the environment: Theorising the links between economy and environment at the local and regional scale." *Journal of Environmental Planning and Policy* 4: 123–38.

Hamel, P. and R. Keil, eds. 2015. *Suburban governance: A global view.* Toronto: University of Toronto Press.

Harrison, J. and M. Hoyler, eds. 2015. *Megaregions: Globalization's new urban form?* Cheltenham: Edward Elgar.

Harvey, D. 1989a. *The urban experience.* Baltimore: Johns Hopkins University Press.

———. 1989b. "From managerialism to entrepreneurialism: The transformation in urban governance in late capitalism." *Geographiska Annaler* 71B: 3–17.

Häußermann, H., D. Läpple, and W. Siebel. 2008. *Stadtpolitik.* Frankfurt: Edition Suhrkamp.

Heeg, S. 2001. *Politische Regulation des Raums. Nationalstaat—Metropolen—Regionen.* Berlin: Edition Sigma.

Heinelt, H. and D. Kübler, eds. 2005. *Metropolitan governance in the 21st century: Governing capacity, democracy and the dynamics of place.* Milton Park: Routledge.

Hirst, P. 2000. "Democracy and governance." In J. Pierre, ed., *Debating governance: Authority, steering, and democracy* (13–35). Oxford: Oxford University Press.

Hirt, S. and A. Kovachev. 2015. "Suburbia in three acts: The East European story." In P. Hamel and R. Keil, eds., *Suburban governance: A global view* (177–97). Toronto: University of Toronto Press.

Hitz, H., R. Keil, U. Lehrer, K. Ronneberger, C. Schmid, and R. Wolff, eds. 1995. *Capitales fatales: Urbanisierung und Politik in den Finanzmetropolen Zürich und Frankfurt*. Zürich: Rotpunkt-Verlag.

Hoffmann-Martinot, V. and J. Sellers, eds. 2005. *Metropolitanization and political change*. Germany: Verlag fuer Sozialwissenschaften.

Hudson, R. 2009a. "Resilient regions in an uncertain world: Wishful thinking or practical reality?" *Cambridge Journal of Regions, Economy and Society* 3(1): 1–15.

Hudson, R. 2009b. "The costs of globalization: Producing new forms of risk to health and well-being." *Risk Management* 11(1): 13–29. Accessed at www.jstor.org/stable/27670017.

Hudson, R. 2008. "Material matters and the search for resilience: Rethinking regional and urban development strategies in the context of global environmental change." *International Journal of Innovation and Sustainable Development* 3(3/4): 166–84. DOI: 10.1504/IJISD.2008.022224.

Jessop, B. 1997. "The governance of complexity and the complexity of governance: Preliminary remarks on some problems and limits of economic guidance." In A. Amin and J. Hausner, eds., *Beyond markets and hierarchy: Interactive governance and social complexity* (111–47). Cheltenham: Edward Elgar.

Jonas, A. E. G. and K. Ward. 2007. "Introduction to a debate on city-regions: New geographies of governance, democracy and social reproduction." *International Journal of Urban and Regional Research* 31: 169–78.

Jonas, A. E. G and D. Wilson, eds. 1999. *The Urban growth machine: Critical perspectives two decades later*. Albany: SUNY Press.

Jones, M. 2004. "The regional state and economic regulation: Regional regeneration or political mobilisation?" In D. Valler and A. Wood, A., eds., *Local and regional economies: Institutions, politics and economic development*. Aldershot: Ashgate.

Jones, M. and G. MacLeod. 2004. "Regional spaces, spaces of regionalism: territory, insurgent politics and the English question." *Transactions of the Institute of British Geographers* 29(4), December: 433–52.

Jouve, B. and P. Booth, eds. 2004. *Démocraties métropolitaines*. Sainte-Foy: Presses de l'Université du Québec.

Kantor, P. and H. Savitch. 2005. "How to study comparative urban development politics: A research note." *International Journal of Urban and Regional Research* 29(1): 135–51.

Keil, R. 2002. "'Common sense' neoliberalism: Progressive conservative urbanism in Toronto, Canada." *Antipode* 34(3): 578–601.

———. 2009. "The urban politics of roll-with-it neoliberalization." *CITY* 13(2–3), June–September: 231–45.

———. 2011. "Global cities: Connectivity, vulnerability and resilience." In B. Hahn and M. Zwingenberger, eds., *Global cities*. Heidelberg: Universitätsverlag Winter.

Keil, R., P. Hamel, E. Chou, and K. Williams 2015. "Modalities of suburban governance in Canada." In P. Hamel and R. Keil, eds., *Suburban governance: A global view* (80–109). Toronto: University of Toronto Press.

Keil, R. and S. Kipfer. 2003. "The urban experience." In L. Vosko and W. Clement, eds., *Changing Canada: Political economy as transformation* (335–62). Montreal and Kingston: McGill-Queen's University Press.

Keil, R. and S. Macdonald. 2016. "Rethinking urban political ecology from the outside in: Greenbelts and boundaries in the post-suburban city." *Local Environment*. DOI: 10.1080/13549839.2016.1145642.

Keil, R. and R. Mahon. 2009. *Leviathan undone? Towards a political economy of scale*. Vancouver: University of British Columbia Press.

Keil, R., X. Ren, and N. Brenner. 2016. *The globalizing cities reader*. London: Routledge.

Kübler, D. 2006. "Metropolitan governance and democracy in Western Europe: A comparative perspective." Paper presented at the IMO conference, Montreal, April 24 and 25.

Lagendijk, A. 2007. "The accident of the region: A strategic relational perspective on the construction of the region's significance." *Regional Studies* 41(9): 1193–208.

Langhagen-Rohrbach, C. 2003. "Stadtplanung in Frankfurt am Main und in Zürich. Wer macht die Stadt?" *Rhein-Mainische Forschungen* (124): 181–206.

Langhagen-Rohrbach, C. and R. Fischer. 2005. "Regionalwerkstatt Frankfurt-Rhein-Main. Region als Prozeß?" *Standort* 29(2): 76–80.

Lauria, M. 1997. *Reconstructing urban regime theory: Regulating urban politics in a global economy*. Thousand Oaks, CA: Sage.

Le Galès, Patrick. 2002. *European cities: Social conflicts and governance*. New York: Oxford University Press.

Le Galès, P. and D. Lorrain. 2003. "Gouverner les très grandes métropoles." *Revue Française d'Administration publique*: 105–17.

Leitner, H., J. Peck, and E. Sheppard, eds. 2007. *Contesting neoliberalism: Urban frontiers*. London: Guilford Press.

Logan, J. and H. Molotch. 1987. *Urban fortunes*. Berkeley: University of California Press.

Macdonald, S. and R. Keil. 2012. "The Ontario greenbelt: Shifting the scales of the sustainability fix?" *Professional Geographer* 64(1): 125–45.

MacLeod, G. 2011. "Urban politics reconsidered: Growth machine to post-democratic city?" *Urban Studies* 48(12), September: 2629–60.

MacLeod, G. and M. Jones. 2007. "Territorial, scalar, networked, connected: In what sense a 'regional world'?" *Regional Studies* 41(9): 1177–91.

———. 2011. "Renewing urban politics." *Urban Studies* 48(12): 2443–72.

Mayer, M. 2006. "Contesting the neoliberalization of urban governance." In H. Leitner, J. Peck, and E. Sheppard, eds., *Contesting neoliberalism: Urban frontiers* (90–115). New York: Guilford Press.

———. 2012. "Metropolitan research in transatlantic perspective: Differences, similarities, and conceptual diffusion." In D. Brantz, S. Disko, and

G. Wagner-Kyora, eds., *Thick space: Approaches to metropolitanism*, 105–22. Bielefeld: transcript 2012.

McCann, E. and K. Ward. 2010. "Relationality/territoriality: Toward a conceptualization of cities in the world." *Geoforum* 41: 175–84.

McFarlane, C. 2010. "The comparative city: Knowledge, learning, urbanism." *International Journal of Urban and Regional Research* 34(4): 725–42.

McFarlane, C., and J. Rutherford. 2008. "Political infrastructures: Governing and experiencing the fabric of the city." *International Journal of Urban and Regional Research* 32: 363–74.

Mills, M., G. G. Van de Bunt, and J. De Brujin. 2006. "Comparative research: Persistent problems and promising solutions." *International Sociology* 21(5): 619–32.

Newman, P. and A. Thornley. 2003. *Planning world cities: Globalization and urban politics*. London: Palgrave Macmillan.

Paasi, A. 2003. "Region and place: regional identity in question." *Progress in Human Geography* 27: 475–85.

Painter, J. 2008. "Cartographic anxiety and the search for regionality." *Environment and Planning A* 40: 342–61.

Parker, S. 2004. *Urban theory and the urban experience: Encountering the city*. London and New York: Routledge.

———. 2006. "Managing the political field: Italian regions and the territorialisation of politics in the Second Republic." *Journal of Southern Europe and the Balkans* 8(2), August: 235–53.

Parker, S. and M. Harloe. 2015. "What place for the region? Reflections on the regional question and the International Journal of Urban and Regional Research." *International Journal of Urban and Regional Research* 39(2), March: 361–71. DOI: 10.1111/1468-2427.12175.

Peck, J. and A. Tickell. 2002. "Neoliberalizing space." In N. Brenner and N. Theodore, eds., *Spaces of neoliberalism* (33–57). Boston: Blackwell.

Peters, B. G. 2000. "Governance and comparative politics." In J. Pierre, ed., *Debating governance: Authority, steering, and democracy* (36–53). Oxford: Oxford University Press.

Phelps, N. A. and A. T. Vento. 2015. "Suburban governance in Western Europe." In P. Hamel and R. Keil, eds., *Suburban governance: A global view*. Toronto: University of Toronto Press.

Pierre, J. 2005. "Comparative urban governance." *Urban Affairs Review* 40(4): 446–62.

Reiss-Schmidt, S. 2003. "Zwischen Heimatgefühl und Weltstadtanspruch: Die Region Frankfurt/Rhein-Main." *DISP* 152(1): 80–86.

Rhodes. 2000. "Governance and public administration." In J. Pierre, ed., *Debating governance: Authority, steering, and democracy* (54–90). Oxford: Oxford University Press.

Robinson, J. 2006. *Ordinary cities: Between modernity and development*. London: Routledge.

Rodgers, S., C. Barnett, and A. Cochrane. 2014. "Where is urban politics?" *International Journal of Urban and Regional Research* 38(5), September: 1551–60. DOI: 10.1111/1468-2427.12143.

Rodríguez-Pose, A. and R. Sandall. 2008. "From identity to the economy: Analyzing the evolution of the decentralization discourse." *Environment and Planning C: Government and Policy* 26: 54–72.

Sancton, A. 2005. "The governance of metropolitan areas in Canada." *Public Administration and Development* 25: 317–27.

Savitch, H. and P. Kantor. 2002. *Cities in the international marketplace.* Princeton: Princeton University Press.

Savitch, H. and R. Vogel, 2004. "Suburbs without a city: Power and city-county consolidation." *Urban Affairs Review* 39: 759–90.

Savitch, H. and R. Vogel. eds. 1996. *Regional politics: America in a post-city age.* Thousand Oaks, CA: Sage.

Schmid, Christian. 1996. "Urbane Region und Territorialverhältnis—Zur Regulation des Urbanisierungsprozesses." In M. Bruch and H.-P. Krebs, eds., *Unternehmen Globus* (224–54). Münster: Westfälisches Dampfboot.

Sellers, J. M. 2002 "The nation-state and urban governance toward multilevel analysis." *Urban Affairs Review* 37(5): 611–41.

———. 2005. "Re-placing the nation: An agenda for comparative urban politics." *Urban Affairs Review* 40(4): 419–45.

Sellers, J. M. and V. Hoffmann-Martinot. 2006. "Toward an agenda for the Transnational study of local and metropolitan governance." Paper presented at the UAA Annual Meeting, Montreal, April 19–22.

Sieverts, T. 2003. *Cities without cities: An interpretation of the Zwischenstadt.* London and New York: Spon Press.

Simmons, J. and L. Bourne. 2003. *The Canadian urban system 1971–2001: Responses to a changing world.* University of Toronto: Urban and Community Studies. www.citiescentre.utoronto.ca/Assets/Cities+Centre+2013+Digital +Assets/Cities+Centre/Cities+Centre+Digital+Assets/pdfs/publications/ Research+Papers/200+Simmons+Bourne+2003+Canadian+Urban+System.pdf

Soja, E. 2015. "Accentuate the regional." *International Journal of Urban and Regional Research* 39(2), March: 372–81. DOI: 10.1111/1468-2427.12176.

Stoker, G. 2000. "Urban political science and the challenge of urban governance." In J. Pierre, ed., *Debating governance: Authority, steering, and democracy* (91–109). Oxford: Oxford University Press.

Stone, C. 2006. "Power, reform and urban regime analysis." *City & Community* 5(1): 23–38.

———. 1989. *Regime politics.* Lawrence: University of Kansas Press.

Stone, C. and H. Sanders. *The politics of urban development.* Lawrence: University of Kansas Press.

Swyngedouw, E. 2005. "Governance innovation and the citizen: The Janus face of governance-beyond-the-state." *Urban Studies* 42(11), October: 1991–2006.

Tomàs, M. 2015. "If urban regions are the answer, what is the question? Thoughts on the European experience." *International Journal of Urban and Regional Research* 39(2), March: 382–89. DOI: 10.1111/1468-2427.12177.

Turok, I., D. Bailey, G. Bristow, J. Du, U. Fratesi, J. Harrison, A. Lagendijk, G. MacLeod, T. Mickiewicz, S. Usai, and F. Wishlade. 2014. "Editorial: New times, shifting places." *Regional Studies* 48(1): 1–6. DOI: 10.1080/00343404.2014.884357.

Walks, R. A. 2004a. "Place of residence, party preferences, and political attitudes in Canadian cities and suburbs." *Journal of Urban Affairs* 26(3): 269–95.

———. 2004b. "Suburbanization, the vote, and changes in federal and provincial political representation and influence between inner cities and suburbs in large Canadian urban regions, 1945 to 1999." *Urban Affairs Review* 39(4): 411–40.

———. 2005. "The city-suburban cleavage in Canadian federal politics." *Canadian Journal of Political Science* 38(2): 383–413.

Walters, W. 2004. "Some critical notes on 'governance.'" *Studies in Political Economy* 73 (Spring/Summer): 27–46.

Young, D. and R. Keil. 2014. "Locating the urban in-between: Tracking the urban politics of infrastructure in Toronto." *International Journal of Urban and Regional Research*. DOI: 10.1111/1468-2427.12146.

Young, D., P. B. Wood, and R. Keil, eds. 2011. *In-between infrastructure: Urban connectivity in an age of vulnerability.* Kelowna, BC: Praxis (e)Press.

CHAPTER 2

Social Agency and Collective Action in the Structurally Transformed Metropolis
Past and Future Research Agendas

Julie-Anne Boudreau and Pierre Hamel

Introduction

THE VARIOUS CHAPTERS of this book show how expanding metropolitan regions are transforming cities through new types of linkages. Cities and metropolises are related to global networks of social, economic, and cultural transactions that are "engendering novel spatial formats" (Sassen 2011: 101). They bring about "new state spaces" in various economic and political contexts (Brenner 2004; Xu and Yeh 2011: 3). Although there is a relative general consensus on the importance of these transformations, there is still little work focusing on the role social actors, and more generally of citizens, in these processes. In other words, research on structural changes in contemporary cities has not paid sufficient attention to agency and collective action. On the other hand, social movement theory, concerned at the outset with the conduct of social actors, has been trapped in a reductionism that gives priority to actors' discourse, leaving aside the dialectical interaction between structural constraints and the factors favourable to agency or to collective behaviour.

In this chapter, we wish to propose an alternative reading of citizenship and collective action in a context of globalized urbanity. First, we begin by critically assessing the work of social movement theory in order to propose a conceptual way out of the type of reductionism that has characterized social movement theory to date. In that respect, we rely on a perspective based on a dialectical understanding of action. Even though this perspective brings back a traditional sociological concept, namely "ambivalence," it provides a framework for understanding the normative orientation of action. Relying on a functionalist vision between an actor and an end, this perspective also introduces a tension between the subjective components of action and the objective world out there. As expressed by social actors engaged in processes of collective action, hesitation between a position of standing back and a position of participation remains strong. Secondly, we develop a sociological definition of citizenship grounded in the 1990s debates around the notion of urban citizenship. Finally, we will suggest an agenda for future research.

Understanding the Ambivalence of Collective Action

In sociology, as well as in other fields of social sciences, the study of new forms of collective action is not recent (Fligstein and McAdam 2012). It goes back to the 1960s and 1970s, when researchers sought to understand what was happening in society around them and began to speak in terms of "new social movements." From that point, a series of different theoretical hypotheses—responding to one another—were tested with the aim of better understanding the specificities of these new forms of action or new collective actors. Action and actors mobilized around diverse social, cultural, and political issues and a wide variety of practical problems related to health, the environment, sexual and gender identities, the recognition of fundamental rights against discrimination, and so on.

As of the 1960s, studying social movements became a highly contested field of research (Diani 1992). Multiple confrontations prevailed among researchers in their attempts to explain the origins and scope of these "new movements" active outside of the workplace by comparison to the labour movement of the late nineteenth and early twentieth centuries. Over the last fifty years, researchers have rarely agreed about the object of inquiry, or whether we should call it social movements, collective action, or a novel form of experience (Cefaï 2007). On one hand, social movements are defined on the basis of their grievances and conflicting interests in regard to dominant actors. On the other hand, however, social movements are understood as being central to social change, bringing in a sense of totality that other actors are not necessarily fighting for (Hamel, Lustiger-Thaler, and Maheu 2012).

In addition, despite the abundance of theoretical and empirical research, including case studies, comparative and historical analyses, and cross-national observations (Snow, Soule, and Kriesi 2004; Filieule, Mathieu, and Péchu 2009), it remains very difficult to satisfactorily explain the emergence of collective action. Why on some occasions do people decide to mobilize and at other times they do not? Why do citizens sometimes choose collective action to combat social injustice and social inequality and at other times do not? And what kind of movement is mobilized on what occasion (Walder 2009)?

The sociology of social movements has made some important progress in identifying the necessary conditions for the expression of collective action (Hamel, Lustiger-Thaler, and Maheu 2012). A consensus exists among researchers concerning the role of organizational factors, the resources available, and the framing activities by lead actors in the development of social mobilization (Snow and Soule 2010). Still, researchers are often trapped in a very simplistic reading of action, unable to recognize the tension existing between structural trends and contradictions that are constraining actors' behaviours and the normative dimensions involved in actors' subjectivity.

By highlighting the *ambivalence of action*, the approach we wish to focus on starts with a theoretical definition of the object. Social movements as well as collective action are theoretical constructs that hardly coincide with social actors themselves. A fruitful analysis of collective action relies on accepting that there is considerable distance between real social actors and the theoretical concept of collective action mobilized by the researcher. As Louis Maheu (2005) explains, one way out of the narrow understanding of collective action expressed by social movement theory is to overcome the phenomenological bias of most studies of collective action—researchers focusing mainly on actors' discourse and representation—through better articulating social actors' ability to act with the structural constraints they face. The analytical focus is shifted onto the ambivalence of action, bringing to the fore the fact that social movements define the social in a paradoxical way. These collective actors are simultaneously stuck in antagonistic, conflict-ridden relationships and in a dialogue with opponents with whom they share the same common field of social relations.

We will not explain this approach in detail here. Suffice it to say that we wish to highlight actors' *behaviour* in the current modern and global context by considering the ambivalence of action. Consistent with this perspective, we would like to stress the fundamental characteristics of social movements, starting with their willingness to challenge relations of domination. It is important to reiterate the fact that movements are defined by their capacity to challenge relations of domination. In the case of contemporary social movements, their contestation is often deployed in the institutional field in comparison to historical or classical movements evolving most of the time outside institutions. In that sense, we agree with the following: "Social movements contest the relations of domination that prevail on the political scene and beyond, that is, within social and cultural life. They also bring in a vision of totality regarding the social. They contest dominant models of decision-making, starting with what is transpiring in the institutional field" (Hamel, Lustiger-Thaler, and Maheu 2012, 178).

From then on, it is important to recall the opposition between two standpoints for looking at movements: one defined from a sector-based approach—interested in actors' behaviour defined as a component of a partial social system—and the other referring to a horizontal point of view able to question the ability of movements to "bring in a vision of totality about the social" (ibid.). From this second perspective, even though action repertoire and actors' strategies remain important, they are not the main focus of the analytical process. Social movements are considered a point of entry to better understand the social structure at work in a specific societal context. The capacity of actors to introduce a "vision of totality about the social" is congruent with their personal and collective commitment in regards to their normative convictions. This can be materialized in what we label a process of *re-composition of action*. Consequently, in order to assess the extent to which collective action succeeds in achieving actors' intended purpose, one can look at the dual processes of action *de-composition* and action *re-composition* that are often related precisely to the ambivalence of action. To what extent we are witnessing a *re-composition* of action, despite the structural contradictions actors are facing, is a good way to assess the scope of collective action. One can consider that action is re-composed when there is a process of disruption with dominant forces in regard to their privileges and routines. It is only when such a disruption prevails—even if it is often preceded by a de-composition of action or mixed with it—that social actors are able to successfully challenge relations of domination defined and reproduced by the elites.

It is also in that respect that the process of collective action is inherently ambivalent. It can change direction, tactics, enemies, and targets at any time. The variation in the social, cultural, or political orientation of movements is something difficult to assess (Walder 2009). The actors in place and the lines of conflict can never be taken for granted. It is not a matter of whether action is sometimes working toward activists' intended goals, or whether it appears as if they are "losing." It is something diversified and nuanced, with which social movement theory has had difficulty coping with in the past (Cefaï 2007). Most of the time, social movement theory has been trapped in a simplistic assessment of mobilizations, blind to the social, cultural, and political diversity of actors' engagement or to the processes of decomposition and re-composition of action as it unfolds.

The central tenet of social movement theory is that the state-citizen relationship is inherently antagonistic in that it is based on competitive and often confrontational claim-making. Yet, this is only one way to inter- act with the state. Negotiation is another (for instance, bribing a corrupted official). Hiding from the state is yet another way (e.g., squatting). Many individuals prefer to hide, or keep a low profile, rather than confront authorities, and this can also be considered a form of political engagement. Bayat (2004: 81, 94) suggests that political subjectivity comes more in the form of a "quiet encroachment of the ordinary," which he defines as "noncollective, but prolonged, direct action by individuals and families to acquire the basic necessities of life (land for shelter, urban collective consumption, informal work, business opportunities, and public space) in a quiet and unassuming, yet illegal fashion.... the struggle of the actors against the authorities is not about winning a gain, but primarily about defending and furthering what has already been won." In other words, political action is not necessarily socially and politically transformative or revolutionary. Another example is the reemergence of urban riots, a type of action that cannot be directly linked to articulated political demands. French suburbs, Athens, London, and other European cities have become sites of what many have described as "pre-political" protest by young people. For some groups, riots can be the only way to enter the political space and find a way to negotiate (Rea 2006; Balibar 2007).

It is with this sensitivity to the unpredictability and ambivalence of action in mind that we now move forward and examine the notion of citizenship, a requisite one for thinking of collective action in the context of global modernity.

Toward an urban sociological definition of citizenship

The notion of citizenship is first and foremost a normative reality that can be traced back to the Hellenic public sphere, where it was possible for citizens to deliberate public affairs among equals. Due to its abstract char- acter—the status of a person, including rights and duties, living within the territorial and political limits of a state under the rule of law—this nor- mative model has been criticized by modern thinkers. Behind abstract equality, many authors decried, lay social exclusion: women and slaves could not take part in open public discussion. From that point, modern citizenship developed on the basis of a different conception of equality, grounded in the idea of the universality of human nature (Thériault 1999).

This directly contributes to the definition of human rights. With the democratic revolutions of the eighteenth century, modern liberal states began with the idea of achieving a certain equalization of social conditions for everyone. In the modern context, however, equality remained an abstract principle. Modern societies remained unequal societies. In Western capitalist societies, even though redistributive social policies defined by welfare states helped in reducing classical inequalities, new social inequalities related to social and cultural—gender or ethnic—differences continued to grow (Dubet 2000).

Modern citizenship, as conceived by T. H. Marshall (1950), was in many ways the result of the struggles and claims of the workers' movement of the late nineteenth and early twentieth centuries. There is now an urgent need to update this perspective in order to take into account the recent transformations in social organizations and within an economic system that is under structural pressure from multiple globalizing processes, including the formation of city-regions and mega city-regions. In this sense, the "right to the city," which was not even conceived as important by Marshall, can no longer be avoided in any definition of social citizenship. This implies that we must consider different perspectives on social conflicts, social struggles, and mobilizations that are thriving in city-regions.

With the rise of anti-globalization movements at the end of the 1990s, the relation between urban movements and resistance to neo-liberal globalization inspired much research on the dialectic between global and local as new sites of resistance (e.g., Hamel, Lustiger-Thaler, and Mayer 2000; Merrifield 2002; INURA 2003; Köhler and Wissen 2003; Conway 2004). After coming together in the World Social Forum and other global gatherings, these movements sparked off new alliances within urban movement scenes. The interplay of these different clusters of "glocal" movements, from Occupy to the Indignados, from the Social Fora to localized anti-gentrification struggles, has created a novel multiscalar architecture of urban protest.

This said, even though most of the time urban movements are connected to local territorial scales—meaning in relation either to a specific local area, a neighbourhood, or within city limits—as the "urban" in Henri Lefebvre's perspective is increasingly linked to city-regional dimensions, social actors have no choice but to re-define their action toward jumping scale with a particular emphasis on city-regions. This was to be expected. However, so far, in fact, urban protest has rarely succeeded in being redeployed at the metropolitan scale. Even though social actors find the city-regional scale relevant in terms of representation—they agree that the social and cultural image of the city can no longer coincide with the traditional or classical definition of the city—it does not mean that they easily define action strategy from this standpoint.

Without suggesting that the idea of urban citizenship should replace traditional definitions of citizenship (either liberal or social citizenship), one cannot but accept that with the emergence of global urbanity and urbanism, the "right to the city" is more than ever on the social and political agenda. As David Harvey (2008) has mentioned, the crises that are emerging around the new trends of urbanization are giving rise to new conflicts between affluent and deprived people, making possible new alliances among workers and urbanites. This is what the "right to the city" can convey by revising the definition of human rights and consequently the notion of citizenship: "The right to the city is far more that the individual liberty to access to urban resources: it is a right to change ourselves by changing the city. It is, moreover, a common rather than an individual right since this transformation inevitably depends upon the exercise of a collective power to reshape the processes of urbanization. The freedom to make and remake our cities and ourselves is, I want to argue, one of the most precious, yet most neglected of our human rights" (Harvey 2008, 23).

The notion of urban citizenship stresses the importance of recognizing the legitimacy of political action for people without legal citizenship (Holston 1995; Holston and Appadurai 1996; Sassen 1996; Dikeç and Gilbert 2002; Mitchell 2003). Looking at the urban history of the United States, Robert Beauregard insists that with the "loss of bourgeois urbanity and of faith in the government came a loss of civic virtue" (2006: 187). He argues that renewed urban civic life passes through the restoration of public space, social segregation being incompatible with the idea of citizenship. For that matter, "urban citizenship entails obligations to share public space, to be tolerant of diverse lifestyles and forms of expression, and to contribute to the democracy and cultural life that supports these rights and obligations" (ibid., 188).

The right to be politically active even without legal citizenship status brings forth the issue of the possibility or ability to act. The studies referred to in the previous paragraph locate political mobilization in everyday life, because people *inhabit* a world in which they wish to act. However, by focusing on the legitimacy to act without legal citizenship, this literature remains unable to explain why people decide to act. We consequently need to seek other theoretical resources to construct a truly sociological definition of citizenship that would enable us to go beyond the shortcomings of social movement theory and its reductionist reading of collective action.

Even if nowadays the state continues to play an important—if not decisive—role in regulating social and economic problems in cities, the traditional and centralized approach to public action proved inadequate to meet emerging social demands. The conflict between redistribution and recognition as conceived by Nancy Fraser (2003) needs to be addressed from a critical standpoint. Consequently, it is crucial to question the "state-centrism" of both social movement theory and the urban citizenship literature from a pragmatic perspective and to take into account the recent forms of collective action operating in areas that were previously considered external to the political field (Keucheyan 2010). Starting in the 1990s, sociologists began to rethink the notion of citizenship as a central element of "new critical theories" (ibid.) and to reject Marshall's state-centric approach. This meant that our understanding of citizenship needed to go beyond the acquisition of rights, including rights to the city.

Recent social and cultural transformations beyond the scope of state regulation have to be considered more closely. This is what the notion of "governmentality" (*gouvernementalité*), as elaborated by Michel Foucault, can help to highlight. From this perspective, it is possible to look at citizenship less as a "legitimate institution" generated from the sovereign powers of the State, and instead more as specific social practices through which power is implemented. This means tearing down the strong opposition between subject and sovereign (between governing and governed people) which was characteristic of Marshall's definition of social citizenship, and entering the field of government: "To govern means 'to structure the possible field of action of others' (Foucault); it is an action over action, a conduct of others' conduct. This means that the governed are active subjects; in the same moment that they obey, they are free to act within a range of possible actions. In this way, government is the source of a critical attitude (or counter-conducts); it always involves some resistance against it, expressing the will not to be governed, or at least not in such a way." (Procacci 2001: 347). With this point of view, we are distancing ourselves from a classical definition of citizenship that is usually based on an abstract designation of citizens. The emphasis instead is on activity and new forms of subjectivity and conduct. Thus, citizenship is grounded in the social field. It that respect, it can open a breach in the political rationality of liberal rights. From then on, it is possible to better understand that "[t]he political transformation of the relationship of citizens to the state originates neither at the level of the state nor at the level of individuals, but at the level of society, and independent field of practices and knowledge with respect to the juridical and the economic sphere" (ibid., 350).

This reading of citizenship coincides with Béatrice Durand's (2010) contention that despite their weight, nations do not have a monopoly over democratic political organizations. This is similar to authors who highlight the erosion of citizen political power as we witness the weakening of legislative powers in contemporary states (Sassen 2010). These analyses invite us to consider citizenship through the lens of emerging social practices, collective action, or new forms of citizen participation in urban affairs. But they also implicitly initiate debates around issues of social integration, as the increasing weight of minorities and/or cultural and religious pluralism has been transforming in a radical way the social landscape of city-regions.

Political action in the city is deeply entrenched in everyday life, which means that it is defined by interdependencies, unpredictability, and non-strategic actions. This challenges some of the underlying assumptions of social movement theory, which has been constructed on an antagonistic ontology aiming to uncover the workings of domination in order to foster resistance. But, resistance is also about unorganized, diffuse, and non-strategic action that constantly shifts goals and directions, and that creates numerous ruptures. The researcher's duty, therefore, is to look for political acts in unexpected places, encountering urban resistance in practices of guerrilla gardening, in the occupation of public parks, or in alternative sports such as skateboarding, collective kitchen, or dumpster diving.

An agenda for future research

We end this chapter with proposals for future research based on the theoretical propositions offered here. We began by highlighting the difficulties of social movement theory by (1) taking into account the structural constraints on action and (2) explaining why people mobilize at certain moments and in certain places and not at other times and spaces. We then explored how urban citizenship literature has tried to overcome these difficulties by shifting the analytical lens to contemporary urban action at multiple scales, from the anti-globalization movement to local immigrant rights or anti-gentrification struggles. One of the important contributions of this literature is that it takes the structural transformations occurring in our cities as its starting point. It challenges the state-centric approach that has characterized social movement theory and the various definitions of citizenship, including Marshall's social citizenship, by grounding the analysis not in legal rights and responsibilities, but in everyday urban reality as it is affected by global economic, cultural, and political forces. However, the notion of urban citizenship remains unable to satisfactorily explain why people decide to act or not.

Building on the insights from urban citizenship literature, we argued that two further theoretical challenges are required if we are to better analyze contemporary collective action. Firstly, rather than focus the research on the normative goals of social movement actors and whether they achieved them or not, it might be more fruitful to zoom in on the process of action itself, on the unfolding of action. This entails recognizing that action is highly ambivalent—as a conflict unfolds, actors shift allegiances, goals, and targets. It is these processes of de-composition and re-composition that we need to uncover, because it is generally here that there is a rupture in the linearity of strategically planned action and that relations of domination are truly challenged. These ruptures, changes of direction, and diffusion of goals are often responses to shifting structural constraints. As we described at the end of section one, this approach enables us to see forms of political engagement we previously could not see with the tools of social movement theory (riots, practices of negotiation, hiding, etc.).

This brings us to a second challenge: it is crucial to question the "state-centric" bias of social movement theory and even of urban citizenship literature (to a certain degree). We suggest instead taking a more pragmatic standpoint and bringing to the forefront such forms of collective action that have long been considered outside of the political realm. We rely on Foucault's work on "governmentality" to demonstrate how collective action operates in a field of action composed of various chain reactions rather than fixed antagonistic interests (the dominant and the dominated, the State and civil society). We focus on unintended, diffuse, non-strategic small acts. This means the question of why people mobilize becomes irrelevant, because we zoom in on actions that are not intentionally, willfully, strategically political. In this context, we see the role of critical research as uncovering such acts, assembling them, and giving them political coherence.

Crudely speaking, critical social sciences have been marked by two opposite forms of thought: structural determinism influenced by Marx on the Left, and radical individualism influenced by Hayek on the Right. Both streams of thought sought to challenge and revolutionize reformist social sciences that were developing in the twentieth century in order to consolidate the Keynesian and corporatist nation-state. As the hegemony of such a frame of thought and socio-political form of organization eroded at the end of the 1960s with the rise of new social movements, colonial struggles, and profound global economic transformations, new critical voices made their way in social sciences under the labels of post-modernism and post-colonialism.

Critique, as Bruno Latour (2004) suggests, is a matter of assemblage more than dissection (modern rationality) and dichotomies (Marxism). By this he means that in order to uncover new sites of potential critical intervention, we ought to stop breaking reality into neat, manageable boxes (geographically by focusing on clearly defined states and societies, but also analytically through the categorization and formalization of a reality otherwise impossible to describe).

The critical perspective offered by Marxism and social movement theory, with its fundamentally dichotomous view of the world (dominant-dominated, capital-labour, Global North–Global South) is problematic as it hides the messiness of reality. Assembling ideas, voices, and facts should be the task of the researcher, to reproduce or render the messiness of urbanity. As social scientists, we do not have a monopoly over determining what is unjust by, for instance, revealing the structural workings of capitalism. Assembling ideas, facts, and voices can be a channel for acting against spatial injustices. This means encouraging flexible forms of comparison. The objective of comparing should not be simply to highlight contrasts and similarities, but rather to use a different lens to shed light on a local process. For instance, in comparing homeless activism in the U.S. to slum dwelling in India, Ananya Roy does not hesitate to "use one site to pose questions of another" because she sees transnationalism as an "interrogative technique" (Roy 2003: 466).

Concluding Remarks

Social movements and other forms of political action, deeply entrenched in everyday life and expressing a sense of singularity, remain fragile. Even though collective behaviours can at times manifest in an explicit resistance to social and political exclusion, their recognition by elites or by a large public is never gained once and for all. These actors are continually experiencing a kind of discrimination that only a pragmatic reference to the principle of equality—in defence of minority rights—may help to overcome. In voicing their difference, these social actors are looking for social justice. In doing so, they are challenging the universal and abstract definition of the individual that is consistent with an intangible definition of citizenship. In its place, a social definition of the individual is suggested. In this context and as a last resort, as republican universalism no longer guarantees an equal treatment of all citizens, it is the promotion of a specific identity that can represent a valuable resource against contempt (Ion 2012). This observation brought us to review the theory of social movements and to suggest a definition of citizenship able to reflect the social and cultural diversity characterizing expanding metropolitan regions.

References

Balibar, E. 2007. "Uprisings in the banlieues." *Constellations* 14(1): 47–71.
Bayat, A. 2004. "Globalization and the politics of the informals in the global south." In A. Roy and N. Al Sayyad, eds., *Urban informality: Transnational perspectives from the Middle East, Latin America, and South Asia* (79–102). Lanham, MD: Lexington Books.
Beauregard, R. A. 2006. *When America became suburban*. Minneapolis: University of Minnesota Press.
Brenner, N. 2004. *New state spaces*. Oxford: Oxford University Press.
Cefaï, D. 2007. *Pourquoi se mobilise-t-on? Les théories de l'action collective*. Paris: La Découverte.
Conway, J. 2004. *Identity, place, knowledge: Social movements contesting globalization*. Toronto: Fernwood.
Diani, M. 1992. "The concept of social movement." *Sociological Review* 40(1): 1–25.
Dikeç, M. and L. Gilbert. 2002. "Right to the city: Homage or a new societal ethics?" *Capitalism, Nature, Socialism* 11(2): 58–74.
Dubet, F. 2000. *Les inégalités multipliées*. La Tour d'Aigues: Les éditions de l'Aube.
Durand, B. 2010. *La nouvelle idéologie française*. Paris: Stock.
Filieule, O., L. Mathieu, and C. Péchu, eds. 2009. *Dictionnaire des mouvements sociaux*. Paris: Presses de Science Po.
Fligstein, N. and D. McAdam. 2012. *A theory of fields*. Oxford: Oxford University Press.
Fraser, N. 2003. "Social justice in the age of identity politics: Redistribution, recognition and participation." In N. Fraser and A. Honneth, eds., *Redistribution or recognition? A political-philosophical exchange* (7–109). London: Verso.
Hamel, P., H. Lustiger-Thaler, and M. Mayer, eds. 2000. *Urban movements in a globalising world*. London: Routledge.
Hamel, P., H. Lustiger-Thaler, and L. Maheu. 2012. "Global social movements: Politics, subjectivity and human rights." In A. Sales, ed., *Sociology today: Social transformations in a globalizing world* (171–94). London: Sage.
Harvey, D. 2010. "The right to the city." *New Left Review* 53: 23–40.
Holston, J. 1995. "Spaces of insurgent citizenship." *Planning Theory* 13: 35–51.
Holston, J. and A. Appadurai. 1996. "Cities and Citizenship." *Public Culture* 8: 187–204. International Network for Urban Research and Action, ed. 2003. *The contested metropolis: Six cities at the beginning of the 21st century*. Basel: Birkhäuser-Verlag.
Ion, J. 2012. *S'engager dans une société d'individus*. Paris: Armand Colin.
Keucheyan, R. 2010. *Hémisphère Gauche. Une cartographie des nouvelles pensées critiques*. Paris: La Découverte.
Köhler, B. and M. Wissen. 2003. "Glocalizing protest: Urban conflicts and global social movements." *International Journal of Urban and Regional Research* 27(4): 942–51.

Latour, B. 2004. "Why has critique run out of steam? From matters of fact to matters of concern." *Critical Inquiry* 30: 225–48.

Maheu, L. 1995. "Introduction." In L. Maheu, ed., *Social movements and social classes: The future of collective action* (1–17). London: Sage.

———. 2005. "Mouvements sociaux et modernité avancée. Le retour obligé à l'ambivalence de l'action." In L. Guay, P. Hamel, D. Masson, and J.-G. Vaillancourt, eds., *Mouvements sociaux et changements institutionnels. L'action collective à l'ère de la mondialisation* (9–34). Québec: Presses de l'Université du Québec.

Marshall, T. H. 1950. *Citizenship and social class and other essays.* Cambridge: Cambridge University Press.

Merrifield, A. 2002. "Seattle, Quebec, Genoa: Après le déluge . . . Henri Lefebvre?" *Environment and Planning D: Society and Space* 20(2): 127–34.

Mitchell, D. 2003. *The right to the city: Social justice and the fight for public space.* New York: Guilford Press.

Procacci, G. 2001. "Governmentality and citizenship." In K. Nash and A. Scott, eds., *The Blackwell companion to political sociology* (342–51). Oxford: Blackwell.

Rea, A. 2006. "Les émeutes urbaines: Causes institutionnelles et absence de reconnaissance." *Déviance et Société* 30(4): 463–75.

———. 2003. "Paradigms of propertied citizenship: Transnational techniques of analysis." *Urban Affairs Review* 38(4): 463–91.

Sassen, S. 1996. "Whose city is it? Globalization and the formation of new claims." *Public Culture* 8: 205–23.

———. 2010. "Vers une multiplication d'assemblages specialisés de territoire, d'autorité et de droits." In A. Petitat, ed., *Être en société. Le lien social à l'épreuve des cultures* (63–77). Québec: Presses de l'Université Laval.

———. 2011. "Novel spatial formats: megaregions and global cities." In J. Xu and A. G. O. Yeh, eds., *Governance and planning of mega-city regions: An international comparative perspective* (101–26). New York and London, Routledge.

Snow, D. A. and S. A. Soule. 2010. *A primer on social movements.* New York and London: W. W. Norton.

Snow, D. A., S. A. Soule, and H. Kriesi, eds. 2004. *The Blackwell companion to social movements.* Oxford: Blackwell.

Thériault, J.-Y. 1999. "Présentation. La citoyenneté: entre normativité et factualité." *Sociologie et sociétés* 31(2): 5–13.

Walder, A. G. 2009. "Political sociology and social movements." *Annual Review of Sociology* 35: 393–412.

Xu, J. and A. G. O. Yeh. 2011. "Governance and planning of mega-city regions. Diverse processes and reconstituted state spaces." In J. Xu and A. G. O. Yeh, eds., *Governance and planning of mega-city regions: An international comparative perspective* (1–25). New York and London, Routledge.

CHAPTER 3

Movements and Politics in the Metropolitan Region

Margit Mayer

Introduction

SPRAWLING METROPOLITANIZATION and other forms of concentrated as well as extended landscapes of urbanization challenge existing schemes for both state intervention and social movement activism. They challenge traditional state strategies because they crisscross existing territorially based regulatory bodies. And urban movements that have traditionally targeted municipal actors or mobilized against "outside forces" threatening the social and cultural fabric of their urban spaces are increasingly challenged to identify targets responsible for large-scale transformations affecting the socio-spatial conditions of familiar and not so familiar urban terrains.

While some research has been undertaken exploring the reterritorialization of the state and emergent forms of regional governance, not much systematic work is done with regard to movement activism in and for the changing urbanized regions, and even less with a transnationally comparative perspective. Some authors have put forth hypotheses about how the emergence of new political institutions on the basis of some regional coherence might open spaces for alternative designs to better meet criteria of ecological sustainability or social welfare, but most of the speculations about how governance rearrangements at the metropolitan scale might advance democratic possibilities remain just that: speculations, without either empirical or other systematic evidence undergirding such hopes.

This chapter will not be able to present conclusive research confirming specific relationships between new governance arrangements in the increasingly boundless metropolitan areas and (chances for) progressive activism, but it suggests some directions where it might be productive to look. It does so by pointing to instances of incipient forms of mobilization that transcend the models of classical urban-based activism and to some networks that span the (eroding) boundaries between classical urban centres and what are no longer "peripheries."

New Types of Urban and Regional Politics

Because of the increased importance of urban regions, and to better address their peculiar issues such as traffic and environmental problems as well as economic competitiveness, urban planners and theorists have been highlighting the need for greater city-regional intergovernmental cooperation. Many urban and regional theorists have claimed that governance has found an increasingly relevant scale in the region, and that new regulatory and decision-making capacities have emerged at this scale (cf. Jonas and Ward 2007; Harrison 2008; Harrison 2010). In fact, however, institutional reform of metropolitan areas has remained elusive (Kantor 2008; Lefèvre and Weir 2012). In spite of various national and regional state efforts since the 1960s, most major North American and European metropolitan areas by the end of the twentieth century did not have true metropolitan governments. This perceived deficit led to new approaches emphasizing the promotion of innovative forms of regional engagement that would draw civil society and local governments into regional problem-solving networks (Lefèvre and Weir 2012: 631; Orfield 2002). Yet, even with some federal incentives, signs of political cooperation within metropolitan areas have remained scant, and stable institutional arrangements capable of addressing the problems faced by large urban areas have rarely been built.

In Europe, the 1990–2010 decades saw many institutional experiments and reforms, but most of them "have not yet been implemented" (Lefèvre and Weir 2012: 633). In Germany, for example, the first metropolitan authority was created in 1994, when Stuttgart and the surrounding municipalities, with the support of the state of Baden-Württemberg, constructed the Verband Region Stuttgart (VRS). In 1996, a similar creation was born in Hannover, and in 2009 in Aachen. These authorities were set up to balance the sharpening inequalities between central cities and their surrounding regions. In 1999, the French government approved a law creating new metropolitan governments in all areas over 500,000 residents, and the Italian government passed a law to facilitate the establishment of Metropolitan Cities—but most of these institutional reforms have not been carried through (Lefèvre and Weir 2012: 633–34). Even when imple-mented, the resulting structures have been weak: today, the VRS has very few responsibilities, a weak budget, and almost no authority over local governments. While formal institutional reform had limited impact, over the last two decades a variety of more experimental projects to promote metropolitan governance, such as Regional Development Agencies or stra-tegic planning processes frequently run by complex organizational struc-tures, have been quite effective. Also noteworthy are more informal pro-cesses of political coordination that enable city-regions to achieve competitiveness even without much formal intergovernmental innovation. Kantor (2008) argues that governmental actors rely on tacit recognition of mutual governmental interests that become institutionalized to sustain patterns of policy convergence: not coordination, but cooperation in the sense of well-institutionalized patterns of intergovernmental relations that are sustained by continuous political investment to support, if only tacitly, common policy objectives of regional scope (Kantor 2008: 116). On the Canadian side, a variety of efforts have been under way to build city-regional political space, with varying results: the path toward city-region-alism in the Toronto region has been "more fluid, ad hoc and project-based than in Montreal, where it is virtually absent" (Boudreau et al. 2007: 47).

Since city-regional territories are, as all social space, produced through material politics and struggles framed at diverse scales—simultaneously down-scaled from the global scale and upscaled from the local geographies of competition and conflict (Jonas and Ward 2007: 172)—the emerging patterns of regional governance reflect an enormous diversity of place-spe-cific national and regional legacies and traditions. Thus, the European forms of regional collaboration—around specific policy sectors such as public transport and planning (e.g., the Frankfurt case discussed by Keil and Siegl in this volume)—have been rather broad and inclusive and backed by central and sub-national governments. European national gov-ernments have strongly supported local governmental consolidation and mergers, and local governments had little power to block central govern-ment reform efforts. Also, European central governments are usually more directly involved in the government of urban areas than in North America, and have been more willing to intervene in local matters (Lefèvre and Weir 2012: 627–28). By contrast, in North America instances of regional col-laboration function mostly as business campaigns to market the region. Here, regionalism's greatest successes have been business-backed, proj-ect-specific efforts designed to improve the long-term economic viability of the region. In particular, the U.S. experience has been marked by a traditional bias in favour of local control, and uniquely shaped by the strength of its own peculiar type of suburbanism.

While the conventional American suburbs—white and wealthy—have increasingly been superseded by more heterogeneous ones (in class as well as ethnic terms) and complemented by new types of "Metroburbia USA" (Knox 2008)—also known as edge cities, technoburbs, boomburgs, or peri-urban development—the fastest growing outer suburbs have been "almost all overwhelmingly white, wealthier than the rest of the country and conservative leaning" (Giroux 2005 quoted in Peck 2011: 903). Here, gating is "just one manifestation of a much wider and deeper privatization of (sub)urban governance ... yielding an expansive complex of home-owner associations, quasi-private community management regimes, and 'association-governed communities', or AGCs" (Peck 2011: 904). Politi-cally, the expansion of these types of edge cities can thus be read as "eva-sion and subversion of pan-urban regulatory coordination" and thus as "a counter to big-city government and its 'redistributionist machinery'" (Peck 2011: 908–9).

The U.S. case provides the extreme pole on a broad spectrum of spa-tially and politically more and less pronounced Fordist compromises, but suburban politics have usually centred, both in North America and in Europe, on land development and a pro-growth agenda as part of the Fordist spatial fix where the traditional suburb served primarily a residen-tial function in the metropolitan division of labour. The European context is shaped by its unique (sub)urban history, where (industrial) suburbs first emerged between the two world wars with the construction of poor-quality individual cottages for the working classes. After the Second World War, the centrality of the historic central city was not challenged by urban sprawl and suburbanization as in North America, but suburbs did expand here as well. With the support of national governments, huge, mostly spatially peripheral, complexes of affordable housing (housing estates in Britain, *grands ensembles* in France) were built, separate from the sprawling sub-urbanization (supported by tax policies) carried out by the middle classes. As a result, European central cities never became as intrinsically associated with "urban" problems such as crime, poverty, joblessness, etc., as in North America (cf. Ekers et al. 2012: 411–12).

On both continents, the ideology and politics of suburbia has been subject to transformation "even from the moment of quintessential 1950s mass suburban developments in the United States" (Phelps and Wood 2011: 2598). As a wider range of business interests beyond the landed interests began to engage in the politics of (post)suburbia, and as edge cities became sites of innovation and external economies themselves, the politics of postsuburbia began to revolve not only around the exchange value of property associated with the conversion of agricultural land into new suburbs, but increasingly around economic development, transport, and other infrastructure issues. In an effort to ameliorate some of the negative effects of the Fordist spatial fix, postsuburban politics also began to focus more on the *qualities* of the urban environment, adding protection of residential amenities, attention to design (e.g., pedestrian-friendly) and consumption issues to its repertoire (Phelps and Wood 2011: 2599, 2603).

There are other incarnations of (post)suburbs besides the flourishing ones just mentioned: declining and shrinking suburbs and deteriorating former social housing estates on the outskirts of cities emerged long before the 2008 crisis. In these types of regions, the pursuit of growth has played a more central role in local politics than the amenity-enhancing strategies practised in competitive boomburbs. But since predatory lending and speculation were widespread in inner as well as outer suburbs and exurbs, many of these promising spaces on the frontier of particularly U.S. (post)-suburbia have had to abandon even growth strategies (cf. Tobar 2012; Saillant and Marcum 2012).

Shared by all the national and regional path dependencies and variations in the shift from (more or less) Keynesian sub/urbanism to the contemporary neo-liberal landscapes of urbanization is the general tendency of the erosion of Fordist economic institutions and Keynesian welfare states. These Fordist arrangements had been prioritizing (though to varying degrees) the national scale over subnational ones, and thus their erosion created a need for new territorial structures to draw down regulatory authority from sovereign nation states. Increasingly, city-regions became the new building blocks of the global economy (cf. Scott et al. 2001; Jonas and Ward 2007: 169), but these developments and the discourses pushing them took on nationally specific forms.

With the relatively stronger political weight of suburban powers in Canadian and U.S. urban regions, the North American arrangements prioritized metropolitan issues far sooner than was possible in Europe, where the traditional focus on the classical city centre has continued to highlight urban over metropolitan issues (cf. Mayer 2012). But everywhere, suburbanization processes have become subsumed within emerging "megalopolis spaces" (Lang and Knox 2009). The peculiar sociospatial patchworks of concentrated urban regions emerging on both continents are made up of varying compositions of different formations such as middle-class suburbs, outer suburban development, "out-of-town" retail and office developments, as well as (more densely populated) *banlieues* (encircling the cities of France)[1] or peripheral housing estates harbouring de-industrialized (British, German, Dutch etc.) working-class and/or migrant communities in desolate areas. Corresponding to this diversity, a variety of political responses not quite geared toward the new "relational reality of the in-between city" (Young and Keil 2010: 93) have been observable. These responses to the new forms of urbanization are still very much in flux and often not yet aligned with the contours of the growth of decentralized development. Nevertheless, clearly discernable are incipient efforts at creating regional policies and institutions, each characterized by locally specific traditions of strategic planning, practices of collaboration, and incremental institutional building across today's patchworks of splintered and segregated regions.

These policies appear to either adapt (in the European case) the neo-liberal urban development policy repertoire to "voids" on the map of regional development (such as declining peripheries that appear ripe for development), or to diffuse from the edge cities that had provided extremely fertile ground for their emergence (in the U.S. case). Substantively, this repertoire includes the following strategies:

- Signature events and various forms of festivalization are tried-and-tested strategies for accelerating investment flows into areas with "potential," and are today applied to formerly peripheral and dilapidating outskirts such as Wilhelmsburg, south of Hamburg's city centre, which has been upgraded through an International Garden Show and the International Building Exhibit (cf. Arbeitskreis Umstrukturierung Wilhelmsburg 2013). Such strategies give rise to efforts by "right to the city" movements to mobilize the affected populations.

- Entrepreneurial forms of governance, out-sourcing, and the use of task- and project-driven initiatives were first developed in edge cities and in efforts to enhance coherence across fragmented jurisdictions. The setting up of special agencies to deliver target-driven initiatives that focus on specific concrete objectives proved useful in allowing developers and investors to play more leading roles in (informalized) political processes. Today, the proliferation of shadow and private governmental forms is widely employed in urban as well as suburban and regional contexts, with the effect that a burgeoning private sector technocratic strata is now increasingly mobilized in the service of highly particularistic interests—giving rise to struggles over (the growing absence of) representative democracy (cf. Phelps and Wood 2011: 2602).

- A further key element of neo-liberal urban politics has been the privatization not just of public services, but also of space: this, too, was first widely applied in the rollout of exurban settlements, where gated communities first emerged and collective infrastructures were scant from the beginning. Nowadays, even the "European city"—the envy of many American planners and urban scholars—is no longer the "public," "open," and "accessible" space its normative definition (if not its historical reality) suggests, but is riddled with restricted access areas and private spaces dedicated to elite consumption (cf. Novy and Mayer 2009), triggering a variety of protests by those who have been excluded.

• Finally, the neo-liberal tool kit to deal with the exacerbating polarization processes is not only applied within central cities, but replicated across the ever-widening patchwork of regional urbanization. While potentially high-value pockets are being turned over to more and more intense forms of gentrification including pricy micro-apartments,[2] the area-based programs that were previously applied to "blighted" neighbourhoods have become superseded by blunt displacement policies pushing the poor out to further peripheries or into invisible interstices of blight. While formerly marginal social housing complexes have their top floors turned into penthouses, new slums are erected in internal and external "peripheries"—with container housing (for asylum seekers outside of German towns, for welfare recipients outside of Polish towns) or official and unofficial tent cities across North America (Vollmann 2011; National Coalition for the Homeless 2010).

It is the content of these policies that triggers conflicts and frequently resistance, but this too is unevenly spread across the checkered urbanized landscape. While riots have erupted in the impoverished and marginalized suburbs of Paris and Stockholm as well as London and spreading to other British cities, still movement milieux and infrastructures are more entrenched in traditional urban contexts (cf. Mayer et al. 2016). This fact not only presents advantages for mobilization and coalition building, it also restrains urban movements from addressing these policies' exclusionary or discriminating effects, as they remain focused on traditional "right to the *city*" demands. Even though conflicts and contestations around dispossession and enclosures explode, with varying intensities, across the urbanized landscapes, there remain huge distances between the life worlds, languages, and demands of urban progressive and leftist movements on the one side and those of transfer recipients, migrants, unemployed youth, and other poor and marginalized groups on the other. The next section will take a closer look at the diversity of movements specific to the metropolitan region in order to detect emerging patterns.

New Types of Movements in the Urban Region

As the region develops multiple centres and peripheries, and as official regional policy reproduces ownership politics at the expense of tenants, workers, and non-citizens, "new forms of collective action *may* well emerge from the diverse polities that populate the postsuburban region, especially at the vast decentralized workplaces and factories, at the metabolic frontier (Greenbelt) and in the newly emerging field of social welfare delivery in the exurban belt," is the prognosis made by Addie and Keil (2015: 414, emphasis added).

This section traces what new forms of collective action, and what new challenges, have emerged or appear to be emerging (a) in response to the re-scaling of urban/regional politics and a round issues of collective consumption and provision across the city-region, and (b) in response to the substance of the neo-liberal policies that are building on and exacerbating the polarizing, cleaving, and privatizing tendencies shaping the contemporary metropolitan landscape.

Rescaling / broadening movement politics

Movement groups have shifted their mobilizing work to supra-urban scales and tried to organize peripheral communities. However, this is found less frequently in Europe than in North America, where sprawling urban regions have a much longer history. In places like Los Angeles or Toronto, the cleavages have not been running as much between the city and its suburbs, as residential segregation has existed more within than between jurisdictional lines (Pastor 2001: 752–53). Thus, for example, groups in poverty areas have discovered that the best way to improve conditions in their locale is by targeting and transforming regional policy (ibid.: 775; OCAP 2006).

Within North America, the number of metro-wide efforts focused on equity between various communities is far higher in the U.S. than in Canada, which is why this section reports on more U.S. examples. Such efforts have often been undertaken by activist community-based organizations together with labour unions, such as Justice for Janitors, Los Angeles Metropolitan Alliance, or the Labor/Community Strategy Center's bus riders union (Soja 2010: 142ff.; Pastor et al. 2009). Some similar metro-wide networks have emerged in Canada, such as, e.g., the Metro Network for Social Justice (MNSJ) in the Toronto area. It emerged as a metropolitan-wide coalition and was strongly shaped by its interactions with the metropolitan government and the Metro Council's attempts to cut back the local welfare state in the 1990s. It, too, was a "labor-community coalition" concerned with social welfare and economic justice (Conway 2006: 2). In her earlier work on the Metro Network for Social Justice, Conway found that "[c]oalitions of this nature are a distinctly Canadian innovation and a fruit of popular struggles against free trade in the 1980s.... They 'represented' a wide range of concerns—peace, international development, racial and sexual equality, housing, welfare rights, food security, childcare, disability rights.... The single largest group was of community-based social service agencies" (2000: 45)—but soon enough the model became quite widespread, and even more so in the U.S. than in Canada.

Interesting differences between the U.S. and Canada emerge in transit activism. While the LCSC in Los Angeles has organized a largely minority bus riders union, which used a combination of legal and community pressure to force better bus service from the regional Metropolitan Transit Authority, transit activism in Toronto has chosen a different focus. The Streetcars for Toronto Committee in the 1970s has been more concerned with service quality and spatial access (threatened by cutbacks), but "the notion of disparity between the different types of users was not a top consideration. They were primarily looking at equal access, not equitable access" (Hertel et al. 2015: 20). This focus has continued with contemporary transit activism in the Toronto region carried on by groups such as the Fair Fare Coalition, TTC riders, and the Greater Toronto Workers Assembly: they primarily contest the discrimination of suburban users and of those from outside the TTC system, where low-income residents, new immigrants, and visible minorities are increasingly living in areas without access to good transit.

Like the Toronto-based Metro Network for Social Justice, the LA Metropolitan Alliance has taken on a broader agenda. It consisted, among others, of Action for Grassroots Empowerment and Neighborhood Development (AGENDA), a regionally oriented advocacy organization, which emerged after the 1993 riots in order to engage grassroots leaders in policy development and implementation. While building its membership and mass base in disadvantaged South Central LA, it also focused on building bridges between the region's low-income communities to press decision-makers for changes in regional approaches to infrastructure spending. Sensing the potential of "community-based regionalism" (Pastor 2001), Metro Alliance/AGENDA went after DreamWorks, Steven Spielberg's effort to create the first new movie studio to be built in Los Angeles in fifty years. Metro Alliance/AGENDA developed a model strategy because it was quite successful in challenging the studio's placement in West LA: it held "public hearings" through 1998 in City Hall and South LA, charging that the company was rewarded with a $70 million subsidy from the city of Los Angeles without any conditions (such as hiring). AGENDA negotiated with DreamWorks to create training programs to help inner-city youth gain employment in the entertainment industries. This strategy turned into a model for similar community-based movements for regional equity and for similar alliances to be formed. In response to the growth policies pursued by many urban regions, community–labour coalitions would intervene in specific subsidy deals to ensure that not just corporations and developers, but also disadvantaged communities would benefit—through agreements on first source hiring, living wages, apprenticeship set-asides, affordable housing, money for community facilities, and other local benefits (e.g., *Minnesota Alliance for Progressive Action*, *Maine Citizens Leadership Fund*, *Good Jobs First*, *East Bay Alliance for a Sustainable Economy*).

Activist community organizations across the U.S. and Canada have thus jumped municipal boundaries in a variety of policy areas and addressed regional institutions: not only Metropolitan Transit authorities, but also the Air Quality Management District of LA and/or other institutions tasked with environmental regulation. Environmental problems that transcend municipal boundaries have provided ample cause for movement groups to mobilize across territories: whether in defence of threatened conservation zones (as with the Oak Ridges Moraine on the suburban fringe of the Greater Toronto Area; cf. Sandberg et al. 2013) or in efforts to organize peripheral communities (such as the *Toronto Environmental Alliance*), contestations have emerged on metropolitan/regional bases, frequently targeting multi-city special authorities. In the LA region, *Communities for a Better Environment* has been tackling environmental degradation with a largely Latino constituency and a geographic coverage that targets a broad area of South LA, including parts of the city, unincorporated areas of the county, and inner-ring suburbs. Among its successes was suing the regional Air Quality Management District, which forced it to suspend a credit trading program that concentrated pollutants in a minority neighbourhood (Pastor 2001: 775). Yet another policy area—job creation—was also addressed on the metro-wide scale, for example, when the *Alameda Corridor Jobs Coalition* arose in response to the Alameda Corridor Project, which was to build a high-speed rail line through the heart of South LA, from the ports to downtown warehousing operations. The coalition successfully lobbied the Alameda Corridor Transportation Authority for a commitment to place local residents in training slots.

Upscaling to the region has become advantageous for local movements, not only because causal processes increasingly operate at broader-than-local scales, but also because it enhances the potential to build alliances linking cities and suburbs. In spite of such advantages, so far we see far less metro-wide networking taking shape in Europe. Even in North America the disjunctures between scales of systemic processes and fiscal resources, on one hand, and scales of mobilization on the other, still pose thorny problems. Byron Miller concluded from his study of instances of resistance to neo-liberal policies in Alberta and Calgary that a major challenge facing activists is the construction of geographically extensive multi-locational networks that allow the rescaling of resistance as needed (Miller 2007: 245).

However, no one scale can ever be the "one and only" scale at which intractable social and economic problems can be resolved within the context of capitalist urbanization. Economic and political elites keep reshuffling and scale-shifting the regulatory arrangements to deal with contested issues, thus constantly rearranging power relations between ruling and challenging groups. A comparative analysis is always useful to alert against reifying particular scales, and thus it is revealing that the contestation of particular policies or services in newly gelling "in-between spaces," former peripheral areas, or on expanded regional levels has not taken shape in the same ways in European countries.

Even though German cities are also increasingly situating themselves and competing globally as metropolitan actors—stressing large-scale infrastructural projects and building regional identities and cohesion, as shown in the first section—this has not (yet) affected the exurban or non-urban communities in the ways North American social landscapes have become transformed. While small towns and villages obviously have also transformed in sociospatial and regulatory ways, stubborn structural differences in terms of social structure, public services, automobility, or electoral behaviour, persist. Even with regard to the most urbanized/globalized Frankfurt city-region, Keil (2011: 2511) noted that services that support a (creative) class (such as flexible daycare facilities) "cannot be found in small villages and towns of the region and force this workforce into a central location for work and housing," while at the same time "artists and other creatives would not consider moving into the periphery."

The persistent perception of a relatively clear dichotomy between centrality and periphery among broad sections of the population, the relative lack of edge cities, and the panoply of diverging everyday behaviours and preferences between those living in the countryside, peripheral areas, or suburbs, versus those living in cities, are reflected not only in a comparatively underdeveloped body of German research on the sociology of city-regions, but also in a scarcity of social movements addressing social ills and grievances on a regional scale[3] or outside of the urban framework. Environmental and climate problems, however, and conflicts over various socio-material infrastructures of urbanization and transport do trigger mobilization outside of and beyond the usual urban parameters. Protests against airport constructions or airport expansions stand out, triggered mostly because of their detrimental side effects on nearby residents. Plans for major transport hubs have mobilized so-called *Wutbürger* (enraged citizens) protesting the noise, environmental degradation, and the diminution of the quality of life and property values which, for example, the new Berlin-Brandenburg airport would bring to surrounding suburban landscapes. This 2011–13 movement has been far less radical and less broad than the resistance against the expansion of the Frankfurt airport in the early 1980s, when urban militants managed to join forces with many different regional actors upset by the ecological and social costs (Karasek 1981; Bürgerinitiative gegen die Flughafenerweiterung Frankfurt am Main 1981).

"Enraged citizens" have also been making headlines in the fifteen-year-long struggle against the economic and development priorities characterizing the rebuilding of the Stuttgart train station. This major restructuring project, "Stuttgart 21," not only entails burying the train station underground in order to develop central city land, but also aims to accelerate rail transport by directly connecting the station to the airport and the fair grounds, and both to a high-speed route toward Ulm. The costly reconstruction of the Stuttgart train station makes sense only in connection with this high-speed highway, a new subterranean airport train station, and thirty-three kilometres of tunnels underneath the city of Stuttgart. The powerful resistance movement has, however, mostly been carried by environmental and urban activist groups and far less so by regional organizations (Schlager 2010). In the 2011 popular referendum, the majorities for carrying on with Stuttgart 21 came overwhelmingly from the surrounding exurban districts.

Future uses of closed-down airports have also spawned contestations between various interested parties from the region. In Berlin's closed Tempelhof airport, the fight is, however, about urban (public/private) land use, as this has been a rare inner-city airport (Sontheimer 2013). Struggles over current plans and political choices for the development of a former airport area can better be studied at Hellinikon International Airport of Athens, where citizens' mobilizations have campaigned for a variety of alternative proposals, the creation of a Metropolitan park among them (cf. Vatavali and Prentou 2012).

While these and other instances of movement politics across urbanized regions often correspond to emerging governance arrangements at the metropolitan scale, the (positive or negative) relation between the movements and new regulatory and decision-making capacities at that scale remains unclear, as not enough systematic research is available. For the time being, more conclusive findings can probably be established by focusing on the substance of contestations over neo-liberal urbanization processes and their sociospatial impacts.

Differentiating and uniting movement politics between "centres" and "peripheries"

Though struggles over social issues and social rights in Europe have not upscaled in ways comparable to those in North America's sprawling urbanized landscapes, they have also been transforming—though in ways markedly different from North American movements. For one, the Southern European crisis has pushed initially urban-scale Indignado movements to wherever evictions and foreclosures happened most frequently, triggering the same diffusion effects that have been observable with the American Occupy movements. After the clearance of encampments, activists began to focus their activities on defending or (re)claiming foreclosed properties for "ordinary" people, supporting hurricane victims, or organizing solidarity for striking workers at various locations. As in the U.S. and Canada, this fanning out process would bring urban, frequently middle-class-based activists in touch with marginalized groups inhabiting internal or external "peripheries"—in any case, with groups that had been at the periphery of progressive social movements. In the core European countries, where the financial and economic crisis has not hit in the same way, bridging the distances between classical Right to the City (RttC) groups and "peripheral" groups has been more challenging. Urban RttC networks here are usually made up of combinations of the following groupings:

- radical autonomous or anarchist groups and various leftist organizations;
- middle-class urbanites seeking to defend their accustomed quality of life;
- precarious groups in the informal sector, in creative industries, or among college students;
- artists and other creative professionals, which may cut across the backgrounds mentioned so far;

- frequently, local environmental groups that fight problematic energy, climate, or development policies (frequently addressing problems that stretch beyond city boundaries);
- and finally, but rarely actively engaged in such networks: the marginalized, excluded, oppressed, and people of colour (cf. Mayer 2013a).

Conscious of this latter deficit, groups within the Hamburg RttC network have attempted to organize low-income tenants and migrants in formerly peripheral social housing districts such as Wilhelmsburg and Altona, which have recently come under gentrification pressures. As described in the first section of this chapter, these areas of high-rise buildings for workers initially conformed to relatively high standards for mass consumption, but became increasingly neglected over time. In spite of widespread discontent with these conditions and egregiously inadequate services provided by the responsible social housing company, the RttC groups managed to attract only few residents to neighbourhood meetings and to involve only few local tenants in their campaigns and actions. They self-critically describe their lack of adequate language and the unintended result of finding themselves turned into the residents' "representatives" rather than building joint struggles (Hohenstatt 2011).[4]

Because of the difficulties of mobilizing residents of downgraded "marginal" areas and of overcoming the distances between traditional urban activists and those dispossessed even more severely by contemporary neoliberal urbanism, a movement sparked by mostly migrant tenants in a similar former public housing district in Berlin was greeted with much excitement. *Kotti & Co* (named after the central square around which the housing complexes are concentrated) represents a rare instance where an action repertoire resonating with urban and occupy movements was kicked off by seemingly marginal groups. In protest against the rising rents in their housing complexes, low-income migrants and families on welfare in May 2012 erected a *gecekondu* in the middle of Kreuzberg, invoking the informal settlements sprouting overnight in Turkish cities. They were soon supported by neighbours and activists, who would bring food and volunteer for night shifts, and by academics, who helped organize a conference to pressure the local authorities. This movement was initiated by long-time residents, many of whom had come to Berlin thirty or more years ago as "guest workers," when then-blighted Kreuzberg was peripheral (next to the wall) and one of the few districts where they could settle. Over the years, they have helped turn the former "problem area" into an attractive "multicultural" district. Together with squatter movements, they rehabbed old tenements slated for demolition, and they made the drab Fordist social housing blocs come alive. They welcomed students and squatters, then artists and gentrifiers, and more recently masses of tourists and globally mobile home hunters choosing Berlin for their second or vacation homes. They are not opposing the newcomers, even though the latest wave in particular has been driving up prices. But they do demand solutions that will not lead to their own displacement. The welfare office, however, requires them to find cheaper housing on Berlin's periphery[5]— what *now* constitutes Berlin's periphery.

Unwilling to move to peripheral Marzahn (cf. Kil and Silver 2006), the protesters have generated alliances across large swaths of the city-region by building links and organizing joint actions with tenant groups, anti-gentrification activists, and other squatters, among them senior citizens who occupied their closed-down community centre in the far northern district of Pankow, defending it for months until the city helped find a solution that allows them to keep their centre. *Kotti & Co* was led to upscale their strategy to the provincial level through their experience of trying to negotiate with the owners and housing associations.[6] Similarly, a budding coalition fighting the escalating evictions in Berlin is realizing that in order to more effectively prevent evictions, it will have to "expand its activities beyond the politically and socially rather homogenous alliance and beyond Kreuzberg" (Müller 2013: 13).

Meanwhile though, the convergence of tenants' rights activists with senior citizens in Pankow and Turkish families defending central city housing and the right to remain in the city has created a political space in which collective actors could form (rather than a region acting collectively). Though spanning a growing collectivity of actors from "central" as well as more or less "peripheral" areas, this converging political space does not yet include agency from the "new," more distant margins, constantly being pushed further and further out.

There are further manifestations of self-empowerment and mobilization around issues of social rights and collective consumption and provision, spilling over the conventional urban boundaries. In contrast to a variety of movement organizations that advocate or mobilize around the rights of (undocumented) migrants such as "No One Is Illegal," refugees have increasingly begun to self-organize. For some years now, they have been building resistance against the shameful treatment they receive within the EU and formed organizations (such as *The Voice Refugee Forum* and *Caravan for the Rights of Refugees and Migrants*), but recent protests making use of urban encampments as well as cross-regional marches have galvanized more public reaction than ever before. After the suicide of

Mohammad Rahsepars from Iran in early 2012 in an asylum seekers' accommodation in Würzburg/Bavaria, refugees camped out in the centre of the city for months demanding free mobility, an end to deportations, to humiliating treatment, and to being housed in desolate container camps. Protest camps spread throughout Germany, and in September refugees undertook a 600 km march from Würzburg to Berlin, in direct violation of "Residenzpflicht," the current law forbidding refugees to leave the district they have been assigned to. After arriving in Berlin, they set up a protest camp at Oranienplatz, where about 120 activist refugees from Sudan, Macedonia, Iran, and Afghanistan have been holding out, some living in a nearby squatted former school building. Six thousand people joined their demonstration to the German parliament in support of their demands. At a "Refugee Struggle Congress" in Munich in March, where the formation of independent councils of refugees was planned and a separate "citizens' plenary" explored ways to support the protests of the "non-citizens," participants skyped with refugee activists in Vienna. With these mobilizations, the refugee activists have put the violation of their social and political rights on the agenda, and, importantly, have seized the right—still officially denied to them in most provinces—to move about freely; they have been converging from all kinds of (rural, ex- and suburban) districts onto public spaces, churches, and vacant buildings in central cities; and conversely, they have organized a "Refugees' Revolution Bus Tour" to visit, together with supporters, the "reception camps" where refugees are "processed," often for years, in order to spread information about their protests and invite others to join their demonstrations, often enduring police violence (Schwarzer 2013; Refugee Tent Action 2013).[7]

With massive new waves of refugees flooding into Germany and other European countries, and with responsibilities for processing and regulating these new inflows and for taking care of the needs of the new arrivals being shuffled up and down the political hierarchies, contestations transcend municipal boundaries. Though caused by geopolitical and global actors, they erupt and will need to be addressed where they manifest: within city-regional contexts. Thus, while on first consideration mobilizations by and for refugees may appear to be unrelated to movements around issues of extended urbanization, from the perspective of an up-to-date conception of urbanization, this is not so. While urbanization is traditionally conceived in terms of agglomeration—i.e., as dense concentration of population, infrastructure and investments within a less densely settled territorial plane—Brenner and others have highlighted that this process of agglomeration has been premised upon, and contributes to, transformations of socio-spatial organization across the rest of the world, which materialize "in densely tangled circuits of labor, commodities, cultural forms, energy, raw materials" (Brenner 2013: 103). These circuits "radiate outward from the immediate zone of agglomeration and implode back into it" (ibid.; cf. also Brenner and Schmid 2012; Merrifield 2012). Migrants and refugees are an integral human part of these flows and contribute to shaping the socio-spatial morphology of—in this case—the German urban region, while simultaneously intertwining it with the extended worldwide urban fabric. As the refugees seek asylum and struggle for recognition and rights in German society, they provide German movements the opportunity to link their own urban/regional activities to the worldwide struggles for the global commons carried out "by peasants, small landholders, farm workers, indigenous populations … across the variegated landscapes of extended urbanization. Here, too, the dynamics of accumulation by dispossession and enclosure have had creatively destructive effects upon everyday life … and socio-environmental conditions" (Brenner 2013: 108).

Thus, the presence of migrants in German and other European city-regions signals not only the presence of the periphery in the centre, but their struggles are also turning "first world" city-regions into arenas of anti-colonial and anti-racist struggles. Refugees and (undocumented) migrants from the global South inhabit this political space together with other urban outcasts—homeless people, day labourers, ex-felons, people of colour, and many others that have been "de-industrialized," made redundant or otherwise marginalized for being poor or not fitting prescribed standards. Their rights are the least recognized and respected within the dynamics of accumulation by dispossession and enclosure; they are most easily pushed into internal and external peripheries, camps, and prisons. For the emerging urbanized landscapes not to reproduce sharp polarizations within their variegated patterns, for them not to exacerbate the distance but enhance the connectivity between centres and peripheries, the differently placed movements will have to link arms and jointly struggle against the exclusionary tendencies and the differential valuation of the rights of more and less vulnerable (non)citizens.

Conclusion

While we have no conclusive research identifying specific relationships between new regional governance arrangements, metro-wide politics and progressive activism, the overview presented here does provide some leads and directions that should prove productive for more systematic research into the trends and patterns of movement activism within and for changing urbanized regions. The comparison between the North American and European experiences has been instructive, as their similarities and differences prevent us from reifying any particular scale.

Movements spanning the multiple centres and peripheries of the region have emerged more easily and widely in North America: while Canadian and U.S. metropolitan areas have seen different kinds of regional networks and mobilizations around a variety of issues evolve and consolidate, in Europe we find fewer and more embryonic forms of mobilization transcending the classical urban-based activism. To what extent this lag might be a result of less developed or less stable city-regional intergovernmental cooperation, regulatory capacity, and institutional arrangements is not clear, especially since the forms of regional collaboration that do exist in various European metropolitan areas are frequently broad and inclusive and enjoy backing by supra-regional governments.

Our tracing of the transformation of specific suburbias and their changing politics in the shift from Keynesian (sub)urbanism to the contemporary neo-liberal landscapes of extended urbanization has revealed that the stronger suburban powers on the North American continent and the strong role played by the business sector in pushing regional collaboration, particularly in the U.S., may be responsible both for the earlier political prioritization of metropolitan issues as well as for triggering resistance on that scale. Triggers for such resistance would either be the business-driven, hence frequently exclusive, orientation of regional policies or the experience of community-based activists fighting local disadvantages, as when regional strategies proved most effective for improving their conditions. Community-based regionalism thus has emerged more easily as a strategy in a variety of policy areas, both, because the processes causing environmental degradation, traffic congestion, or social and employment problems operate at broader than local scales, and because it enhances the potential to build alliances across urban, suburban, and periurban quarters.

Even though in Europe it is also city-regions that function as the new building blocks of the global economy, its local/regional civil societies are still more differentially congealed in the life worlds of the city, the countryside, the suburb or *banlieue*. This is what accounts for the relative scarcity of region-wide networks and alliances in Europe. Only major infrastructural projects have spawned distinct mobilizations outside of and beyond the traditional urban parameters. However, extended urbanization has also transformed struggles over social issues and social rights: in Southern Europe urban activists were led to reach out to internal and external peripheries in their efforts to support foreclosure and other austerity victims; in Northern Europe activists reach out to those (former) peripheries that are coming under gentrification pressures. Even as they link up with other (anti-eviction, anti-displacement) struggles across the city, the new political space they create has so far rarely included agency based in the distant periphery. But these developments are very much in flux and may well intensify in the near future.

Notes

1 In France the term *banlieue* is used as a synonym for racial violence, poverty, drug and human trafficking, ethnic and religious conflict, thereby demonizing the deprived living in the outskirts. In Quebec it simply means "suburb." What in France manifests as peripheral declining region, the *banlieue*, corresponds to the rather different sociospatial formation of the Afro-American ghetto in the U.S. Each is the result of specific institutional logics of segregation, each erupting in periodic bursts of revolt. While the U.S. ghetto is the creature of racially skewed and market-oriented state policies that trapped poor blacks at the bottom of the spatial order of the polarized city (Wacquant in Young and Keil 2014: 1593), the French state has repeatedly cycled through phases of regulating and abandoning the urban outskirts. The "return of the state" to the *banlieues* announced by Prime Minister Jean-Marc Ayrault after the 2005 *banlieue* riots signals the latest attempt to deal with the de facto detachment between French central cities and their surrounding "badlands" (Dikec 2007). While reprioritizing the "most vulnerable" areas in the outskirts, the plan also sought to integrate the inner city of Paris with the quarters located outside the Boulevard Périphérique, to increase housing development and to construct new train links. The plan was presented as "decentralization of power"—but it entailed various risks, among them that the richest suburbs would invest solely into private housing, forcing the poorest residents into highly concentrated areas of poverty (White 2013).
2 As in the tony areas of the (extremely variegated) Bay Area or New York City region (cf. Romney 2012; Denney 2013).
3 To the extent that metropolitan-wide governance structures emerged, the fact that (municipal) governance is shaped more by party politics than in North America leaves a bigger gap between grassroots coalitions for social and civil rights and political parties—and thus helps explain the relative silence of German (urban) movements vis-à-vis metropolitan-wide issues.
4 Cf. the website of the group Arbeitskreis Umstrukturierung Wilhelmsburg: http://akuwilhelmsburg.blogsport.eu
5 In a city of 3.5 million people, a district made up of 150,000 housing units (approximately 500,000 people), which is affected by this turnover to privatization, constitutes a sizeable problem. In 2011 the rents of 100,000 households on Hartz IV (the German welfare/workfare program) registered above the limit permitted by the welfare office; 65,000 of these households were requested to lower their housing costs. For most, this has meant doubling up or moving to the outskirts, as there is practically no more affordable housing in the central districts. From 2002 to 2010 the number of evictions rose by 65%, in 2010 alone by 11% to 5,603 evictions, in 2013, twenty-two per day (Müller 2013: 12).

6 "It became clear that we needed to act politically rather than through litigation, and on the provincial rather than on the municipal level, so as to push for a change in the law" (Kaltenborn 2012: 93; author's translation).
7 Cf. http://asylstrikeberlin.wordpress.com/ and http://refugeesrevolution.blogsport .de.

References

Addie, J.-P. D. and R. Keil. 2015. "Real existing regionalism: The region between talk, territory and technology." *International Journal of Urban and Regional Research* 39(2): 407–17, March. DOI: 10.1111/1468-2427.12179.

Arbeitskreis Umstrukturierung Wilhelmsburg. 2013. *Unternehmen Wilhelmsburg. Stadtentwicklung im Zeichen von IBA und igs*. Hamburg: Assoziation A.

Boudreau, J.-A., P. Hamel, B. Jouve, and R. Keil, 2007. "New state spaces in Canada: Metropolitanization in Montreal and Toronto compared." *Urban Geography* 28(1): 30–53.

Brenner, N. 2013. "Theses on urbanization." *Public Culture* 25(1): 85–114.

Brenner, N. and C. Schmid. 2012. "Planetary urbanization." In M. Gandy, ed., *Urban Constellations*. Berlin: Jovis.

Bürgerinitiative gegen die Flughafenerweiterung Frankfurt am Main, ed. 1981. *Keine Startbahn West—Argumente, Bilder und Berichte*. Offenbach: Verlag 2000.

Changfoot, N. 2007. "Local activism and neoliberalism: Performing neoliberal citizenship as resistance." *Studies in Political Economy* 80 (autumn): 129–49.

Conway, J. 2000. "Knowledge and the impasse in left politics: Potentials and problems in social movement practice." *Studies in Political Economy* 62 (summer): 43–70.

———. 2006. *Praxis and politics: Knowledge production in social movements*. New York: Routledge.

Dikec, M. 2007. *Badlands of the republic: Space, politics and urban policy*. London: Wiley.

Denney, C. 2013. "Berkeley Central – you can't afford it." *Berkeley Daily Planet*, March 22. www.berkeleydailyplanet.com/issue/2013-03-22/article/ 40910?headline=Berkeley-Central-You-Can-t-Afford-It--By-Carol-Denney.

Ekers, M., P. Hamel, and R. Keil. 2012. "Governing suburbia: Modalities and mechanisms of suburban governance." *Regional Studies* 46(3): 405–22.

Giroux, G. L. 2005. "A line in the suburban sand." *Congressional Quarterly Weekly* 63: 1714–19.

Harrison, J. 2008. "The region in political economy." *Geography Compass* 3: 814–30.

———. 2010. "Networks of connectivity, territorial fragmentation, uneven development: The new politics of city-regionalism." *Political Geography* 29: 17–27.

Hertel, S., R. Keil, M. Collens. 2015. *Switching tracks: Towards transit equity in the Greater Toronto and Hamilton Area*. City Institute.

Hohenstatt, F. (Arbeitskreis Umstrukturierung Wilhelmsburg) and N. N. (Plattform gegen Verdrängung Altona). 2011. "Bündnisse und Netzwerke: Ethnische Minderheiten, Parteien und Bewegungen." Presentation on Panel

Revolutionäre Realpolitik #4 at the Rosa Luxemburg Stiftung-sponsored Conference, "Transformative organizing strategies to challenge the cuts and change society." www.rosalux.de/documentation/44134/revolutionaere -realpolitik-in-zeiten-von-kuerzungspolitik-und-krise.html.

Jonas, A. E. G. and K. Ward. 2007. "Introduction to a debate on city-regions: New geographies of governance, democracy and social reproduction." *International Journal of Urban and Regional Research* 31(1): 169–78.

Jones, M. 2013. "'Polymorphic spatial politics': Tales from a grassroots regional movement." In W. Nicholls, B. Miller, and J. Beaumont, eds., *Spaces of contention* (103–20). Aldershot: Ashgate.

Kaltenborn, S. 2012. "'Die Stadt von morgen beginnt heute': Kotti & Co protestiert gegen die Berliner Wohnungspolitik. LuXemburg. Gesellschaftsanalyse und linke." *Praxis* 4: 92–95.

Kantor, P. 2008. "Varieties of city regionalism and the quest for political cooperation: A comparative perspective." *Urban Research and Practice* 1(2): 111–29.

Karasek, H. 1981. *Das Dorf im Flörsheimer Wald. Eine Chronik des alltäglichen Widerstands gegen die Startbahn West*. Darmstadt: Luchterhand.

Keil, R. 1994. "Global sprawl: Urban form after Fordism." *Environment & Planning D* 12: 31–36.

———. 2011. "The global city comes home: Internalised globalisation in Frankfurt-Rhine-Main." *Urban Studies* 48(12): 2495–517.

Kil, W. and H. Silver. 2006. "From Kreuzberg to Marzahn: New migrant communities in Berlin." *German Politics and Society* 24(4): 95–121.

Knox, P. L. 2008. *Metroburbia USA*. New Brunswick, NJ: Rutgers University Press.

Lang, R. and P. L. Knox. 2009. "The new metropolis: Rethinking megalopolis." *Regional Studies* 43(6): 789–802.

Lefèvre, C. and M. Weir. 2012. "Building metropolitan institutions." In K. Mossberger, S. E. Clarke, and P. John, eds., *The Oxford Handbook of Urban Politics* (624–41). New York: Oxford University Press.

Madden, D. 2012. "City becoming world: Nancy, Lefebvre, and the global-urban imagination." *Society and Space D* 30(5): 772–87.

Mayer, M. 2008. "To what end do we theorize sociospatial relations?" *Environment and Planning D: Society and Space* 26(3): 414–19.

———. 2012. "Metropolitan research from a transatlantic perspective: Differences, similarities, and conceptual diffusion." In D. Brantz, S. Disko, and G. Wagner-Kyora, eds., *Thick space: Approaches to metropolitanism* (105–22). Bielefeld: transcript.

———. 2013a. "First world urban activism: Beyond austerity urbanism and creative city politics." *CITY* 17(1): 5–19.

———. 2013b. "Multiscalar mobilization for the just city: New spatial politics of urban movements." In W. Nicholls, B. Miller, and J. Beaumont, eds., *Spaces of contention* (163–96). Aldershot: Ashgate.

Mayer, M., C. Thörn, and H. Thörn, eds. 2016. *Urban uprisings: Challenging neoliberal urbanism in Europe*. London: Palgrave Macmillan.

Merrifield, A. 2000. "The urbanization of labor: Living wage activism in the American city." *Social Text* 18(1): 31–54.

————. 2012. "The urban question under planetary urbanization." *International Journal of Urban and Regional Research*. Early view 2012: www.ijurr.org/details/article/2881901/The_Urban_Question_under_Planetary_Urbanization.html.

————. 2013. "The planetary urbanization of non-work." *CITY* 17(1): 20–36.

Miller, B. 2007. "Modes of governance, modes of resistance: Contesting neoliberalism in Calgary." In H. Leitner et al., eds., *Contesting neoliberalism: Urban frontiers* (223–49). New York: Guilford Press.

Müller, M. 2013. "Miete essen Einkommen auf. Das Wohnen in deutschen Städten wird teurer." *Analyse & Kritik* 581: 12–13.

National Coalition for the Homeless. 2010. *Tent cities in America: A Pacific coast report*. www.nationalhomeless.org/publications/tent_cities_pr.html.

Novy, J. and M. Mayer. 2009. "As 'just' as it gets? The European city in the 'just city' discourse." In P. Marcuse, J. Connolly, J. Novy, I. Olivo, C. Potter, and J. Steil, eds., *Searching for the just city: Debates in urban theory and practice* (103–19). New York: Routledge.

OCAP (Ontario Coalition Against Poverty). 2006. "What is OCAP? An introduction to the Ontario Coalition against Poverty." http://ocap.ca/files/whatis.pdf.

Orfield, M. 2002. *American metropolitics: The new suburban reality*. Washington, DC: Brookings Institution Press.

Pastor, M. 2001. "Looking for regionalism in all the wrong places: Demography, geography, and community in Los Angeles County." *Urban Affairs Review* 36(6): 747–82.

Pastor, M., C. Benner, and M. Matsuoka. 2009. *This could be the start of something big: How social movements for regional equity are reshaping metropolitan America*. Ithaca, NY: Cornell University Press.

Peck, J. 2011. "Neoliberal suburbanism: Frontier space." *Urban Geography* 32(6): 884–919.

Phelps, N. A. and A. Wood. 2011. "The new post-suburban politics?" *Urban Studies* 48(12): 2591–610.

Refugee Tent Action. 2013. *On the position of 'asylum-seekers' and 'asylum-seekers' struggles in modern societies*. 17 March. http://refugeetentaction.net/index.php?option=com_content&view=article&id=208:on-the-position-of-asylum-seekers-and-asylum-seekers-struggles-in-modern-societies&catid=2&Itemid=133&lang=en.

Romney, L. 2012. "San Francisco considers allowing nation's tiniest micro-apartments." *Los Angeles Times*. September 24.

Rosa Luxemburg Stiftung. 2011. Transformative organizing strategies to challenge the cuts and change society conference. Max (Plattform gegen Verdrängung Altona, Hamburg), Flo (Arbeitskreis Umstrukturierung Wilhelmsburg, Hamburg) on Community Organizing around Urban and Community Conflicts. www.rosalux.de/documentation/44134/revolutionaere-realpolitik-in-zeiten-von-kuerzungspolitik-und-krise.html.

Saillant, C. and D. Marcum. 2012. "Southland cities struggle to avoid joining Stockton in bankruptcy." *Los Angeles Times*. June 27.

Sandberg, L. A., G. Wekerle, L. Gilbert, 2013. *The Oak Ridges Moraine battles: Development, sprawl, and nature conservation in the Toronto region*. Toronto: University of Toronto Press.

Schlager, A. 2010. "Die Proteste gegen 'Stuttgart 21': Analyse und Schlussfolgerungen für linke Politik." In C. Hildebrandt and N. Tügel, eds., *Der Herbst der 'Wutbürger.'* Soziale Kämpfe in Zeiten der Krise (RLS 12).

Schwarzer, A. 2013. "Campen in der Kälte. Seit einem Jahr protestieren Non-Citizens für gleichberechtigte Teilhabe." *Analyse & Kritik* 581: 11.

Scott, A. J., J. Agnew, E. Soja, and M. Storper. 2001. "Global city regions." In A. J. Scott, ed., *Global city regions: Trends, theory, policy* (11–30). Oxford: Oxford University Press.

Scott, M. 2011. "G20 mobilizing in Toronto and community organizing: Opportunities created and lessons learned." *Interface: A Journal For and About Social Movements* 3(1): 185–89.

Soja, E. W. 2010. *Seeking spatial justice.* Minneapolis: University of Minnesota Press.

Sontheimer, T. 2013. *Das Tempelhofer Feld als umkämpfter öffentlicher Raum.* Freie Universität Berlin, Fachbereich Politik- und Sozialwissenschaften. B.A. thesis.

Tobar, H. 2012. "Foreclosures and resulting blight infest once-safe neighborhoods." *Los Angeles Times.* May 29.

Vatavali, F. and P. Prentou. 2012. "The former Hellinikon International Airport at Athens." Presentation at *Encounter Athens Workshop.* encounterathens.word press.com/2012/03/09/the-former-hellinikon-international-airport-of-athens/

Vollmann, W. T. 2011. "Homeless in Sacramento: Welcome to the new tent cities." *Harper's Magazine,* March: 29–46.

Weir, M. 2011. "Creating justice for the poor in the new metropolis." In C. R. Hayward and T. Swanstrom, eds., *Justice and the American metropolis* (237–57). Minneapolis: University of Minnesota Press.

White, J. 2013. "The return of the state to the Parisian banlieue." *Opendemocracy.* March 19. www.opendemocracy.net/opensecurity/joel-white/return -of-state-to-parisian-banlieue

Young, D., and R. Keil. 2010. "Reconnecting the disconnected: The politics of infrastructure in the in-between city." *Cities* 27(2): 87–95.

———. 2014. "Locating the urban in-between: Tracking the urban politics of infrastructure in Toronto." *International Journal of Urban and Regional Research* 38(5), September: 1589–608.

CHAPTER 4

Governing the Built Environment in European Metropolitan Regions
Financialization, Responsibilization, and Urban Competition

Susanne Heeg

Introduction: Governing the Built Environment in European Cities

METROPOLITAN REGIONS in Europe seem to be the winners of contemporary demographic as well as economic growth. This seems to explain the growing pressure on the metropolitan housing market. Rents as well as housing prices are on the rise and are thus contributing to difficult living conditions in metropolitan regions, particularly for low-income households. This is taking place throughout Europe regardless of welfarist, market-driven, or developmentalist orientations of the respective national states of which the metropolitan regions are a part. Housing in particular and urban space in general seem to be ever more expensive and contested goods in metropolitan regions (Twickel 2012; Boulay 2012; García 2010). In this chapter I contextualize these processes regarding the built environment. This involves the analysis of the structure of real estate investments as an outcome of investment strategies of private investors and of policy interventions of local governments in times of global financial crisis and European debt crisis.

From the perspective of private investors, metropolitan regions offer a broad range of investment opportunities in real estate. Local governments react with attempts to channel these investments either with subsidies or by launching policy initiatives in order to facilitate private investments. The interplay between private actors and local governments currently materializes in the form of fragmented metropolitan regions.

Whereas inner cities are increasingly clean, glitzy, shiny, and much desired urban spaces, peripheral areas within cities seem to be neglected. Quite often, they lack jobs, infrastructure (education, health, retail, etc.), and connectivity. As emphasized in the introduction to this book, inequalities and conflicts of interest between the centre and the periphery are quite strong in metropolitan regions. Still, even the peripheral areas seem to be attractive investment locations: for almost ten years, institutional investors such as hedge funds or real estate private equity funds (REPE) have invested and traded in the formerly municipal housing stock (Holm 2011). So, when inner cities and peripheral urban areas witness investments, are suburban regions—which have been strategic sites for investments in the postwar period—still important as investment sites? Municipal governments in the suburbs strive for new housing, business, and leisure developments in order to contribute to the local well-being. Up to now, many but not all suburban municipalities seem to be attractive locations for office, industrial, and particularly for housing investment. Municipalities benefiting from growth are usually those that profit from socio-economic developments in the central city. Back office jobs are relocated to suburban areas, and households continue moving to the suburbs in search of better living conditions.

In this regard, this chapter gives an overview of processes shaping the built environment in dynamic metropolitan regions within Europe. How do policy initiatives and investment strategies of private and institutional investors coalesce in producing fragmented metropolitan regions? What are the reasons for spatially different investment strategies within metropolitan regions? What do the strategies look like? What are the outcomes and what is the influence of private interests, political actors, and local governments? Answers to these questions require the analysis of the power structure of alliances of different private, non-governmental, and public actors within metropolitan regions and their impact on spatial structures.

However, processes within metropolitan regions are not exclusively the result of processes within the respective local and regional units, but also of macro-economic and macro-social processes. So, the patterning of metropolitan regions is not only multi-dimensional, but at the same time multi-scalar. In metropolitan regions, investment strategies of global investors meet local upgrading strategies and encounter dreams of home ownership. While the global investors are in search of attractive investment opportunities, local governments advocate for attractive investment and housing environments. In order to analyze this interrelationship, it is necessary to pay attention to urban competition, the emergence of a finance-dominated accumulation regime, and transformation of the welfare state. With the discussion of separate but interdependent developments as global investments, a fierce struggle for private investments within metropolitan regions and the shift toward home ownership, it is possible to get a glimpse of what structures the built environment in metropolitan regions. Theoretically, this demands the inclusion of discussions about the shift to finance-dominated accumulation regime, the transformation of the built environment into financial assets (also referred to as financialization),[1] the call for "personal responsibility" and "self-responsibility" (also referred to as responsibilization; see Shamir 2008), and urban competition. These socio-spatial approaches come together in linking the structure of the real estate industry, the built environment, and the power of actors to the development of places and spaces in metropolitan regions. This chapter attempts to connect different theoretical strands for a better understanding of the development of the built environment in metropolitan regions. I argue that contemporary metropolitan forms can only be understood in light of the growing importance of finance for social and spatial organization.

In order to examine the multi-dimensional and multi-scalar developments within metropolitan regions in Europe, we begin with a discussion of the finance-dominated accumulation regime, welfare state reorganization, and the accompanying responsibilization of individuals. Next, the impact of these processes on the built environment and the real estate industry will be explained ("financialization of the built environment"). Thirdly, the impacts of these developments on and in metropolitan regions characterized by inter-regional competition will be analyzed.

Finance Dominated Accumulation Regime and Responsibilization

Within regulation theory, it is argued that fundamental shifts have taken place affecting institutional compromises in the field of labour, wage relation, forms of competition, and organization of social welfare. According to this discussion, a new finance-dominated or finance-led accumulation regime came into being in the 1980s and was consolidated thanks to neo-liberal governmental policies that strove to reduce social expenditure, including health-care benefits, retirement pensions, and unemployment benefits (Serfati 2000). An important aspect of this transformation is the global expansion of financial capital in search of profitable investments. The new formation is no longer structured by technical-industrial innovations or new ways of organizing labour—as was the previous Fordist formation—but by financial innovations (Aglietta 2000). Starting in the

U.S. and expanding into more and more countries, the deregulation of the financial sector, the proliferation of new financial instruments, and the liberalization of international capital flows have contributed to a shift toward market-based financial systems. Consequently, institutional investors emerged as major players in financial markets with a shareholder instead of a stockholder value orientation. Among these investors, pension funds, insurances, and different forms of investment funds are of major importance because they channel money via direct (buying properties) and indirect investments (in real estate private equity funds, open-ended and closed real estate funds, publicly listed property companies, etc.) into the built environment of metropolitan regions.[2]

In all European countries, a cutback of the welfare state has taken place which creates new challenges for individuals. According to Blank et al. (2012), a shift in social leitmotifs has taken place, and as a result it is no longer the welfare state but the individuals who are responsible for individual risks. In many European welfare states such as Germany, the Netherlands, Sweden, etc., there have existed obligatory social insurance systems and social services which took on the responsibility—quite often in an authoritative, paternalistic manner—for old age, diseases, disabilities, and other fundamental problems in the course of life. In the meantime, a collective responsibility for the risks of life no longer exists; rather, there is an individual responsibility to arrange and provide for permanent changes according to social and economic developments. It is necessary nowadays to safeguard privately against the risks of old age, unemployment, poverty, illness, or invalidity. Instead of a system of social redistribution and reallocation ("pay-as-you-go system") that protected against individual risks, now in more and more social realms capital-covered system are applied (pension funds, private and additional health insurances, and more financial products).

The necessity for engagement in self-provision is accompanied by the call to build up assets that are supposed to supplement wage labour. Up until twenty years ago, in many European countries spare money was put into savings accounts; nowadays money is no longer saved but invested (Legnaro et al. 2005: 27). However, the opportunity to optimize assets is transforming into the challenge to engage in an adept, skilled, and anticipatory investment. This freedom of self-improvement—against the paternalism of the welfare state—is a social demand to redefine oneself in the context of an increasingly deregulated financial and labour market. In this context, it becomes a normal aspect of modern life to command a portfolio of various assets in the form of funds, certificates, commercial papers, and/ or in the form of real estate (mostly housing).

These fundamental transformations affecting the position and tasks of individuals can be described as "responsibilization." However, the financialization of pension and health systems through pension funds and insurances ties the fate of individual beneficiaries and workers to the fate of financial markets. "Old arrangements of social rights have been replaced and continue to be replaced by new arrangements in which social rights and guarantees are transferred from the state to financial markets. Indeed, the restructuring of welfare states has resulted in a 'great risk shift' in which households are increasingly dependent on financial markets for their longterm security" (Aalbers 2008: 151). Principles of markets are introduced into everyday life and social processes (Vogl 2011: 134). A synchronization of economic and social reproduction is the ultimate aim.

These processes line up with the development of new investment opportunities. Pension schemes, health infrastructure, housing, water, sewer, and electricity networks are subjected not only to marketization processes but also to the transformation in financial products, which compete with other investment opportunities such as government bonds, shares, etc. In this sense, the finance-dominated accumulation regime brings together the responsibilization of individuals and the creation of investment opportunities where there were none before.

However, the transformations affect not only the valorization and calculation of (formerly) public goods, the role of labour, and welfare, but also the built environment. The built environment is seen—not only by financial institutions but also by individuals—as an asset in which money can be invested and disinvested by redirecting capital from low payoffs to potentially higher ones (Harvey 1985). The built environment is a "role model" in connecting financialization and responsibilization as processes characteristic of contemporary social formation: firstly, the built environment is transformed into financial products, and secondly, housing becomes important less because of its use value, but as a financial asset. Both processes are part and parcel of the call for responsibilization.

Built Environment

Housing as well as industrial and office properties are nowadays perceived as financial assets. Big chunks of public housing have been privatized and the new owners incorporate it into their financial calculations. Companies try to benefit from selling their buildings to institutional investors. Because properties are perceived as unproductive capital, they are incorporated into funds or leaseback arrangements. Nowadays there exists a wide range of investment vehicles in regard to the built environment. Real estate investment trusts (REITs), publicly listed property companies, real estate private equity funds (REPE), open-ended and closed real estate investment funds, and other forms have made it possible to collect vast sums of money from households (i.e., private investors) and institutional investors. What make these investment vehicles attractive are their different risk and profit profiles as well as disinvestment opportunities, so that they serve different requirements and demands. Taken together, these investment vehicles are preconditions for the financialization of the built environment.

But what do REITs, real estate investment funds, REPE, etc., have to do with responsibilization? Pension funds, insurance companies, or private asset managers invest in the above-mentioned channels[3] because they give them access to a group of knowledgeable people and organizations. In particular, pension funds and insurance companies manage giant pools of money consisting of savings from households and individuals, and are therefore key players in the financial market (Huffschmid 2009: 61ff.; Bellofiore 2002). A substantial percentage of the collective savings of all households and individuals is channeled through insurances, pension, and other investment funds into real estate investment funds as an indirect access to the property market (Theurillat 2010). Nowadays, real estate is an essential component of a diversified portfolio, particularly when interest rates and profits on the stock market are low and fear of inflation prevails. Commercial papers in real estate have increased the attractiveness of investment in properties because money is no longer fixed for a long time period; rather, these papers offer the promise that they can be sold at almost any time.

The investment in commercial papers is closely related to responsibilization because it goes along with the transfer of money into the investment vehicles of banks, insurances, and pension funds in order to build up assets for strenuous times. Many people became indirect investors in property and in so doing were essential contributors in the finance-dominated accumulation regime. This has an impact on the built environment and thus on the development of the built environment in metropolitan regions. This is particularly true when it comes to investments in housing and home ownership.

Particularly in the northern Scandinavian countries, but in Germany, Switzerland, and Austria as well, home ownership has become more important due to responsibilization. In Britain, home ownership became a social ideal during the Thatcher era. Despite the fact that home ownership has been traditionally important in many southern European countries, even in Spain and Italy home ownership has increased (see Table 4.1).

This has to do with the privatization of social, public, and cooperative housing, which reduced opportunities for renting and made home ownership compulsory (for Italy and Spain, see Magalhães 2001).

The reason for increasing home ownership is to shift responsibility to the social subjects: "The RTB ["Right to Buy," a strategy of the Thatcher government to justify the sell-out of public housing] forces human beings to provide for themselves and for next of kin and not to transfer this responsibility to the state.... politics should engage in creating responsible human beings and not to force them to rely on external power as the state" (King 2010: 225; author's translation). The challenge for low-income households is that while the percentage of protected (that is social, public, and collective) housing decreases, it is financially a very heavy burden to buy a home. In metropolitan areas, rising rents are a consequence of the decline of protected housing units. This is common in many metropolitan areas throughout Europe.

As a result, home ownership has increased considerably in European states (see Table 4.1). Despite compulsory job mobility, job instabilities, and concomitant problems such as credit loan defaults, it seems that home ownership is widely accepted as a possible safeguard against economic hardship and as security for old age. Even in Germany, which, together with Switzerland and Sweden, had the lowest percentage of homeowners (see Behring and Helbrecht 2003), home ownership has become more important.

Political incentives, such as tax reductions and financial support for purchase and rehabilitation, as well as new forms of financing, facilitated an increase in home ownership. But the main reason is the fundamental

Table 4.1   Percentage of homeowners in Europe

	% in 1990	% in 2012
Spain	76	85
Ireland	81	75
Norway	59	77
Great Britain	68	69
Italy	67	77
The Netherlands	44	60
France	54	58
Germany	38	46
Switzerland	31	35

Sources: For 1990 see Boelhouwer et al. 2005; for 2012 see ifs 2012: 3.

shift from welfare to workfare and the accompanying pressure to provide for oneself. Many households—particularly in Great Britain, Ireland, and Spain—have enjoyed easy access to credit and mortgage, with the result that the dream of owning one's own home has become feasible (Kitchin et al. 2012; Martin 2011; López and Rodríguez 2011). Part of this development has been the normalization of a calculative behaviour in individuals in the attempt to balance risk and yields; however, the housing crisis of the last few years has proven that calculations get difficult in unstable contexts (with changing housing prices, precarious employment, pressure on wages, etc.). In many countries, the outcome of these transformations is insolvency, foreclosures, and/or problems in refinancing that go along with difficulties in keeping up with the costs of home ownership. Map 4.1 gives an overview of how the proportion of the home ownership

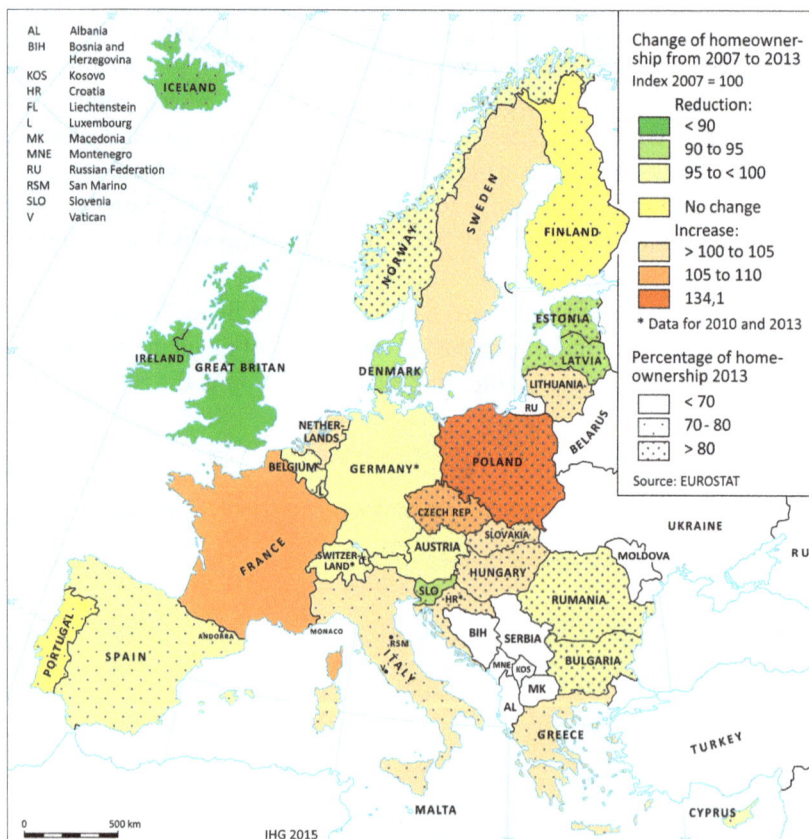

AL   Albania
BIH   Bosnia and Herzegovina
KOS   Kosovo
HR   Croatia
FL   Liechtenstein
L   Luxembourg
MK   Macedonia
MNE   Montenegro
RU   Russian Federation
RSM   San Marino
SLO   Slovenia
V   Vatican

Change of homeownership from 2007 to 2013
Index 2007 = 100
Reduction:
< 90
90 to 95
95 to < 100
No change
Increase:
> 100 to 105
105 to 110
134,1
* Data for 2010 and 2013

Percentage of homeownership 2013
< 70
70 - 80
> 80
Source: EUROSTAT

Map 4.1   Changes in percentage of population living in ownership in Europe of the 28 member states, 2007–13. *Sources*: Eurostat, income, and living conditions, 2015.

population has changed within the last ten years—covering the period before and after the financial and European debt crisis.

Here is not the space to discuss causes and outcomes of the housing crises, but the liberalization and globalization of financial markets as well as the responsibilization are part of such an explanation.

Urban Competition and Property-Led Development in Metropolitan Regions

According to Peter Hall, European cities were traditionally dense and compact, and depended almost exclusively on public transport (Hall 1997). This changed after World War Two, when cities in all Western European countries experienced suburbanization. Starting in Britain and the Benelux countries in the 1950s, the process spread to Germany and Scandinavia in the 1960s and then finally affected the countries formerly thought immune—France, Italy, Spain, and Portugal—in the 1970s and 1980s (Hall 1997: 214ff.). Since then, cities and municipalities in the suburbs of important cities have gained both population and employment and have merged into metropolitan regions. At present, metropolitan regions represent integral units with respect to work, life, sports, leisure, etc., with an overlapping infrastructure.

Despite this characterization, metropolitan regions are far from being homogenous or coherent spaces—neither in a political nor in a social sense. As pointed out in the introduction by the editors, place-specific dependencies and contextual embedding within historical and geograph- ically distinct political-economic and social networks has produced diver- gent and contested urban morphologies, administrative boundaries, and governance regimes. Metropolitan regions are divided by territorial boundaries, different economic growth potentials, and socio-spatial devel- opments. Because of these differences, metropolitan regions do not act "naturally" as collective actors but speak—against a background of trans- formation of constraints and opportunities—with different voices (Keil 2011). What makes this situation even more complicated is that all the different municipalities within a metropolitan region are autonomous political entities that engage in urban entrepreneurialism in order to shape local socio-economic development—quite often against the neighbouring municipality. Although more and more voices express the need to coop- erate and to establish new institutional arrangements, many metropolitan regions are not institutionally integrated but consist of municipalities and cities pursuing distinct aims and strategies. Until now, efforts to create joint strategies have been rare and difficult, although the debate on how to build up coherent regional infrastructure and governance is on the way.[4]

What contributes to the prevalence of competition in comparison to cooperation is that municipalities might on one hand benefit economically from autonomy if they manage to offer superior local conditions to economic and otherwise important actors. On the other hand, they are still responsible for their economic and social development. This means opportunities as well as challenges. However, these opportunities and challenges play out in difficult times. To a varying degree and speed, urban and municipal governments have been confronted for more than thirty years with growing social and financial burdens due to political devolution at the regional and local level, cutbacks in financial redistribution within the political system, and increasing unemployment due to economic reorganization (MacLeod 2001; Heeg 2001).

Deindustrialization, widespread unemployment, and fiscal austerity at both the national and local levels have enforced changes in local politics. Currently, local governments rely less on federal grants but are obliged to shape their own economic fortunes. According to David Harvey (1989), this context has enforced a shift toward urban entrepreneurialism typically resting on public–private partnerships with a focus on investment and economic development. This goes along with a much stronger appeal to market rationality and privatization instead of efforts to ameliorate social conditions within a particular territory. In that sense, urban entrepreneurial strategies build necessarily on a broader coalition of forces. Within these coalitions, urban governments and administration have a facilitative and coordinating role to play. Main addressees of local governmental endeavours are private and non-governmental actors. The aim is to stimulate or attract private business and thereby generate tax revenues and jobs. It is assumed that only private enterprise can stimulate economic growth, and create new and keep existing jobs. In this sense, the power to organize space and to shape infrastructures derives from a whole complex of forces consisting of diverse social agents. Not only do local governments and their administrations shape space, but so do private, social, and non-governmental actors. Within these new partnerships, coalitions, and alliances, real estate actors are of prime importance. Private real estate capital takes centre stage for the task of adapting the built environment to changing socio-economic demands and dynamics. Property—in the form of office, industrial, hotel, homes, and other building structures—is seen as a precondition for economic and social growth. Taken together, this implies the adoption of property-led development strategies in urban/local planning. In order to stimulate economic growth and innovation, a more flexible, liberal, less regulated planning is institutionalized. This approach is based on a partnership between private real estate capital and public planners and entails a developer-friendly planning process.

It is usually argued that the aim of the partnerships is to finance the reshaping and reconstruction of the built environment through private investments. This is accompanied by an opening up to the interests of the real estate industry. In stark contrast to the more passive role of private actors during the managerial era (Harvey 1989), the entrepreneurial urban era goes along with an active and enabling role for private real estate capital. Managerial urban politics centred on the idea that the built environment should improve mobility and provide basic infrastructure for local residents (Ward 2002). The shift implies a qualitative change: private sector interests become paramount due to their central role in project development and financing (Breitbach and Mitchell 2003). The role of the public sector is reduced to facilitating the functioning of the real estate market; "a healthy real estate market is necessary in order to motivate firms to stay in the region and to attract new enterprises.… Only if the local economic development agency manages to offer appropriate sites and buildings will the municipality be capable of emerging victorious from urban competition" (Markert and Zacharias 2006: 122; author's translation). In this context, the main aim of applying property-led development approaches is to facilitate renewal as well as new developments in industrial and commercial premises (Breitbach and Mitchell 2003). It is assumed that a missing "hardware" of building structures works as a hindrance to cumulative regional agglomeration effects. Gornig and Spars (2006: 569) claim that "The real estate and construction sector has a key position in facilitating economic growth because of its ability to overcome agglomeration impediments. Particularly important is the far-sighted planning and 'storage' of real estate supply according to the development of demand. This will stem possible price increases in rent and land caused by conditions of scarcity in metropolitan regions" (author's translation). According to Gornig and Spars, it is necessary to ensure the supply of appropriate sites and buildings in order to enable increasing returns for local industries.

The built environment is supposed to guarantee physical and spatial inputs to meet the requirements of new and changing production processes as well as new households. The anticipated cycle of accumulation "is one that begins with the development of property; such development attracts new capital; new capital creates new jobs, which in turn attracts an in-coming labour force; but it also creates tax and development-pressures on surrounding farmland" (Breitbach and Mitchell 2003: 223). It seems that property-led development becomes important as a last-ditch attempt to shape and mobilize urban and local potentials when there is a limited scope for endogenous, independent strategies within an increasingly deregulated and financialized global market. However, fixing urban development through property-led development is far from guaranteed (Heeg 2003).

The current debt crisis—as a consequence and by-product of the financial crisis of 2008—stirs property investments. Low-performing stock markets make real estate investments currently very attractive. Excess capital liquidity is searching the globe for high-performing investments and touches down in metropolitan areas. Properties in promising locations in metropolitan regions are currently very much in demand. However, the interest in properties and its uses is different in the central city, peripheral areas of cities, and suburbs.

The "hottest" investments are currently office buildings and condominiums in central city areas and detached houses, as well as industrial and logistic properties in the suburbs. After several years, in which scarcely any transaction in large housing estates took place, these investments in peripheral areas are again attractive for opportunistic investors[5] as REPE, hedge funds, and REITs. The boom in all these investments has contributed to increasing prices as well as rents throughout metropolitan regions. However, not only are global investors busy buying properties, but individuals are also eager to invest surplus money into condominiums and detached homes. The rush of individuals into property and home ownership is the most important factor for massive price increases. The process, as emphasized earlier, has spatially different features.

Central cities are the winners in the game. In a journal by the Industry and Trade Chamber of Frankfurt, Wilhelm Brandt, the spokesperson for CA Immo, one of the biggest German developers, emphasized "the return of urbanity" (Brandt 2007: 18ff.). He argued that all metropolitan regions experience a movement back to the cities. The highly developed infrastructure and the amenities in the city open up an attractive place to live and work. In addition to CA Immo, many developers and other investors have recognized the potentials of the central city, either in the form of luxury housing or in office investment. At the moment, many European cities (of metropolitan regions) are undergoing a kind of real estate gold rush. Investors are desperately looking for developable premises in the form of undeveloped or built-up areas. Three types of properties attract particular attention: former industrial or harbour areas that are close to the inner city and are approved for redevelopment as condominium blocks and/or office buildings; old historic residential buildings that need refurbishing and promise high yields after their conversion to condominiums; and, finally, office buildings in the inner city that are "all-time income-generating-machines." Although many cities in Europe—such as London, Paris, or Frankfurt—experience high vacancy rates in office buildings, inner-city office buildings with modern technical infrastructures still find office tenants willing to pay high rents (Goslich 2012: 18ff.). The high probability of finding new tenants makes these buildings very attractive to institutional investors as pension funds that seek stable income-generating revenues. A fierce competition accelerates rising prices so that the price gradient from the inner city to other parts of the city and the suburbs is steep. The central city promises positive returns, so that many core investors are active. Open-ended and closed real estate investment funds invest as risk averse—or so-called "core investors"—in industrial and office properties located in areas that are much in demand.

In particular, the price for working and living in the city has increased since the financial and debt crisis. Material expression is the competition between commercial (mostly office) and housing developments. REITs as well as specialized real estate funds prefer investments in inner-city housing stock (quite often old buildings with considerable potential in yield appreciation via rent/price increase), where housing/residential development schemes can compete with office developments due to high vacancy rates and high purchasing power of investors (who pass the price on to the future tenants or purchasers of condominiums). The segment includes mostly luxury housing, loft living, and historic old building structures. Taken together, this favours, on one hand, gentrification and on the other hand an expulsion of low-income households out of the central city. One effect is the displacement of the poor into the housing stock in peripheral areas of the city. Even though this displacement seems contradictory, it makes the formerly public housing stock in the peripheral areas of the city attractive for risk-taking investors. For the poor who do not have many options, the housing stock is one of the increasingly sparse possibilities of having a roof over their head. The poor are welcomed tenants by risk-taking institutional investors. The profit margins are the result of increased rents and especially decorating work that implies quite often that no investment into the materiality of the housing stock takes place. Instead, the quality is eroding (Holm 2011; Doling 1994).

In the central city as well as in the suburbs, many private investors try to activate their financial assets and to get a credit/mortgage (Boelhouwer et al. 2005). The attempt to safeguard assets against inflation explains the current rush to home ownership. Moreover, the low interest rates seem to make mortgages attractive. The hope is to protect financial assets and spare money against inflation and thus provide for old age. In order to meet these investment interests, in the suburbs as well as in the inner cities, local governments agree to new developments. The steady supply of attractive housing is seen as a prerequisite for attracting "high-potentials," technical innovators, and the creative class. Simultaneously, meeting the demand for future economic and demographic development goes along with flexible and project planning in order to shape the built environment accordingly (Behrend and Theiss 2010: 5).

The demand for housing (and other property types such as industrial, retail, and logistic properties) is so high, that many municipalities within metropolitan regions can scarcely meet the demand. Housing project after housing project is planned. However, this means that suburbs threaten their amenities due to excessive and uncoordinated building developments.

Conclusion: Bringing It All Together

Metropolitan regions seem to be a preferred investment objective. However, these regions are not homogenous investment locations. Real estate professions such as consultancies, developers, and investors contribute to and shape internal metropolitan pattern. They apply the "principle of uniformity" and use boundaries that divide the region into different, internally uniform areas: The practice of demarcating a neighbourhood is a form of market coordination—the greater the consensus on the boundaries, the greater the coordination. This creates high prices in attractive areas on one hand and a deteriorating building stock in peripheral areas on the other. The second process seems to support redlining in some cases (Aalbers 2011). What is central and what is peripheral, however, is not stable, but changes over time.

Contemporary metropolitan regions are more and more an outcome of parallel processes of fusion and fragmentation. They are increasingly enmeshed as well as structured by uneven development. Differential real estate investments are product and motor of the uneven development of capitalism. Uneven development within metropolitan areas is not a natural result but an outcome of delineating processes in territory, of prejudiced urban managers and gatekeepers, of the structure and regulation of the residential mortgage market, of statistical discrimination, or of neighbourhood decline and the devalorization of capital invested in the built environment (Aalbers 2011: 51). In this sense, the financialization of the built environment facilitates uneven development, fragmentation, and an increased volatility in capital flows. At the moment vast sums of money flow into property, but the effects are not more (low- or middle-income) housing but an increasing valorization and upgrading of the housing stock as well as a devalorization of subspaces. It is very likely that the differential development of subspaces will contribute to an increased competition between municipalities of the metropolitan region for real estate investments. Whether private investments as well as urban competition will help alleviate regional fragmentation is doubtful.

Notes

1 According to Ben Fine, financialization refers to (1) the expansion and proliferation of financial markets over the past thirty hears; (2) the expansion of speculative assets as opposed to investment in the "real economy"; (3) the expansion and proliferation of financial instruments and services; (4) the increasing dominance of finance over industry; (5) a strategy of redistribution to an international renter class (Lordon 2000); and (6) a strategy of debt-driven consumption (Fine 2009: 3ff.). Relevant for the discussion here are aspects 1, 2, and 3. They refer to the growing importance of financial markets and instruments that are also of paramount importance in the governance of the built environment (Heeg 2011).

2 Not all metropolitan regions are the targets of these investments. I discuss here those metropolitan regions that undergo economic and demographic growth (see Scott and Forbes 2012: 9).

3 An exception is open-ended funds.

4 For a discussion of urban, regional, and metropolitan governance, see MacLeod 2001, Heinelt 2011, Keil 2011, and Altrock 2011.

5 Opportunistic funds tend to focus on riskier strategies and utilize a higher degree of leverage to generate greater appreciation—in contrast to value added and core investors (see later in this chapter). Core funds are characterized as lower-risk vehicles that invest in stabilized, income-producing real estate. Value-added funds are characterized by capital invested to enhance income, resulting in higher appreciation than core funds (BlackRock 2010: 1).

References

Aalbers, M. 2008. "The financialization of home and the mortgage market crisis." *Competition & Change* 12(2): 148–66.

———. 2011. *Place, exclusion, and mortgage markets*. Chichester: Wiley-Blackwell.

Aglietta, M. 2000. *Ein neues Akkumulationsregime: Die Regulationstheorie auf dem Prüfstand*. Hamburg: VSA.

Altrock, U., ed. 2011. *Gewinnen, Verlieren, Transformieren. Die europäischen Stadtregionen in Bewegung*. Berlin: Reimer.

Behrend, R. and A. Theiss. 2010. *Zukunftsperspektiven für FrankfurtRheinMain. Perspektiven für den Wohnungsmarkt in FrankfurtRheinMain 2020*. Frankfurt am Main: Frankfurt am Main IHK Forum. www.frankfurt-main.ihk.de/pdf/standortpolitik/Zukunftsperspektiven_Wohnungsmarkt_FrankfurtRheinMain_2020.pdf.

Behring, K. and I. Helbrecht. 2003. "Mieter oder Selbstnutzer in Europa? Ursachen der unterschiedlichen Eigentümerquoten in Europa in ausgewählten europäischen Staaten." *Informationen zur Raumentwicklung* (6): 343–53.

Bellofiore, R. 2002. "Der Kapitalismus der Rentenfonds." In M. Aglietta, J. Bischoff, P. Boccara, W. F. Haug, and J. Huffschmid, eds., *Umbau der Märkte*. Hamburg: VSA.

BlackRock, ed. 2010. *Impact of market cycle on core, value-add and opportunistic real estate*. www2.blackrock.com/webcore/litService/search/get Document.seam?contentId=1111111822&Source=SEARCH&Venue=PUB_ INS.

Blank, F., B. Ewert, and S. Köppe. 2012. "Leistungsempfänger, Bürger oder Konsumenten? Nutzer in der Sozialpolitik." *WSI Mitteilungen* 65 (3): 168.

Boelhouwer, P. J., J. F. Doling, and M. Elsinga eds. 2005. *Home ownership: Getting in, getting from, getting out*. Delft: DUP Science.

Breitbach, C. and D. Mitchell. 2003. "Growth machines and growth pains: The contradictions of property development and landscape in Sioux Falls South Dakota." In A. MacLaran, ed., *Making Space: Property development and urban planning*. London: Arnold.

Boulay, G. 2012. "Real estate market and urban transformations: Spatio-temporal analysis of house price increase in the centre of Marseille (1996–2010)." *Articulo* (9): 2–19.

Brandt, W. 2007. "Rückkehr der Urbanität." *IHK Wirtschaftsforum* (10): 18–19.

Doling, J. 1994. "The privatisation of social housing in European welfare states." *Environmental Planning* C 12(2): 243–55.

Eurostat 2015. "Income and living conditions: Distribution of population by tenure status." http://appsso.eurostat.ec.europa.eu/nui/submitViewTableAction .do

Fine, B. 2009. "Neo-liberalism in retrospect? – It's financialisation, stupid!" Presentation at the Developmental Politics in the Neo-Liberal Era and Beyond Conference, October 22–24, 2009, Center for Social Sciences, Seoul National University. http://eprints.soas.ac.uk/7993/1/seoulart.pdf.

García, M. 2010. "The breakdown of the Spanish urban growth model: Social and territorial effects of the global crisis." *International Journal of Urban and Regional Research* 34(4): 967–80.

Gornig, M. and G. Spars. 2006. "Bedeutung der Bau- und Immobilienwirtschaft für die Wettbewerbsfähigkeit von Städten und Regionen." *Informationen zur Raumentwicklung* 10: 567–74.

Goslich, L. 2012. "Immer noch gilt Lage, Lage, Lage. Gewerbeimmobilien bieten gute Chancen für erfahrene Privat-Anleger." *Süddeutsche* Zeitung. November 28, 2012.

Hall, P. 1997. "The future of the metropolis and its form." *Regional Studies* 31(3): 211–20.

Harvey, D. 1985. *The urbanization of capital: Studies in the history and theory of capitalist urbanization*. Baltimore: Johns Hopkins University Press.

———. 1989. "From managerialism to entrepreneurialism: The transformation in urban governance in late capitalism." *Geographiska Annaler* 71(1): 3–17.

Heeg, S. 2001. *Politische Regulation des Raums. Metropolen – Regionen – Nationalstaat*. Berlin: edition sigma.

————. 2003. "Städtische Flächenentwicklung vor dem Hintergrund von Veränderungen in der Immobilienwirtschaft." *Raumforschung und Raumordnung* (5): 334–44.

————. 2011. "Finanzkrise und städtischen Immobilienmärkten: räumliche Auswirkungen in und zwischen Städten." In A. Demirović et al., eds., *Vielfach-Krise: Im finanzmarktdominierten Kapitalismus*. Hamburg: VSA.

Heinelt, H. 2011. *Metropolitan governance: Different paths in contrasting contexts: Germany and Israel*. Frankfurt am Main: Campus.

Holm, A. 2011. "Politiken und Effekte der Wohnungsprivatisierungen in Europa." In B. Belina et al., eds., *Urbane Differenzen. Disparitäten innerhalb und zwischen Städten*. Münster: Westfälisches Dampfboot.

Huffschmid, J. 2009. "Nicht die Krise, der Finanzkapitalismus ist das Problem. Vom »normalen« Funktionieren von Umverteilung und Instabilität." In M. Candeias and R. Rilling, eds., *Krise. Neues vom Finanzkapitalismus und seinem Staat*. Berlin: Karl-Dietz-Verlag (Texte der Rosa-Luxemburg-Stiftung 55).

ifs – Institut für Städtebau, Wohnungswirtschaft und Bausparwesen. 2012. Selbstgenutztes Wohneigentum/Eigentumsquote. http://typo3.p165294.webspace config.de/fileadmin/Daten_Fakten/Wohneigentumsquoten_in_Deutschland_und_Europa.pdf.

Jacobs, J. 1992. *The death and life of great American cities*. New York: Vintage.

Keil, R. 2011. "The global city comes home: Internalised globalisation in Frankfurt Rhine-Main." *Urban Studies* 48(12): 2495–517.

King, P. 2010. "Die Privatisierung von Sozialwohnungen: Das 'Right to Buy' in Großbritannien." In K. Funk, ed., *Gesellschaftspolitische Vorteile des Wohneigentums. Aspekte des Wohneigentums*. Berlin: Liberal Verlag.

Kitchin, R., C. O'Callaghan, M. Boyle, J. Gleeson, and K. Keaveney. 2012. "Placing neoliberalism: The rise and fall of Ireland's Celtic tiger." *Environmental Planning A* 44(6): 1302–26.

Lefebvre, H., E. Kofman, and E. Lebas. 1996. *Writings on cities*. Oxford: Blackwell.

Legnaro, A., A. Birenheide, and M. Fischer. 2005. *Kapitalismus für alle. Aktien, Freiheit und Kontrolle*. Münster: Westfälisches Dampfboot.

López, I. and E. Rodríguez. 2011. "The Spanish model." *New Left Review* 69: 5–29.

Lordon, F. 2000. *"Aktionärsdemokratie" als soziale Utopie? Über das neue Finanzregime und Wirtschaftsdemokratie*. Hamburg: VSA.

MacLeod, G. 2001. "New regionalism reconsidered: Globalization and the remaking of political economic space." *International Journal of Urban and Regional Research* 25(4): 804–29.

Magalhães, C. S. de. 2001. "International property consultants and the transformation of local markets." *Journal of Property Research* 18(1): 99–121.

Markert, C. and T. Zacharias. 2006. "Wirtschaftsförderung und Immobilienwirtschaft. Partner in der operativen Stadtentwicklung." *Standort* 3: 118–22.

Martin, R. 2011. "The local geographies of the financial crisis: From the housing bubble to economic recession and beyond." *Journal of Economic Geography* 11(4): 587–618.

Scott, L. and J. Forbes. 2012. *Emerging trends in real estate: Europe*. New York: Price Waterhouse Coopers.

Serfati, C. 2000. "Globalised finance-dominated accumulation regime and sustainable development." *International Journal of Sustainable Development* 3(1): 40–62.

Shamir, R. 2008. "The age of responsibilization: on market-embedded morality." *Economy and Society* 37(1): 1–19.

Theurillat, T., J. Corpataux, and O. Crevoisier. 2010. "Property sector financialization: The case of Swiss pension funds (1992–2005)." *European Planning Studies* 18(2): 189–212.

Twickel, C. 2012. "Sollen Sie doch nach Marzahn ziehen!" *Spiegel online*. November 30, 2012. www.spiegel.de/kultur/tv/maybrit-illner-talk-ueber -mietensteigerungen.html

Vogl, J. 2011. *Das Gespenst des Kapitals*. 4. Aufl. Zürich: Diaphanes.

Ward, S. V. 2002. *Planning the twentieth-century city: The advanced capitalist world*. Chichester: Wiley.

CHAPTER 5

The Global City-Region
A Constantly Emerging Scalar Fix

Bernd Belina and Ute Lehrer

New Regionalisms, Old Competitions

THE INTER-SCALAR RELATIONSHIPS, which are produced, reproduced, and transformed through global city formation, have been discussed in urban studies for some time (Keil and Mahon 2009). In this context, the role and relevance of regions, regionalizations, and regionalisms has garnered new interest. More than a decade ago, Scott, Agnew, Soja, and Storper, for example, claimed that "city-regions increasingly function as essential spatial nodes of the global economy and as distinctive political actors on the world stage" (2001: 11), with the latter—the global city-region as political actor—still under construction: "The creation of new and responsive frameworks of regional governance capable of sustaining economic development, instigating a sense of cooperative regional identity, and promoting innovative ways of achieving regional democracy and economic fair play is the great challenge for the future" (Scott et al. 2001: 21).

While we acknowledge both the diversity within this strand of recent urban studies literature and the critique directed at it from various directions, we believe it is safe to state that this view is shared by many across theoretical and political spectrums in one way or another. The city-region, and the global city-region in particular, as an economic, political, and social entity—be it territorial or networked, be it relatively fixed or constantly emerging, be it constructed "from above" or "from below" (cf. Allen and Cochrane 2007; Amin 2004; Jonas 2012; Macleod and Jones

2007)—is regarded by many as an increasingly important scale in current capitalism that is produced, more or less directly, as a result of global competition and uneven development. Some go so far as to see the metropolitan region as a privileged site to achieve "spatial justice" (Soja 2010).

We argue that much of this literature, focusing almost exclusively on successful region-building projects, fails to take into account the structures of competition that exist *within* city-regions. Such competition may enable or counter attempts at and strategies of regionalization depending on how these processes articulate with each other. Among these intra-regional structures of competition, some of the more important ones include inter-capitalist competition, the competition between public, semi-public, non-profit, and private agencies, and the competition between municipalities. It is on the latter that we focus in this chapter, suggesting that inter-municipal competition, often induced from the national scale, can be used by corporations to play off municipalities within a region against each other.

Against the view that regards the integration of corporations into global markets as a driver of both economic and political integration on the regional scale, we argue that a dialectic is at work between regional economic integration into clusters and networks on one hand and inter-municipal competition within the region on the other hand, with both sides of the dialectic allowing for strategic use on the part of corporations. Depending on the regional relation of forces and the way in which these have materialized institutionally, thereby producing structural selectivities, this dialectic can result in more or less serious attempts at inter-municipal cooperation and the forming of a politically institutionalized region. We believe that hopes and aspirations for global city-regions as political entities that are at the same time economically competitive, identity producing *and* "spatially just" are often premature. The contradictory relationship between practices, interest and processes aiming at regional cooperation and intra-regional competition will develop path-dependently in different locations and will concern different subject matters. Under conditions of a neo-liberalizing hegemony, we argue, the result is in many cases a fuzzy picture of competing regionalizations and regional actors. We call this a *constantly emerging regional scalar fix* that structures the region in such a way that certain individual capitals and fractions of capital will profit from it.

Spatial scales were theorized by Smith (1984) and others (cf. Swyngedouw 1997 and Brenner 2004) as resulting from tensions between cooperation and competition in economic, political, and social processes. They allow for "the spatial resolution to contradictory social forces; in partic-ular the resolution between opposing forces of competition and coopera-tion" (Smith 1995: 61) within the "dialectic between differentiation and equalization" (Smith 1984: 135). As result and "resolution" of social interaction and struggle, "these scale redefinitions alter and express changes in the geometry of social power by strengthening power and control of some while disempowering others" (Swyngedouw 2000: 70–71; cf. Brenner 2004, MacKinnon 2011). Attempts to produce the political scale of the region, then, are attempts to actively change power relations within the region and beyond. Resulting regionalizations bear the mark of the struggles that formed them and have them inscribed in their insti-tutional as well as spatial structure. In a situation where the gains from competition within the region outweigh those that interregional cooper-ation offers to powerful actors, a situation can arise in which different actors pursue different "scale jumping" strategies and push for different institutionalizations of the region, while others expect more gains from either not participating in these attempts, or from using the different regionalizations to their own favour.

On the surface, we see an ongoing plethora of attempts to institution-alize the region. Resulting regionalizations that are often portrayed in maps showing all sorts of partly overlapping but competing regions hint at, and at the same time hide, the power struggles that produced this fuzziness in the first place. As attempts to form regional institutions usu-ally build on existing municipal territories, one central aspect of the fuzz-iness of the constantly emerging regional scalar fix is the way in which individual municipalities participate in region-building activities. This goes along with questions such as these: How do elites and other residents position "their" municipality within the region? How do they see and use the region, both in practice and in discourse? And why? What are the gains and losses "the region" can offer to various local actors? Or can they gain from competition within the region? The ways in which region-alizations and the production of a regional political scale proceed are crucially determined by how state and non-state actors perceive and plan to use the region.

With our analysis, we would like to reinsert into the debate of the city-region the crucial fact that "[l]ocal jurisdictions frequently divide rather than unify the urban region, thus emphasizing the segmentations (such as that between city and suburb) rather than the tendency toward structured coherence and class-alliance formation" (Harvey 1989: 153). We want to especially focus on how certain social groups—namely capi-tal—can profit from these segmentations resulting from inter-municipal competition, at the expense of other—namely various subaltern—groups. We believe that debates on the relationship between core city and regional peripheries/suburbs can profit from such a focus on the political economy of regionalizations, central economic actors, and the materializations of relations of force on the regional scale in at least three ways. First, such a view takes seriously municipalities outside the core city of city-regions as actively forming the city-region. Second, focusing on central political and economic actors allows for the integration of approaches that concentrate more on the territorial and scalar characteristics of political institutionalizations of regions as well as those that emphasis the networked and topological character of the interactions between regional actors. Third, comparing the functioning of the dialectic between global and regional integration between metropolitan regions takes seriously the commonalities between regions—resulting from the fact that they are formed under capitalist conditions and within capitalist states—while at the same time highlighting differences between regions, understood as different manifestations of the dialectic between global and regional integration.

Empirical Background

We illustrate our argument with empirical evidence from an ongoing comparative research project that looks at the ways in which elites in mid-size suburban municipalities in the Toronto and Frankfurt regions position their municipality within their respective global city-region.[1] How are the identities of these municipalities constructed by local elites, especially with regards to the binaries of local-regional and urban-suburban? Following theorizations of "place" and their "identity" by Massey (1994) and Harvey (1996), we are interested in the social processes and relations that go into this identification, and particularly in the relations of force that condense in the specific, constantly emerging regional scalar fix.

The municipalities chosen for our case study approach are Markham in the Toronto region and Eschborn in the Frankfurt region. While more details on these municipalities are given below, we want to briefly introduce these two global city-regions.

From a global perspective, Frankfurt am Main and Toronto are secondary financial centres (Todd 2005; Taylor 2004; Sassen 1996; Bördlein 1999; Hitz et al. 1995; Kipfer and Keil 2002; Boudreau et al. 2009; Brenner and Keil 2006). Both cities have undergone major restructuring in regards to their industries: In Frankfurt, two out of three manufacturing jobs disappeared between 1970 and 2008, while employment in the service sector expanded steadily, reaching 89% of all jobs in 2008. The most robust growth took place in the financial sector, with an increase of over 82% during the same period. The surrounding communities benefited from relocation of manufacturing and new logistical centres as well as from an increase in service sector and back-office employment. Simultaneously, population grew both in Frankfurt, to 697,509 (with 464,000 jobs), as well as in its surrounding municipalities, constituting an integrated metropolitan region of over 5.5 million in mid-2012.[2] In the Canadian case, while manufacturing declined by18% between 2001 and 2006, the region still remains a major manufacturing engine (Toronto Workforce Innovation 2010). Service employment in finance and insurance increased by 24% between 2004 and 2009. The city of Toronto, with 2.8 million people and 1.4 million jobs,[3] is the centre of a region of 6.1 million residents and 3.4 million jobs.[4] The strength of the financial, cultural, and high tech industries downtown has also driven employment numbers and residential growth in surrounding municipalities.

Instances of Inter-municipal Competition and Corporate Profit in and Through the Region

In what follows, we sketch two instances of inter-municipal competition from our case study regions. They are deliberately different in content and scope and generalizable to different degrees; and their reconstruction is based on different methodologies. What both of these instances have in common, though, is that they shed some light on the contentious relationship between regionalization and inter-municipal competition through the way in which suburban identities are constructed in relation to the region.

Peripheries going global

It is commonly believed that global city-regions are successful in globalized interurban competition (for an overview, see Brenner and Keil 2006) because they condense centralized functions of economic activity, such as financial industries, transportation infrastructure, and communications technologies, in networked global circuits (Castells 1996). Although it is recognized that the production of this centrality entails particular, specialized processes in specific sites (Sassen 1996), the assumption prevails that those processes are themselves tied to centrality. This may no longer be the case. What we find in the global city-regions we are studying are instances of suburban municipalities consciously "going global" themselves.

Our case in point is the municipality of Markham, which was incorporated as a Town in 1969 and has experienced rapid growth in the past decade. With a current population of more than 332,000,[5] it has become the fourth largest community in the Greater Toronto Region and the sixteenth largest within Canada. In order to reflect its new identity as a major player within the region and also to raise its profile for international business investments, it changed its name from "Town of Markham" to "City of Markham" on July 1, 2012 (CBC News 2012). This switch to city status has no implications for Markham's powers as a municipality.

Markham is home to more than 400 corporate head offices and close to 900 high technology and life sciences companies (City of Markham 2013: 3). These two sectors account for 38,000 out of the 140,000 jobs and are at the core of Markham's "economic strategy." In the words of its self-promotional material, the city "will continue to attract highly educated and skilled immigrants; build on its leadership position in the high tech and life sciences sectors; and reach out to global markets, both to bring investments into Markham as well as to provide Markham-based businesses with global opportunities" (ibid.). Attracted by low tax rates and proximity to the larger urban centre of Toronto, the top twenty employers of Markham include companies from manufacturing and the financial industry, such as IBM Canada, TD Waterhouse, American Express, AMD Technologies, CGI Information Systems, Allstate Insurance, General Electric, and Honda Canada.

The proposal to develop a large sports arena in order to attract a hockey team from the highest league was presented as a major economic development scheme (though, eventually, it was voted down at the local Council), as was the Master Plan for developing a downtown area in the traditionally low-density town. This high intensity of development strategies speaks to Markham's tremendous growth ambitions.

What began as a farmers' settlement of European descent in the eighteenth century and, thanks to the combination of many water sources for mills and its good connection to the transportation network, expanded to include also agriculture-based industries, Markham's socio-cultural development in the later part of the second half of the twentieth century took a major turn. In the most recent census track from 2011, some form of Chinese (Mandarin, Cantonese, or non specified) was spoken by more than one third of the population, followed by various languages from the South Asian area, as the largest non-English mother tongue group. As home to 72% of "visible minorities," with 58% of its population born outside of Canada, Markham's cultural diversity is evident (City of Markham 2013: 9). No wonder the urban landscape includes malls catering specifically to Chinese and Indian communities offering a variety of traditional products, apparel, food, and language services. The city also celebrates its cultural diversity and emphasizes community development through civic programs and development projects that include new multi-purpose community centres.

Building on its cultural diversity, Markham has developed many international economic ties, signing "twinning" or "sistering" agreements with other cities for the purpose of enhanced international investment opportunity. To this end, the municipality organizes trips with "delegations to India or China or Israel, to name a few" (interview with Mayor Scarpitti, June 5, 2012), supporting local businesses that search for investment opportunities, strategic partners, markets, and the like. The way the mayor presents this connectivity of Markham to global circuits and flows shows how the municipality is represented as a global player in its own right that does not need the global city-region:

> Since we have so many global citizens here, our delegation includes a lot of local people that are from there, which is a great kind of way to get in to the different businesses, the sectors and even the government officials. It's been a real win-win having the global citizens living here with us. But now when we go back to China and India, anywhere from eighty to over ninety percent of the delegates are ex-pats who are telling them our story. And no one tells it better than them because they speak the language. There are no barriers and so there's a real strength in taking people from our community—business leaders. So, it's building on the strength of the global citizens that we've attracted. (Interview Mayor)

The mayor notes that even the recent change to calling Markham a "city" rather than a "town" had its roots in Markham's perceived reputation in the world: "We were a city in everything but name. So we were the town of Markham ... it was kind of a mixed messaging.... And what we're finding is, especially when we go to India and China—on international trips—when you say you're from the town of Markham, people get visions of dirt roads and unsophistication" (Interview Mayor).

At the same time, the Mayor takes great pains to make clear that Markham profits from being part of the Toronto global city-region: "I think as much as we've carved out our niche within the Toronto region, ... part of our success is because we are a part of the Toronto region ... we have a safe, world-class city as a neighbour." When pushed on the question of inter-municipal competition on the regional scale, he states: "I think there's a healthy competition because when people are being able to compare notes they are able to say, what is the tax structure? What amenities, what types of communities are you creating? What type of labour pool are you attracting to your communities? And, on all of those fronts I think we would score quite well" (Interview Mayor).

Although we have to be careful when interpreting these statements, in our reading they encapsulate not only the uneasy regional compromise between competition and cooperation, but also hint toward the forces profiting from this compromise: businesses that are happy about the "pro-business environment" (City of Markham 2013: 3) and that profit from municipalities that outcompete each other in the realms of "amenities" and "tax structure."

Before we turn to the latter subject matter for our second example, we can summarize with reference to the dialectic between regional and global integration that Markham as a municipality is playing an active part in the global integration of corporations located within its confines. Markham's elites do not regard the city as being at the receiving end of the merits of Toronto's status as a global city, but as a city with a global strategy of its own. Within the dialectic between regional and global integration, this position weakens attempts at political cooperation between the peripheral and the core city.

Competing for tax money

At first glance, the business perspective on regionalization is univocally positive both in Frankfurt and Toronto. In Toronto, the organized regional business community articulates its commitment for a "business cluster strategy" (Wilding and Hillier 2012), while in Frankfurt there are "high expectations" in regards to regional cooperation (May 2012). This positive take on regionalization holds true as long as individual business owners see themselves as part of the collective "regional capital"—because they profit from it. As soon as it becomes possible to use inter-municipal competition within the region to their advantage, individual business owners will do so and "the region" is reduced to a rhetorical device. We want to illustrate this with a story from the Frankfurt region.

Local business tax is the most important tax revenue for German municipalities. It is calculated on the basis of a company's operating profits, which then are multiplied by 3.5% and a rate fixed by the municipality. While a variety of additional elements—such as the value of a company's assets, the rent it pays, losses from previous years, and many other factors—make the calculation more complex, in the political realm as well as for large corporations, the local rate ("Hebesatz") is central in debates and calculations. According to an overview provided by the National Association of the Chambers of Commerce, the local rate in 2007 varied between the legal minimum of 200 points and 490 points. In general, big cities set a higher rate, as they need to sustain more material and social infrastructure than smaller ones (Arbeitskreis Standortverlagerung 2009).

Using their authority to fix the collection rate, municipal governments are torn between raising the rate to create additional income, and lowering it in order to attract new businesses or keep old ones from moving away. One recent example from the Frankfurt region illustrates the way in which setting the collection rate of local business tax is used by the suburban municipality of Eschborn to outcompete the central city of Frankfurt. The small city of 21,000 inhabitants that directly neighbours Frankfurt accounts for 31,300 jobs, 91.5% of which are in the service sector.[6] Among these, financial services account for 14%.[7]

According to the city's self-promotion materials, the city's economic success is based on two main factors: "Managers confirm that the main benefit for them is Eschborn's strategic proximity to Frankfurt Airport and the high-speed train link [to Frankfurt and the rest of Germany]. Another crucial factor in the choice of location is Eschborn's ['competitive tax policy'],[8] as one CEO describes it" (Stadt Eschborn 2013: 34). This constellation is much to the disdain of Frankfurt's elites.

Frankfurt is the centre of continental European financial capital, head-quarters to both the German and the European central banks as well as all major German and many international banks; in addition it is home to many highly specialized service providers for the financial industry. Also, Frankfurt is the location of the major continental European stock market—or at least of its "mailbox."

In 2008, the most important German stock exchange corporation by far, the Deutsche Börse Group, announced the relocation of most of its offices with 2,000 jobs from the city of Frankfurt to the neighbouring town of Eschborn. Only a few jobs, the postal address, and the publicly-visible part of the stock exchange, the floor trading, remain in Frankfurt. While Frankfurt's business tax collection rate is set at 460 points, one of the highest in Germany, Eschborn's is a mere 280 points. Deutsche Börse Group is estimated to save around fifty million euros a year (exact figure unavailable due to tax secrecy) due to the relocation. While politicians in Frankfurt were shocked and frustrated, the mayor of Eschborn, the CEO of Deutsche Börse, and politicians from the federal state of Hessen framed the relocation as a "commitment to the region" (cf. Belina 2013).

In this case, Frankfurt's attempt to compete with neighbouring munic-ipalities and other places across the nation and the globe was not success-ful. Even though Frankfurt had lowered its business taxes several times—from 515 to 500 in 2000, and from 490 to 460 only in 2007, losing an estimated seventy million euros a year (Ochs 2008)—it nevertheless could not hold on to the main parts of the Deutsche Börse.

This ongoing lowering of the business taxes is part of a process within the region that Map 5.1 illustrates. The municipalities in dark grey have reduced their business tax collection rate in the 2000s. This is particularly true for the municipalities in the vicinity of Frankfurt (and Frankfurt itself) that have used the tax rate to outcompete each other. The further we move away from the core and the weaker the economic ties between municipalities and the core city, the less important the tax seems to be as a means in competition and the more municipalities seem to rely on tax income.

Given this background, we can interpret the relocation of the stock exchange as a single corporation's strategic use of the inter-municipal competition that exists within the region. When heralded as a commitment to the region by actors with vested interests, "the region" becomes an ideological device to legitimate tax avoidance, which is partly fostered

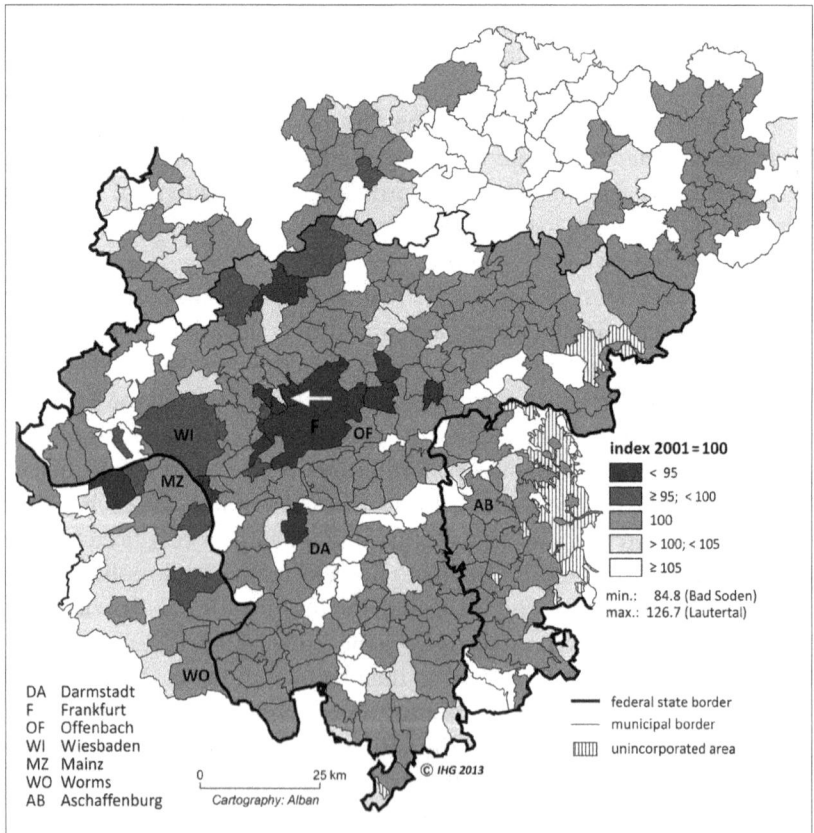

Map 5.1   Change of local business tax collection rate in municipalities of Frankfurt Rhine-Main region 2001–9.

by the government of Hesse, which wants to keep the wealth within the region but is less specific about inter-municipal competition. This creates an environment in which the increased wealth accumulation of one municipality is based on depriving neighbouring ones.[9]

Unsurprisingly, elites in Frankfurt use "the region" in quite different ways, complaining about the "cannibalism" of the hinterland and demanding legislation prohibiting inter-municipal competition via the business collection rate (for details, see Belina 2013). In all of this, "the region," in both practice and discourse, is merely a means toward the end of the Deutsche Börse AG and its shareholders: namely, to save money. This tax money is lost to residents in the region whose municipal infrastructure—in one of the richest regions of Europe—will deteriorate yet again due to the steady deficit of the municipal budgets.

The competition via local business taxes in a region whose core city has a history of several decades of "entrepreneurial city" discourse and politics (Schipper 2013) is one central moment of what has been called the "double logic of competition" (Ronneberger 2012: 21) at work in the Frankfurt region since the 2000s. In other words, while global and national policies posit the region in a competition against other major urban centres such as Munich, Zurich, Paris, and London, national and regional policies put municipalities within the region in competition with each other. The tension between the two results not in a unified regional political entity, but in a constantly emerging regional scalar fix with a variety of regionalizations concerning specific issues such as "marketing, economic development, promotion of culture, local recreation, transportation, water supply or sewage disposal" (Zimmermann and Monstadt 2012: 347; cf. Keil 2011), where municipalities cooperate that would otherwise try to outcompete each other constantly.

With regards to the dialectics between global and regional integration, the possibility of using the local business tax rate as a means of interurban competition on the regional scale, and the way in which Eschborn used it, highlight the obstacles to political integration on the regional scale. For the Deutsche Börse AG, staying within the region is advantageous due to its multiple networked connections within the region as well as the symbolic value of Frankfurt. Its global integration profits from its regional integration. But this does not lead to regional political integration; quite the contrary: its relocation to Eschborn is a case in point of a corporation profiting from inter-municipal competition within the region.

The Dialectic Between Global and Regional Integration

This chapter examined the global city-region as a continuously emerging scalar fix resulting from the dialectic between global and regional integration. We argue that this emerging and constantly oscillating scalar fix is negotiated by a web of self-interested actors, both political/territorial and corporate/networked. The outcome is a regional "structured coherence" that relies not only on the strength of the centre but explicitly depends on a decentralized structure of power sharing, division of labour and functions, and a mix of conflict and cooperation among various regional players. Using two illustrations, we pointed especially to the possibility that rather mundane *cui bono* ("to whose benefit?") questions may help to grasp the complexity of regional networks and their politico-territorial governance.

To understand the way in which regions actually become political entities, we need to take a close look at the social forces at work, their relation to each other, the spatial forms they use—territories, scales, networks, and places—and the resulting power structures between political and corporate actors, among others. Far from being an almost automatic result of capitalist uneven development, the political institutionalization of regions is the result of power struggles in which the region is as much a means as an end. Based on our illustration, what we would expect to find more often than not are relations of force that result in "the region" being a discursive and practical means in the hands of capital and corporate power and political actors close to their interests that will counter any attempt to foster "spatial justice" through the metropolitan region.

Notes

1 This research is supported by a Social Science and Humanities Research Council of Canada grant, Ute Lehrer, Principal Investigator, "Suburban identities in the global city between competition and cooperation: Toronto and Frankfurt," Standard Research Project SSHRC, 2011–2017.
2 www.statistik-hessen.de/themenauswahl/bevoelkerung-gebiet/regionaldaten/bev oelkerung-der-hessischen-gemeinden.
3 www1.toronto.ca/City%20Of%20Toronto/City%20Planning/SIPA/Files/pdf/S/survey2014revised.pdf.
4 www1.toronto.ca/City%20Of%20Toronto/Economic%20Development%2&%20Culture/Business%20Pages/Operate%20&%20Grow%20your%20Business/Business%20Improvement%20Areas/BIA%20Resources/2016-march.pdf.
5 www.markham.ca/wps/portal/Markham/AboutMarkham/FactsStats/.
6 www.eschborn.de/wirtschaft/zahlen-und-fakten.
7 www.eschborn.de/wirtschaft/zahlen-und-fakten/arbeitsmarkt.
8 In the original, it is called "sporting tax policy" (2013: 34) to describe its competitiveness with other locations.

9 In 2012, Eschborn had by far the highest per capita income from local business tax; www.focus.de/regional/wiesbaden/finanzen-gewerbesteuer-sprudelt-weiter -kroesus-eschborn_aid_971478.html; accessed March 25, 2014.

References

Allen, J. and A. Cochrane. 2007. "Beyond the territorial fix: Regional assemblages, politics and power." *Regional Studies* 41(9): 1161–75.

Amin, A. 2004. "Regions unbound: Towards a new politics of place." *Geografiska Annaler B* 86(1): 33–44.

Arbeitskreis Standortverlagerung und Gewerbesteuer der deutschen Industrie- und Handelskammern. 2009. *Standort Deutschland – Standortfaktor Gewerbesteuer*. Accessed February 25, 2014. www.dihk.de/themenfelder/ recht-und-fairplay/steuern/unternehmensteuern/positionen/standortfaktor -gewerbesteuer.

Belina, B. 2013. "Region, Strukturierte Kohärenz und Continuously Emerging Scalar Fix. Zu Kooperation und Konkurrenz in der Global City Region Frankfurt Rhein-Main." In *Die konflikthafte Konstitution der Region. Kultur, Politik, Ökonomie*. Münster: Westfälisches Dampfboot, ed. O. Brand, S. Dörhöfer, and P. Eser, 140–61.

Bördlein, R. 1999. "Finanzdienstleistungen in Frankfurt am Main. Ein europäisches Finanzzentrum zwischen Kontinuität und Umbruch." *Berichte zur deutschen Landeskunde* 73(1): 67–93.

Boudreau, J. A., R. Keil, and D. Young. 2009. *Changing Toronto: Governing urban neoliberalism*. Toronto: University of Toronto Press.

Brenner, N. 2004. "Urban governance and the production of new state spaces in Western Europe, 1960–2000." *Review of International Political Economy* 11(3): 447–88.

———. 2009. "A thousand leaves: Notes on the geographies of uneven spatial development." In R. Keil and R. Mahon, eds., *Towards a political economy of scale*. Vancouver: University of British Columbia Press.

Brenner, N. and R. Keil, eds. 2006. *The global cities reader*. London and New York: Routledge.

Castells, M. 1996. *The rise of the network society*. Oxford: Blackwell.

CBC News. 2012. "Markham to change from town to city." May 30. www.cbc .ca/news/canada/toronto/markham-to-change-from-town-to-city-1.1179129 Accessed August 10, 2015.

City of Markham. 2013. "Economic profile: Year end 2012." Markham: Economic Development Department. Accessed August 11, 2015. www .markham.ca/wps/wcm/connect/markhampublic/087449db-a5b6-49a5 -9ce9-b6366699e795/Economic+Profile+Markham+Year+End+2012.pdf? MOD=AJPERES&CACHEID=087449db-a5b6-49a5-9ce9-b6366699e795.

Harvey, D. 1989. *The urban experience*. Oxford: Blackwell.

———. 1996. *Justice, nature and the geography of difference*. Oxford: Blackwell.

Hitz, H., R. Keil, U. Lehrer, C. Schmid, K. Ronneberger, and R. Wolff. 1995. *Capitales Fatales: Urbanisierung und Politik in den Finanzmetropolen Frankfurt und Zürich*. Zürich: Rotpunkt Verlag.

Jonas, A. E. G. 2012. "Region and place: Regionalism in question." *Progress in Human Geography* 36(2): 263–72.

Keil, R. 2011. "The global city comes home: Internalised globalisation in Frankfurt Rhine-Main." *Urban Studies* 48(12): 2495–517.

Keil, R. and R. Mahon, eds. 2009. *Leviathan undone? Towards a political economy of scale.* Vancouver: University of British Columbia Press.

Kipfer, S. and R. Keil. 2002. "Toronto Inc? Planning the competitive city in the new Toronto." *Antipode* 34(2): 227–64.

MacKinnon, D. 2011. "Reconstructing scale: Towards a new scalar politics." *Progress in Human Geography* 35(1): 21–36.

Macleod, G. and M. Jones. 2007. "Territorial, scalar, networked, connected: In what sense a 'regional world'?" *Regional Studies* 41(9): 1177–91.

Massey, D. 1994. *Space, place, and gender.* Minneapolis: University of Minnesota Press.

May, A. 2012. "'Es steht viel auf dem Spiel' – Ein Gespräch mit IHK-Präsident Dr. Mathias Müller über eine zukunftsfähige Organisationsstruktur für die Metropolregion FrankfurtRheinMain und die neuen Handlungsspielräume des Regionalverbandes." *IHK WirtschaftsForum* 135(4): 8–9.

Ochs, J. 2008. "Abstimmung mit Portemonnaie – und mit Füßen. Der beschlossene Wegzug der Börse aus Frankfurt schockt die Stadt und schiebt einen neuerlichen Keil zwischen die Kommunen der Rhein-Main-Region." *Frankfurter Rundschau,* January 15, 3.

Ronneberger, K. 2012. *Machbarkeitsstudie über eine Untersuchung zur sozial-räumlichen Entwicklung der Metropolregion Rhein-Main unter besonderer Berücksichtigung von Offenbach.* Report, Stiftungsprofessur Kreativität im urbanen Kontext: Offenbach.

Sassen, S. 1996. *Metropolen des Weltmarktes. Die neue Rolle der Global Cities.* Frankfurt am Main/New York: Campus.

Schipper, S. 2013. *Genealogie und Gegenwart der "unternehmerischen Stadt." Neoliberales Regieren in Frankfurt am Main zwischen 1960 und 2010.* Münster: Westfälisches Dampfboot.

Scott, A. J., J. Agnew, E. W. Soja, and M. Storper. 2001. "Global city-regions." In A. J. Scott, eds., *Global city-regions: Trends, theory, policy* (11–30). Oxford: Oxford University Press.

Smith, N. 1984. *Uneven development.* Oxford: Oxford University Press.

———. 1995. "Remaking scale: Competition and cooperation in prenational and postnational Europe." In H. Eskelinen and F. Snickars, eds., *Competitive European peripheries* (59–74). Berlin: Springer.

Soja, E. W. 2010. *Seeking spatial justice.* Minneapolis: University of Minnesota Press.

Stadt Eschborn. 2013. "Give me five."*Eschborn Magazin: for business und mehr*: 34–35. www.eschborn.de/fileadmin/eschborn/Bilder/Wirtschaft/Eschborn_For_Business2013.pdf.

Swyngedouw, E. 1997. "Neither global nor local: 'Glocalization' and the politics of scale." In K. Cox, ed., *Spaces of globalization* (137–66). New York: Guildford Press.

———. 2000. "Authoritarian governance, power, and the politics of rescaling." *Environment and Planning D: Society and Space* 18: 63–76.

Taylor, P. J. 2004. *World city network: A global urban analysis*. London: Routledge.

Todd, G. 1995. "'Going global' in the semi-periphery: World cities as political projects: the case of Toronto." In P. Knox, ed., *World cities in a world system*. Cambridge: Cambridge University Press.

Toronto Workforce Innovation. 2010. "Facts and figures." Accessed August 11, 2015. www.workforceinnovation.ca/factsandfigures/keysectors#Manufacturing.

Wilding, C. and M. Hillier. 2012. "Embrace the regional cluster strategy." *Globe and Mail*, March 29, 2012. Accessed April 9, 2012. www.theglobeandmail .com/news/opinions/opinion/embrace-the-regional-cluster-strategy-toronto/ article2384637/.

Zimmermann, K. and J. Monstadt. 2012. "Regionale Kooperation im Rhein-Main-Gebiet: Eine vorläufige Bilanz." In J. Monstadt, K. Zimmermann, T. Robischon, and B. Schönig, eds., *Die diskutierte Region*. Frankfurt/M. and New York, 345–52.

Canadian Regions

CHAPTER 6

Internalized Globalization and Regional Governance in the Toronto Region

Roger Keil and Jean-Paul D. Addie

Introduction

IN THIS BOOK, we have been asking how urban regions develop collective agency in the face of changing structural conditions, especially the macro-processes of globalization and neo-liberalization. We are interested in understanding the institutional changes brought about in an era of uneven and contested economic and demographic growth that have led to new morphological, spatial, scalar, and topological forms across Europe and North America. Toronto has played a particular role in this context. If we look at the central questions this book wants to address in relation to the extended Toronto region—namely whether collective agency has been established at the regional level—we must say no, at least not in a strong sense of territorial governance. No new level of government has been created between the Greater Toronto Area's (GTA) lower-tier local municipalities (including the City of Toronto), its four upper-tier regional municipalities (Durham, Halton, Peel, and York), and the provincial government (Queen's Park) to reflect the explosion of urban spaces in southern Ontario beyond the traditional political containers created a generation ago. The entrenched territorial logic and political divisions between the City of Toronto and its suburban and exurban hinterland—often discursively framed through the polarized 416/905 divide (as based an their respective area codes)—cast a persistent shadow over debates of regionalism and regional governance. Still, new political spaces and institutions are in the process of being established and new "regional" issues are entering the political agenda (see Figure 6.1). In this chapter we examine these in closer detail.[1]

While there is no single city-regional political space—and regional government overall continues to lie effectively with the provincial government—institutional innovations and process change have created conditions for the emergence of a new politics of regional cooperation beyond the old 416/905 dichotomy and conflict. This incipient regional compact aims at stabilizing the long-term resilience of economic, social, and

Figure 6.1   The Toronto region, including the Greater Toronto and Hamilton Areas, the Greater Golden Horseshoe, Greenbelt, and environs. Map by Robert Fiedler.

environmental relations as a novel form of spatial fix. It is this "structured coherence" (Harvey 1985: 139–40), and how it is produced, that we attempt to uncover here by recasting the question of collective regional agency from a particular point of view: *internalized globalization.* In doing so, we examine how regional actors have begun to reframe the globalization of the region as a question of "how," not "if." Internalized globalization is shaped by the opening of central cities to their wider regions via extended infrastructure networks and the aggressive adoption of internationalization by urban regimes, with the goal of seeding more resilient forms of governance at a variety of scales (for an expansion of this argument, see Keil 2011a and Keil and Siegl in this volume).

Much of the information on which our analysis is based draws from interviews conducted with experts in the areas of housing and transportation, two policy sectors vital to understanding the overall governance and patterns of state intervention in southern Ontario (see chapters by Addie and Abbruzzese in this volume). Interviewees were identified on the basis of their institutional expertise or position as key regional decision-makers. The protocols of these interviews involved a set of exploratory questions that probed the intersections of governance, politics, and planning under conditions of neo-liberalization and globalization. The discursive choices they made in talking about matters of territorial unity at the regional scale (or regional agency) and technologies of regionalization reveal the parameters of creating resilience in the Toronto region. We present their competing and coalescing narratives below.

Real Existing Regionalism: Identity Formation, Material Change, and Technological Adaptation

We have entered an era of regional governance where urban and suburban politics are not easily separated, particularly in regions that aspire to be global. In fact, in a globalized context, suburbanizing regions are beginning to be key spaces where newly emerging relational interconnectivities take hold to redefine metropolitan place and globalized space in equal measure (Addie and Keil 2015; Young and Keil 2014). Amidst the unfurling spatial politics of this dynamic milieu, ideational constructs of "the region" have often been mobilized as a means to internalize, institutionalize, and ultimately normalize new meanings that can then legitimize the exercise of regional collective agency. Such neo-liberal strategies tend to leverage post-political rhetoric that depoliticizes or displaces local tensions by appealing to normative claims of economic competitiveness, resilience, and quality of life (see Deas 2014; Haughton et al. 2013). In Toronto, for example, Richard Florida (2012) has called for cities and suburbs "to act in harmony as one region" lest the region lose its global competitive edge. Local political interests are frequently lost in the mix as a result, most notably in the case of those people living in the ubiquitous "in-between" spaces of the contemporary metropolis (Young and Keil 2010). We therefore pay particular attention to how key decision-makers understand and deploy urban versus suburban identities, properties, or dimensions in articulating their views on regional politics.

The disciplinary logics of internalized globalization compel the construction of urban regions as, in Lefebvre's (1991) term, distinct "representations of space" that are produced, codified, and mobilized through a variety of techniques of spatialization. As we demonstrate in the case of Toronto, regulatory institutions capture the region in a mix of rhetorical and technological change that complies neither with preconceived notions of regionalization nor with the pessimism of total regional dysfunctionality, but instead reflects the ongoing, multiscalar negotiation of diverse communities, interests, and space times. As much recent critical geographic research now attests, regions are not solely the territorial construct *du jour* for economic competitiveness and urban resilience, but contested political constructs (see Paasi 2010; Jonas 2012). The politics and technologies of regionalism do not occur in isolation from other social and political arenas but are fundamentally co-constituted through spatial practices, social processes, and increasingly diffuse forms of governance (Allen and Cochrane 2014).

In attempting to determine the actual processes through which regional collective agency is being sought, we depart from the normative and ideological debates around the new regionalism through the notion of "real existing regionalism" (Addie and Keil 2015). This concept acknowledges the fact that regionalism is neither a mere ideational construct nor a set of predictable practices, but a contested product of discourses (*talk*), territorial relationships (*territory*) and multi-faceted *technologies*. As an analytical framework, we operationalize real existing regionalism to confront the tensions between the discursive constructions and normative interventions that characterize much regionalist conversation today, and the territorial politics (local competition) and technologies that are deployed to give these tensions strategic direction. These technologies are both material (with regards to the design and construction of the built environment or modal choice in transport planning, etc.) and of power (e.g., negotiating the modalities of state, market, and private authoritarian intervention that are employed in governing institutions at the regional scale).

As evidenced across the contributions to this volume, the real existing regionalism of a particular area will be reflective of, and in turn generate, new, locally contingent state spatial strategic choices. At the current conjuncture, those are primarily embedded in and express neo-liberal values and objectives. We expect, therefore, no fundamental conflict over particular regions' strategic direction, yet divergences in kind during a climate of "roll-with-it" neo-liberalization (Keil 2009). While actors at the regional scale are far from powerless in shaping the direction of institutional innovation, they are bound, at this point, by the overall constraints imposed by the discipline of a neo-liberal (or nascent post-neo-liberal) policy environment where the chief regulatory discourse pushes for a post-crisis developmental consensus. The horizon set by elites at this particular conjuncture for *what* regional governance must be sought, is at a more modest scale than during former periods of globalization. We are all expected to aim for less. Yet, while operating fully in the overall governmentalist framework of a roll-with-it reconstruction of post-crisis neo-liberalism, the region has not ceded to be the space of vivid and outspoken contestations about radically different futures. The fact that real existing regionalism operates in the confines of the roll-with-it straightjacket, its technological, ecological, and social dimensions at times imply a sense of more fundamental change, as we see in the Toronto region.

Remaking the Toronto Region Under Internalized Globalization

New ways of talking about, and branding, regional development have taken hold in the Toronto region since the provincial Liberal Party was elected to power in 2003. Under the leadership of Dalton McGuinty (2003–13) and his successor Kathleen Wynne (in office since 2013), the Government of Ontario has actively embraced the role of "regionalizing state." The rhetoric introduced by the mutually reinforcing "Places to Grow" and "Greenbelt" legislation brought in during 2005–6 has established a discursive construction and legal framework around the extended spatial imaginary of the "Greater Golden Horseshoe." At the same time, as Addie details in this volume, Queen's Park authorized the creation of a complementary regional transportation agency, dubbed Metrolinx, for the newly territorialized "Greater Toronto and Hamilton Area" (GTHA). The construction of these territorial frames and technologies have opened new institutional and procedural forms of regional governance to marshal the antagonistic political relations and contradictory social interests found between the dense urbanity of the metropolitan core and the sprawling suburbanity that lies beyond. The resultant growth management strategies look to realize the infrastructural integration and smart and sustainable urbanization deemed necessary to support Toronto's regional economic engine (Addie 2013; Macdonald and Keil 2012). Here, processes through which the regulation of housing and transportation are facilitated are strongly targeted toward creating growth centres and no-growth areas in large contiguous sections of highly developed land across southern Ontario. Consequently, the imperatives of internalized globalization, combined with a desire to curb urban sprawl, are now clearly codified in an integrated program of regional land use and of environmental and transportation policies.

The rescaling of the region and the revamping of growth and mobility management in southern Ontario occurs at a time of dramatic demographic and socio-economic change. The Toronto region has seen a reversal of its social ecology over the past twenty years. The outer suburban belt around the core city has witnessed an influx of endogenous non-European populations and new immigrants (mostly from South and East Asia), leading suburban municipalities such as Mississauga, Brampton, and Markham to acquire strong ethnoburban qualities. At the same time, the former white middle-class suburbs of the postwar years—the old or inner suburbs now located within the amalgamated city of Toronto—have large and highly diverse non-white and immigrant populations (Hulchanski 2010). Terms such as the "racialization of poverty" and "vertical poverty" are now strongly associated with the extensive suburban tower neighbourhoods where the combination of immigration, renter status, and visible minority membership, as well as gender, has become a predictor of structural poverty (United Way Toronto 2011).

Suburban diversity both informs and remakes the emergent region (Keil 2011b). The regional imaginaries presented through the Government of Ontario's growth management strategies belie the highly significant proliferation of qualitatively distinct suburban governance modalities (Hamel and Keil 2015) and suburban "ways of life" (Walks 2013) across the Toronto region. The cultural logic that might have undergirded the conservationist, and often neo-rural, middle-class sensitivies of Toronto's exurban polities in previous years (see Abbruzzese and Wekerle 2011 for a related discussion) has now, once again, been trumped by a more unpredictable mix of internally cohesive cultural identity politics, automobilist growth policies, single family home orientation, ostensive consumerism, and even authoritarian privatism (Ekers et al. 2012). Yet suburban governments have also begun to push toward alternative growth management policies and regional integration from the outside, which have sometimes challenged and superseded the ostensibly more progressive orientation of the metropolitan core (Keenan 2012). Suburban regimes in communities around the Greater Golden Horseshoe are developing a decidedly auton- omous set of strategies to make their mark in an increasingly competitive global city environment. For example, in the ongoing debate on regional transit, Brampton, Caledon, Mississauga, and Oakville staged a Western GTA Summit in the spring of 2013 to press issues of public transit funding and, in doing so, demonstrated a remarkably urban and regional vision more advanced than that of the central municipality of Toronto (Drennan 2013). It is in this mix that the discourse of regional governance must be located.

Talk

Interestingly, most key decision-makers pay more than lip service to the regional dimension of life in the Toronto region. Starting from the eco- nomic necessity of thinking regionally, institutional actors among the civic and political elites recognize the regional scale as the terrain of their oper- ation, as is the case with a leader of a major civic organization:

> For our work, we don't have a religious definition of the Toronto region, so for us it can be quite broad and for some of our initiatives it goes right down to the Golden Horseshoe. So we purposefully don't pick a regional definition. I guess, in terms of what we see more broadly and where we're taking our work is beyond the traditional GTA to encompass definitely Hamilton and, from time to time, Kitchener-Waterloo, depending on the initiative. So we're going more regional than less, and we're seeing the border going out a little bit more broadly then others might define it. But I think people are starting to think in that way, anyway. We're recognizing that as an economic region, we include Hamilton, we include Kitchener- Waterloo. (CEO, Toronto Civic Action Alliance, interview, 2011)

The discursive construction of the region as a meaningful territory of reference is undergirded by the growing assumption that this emerging territorial entity is both unbounded in many ways (evidenced in the extra-regional mobility of both institutional actors and everyday urban inhabitants) *and* held together by the (mostly yet to be built) regional transportation network that ties it together internally:

> The City of Toronto is very much the financial centre that has tentacles out throughout the region, so it's a bit of a focal point for the region and the region being quite big. We have economic ties; we have many economic organizations and businesses that actually operate throughout the region; some of them multinational, some of them local, some of them like [York] University that has campuses in other places. So increasingly we see

organizations that are spreading their operations across the region. We see the people working in those organizations definitely being spread across the organization and it's rare to find a Toronto resident who isn't spending some time in another region or vice versa. We have transportation links very clearly, and I know that's the focus of your work, but we all think of transportation on a regional basis.... We just find everybody is thinking more in terms of a regional basis. (CEO, Toronto Civic Action Alliance interview, 2011)

This view is increasingly evident across urban, suburban, and rural areas of the Toronto region. Speaking from an administrative territory located between the urban centres of Toronto, Mississauga, Brampton, and Hamilton, a Municipal Region official pointed to the impact of shifting regional imaginaries on local resilience and strategic decision-making:

I think the definition of the region is changing over time.... With the province's Places to Grow Act, we find ourselves, as we did our last official plan, talking a lot more about a Greater Golden Horseshoe. And that, in many ways, perhaps makes it a more real answer in terms of what the region means for us.... It's something that continues to evolve in terms of who we sign ourselves up with and who are our partners. The GTA—yes, it's there—but the Greater Golden Horseshoe is becoming much more relevant for us. (Director of Economic Development and Business Services, Municipal Region of Halton, interview, 2010)

Territory

Political actors in the region are keenly aware of the general constraints of a supra-local dynamic that often puts them ostensibly into a reactionary rather than preemptive position. At all levels, a conversation about different territorial assemblages has begun through policy sectors such as housing, transportation, and the environment. Finding institutional solutions to those challenges needs to recognize the multi-scalar character of social and economic life and multi-level nature of political decision-making in Ontario. A representative of a regional business association outlines the landscape of contradictions here:

We want to do something that has not been done before and that is to size up the fiscal capacity of the entire region, understand the fiscal challenges of the entire region going forward, and get a sense of the gap. I think people have done that for Toronto to a certain extent, but we want to do it at another level. It will be kind of crude, we're using it as a blunt instrument. When you look at the solutions to that gap, transit and housing are the two biggest things that are the problem. Toronto can't afford its housing responsibilities and nor could the broader municipal region.... Housing is just too big a ticket item and it's failing at living up to that. (VP Policy and Government Relations, Toronto Board of Trade interview, 2010)

These difficulties are echoed by the strategic thinker of a social welfare organization, which does much of its work in the field of social housing:

> One of the problems with addressing issues on a regional basis, and this is the real vogue in [this] sort of urban thinking, is the kind of city region. [City-regions are] the new nation[s] of the 21st century.... But, in terms of political entities, there is no such thing as a regional entity. What there is in the GTA, for instance, depending on how you define the GTA, there's 33 municipalities, upper tier and lower tier municipalities, all of which have some level of governmental responsibility for issues associated with housing, either planning and zoning, or delivery of affordable housing programs, or delivery of homeless services or things like that.... What there is in the GTA are just a series of informal relationships and historically there has been one big issue that has really driven a wedge into housing within the GTA.... In the last 15, 20 years, in terms of development of various kinds of social housing programs, coop, non-profit, municipal housing programs and so on, the bulk of the new housing always went into the City of Toronto, what is now the large amalgamated City of Toronto. (Director, Affordable Housing and Social Innovation, Wellesley Institute, interview, 2011)

Many activists and policy-makers continue to hold the politics of amalgamation in the 1990s under the provincial government of Conservative Mike Harris responsible for the split in the region when it comes to devising more regionally based policies. In contrast to the ways in which relationships of centre and periphery have been caricaturized in the usual polarized 416/905 discourse. However, the complexity of the regional network of socio-spatial realities in the housing field, for example, are increasingly recognized across the divide: "So one of the arguments of why regions matter is because the image that somehow the region consists of Toronto, which has pockets of poverty [and] is surrounded by a whole bunch of suburbs which are relatively middle class, is in fact not true.... So one of the reasons why the region matters is because the fix, the solution ... the issues and needs are very similar across the region" (Director, Affordable Housing and Social Innovation, Wellesley Institute, interview, 2011).

While local welfare state agencies and civic organizations have begun to aggressively break down the centre-periphery boundaries that have constrained their work in the region, business advocates also note their increased activities, albeit under some degree of internal division:

> We are taking the perspective that our line of influence is the entire GTA
> and that sometimes puts us into a level of conflict with [local organiza-
> tions].... They certainly don't think as regionally. They think about the
> local issues that affect business climate if they do think of public policy....
> We feel that there needs to be a regional perspective to the promotion of
> the economic foundations of a robust economic climate. We think pieces
> of that include coordinating from within the region. A big piece of that is
> promoting the region internationally; we are very weak on that. (VP Policy
> and Government Relations, Toronto Board of Trade, interview, 2010)

This regional orientation stands in contrast to the more traditional interests of some of the municipal institutions even of the central city, such as
economic development organization "Invest Toronto," who are portrayed
as "quite defensive about [*being regionally focused in Toronto*].... They
don't apologize for the fact that Invest Toronto is taking Toronto's interest
sometimes in competition with the rest of the region. So we are in disagreement with that" (VP Policy and Government Relations, Toronto
Board of Trade, interview, 2010).

Not surprisingly, perhaps, the conventional divisions in the socio-
spatial landscape of the region are expressive of a disproportionate distribution of resources, wealth, and need that have perpetuated themselves
through the institutional structures that divided the region into fiefdoms
of territorial interests. Those could ostensibly be reflections of business
interests themselves, but they often also reflect socio-economic and
socio-technological splintering: "if you look at the areas of the city [of
Toronto] that are considered sort of the successful areas of the city, it's
pretty incredible how closely aligned to the subway it is, and when you
see the areas of the city that are struggling, they are the furthest away ...
and I don't think that's a coincidence" (VP Policy and Government Relations, Toronto Board of Trade, interview, 2010).

The representative of an influential civic organization that has traditionally operated in the central municipality but has increasingly looked
beyond Toronto's borders, expressed sympathies for the potential offered
by an approach to governance that involves a more than local
perspective:

> In terms of governance, we don't have any regional government and we
> have very few government institutions that function on a regional basis.
> For some it's ad hoc, for some it's informal, but there are very few formal
> government institutions that function on a regional basis, and so most
> people would say the provincial government is the de facto regional gov-
> ernment for the Toronto region. Then we have the formal structures, the
> municipal government, the regional governments, the City of Toronto,
> and then a leap up to the province. So we look at those institutions that

are functioning on a regional basis and we see quite a lot of promise in those ... those show the power of connecting people across borders and sharing a common agenda and working together to drive change, there's a lot of promise in those models. (CEO, Toronto Civic Action Alliance, interview, 2011)

As important as it is to think of overcoming internal splintering in the governance of particular sectoral distribution systems, it is also necessary to consider the potential unification of disparate regional interests in the face of the federal architecture of government in Canada. Regional unity is considered a necessity in the competition for limited resources dispensed at higher governmental levels both federally and within the province. A gulf has begun to open between the territorial interests mostly represented by politicians, on one hand, and the operatives of the welfare sector, who have started to look at important issues through a regional lens, on the other hand. Asked whether actors in the region have discarded a purely competitive relationship to each other, one respondent explains:

Not everybody has ... but people who are on the ground that are dealing with the issues day in and day out *have*, and time and again we've seen that where you have an issue where you need a concerted regional approach on it and a face that you present to the federal government, etc. Let's face it, most of the money for this comes from the federal government, so if you have all the discussions going on individually with different municipalities in different regions, you don't have the power of a concerted regional voice saying this is important region-wide, and the federal government can play regions off against each other and it's very harmful and you end up with nothing (CEO, Toronto Civic Action Alliance, interview, 2011).

Territorially and institutionally, it is of central importance for regional agency in any sector to create the ability to navigate the highly politicized architecture of the Canadian federation (Keil et al. 2015). The absence, particularly, of national housing and transportation strategies is experienced as severely compromising the ability of building a resilient region through housing and transportation investment. The political boundaries between housing agencies in the region hold strong in administrative terms. Relationships between funders and recipients of funds may be hierarchical, but initiatives of sectoral networking across the region can be an important capacity builder in this respect in the Toronto region, and across other regions, especially as numerous interviewees considered the fragmentation of initiatives and lack of systems thinking as an important impediment to regional coordination and resilience in the housing sector.

Technologies

Technological change comes in two versions to regional governance: technical and governmental. The latter entails the taking of stock in fields of housing and transportation where "biopolitical" benchmarking, population forecasts, etc., are de rigueur. The persistent geopolitical boundaries of the GTA, in addition to the inflexibility of federal census metropolitan areas (CMAs), are a challenge in this regard. Within the Municipal Region of Halton "the communities of Oakville, Halton Hills, and Milton lie in the Toronto CMA, whereas Burlington, a mature community to the west, is actually in the Hamilton CMA. This causes us no end of data issues" (Director of Economic Development and Business Services, Municipal Region of Halton, interview, 2010). However, an emerging regional data bank for housing needs and issues across several municipalities points in a different direction. As a housing expert notes: "The regional [housing] databank which is the first attempt of trying to get back together again the idea that Toronto, and Mississauga, and Brampton, and Oakville actually have some common interest in housing issues and the very modest beginning of that is just simply to recognize that if we come up with a databank of common indicators and can begin to say, yeah, there actually are some issues around aging existing housing stock, long waiting lists for affordable housing" (Director, Affordable Housing and Social Innovation, Wellesley Institute, interview, 2011). The importance of a regional housing strategy was underlined by the CEO of a large multi-sectoral civic organization who confirmed that "the very first thing is to get regional housing data in one place because there has been very little data sharing. So we've actually released a regional housing data bank that for the first time puts all of the data around numbers of units, and income levels, and all sorts of things, in one place" (CEO, Toronto Civic Action Alliance, interview, 2011).

Institutions can be viewed as technologies of power. An important question before the elite decision-makers and thinkers in the Toronto region is to ponder the relevance of explicitly regional institutions of government and governance, a contentious issue given the region's past failures at consolidation, suspicions vis-à-vis potential provincial interests, and continued parochial orientations in municipalities and sectoral agencies. Confronted with the question of the modalities and institutional structures of regional governance and economic coordination itself, one respondent elaborates: "Let's just say it's pretty early days for some of our thinking around that. We struggle a little bit.... We definitely are of the view that we need stronger regional governance. We're not yet in a place,

I'm not sure even in a year's time we'll be there, where we would be contemplating regional governance. My guess is that from just little trial balloons that I have personally floated here and there, that the city and the region isn't ready for something as dramatic as an idea like that at this point" (VP Policy and Government Relations, Toronto Board of Trade, interview, 2010).

The former Chair of the central city's transit agency defends to some degree the territorial interests of the municipality in the regional governance game, due to the vastly different demands for technology and delivery implied in various territorial units:

> Toronto as a region is important but I guess I do see the City of Toronto as the City of Toronto. And perhaps because I am politically aware in understanding the relationships—Mississauga is a different place—we need to work together on some things but this whole debate: a prime example of this is in the marketing of the GTA and the argument that Toronto should be marketed as one region. Well, sure; we need to figure that out internationally, because obviously, internationally, nobody cares about the border of Steeles between Toronto and Markham. Having said that, the City of Toronto has an interest in making sure that, as companies come to the GTA, they decide to locate in the political boundaries of the City of Toronto. (Chair 1, Toronto Transit Commission, interview, 2010)

Regional governance, then, is unlikely to be furthered predominantly through the rescaling of regional institutional government but through networked interdependencies and collaborations among various changing territorial, sectoral, and institutional actors across the larger region. And that will be guided at least for some actors by the principle that sectors are interconnected. One regional housing executive expressed this explicitly: "We have a saying around here: that transit is a housing issue, and housing is a transit issue.... If we don't have the ability for people to work and live in fairly close proximity, we are going to drive the economic viability of this city region into the dumper, and it's rapidly becoming a huge problem" (Director, Housing and Residential Services, York Region, interview, 2011). More specifically, such collaboration among sectoral agencies and territorial actors will take place in an evolving political struggle that ties temporarily specific, spatially parochial, opportunistic interests in with long term resilience hoped to be gained from capital investment into regional infrastructure.

In this sense, transportation, in particular, can be viewed as a conduit of regional governance. Indeed, a local planner from a municipality north of Toronto suggested that "from a transportation level, with our perspective, you *have* to look at it at a larger scale, because certainly in terms of building highways, or even bringing transit up here, looking at how we are interconnected is really key" (Municipal Planner, City of Vaughan, interview, 2010). Transportation is viewed generally at all levels of government, and by most civic organizations and transit providers, as the key to any meaningful strategy to build a resilient region through connecting technology to territorial expansion, regional growth, and Places to Grow. A provincial deputy minister confirmed the guiding vision the government uses to develop in southern Ontario: "There are some particular areas, as I think, that the government has been emphasizing for the last few years. You know there has been a significant rebuilding of the government's social policy responsibilities beginning with hard assets in the area of healthcare, in particular hospitals, and in other areas as well, justice facilities, for example. But the biggest, even as there's been a lot of attention paid to that, the biggest ministry with regard to infrastructure continues to be transportation" (Deputy Minister of Infrastructure Ontario Ministry of Infrastructure, interview, 2011).

An executive officer of Metrolinx, the agency overseeing provincial transportation planning in the GTHA and hence charged with a significant dimension of the realization of Queen's Park's regional vision, offered these insights: "This is now a city-region. The City of Toronto is still very important, the city of Mississauga is still very important, but the line on the map is very blurry now. One city really blends into another" (Executive Vice President, Metrolinx, interview, 2010). One former Chair of the Toronto Transit Commission (TTC) acknowledged the validity and priority of the regional Metrolinx plan: "We feed into that plan, we're asking for amendments to the plan; they're working with us on what those amendments might look like. But, ultimately, it is a regional plan recognizing the regional dynamic that transportation and transit play" (Chair 2, Toronto Transit Commission, interview, 2011).

The board of Metrolinx was reshuffled in 2009 in order to depoliticize decision-making and implementation (see Addie in this volume). While elected politicians who were removed from the board may have viewed this move by the province as an attempt to sideline influence by accountable, elected decision-makers and to put in their place an unelected and democratically unaccountable group of potentially self-interested elites, some network actors welcome the removal of official politics from the terrain of transit planning. One representative of the Agency itself saw it as a welcome way to introduce a more holistic perspective over what he considered parochial and divergent viewpoints that were obstacles in reaching system success (Transportation Policy and Planning Advisor, Metrolinx, interview, 2010). That way, another spokesperson for a large business-oriented civic organization elaborates, the internal connectivity demands in the region itself are tied not only into the movement of people, which takes all the attention in public debate, but into the higher-scale matters of logistics and good movements, which may be the main driving factor for business elites and political decision-makers in breaking down intra-regional obstacles in the first place (CEO, Toronto Civic Action Alliance, interview, 2011). Interviewees in the Toronto region's outer sub-urban municipal regions, in particular, echoed the concern that freight and logistics issues were often downplayed in relation to mass transit within the globalizing region (Planner, Municipal Region of Durham, interview, 2010; Transportation Planner, Municipal Region of Peel, interview, 2010).

Decisions on modal and operating technologies are tied to concerns over political power. Fearing a thinning out and weakening of the City of Toronto's mandate and commitment to high intensity transit in the core city through suburban influence and potentially more automobile-oriented policies, the city's transit agency has traditionally had a hard time with regional integration. In the words of one (former) TTC Chair, "So this regional integration issue is an easy buzzword. It's great because who can argue with better region integration? No one. But practically? Logistically? What we're really talking about, outside of better [provincially operated regional] GO service, because we're probably not going to have one fare, outside of a fare collection card (which is coming), which will make it easier, really, is that kind of region integration, a lot of it is there. The only other topic is; should the TTC expand out?" (Chair 1, Toronto Transit Commission, interview, 2010).

Technologically, thinking about the way in which the region is unified or not often comes back to questions of urban form and land use. This Chair's successor in office confirms the central importance of the spatial identity of the centre in a rapidly expanding regional peripheral economy:

> We have seen over the last 10 years, that while we have increased the residential density within our city, we've lost our employment density, and it's the combination of residential density and employment density that drives the transit and transportation patterns. So, as we've seen some of the employment go to the outer suburbs, our transportation network hasn't kept up with that migration and now we're struggling to figure how it is that we build, as we are about to invest in transit again, we want to make sure that we're building the networks that's meeting the needs of the City, the employment base, the commuters, riders, residence. (Chair 2, Toronto Transit Commission, interview, 2011)

Issues of temporal horizon and spatial scale were front and centre in the recent transit debates in the Toronto region as the City of Toronto's Transit City plan under Mayor David Miller (in office 2003–10) ran up against the more high level transit-oriented ideas at Metrolinx. Space restrictions don't allow us to detail the ensuing battles on Toronto City Council and between different levels of government that have still not led to a solution at the point of this writing; Miller's administration had favoured consolidation of growth into a growth management strategy: more density and transit, more environmental benefits. Transit City was ostensibly about social and environmental change in the core city of Toronto and a move away from prioritizing automobile transportation and low-density development (for a detailed discussion, see Addie 2013; Young and Keil 2010). The transit agency's Chair under Miller confirmed: "Transit City is about more than just moving people, it's about transformation" (Chair 1, Toronto Transit Commission, interview, 2010). Yet, for others, Transit City meant a deviation from stated regional policy and process as outlined in Metrolinx's (2008) Big Move plan, with its higher order transportation priorities (CEO, Toronto Civic Action Alliance, interview, 2011).

Miller's successor, Rob Ford (in office 2010–14), ran for the mayoralty on a strongly anti-Transit City platform and delighted in cancelling the plan the day after he took office. More recently, the moderate conservative and technological modernizer John Tory (who assumed Toronto's mayoralty on 1 December 2014) has vowed to hold on to some existing subway and light rail plans, but affords them lower priority than his predecessors. Instead, Tory has proposed to combine existing rail infrastructure with new track to create a "SmartTrack" regional line, a plan that has subsequently received the (moderate) backing of, and financial support from, provincial and federal governments.

Conclusion

The global character of the relationalities that constitute the region is not in question in this period. It is assumed as the *sine qua non* of regional development (Keil 2011a). Regionalist discourse, territorial practices, and technologies, while often pegged as a possible (resilient) antidote to threats of globalization (Hudson 2009), actually have created, more often than not, the openings for those processes associated with that dynamic. Yet, internalizing globalization does not mean enabling uncritically and without regional demands. Quite to the contrary, the discourses, territorial strategies, and technological solutions deployed in the "real existing" region have to be understood as the terrain on which regional urbanization takes shape (Addie and Keil 2015). The spatial politics of regionalism, as we have demonstrated, are forged and operate through a diverse collection of social and spatial practices. In this context, the seemingly ossified local territorial politic of the 416/905 divide—which often looks likely to inhibit the emergence of collective agency at the regional scale—increasingly butts up against new forms of relational politics that are emerging in the interstices of the existing jurisdictional, administrative, and territorial governance structures, and are capable of bypassing the political and symbolic power of the centre city.

In Toronto, we could see that regional experts and decision-makers are keenly aware of the challenges the region faces. Most of them explicitly see the strength and resilience of the region improved when the regional governance structure can perform some form of "dance" with the challenges of globalization (connectivity, competition, performance) and neo-liberalization (the repeated reference to the importance of strategic private action and business involvement). Yet, there are also strong tendencies to build in social and environmental controls. This is the case for actors in both sectors we have highlighted here (transit and housing) and actors across the public, private, and civic divides. While there is strong evidence here that diffuse networked forms of governance are on the rise among sectoral agencies, we have also seen continued trust in the tried and traditional hierarchical arrangements of elected government and their institutions and agencies. Above all, the provincial government reigns supreme through the use of both classical governmental regulation (Greenbelt and Places to Grow legislations) and sectoral instruments (Metrolinx) as modalities of governance. After more than ten years of Liberal provincial rule in Ontario, the impacts of those policies are getting mixed reviews. It is safe to say that the more recent period of regional regulation through provincial policy contrasts sharply from its predecessor government, which had opened southern Ontario to automobile-oriented, conventional single-family home development built on a sharp divide of urban and suburban forms of settlement. The Liberal regime in place since 2003 has championed different policies in discursive approach (growth control, anti-sprawl rhetoric), technological choice (investment in non-automobile transportation, incentives for more compact-built form) and territorial regulation (an upscaling of policy from the traditional 416/905 split toward a larger frame of reference with the planning and transportation policies put forward for all of southern Ontario).

Yet the real existing regionalism of the Liberal era in southern Ontario has not brought about the fundamental change it had promised to deliver. A recent study by Toronto's Neptis Foundation found devastating deficits in the outcomes of the Greenbelt and Places to Grow plans: "The forecasts did not direct growth away from the rural areas beyond the Greenbelt and towards the more heavily urbanized areas in the Inner Ring. Rather, the Growth Plan is allowing growth to continue outwards, at low densities, to the less urbanized parts of the region beyond the Greenbelt" (Allen and Campsie 2013: iii). Instead of leading to significant re-urbanization of growth nodes in the region, as had been anticipated, most of the growth that will occur in the next twenty years will be displaced into the greenfields beyond the Greenbelt and is likely to look like the common sprawl the combined planning laws of Greenbelt/Places to Grow were supposed to halt. Similarly, the sectoral strategy of regional governance embodied in Metrolinx's Big Move plan has hit a roadblock, as the prevailing talk has become less emphatic and more defensive around the reach, rapidity, and resolve of transit innovation, and as decision-makers have waivered on appropriate modal choices (subways over light rail transit, bus rapid transit over rail, etc.); moreover, territorial cleavages that were to be smoothed out by the depoliticization of the Asgency broke out into full bloom, as politicians at all levels promised more and more unrealistic and financially unsupported modes of transit to a confused and fickle electorate ready to cast their vote toward the most instant set of anticipated rewards.

No wonder, then, that redistributive and environmentally sustainable policies as proposed in Toronto's transportation (as once embodied in the notion of Transit City) and (social) housing sectors have been facing stiff headwinds in this political climate. They have an increasingly tough stand against a language of property ownership, opportunity, disruption, smart technology, on-demand mobility, and personal responsibility; shades of continued neo-liberalization. While the notion of regional governance is gaining ground in the Toronto region, its contours and reach are clearly still under discussion.

Note
We gratefully acknowledge the research assistance of Anna Coté. Some of the argument put forward here is based on Addie and Keil 2015.

References
Abbruzzese T. V. and G. R. Wekerle. 2011. "Gendered spaces of activism in exurbia: Politicizing an ethics of care from the household to the region." *Frontiers: A Women's Studies Journal* 32(2): 186–231.
Addie, J.-P. D. 2013. "Metropolitics in motion: The dynamics of transportation and state re-territorialization in Greater Chicago and Toronto." *Urban Geography* 34(2): 188–217.

Addie, J.-P. D. and R. Keil. 2015. "Real existing regionalism: The region between talk, territory and technology." *International Journal of Urban and Regional Research* 39(2): 407–17.

Allen, J. and A. Cochrane. 2014. "The urban unbound: London's politics and the 2012 Olympics." *International Journal of Urban and Regional Research* 38(5): 1609–24.

Allen, R. and P. Campsie. 2013. *Implementing the growth plan for the Greater Golden Horseshoe: Has the strategic regional vision been compromised?* Toronto: Neptis Foundation.

Deas, I. 2014. "The search for territorial fixes in subnational governance: City-regions and the disputed emergence of post-political consensus in Manchester, England." *Urban Studies* 51(11): 2285–314.

Drennan, R. 2013. "Mississauga summit wants us to move, live and thrive." *Metroland Media, Mississauga.com*. May 9. www.mississauga.com/news/article/1615648--mississauga-summit-wants-us-to-move-live-and-thrive.

Ekers, M., P. Hamel and R. Keil. 2012. "Governing suburbia: Modalities and mechanisms of suburban governance." *Regional Studies* 46(3): 405–22.

Florida, R. 2012. "What Toronto needs now: Richard Florida offers a manifesto for a new model of leadership." *Toronto Life*. October 22. www.torontolife.com/daily/informer/from-print-edition-informer/2012/10/22/what-toronto-needs-now/.

Hamel, P. and R. Keil, eds. 2015. *Suburban governance: A global view*. Toronto: University of Toronto Press.

Harvey, D. 1985. *The urban experience*. Baltimore: Johns Hopkins University Press.

Haughton, G., P. Allmendinger, and S. Oosterlynck. 2013. "Spaces of neoliberal experimentation: Soft spaces, postpolitics, and neoliberal governmentality." *Environment and Planning A* 45(1): 217–34.

Hudson, R. 2009. "Resilient regions in an uncertain world: Wishful thinking or practical reality?" *Cambridge Journal of Regions, Economy and Society* 3(1): 11–25.

Hulchanski, D. 2010. *The three cities within Toronto: Income polarization among Toronto's neighborhoods, 1970–2005*. Toronto: University of Toronto Centre for Urban and Community Studies.

Jonas, A. 2012. "Region and place: Regionalism in question." *Progress in Human Geography* 36(2): 263–72.

Keenan, E. 2012. "How the 905 stole our urbanist mojo." *The Grid*. January 5. www.thegridto.com/city/politics/how-the-905-stole-our-urbanist-mojo/.

Keil, R. 2009. "The urban politics of roll-with-it neoliberalization." *CITY* 13(2–3): 231–45.

———. 2011a. "The global city comes home: Internalized globalization in Frankfurt Rhine-Main." *Urban Studies* 48(12): 2495–517.

———. 2011b. "Global suburbanization: The challenge of researching cities in the 21st century." *Public* 43(1): 54–61.

Keil, R., P. Hamel, E. Chou, and K. Williams. 2015. "Modalities of suburban governance in Canada" In P. Hamel and R. Keil, eds., *Suburban governance: A global view* (80–109). Toronto: University of Toronto Press.

Lefebvre, H. 1991. *The production of space*. Oxford: Blackwell.

Macdonald, S. and R. Keil. 2012. "The Ontario greenbelt: Shifting the scales of the sustainability fix?" *Professional Geographer* 64(1): 125–45.

Metrolinx. 2008. *The Big Move: Transforming transportation in the Greater Toronto and Hamilton Area*. Toronto: Metrolinx.

United Way Toronto. 2011. *Poverty by postal code 2: Vertical poverty*. Toronto: United Way.

Walks, R. A. 2013. "Suburbanism as a way of life, slight return." *Urban Studies* 50(8): 1471–88.

Young, D. and R. Keil. 2010. "Reconnecting the disconnected: The politics of infrastructure in the in-between city." *Cities* 27(2): 87–95.

Young, D. and R. Keil. 2014. "Locating the urban in-between: Tracking the urban politics of infrastructure in Toronto." *International Journal of Urban and Regional Research*, 38(5): 1589–608.

Interviews

Chair 1, Toronto Transit Commission, interview with R. Keil and J.-P. D. Addie, Toronto, January 13, 2010.

Transportation Policy and Planning Advisor, Metrolinx, interview with R. Keil, Toronto, January 19, 2010.

Planner, Municipal Region of Durham, interview with J.-P. D. Addie, Whitby, February 4, 2010.

Executive Vice President, Metrolinx, interview with R. Keil, Toronto, February 12, 2010.

Director Affordable Housing Office, City of Toronto, interview with R. Keil, Toronto, February 12, 2010.

Transportation Planner, Municipal Region of Peel, interview with J.-P. D. Addie, Bramalea, February 22, 2010.

Director of Economic Development and Business Services, Municipal Region of Halton, interview with J.-P. D. Addie, Oakville, March 1, 2010.

Municipal Planner, City of Vaughan, interview with J.-P. D. Addie, Vaughan, March 9, 2010.

VP Policy and Government Relations Toronto Board of Trade, interview with R. Keil, Toronto, October 22, 2010.

Deputy Minister of Infrastructure Ontario Ministry of Infrastructure, interview with R. Keil, Toronto, January 10, 2011.

Chair 2, Toronto Transit Commission, interview with R. Keil, Toronto, January 13, 2011.

CEO, Toronto Civic Action Alliance, interview with R. Keil, Toronto, January 20, 2011.

Director, Affordable Housing and Social Innovation, Wellesley Institute, interview with R. Keil, Toronto, March 9, 2011.

Director, York Region Alliance to End Homelessness, interview with R. Keil, Newmarket, March 21, 2011.

Director Housing and Residential Services, York Region, interview with R. Keil, Newmarket, March 21, 2011.

CHAPTER 7

Governing the Networked Metropolis
The Regionalization of Urban Transportation in Southern Ontario

Jean-Paul D. Addie

Transportation and Regional Relationality/Territoriality

TRANSPORTATION PLANNING and politics in an era of global regionalization illuminate a dynamic milieu of political, infrastructural, and socio-spatial transformation. Advances in "just-in-time" post-Fordist production, containerization, and trade neo-liberalization have engendered the substantial restructuring of both global production networks and regional space (Cidell 2011; Keil and Young 2008). At the same time, global modes of infrastructure governance and financialization (Torrance 2008; Siemiatycki 2013), in addition to the "fast transfer" of transport policies and technologies (Kasarda and Lindsay 2011; Wood 2014), destabilize both established hierarchies of urban political power and conventional territorial understandings of urban regions (see Allen and Cochrane 2007; McCann and Ward 2011). A central facet here has been the role played by the transportation sector as a context and mechanism for the disruptions of experimental neo-liberal urban governance. Here, the institutionalization of the "soft spaces" and "fuzzy boundaries" characteristic of the "new regionalism" have blurred the traditional boundaries—material and imagined—between the city and the suburbs (Allmendinger and Haughton 2012; Soja 2015).

In response, states operating at a number of scales have increasingly turned to the production of regional transportation infrastructure as a spatial strategy to enhance the territorial competitiveness of major urban economies. Evidence from North America and Europe, however, indicates that the infrastructural underpinnings of the regionalized global economy have not emerged as a panacea for the uneven geography of capital accumulation. Kirkpatrick and Smith (2011: 495) demonstrate that the devolution of responsibility from upper levels of government, combined with the rollout of national austerity regimes, have increasingly placed the burden of infrastructure development on local governance units resulting in "a crisis-prone scramble for their next infrastructural 'fix.'" In doing so, the conflicting mobility requirements of global capital, local urban inhabitants, and new metropolitan territorialities are placed into stark relief at the regional scale. Keil and Young (2008) argue that the challenge of accommodating the multiple demands and scalar logics of regional transportation has resulted in a bifurcation between premium infrastructure networks and underserved local transit service in Toronto. Enright (2015) documents comparable struggles to scale a "regime of metromobility" in Greater Paris, where the proposed Grand Paris Express rail network appears likely to enhance socio-spatial inequalities across the metropolitan area, given the plan's strong coupling of infrastructure investment with logics of gentrified urban development (see also Kipfer et al. in this volume).

For Brenner (2004: 176, 260), the rescaling engendered through neoliberal urban locational policies has led the geo-economic role of metropolitanization to surpass older forms of regionalism premised on notions of equity and redistribution. Yet, as Jonas and his collaborators (2013; Jonas et al. 2014) argue, there is also a need to leverage strategic infrastructure investments through territorial fixes to secure the conditions for social reproduction in city-regions. Using the case of Denver's FasTracks commuter rail expansion plan, they have shown that the reconfiguration of metropolitan space catalyzed by the imaginaries of, and investment in, regional(izing) transportation infrastructure can draw local governments, business elites, and civil society together in a new "politics of collective provision" (Jonas et al. 2014). The generation of pan-regional support for such projects, though, often relies on a combination of top-down and bottom-up post-political discourses aimed at overcoming localized territorial politics (ibid., 8–11). Consequently, questions regarding whether or not this new territorial politics actually represents a rescaling of the exercise of power, the formation of regional collective agency, or is capable of realizing inclusive, socially just transport options, remains open. I explore these issues below.

Clearly, the complex multiscalar (and multi-modal) nature of urban transportation poses significant conceptual and methodological challenges as the urban question is reposed at the regional scale. Reacting in part to the evolving spatiality and politics of regionalization, many critical scholars working at the intersection of transportation and the production of urban space have refuted conceptual frameworks premised upon nested territorial configurations and embraced relational ontologies of mobility, flow, and assemblage (e.g., Urry 2003; see Cidell and Prytherch 2015 for an extended discussion). As a component of the broader "relational turn" in urban studies, such approaches pose a distinct challenge to bounded theories of urban and regional politics by pushing beyond normative interpretations of discrete jurisdictional territories (Phelps and Wood 2011: 2600). But even as extra-local actors and institutions shape modalities of urban politics, the conceptual and practical importance of urban/regional territoriality persists. Debates over the territorial and relational dimensions of regional space and regional politics have threatened to devolve into a "debilitating binary division" (Morgan 2007: 1248) that "often seems to depend on one's positioning in ontological debates ... [rather than] a considered examination of the concrete actions and strategies of various agents, actors, interests" (Jonas 2012: 266). Urban politics cannot be seen as solely place-based, just as it cannot be the transient consequence of ephemeral flows. Service provision and collaborative approaches to urban politics and transportation planning are conducted in and through bounded administrative units.

Rather than presenting an absolute ontological division, McCann and Ward (2010) argue the concrete production and governance of both cities and regions needs to be theorized through the productive tensions found within the "relationality/territoriality dialectic." This involves examining how urban actors "manage and struggle over the 'local' impacts of 'global' flows and ... how they engage in global circuits of policy knowledge" (ibid., 177). The mechanisms and processes involved in integrating relational (networked) and territorial (administrative) space are complex and not necessarily progressive. Although governance at the regional scale may be normatively equated with enhanced democratic legitimacy, the region may not be the most appropriate arena for particular groups to pursue their aims and ideals (Tomàs 2015: 387). It is therefore necessary to uncover for which interests particular territorial constructs are necessary or merely contingent (Jonas and Ward 2007: 176).

This chapter takes up the call for studies of regionalization grounded in concrete spaces and processes rather than a priori ontological assumptions through an analysis of urban transportation centred on the Greater Toronto Area (GTA). The following analysis concentrates on the formation and operation of a new regional transportation authority for Greater Toronto; Metrolinx. In tracing the Authority's history, I am particularly concerned with understanding how disputes over the future of urban and regional transport have defined debates over, and the practice of, regionalism in southern Ontario during the post–North American Free Trade Agreement (NAFTA) era of competitive neo-liberal restructuring. Jones and MacLeod's (2004: 435) distinction between the functional "regional spaces" that lie at the centre of the global economy and the "spaces of regionalism" that are socially and politically constructed territorial frames, as I shall argue, is instructive in this context. Foregrounding the tensions between the functional economic region and the administrative region in southern Ontario presents an apposite lens through which to examine the contested construction of a particular "space of regionalism" and a new territorialized infrastructure fix to help secure regional resilience. Throughout this chapter, I draw further from the interview data collected by Roger Keil and myself that informed our analysis in Chapter 6, in addition to extensive critical analysis of planning documents, reports, and newspaper articles, to assess the role of transportation in the production and governance of the Toronto region under advanced neo-liberalization.

Institutionalizing Regional Space as a Space of Regionalism, 1995–2006

The mobilization of the region as a crucial spatial frame for Toronto's transportation infrastructure emerged gradually over a period of two decades. A prolonged period of under-investment in the region's transportation infrastructure following the Government of Ontario's (Queen's Park) abandonment of spatial Keynesianism in the mid-1970s, combined with the development-oriented growth regime in place through the 1980s, resulted in an urban planning process seen as producing sprawling suburban landscapes dependent upon automobile transport (OECD 2010; Soberman et al. 2006). By the early 1990s, functional concerns surrounding urban sprawl and the circulation of people and goods were increasingly being recognized as impediments to the GTA's economic prosperity. The Toronto Board of Trade emerged as an early backer for the creation of a regional transportation authority and continues to see itself as a "consistent advocate" on the issue, since congestion has remained a key issue for their membership in the wake of NAFTA (Policy Director, Toronto Board of Trade, interview, 2009). A resurgent regionalism arose in the GTA as a competitive spatial politics; the infrastructural necessities of global capital framed the region as the spatial medium though which globalization could be marshalled and territorialized in place. The trope of Toronto as a networked "regional space" continues to be perpetuated in policy circles by the uncritical elevation of the region as singular, coherent economic engine (e.g., Golden 2012).

Despite the Government of Ontario's established reservations regarding the empowerment of sub-regional political spaces, the Toronto region's accelerated urbanization necessitated governmental intervention to coordinate urban growth and infrastructure development. Municipal amalgamation in 1998 had not resolved the contradictions inherent within the two-tier government structure of Metropolitan Toronto since the functional networks of the region already extended well beyond the new city's boundaries. Yet in contrast to the aggressive restructuring of local and provincial powers enacted through Premier Mike Harris's neo-liberal "Common-Sense Revolution," his Progressive Conservative government's (in office 1995–2002) approach to regional infrastructure provision was decidedly cautious. Following a consultative forum held in 1997, Queen's Park established the Greater Toronto Services Board (GTSB) as an institutional fix—overseen by a board comprised of local sitting politicians—to coordinate region-wide infrastructure strategies.

The GTSB was introduced into a shifting and contested political landscape. As municipalities looked to securing their political position within southern Ontario's unfurling state restructuring, local politicians evinced little interest in a planning body with region-wide powers. The newly amalgamated City of Toronto in particular did not embrace the prospect of uploading planning authority. Queen's Park subsequently received the greatest support for the GTSB in the outer suburbs. The GTSB operated tentatively in response to the GTA's entrenched political parochialism and its weak mandate and limited powers led to the board being continually undermined by local governments pursuing their own agendas (Frisken 2007: 257–65). In practice, the GTSB primarily acted as the body authorizing capital and operating budgets for the province's GO Transit operations as its coordinating functions were marginalized. Having failed to embed the board within the GTA's evolving institutional landscape, Queen's Park dismantled the agency and resumed charge of GO Transit in September 2001.

Notwithstanding its limited capacity and short lifespan, the GTSB did serve as the genesis for regional transportation governance in the GTA as a prototype institutional body and forum for emerging thinking on regional transportation issues. Toward the end of the board's tenure, intra-regional frustrations with congestion finally coalesced into a broad consensus backing an empowered regional transportation body.[1] In the wake of the GTSB's demise, the Harris government formed the Central Ontario Smart Growth Panel (COSGP) to address the pressing challenges of congestion and waste disposal in an area five times the size of the GTA.[2] While it would be Dalton McGuinty's Liberals who ultimately animated a new regional agenda for southern Ontario, the work of the COSGP strongly informed their vision, and several of the its key recommendations were adopted as the basis for the landmark *Greenbelt* and *Places to Grow* acts (see Keil and Addie in this volume). Indeed, despite the partisan manipulation of the stark and real differences within the GTA, it is possible to see a continuity in the regionalization strategies being rolled out by Queen's Park back from the post-2003 Liberals, through Harris's regime, to the initial regional restructuring instigated by Premier Bob Rae's NDP government (1990–95) in response to the challenge of NAFTA (Courchene 2001).

Building from steps forward taken by McGuinty's regionalizing agenda and governance framework, on April 24, 2006, Ontario's Minister of Transportation introduced long-awaited legislation to Queen's Park proposing the formation of a regional transportation authority for southern Ontario. The *Greater Toronto Transportation Authority Act* passed on June 22, 2006, establishing Metrolinx (rebranded as such in December 2007) as a Crown Agency charged with managing and coordinating transportation across a new territorial jurisdiction: the Greater Toronto and Hamilton Area (GTHA). While remaining accountable to the provincial Ministry of Transportation, Queen's Park bestowed Metrolinx with substantial powers to manage the development of transportation infrastructure, own and operate transit assets, and stimulate the growth patterns established by Places to Grow (see Government of Ontario 2006). To this end, the Agency's responsibilities included preparing a multi-modal regional transportation plan (RTP) and coordinating the GTHA's nine local public transit systems and GO Transit (which merged with Metrolinx in 2009).

Queen's Park reviewed numerous national and international regional transportation systems leading up to the creation of Metrolinx (Ontario Ministry of Transportation 2007). Greater Vancouver's Translink system, in particular, presented an attractive Canadian model for planning and operating regional transportation, but the differing political, infrastructural and urban contexts of Greater Vancouver and Greater Toronto posed significant barriers to the application of its governance structure in southern Ontario. Most notably, Translink is required to report to the Greater Vancouver Regional District, a regional planning body established in 1967 with significant powers to deliver services and set policy across Metro Vancouver. Greater Toronto lacked a comparable oversight authority following the demise of the GTSB. The successful establishment of a regional transportation authority for the Toronto region would also need to overcome the myopic interests of local politicians, a governance challenge that has also affected Translink's operations. Gordon Chong (2005), former chair of the GTSB and vice-chair of GO Transit, had suggested sitting politicians hold a minority position (if any) on a Greater Toronto transportation authority. The institutional framework adopted by Queen's Park, however, did not reflect his recommendations. During the RTP planning process, Metrolinx's eleven-person board primarily consisted of sitting politicians.[3]

A Vision of, and for, the Region, 2006–8

The creation and structure of Metrolinx represented a locally defined moment of institutional restructuring, one that necessitated the rescaling of transportation governance to reflect the impact of changing patterns of mobility and networks of connectivity within southern Ontario as a functional "regional space." A Municipal Region official painted a dramatic picture of the dynamism at play here: "you have patterns that are just all over the place in terms of people living in Markham and working downtown, living downtown and working in Markham or Mississauga. The patterns have been blown apart, I think" (Director of Economic Development and Business Services, Municipal Region of Halton, interview, 2010). Former Toronto mayor David Crombie argued as early as 2003 that "we should be looking beyond Greater Toronto to the Golden Horseshoe…. The current boundaries represent an older regionalism and an older reality that no longer exists" (cf. Monsebraaten 2003: H01). Crombie's appeal to the extended regional spatial imaginary of the Greater Golden Horseshoe, however, belied the continued impact of the territorially defined political jurisdictions that were institutionalized in the GTHA as a "space of regionalism." From the outset, Metrolinx operated less as an independent regional governance body and more as an inter-regional enabler fostering cooperation and synergies between local levels of government as it marshalled new investments and revenue sources made available by Queen's Park and Ottawa. Metrolinx planners viewed their role within the region as one of coordination and facilitation between municipalities and the province (Transportation Policy and Planning Advisor, Metrolinx, interview, 2010). However, opposed to the antagonistic communications between fragmented, territorially defined interests that had characterized the GTSB's brief existence, the Agency, at least initially, was viewed as successful in bringing together voices from throughout southern Ontario in a new regional spirit of collaboration (Planner, Municipal Region of Durham, interview, 2010).

Metrolinx approached regional transportation planning in a manner that both responded to and actively encouraged the emerging geography of the Toronto region. The Agency approved the final version of its RTP, *The Big Move*, on November 28, 2008. The Big Move plan fused the fifty-two major transit improvements laid out in MoveOntario 2020 (a cornerstone of Premier McGuinty's 2007 re-election campaign) with the smart growth land management strategies and city-regional vision established by Places to Grow. Metrolinx's vision for the GTHA's future transportation network, shown in Figure 7.1, proposed reconfiguring the radial central hub-and-spoke structure of the GTHA's existing transportation system toward a highly integrated web connecting the regional urban fabric. A polycentric hierarchy of strategically significant "mobility hubs" are intended to function as major places of connectivity that can seamlessly integrate regional rapid transit service and different modes of transportation in place (from walking to high-speed rail), while fostering urban intensification around the regional growth centres identified by Queen's Park.[4]

Linking urban space through the development of such networked connectivity offers an important step in the physical, social, and political integration of fragmented regions. In this regard, the Big Move's mobility hubs not only presented a rationalized framework for the movement of people across the Toronto region, but as place-based developments with strong promotional renderings, they also helped galvanize local support for the provincial government's emerging regional imaginary (see Figure 7.2). Interviews conducted with municipal region planners across the

Figure 7.1 "The Big Move": Metrolinx's fifteen-year plan for the regional rapid transit and highway network. *Source*: Copyright © Greater Toronto Transportation Authority, 2008.

GTHA indicated strong support for such nodal development as a means to redress perceived service deficiencies and spatially and modally spread transportation investment throughout the region. Introducing The Big Move, the Chair of Metrolinx not only praised the levels of cooperation between local actors in formulating the plan, but further suggested it represented a fundamental shift in their prevailing spatial imaginary: "The RTP will not only reclaim our region's traditional transportation advantage, but also bolster our global competitiveness, protect our environment, and improve our quality of life. *For the very first time, like so many of our global competitors, we are thinking like a single region*" (Metrolinx 2008: 1; emphasis added).

Diverse economic, environmental, and social concerns have prompted actors to mobilize regional space as a means to animate locational advantages, concentrate socio-economic assets, and channel inward investment for global competitiveness. Discursive references to environmental sustainability and the negative impacts of unrestricted suburban expansion percolated throughout The Big Move. Still, the underlying justification for implementing the RTP was couched in the trope of economic competitiveness. That this was the case is not surprising, especially as the plan was released at the height of the 2008–9 financial crisis. In periods of economic crisis, land-use and transportation decisions taken by public agencies provide a vital strategic mechanism for the state, acting "as a

Figure 7.2   "Yonge looking north—Richmond Hill." Renderings illustrate the multi-modal transportation networks—including commuter rail, BRT, and automotive traffic—brought together by the Province of Ontario's proposed mobility hubs. *Source*: Copyright © York Region Rapid Transit Corporation (vivaNext) 2012.

conduit for the interests of private capital" to stimulate capital flows to switch into the built environment (Ekers et al. 2012: 412; Phelps and Wood 2011). The financial crisis did not induce a renewed regionalism in southern Ontario, but it did crystallize the economic rationales driving the push for transportation coordination. Consequently, the political discourses surrounding Metrolinx's RTP in large part disclosed the perceived utility of regionalization as an institutional medium and strategy of crisis management. The Big Move put forward an integrated regional spatial imaginary through which networked connectivity transcends the limitations of a transportation landscape whose institutions and infrastructure have been delineated by sub-regional and territorially defined interests. Commenting on the growing recognition of relational connectivity in the GTHA, a former Metrolinx Chair suggested the Agency had catalyzed a sense of "regional citizenship," noting "even three years ago, the city of Hamilton saw itself as a competitor to the city of Toronto. Today I think there is a growing recognition … that Hamilton is part of the bigger city-region and there needs to be regional coordination and cooperation. It's in everybody's best interest" (Chair, Metrolinx, interview, 2010).

The Persistence of Territorial Politics, 2008–13

The Big Move, however, was a high watermark for transportation planning and policy synergies in southern Ontario. Although Metrolinx's institutional architecture proved adept at establishing a political consensus among local units of government regarding an overall regional vision, it became increasingly apparent, especially to Queen's Park, that the territorial interests of politicians sitting on the Agency's board presented a conflict of interest between local and regional development. Conflicts that could be deferred during the RTP planning phase could not be avoided as Metrolinx shifted toward implementing The Big Move. Metrolinx staff were cognizant of the difficulties "political" board members faced when voting for projects which would not be the best for their constituents (Executive Vice President, Metrolinx, interview, 2010). A lack of fiduciary responsibility—predominantly surrounding a fissure between a "Toronto Caucus," led by Mayor Miller and Adam Giambrone (Chair of the Toronto Transit Commission (TTC) 2006–10), and suburban representatives on the Metrolinx board—raised fears that projects would be promoted based on political clout rather than the technocratic recommendations of planners and engineers. Political posturing between these groups clearly infringed on Metrolinx's ability to get shovels in the ground following the release of The Big Move.

The antagonistic relations between Toronto, its suburban neighbours, and the provincial government unfurled through a contested politics of scale, one that had been recalibrated during Ontario's neo-liberal revolution and associated state restructuring during the 1990s. Although transportation had emerged as a central political issue by the early 2000s, the dynamic processes through which the new political landscape of the Greater Toronto region was being forged produced multiple and multi-scalar politics of representation. The City of Toronto and Queen's Park proposed differing imaginaries of regional space which, echoing MacLeod and Jones's (2007: 1186) relational-structuration approach to territoriality, "discursively (re-)present[ed] their struggles and strategies ... [while] offering an already partitioned geographical 'scaffolding' in and through which such practices and struggles take place."

The City of Toronto, through its 2002 Official Plan, sought to integrate transportation and land-use planning to accommodate future growth, while reducing auto-dependency by making transit, cycling, and walking more attractive options. The TTC (2003) supported the aims of the city's Official Plan by establishing a new policy framework intended to facilitate the "smart" re-urbanization of Toronto. By 2006, Toronto's Mayor Miller corralled these emerging objectives into "Transit City," an $8.3 billion proposal to construct 120 km of light rapid transit (LRT) with supplementary bus rapid transit (BRT) that would integrate the urban fabric of the amalgamated city and provide a direct rapid transit connection to Pearson International Airport. Transit City was not simply forwarded as a transit plan but as a catalyst for urban restructuring. Miller and Giambrone saw European-style LRT offering the means to transform modernist auto-centric landscapes—characterized by low densities, tower blocks, and strip malls—by catalyzing intensification and mixed-use development along key suburban boulevards. Transit City further indicated the city's commitment to invest in Toronto's marginalized inner suburban neighborhoods to both their many low-income and visible minority residents, and to Toronto's globalized development industry (Chair, Toronto Transit Commission, interview, 2010).

Despite several smart growth synergies and Transit City's incorporation into The Big Move, contradictions in scale and purpose were readily apparent between Queen's Park and Toronto's transit plans. Transit City was premised on a discursive imaginary, modal technology, and spatial framework that reinforced a territorially bounded *municipality*-based understanding of urban mobility. For example, in considering Transit City's proposed Eglinton Crosstown LRT route, a former chair of the TTC asserted that since relatively few people would take the entire trip from Kennedy to Pearson Airport, "high speed is not as critical as quality local service" (Chair, Toronto Transit Commission, interview, 2010). In contrast, Metrolinx planners argued for a faster line with fewer local stops based on the overall needs of a regional system (Executive Vice President, Metrolinx, interview, 2010; Transportation Policy and Planning Advisor, Metrolinx, interview, 2010). Queen's Park, in line with its overarching growth management strategies, favoured a strategy of outward multi-modal transport expansion to facilitate urban in-fill and densification around key regional mobility and growth hubs, including the extension of the TTC's subway lines into York Region. With project financing for Transit City contingent upon provincial and federal funding, this conflicting scalar politics fuelled fears in Toronto's urban core that future transportation development would undermine Torontonians' interests within the wider region. The persistence of city–suburban antagonisms within the amalgamated city, however, proved the greatest threat to Transit City. Despite the proposal's transformative goals and intended investment in the inner suburbs, Rob Ford, a right-wing populist from Etobicoke, swept to victory in the 2010 Toronto mayoral election after carrying all the city's inner suburban wards and campaigning to cancel the LRT plan in favour of limited subway construction. The Ford era in Toronto witnessed a cacophony of alternative transit proposals but produced little more than political in-fighting and governmental inertia regarding the city's transport future.

Governing the Contested Landscapes of Regional Transport since 2008

By the time of The Big Move's release, the need to introduce some form of integration between the GTHA's fragmented and disconnected transit operations was a generally accepted principle throughout the wider region, in addition to being a stated objective of Metrolinx. Queen's Park backed the "Presto" smartcard as their preferred mechanism to integrate fare payment systems on all transit networks overseen by Metrolinx, as well as mass transit in Ottawa. Following trial runs in 2007 and 2008, full implementation of Presto was rolled out in November 2009. By 2014, Presto was accepted across Brampton Transit, Burlington Transit, Durham Region Transit, GO Transit, Hamilton Street Railway, MiWay, Oakville Transit, OC Transpo, and York Region Transit. While suburban municipalities and their transit providers embraced the new farecard, the system was only initially trialled at Union Station in Toronto and only fourteen subway stations had introduced Presto technology by 2012. Importantly, the Presto Card continued to mandate that riders pay a double fare when transferring between systems. Full fare integration, although technologically possible, would require excessive annual funding in perpetuity to cover losses incurred by the loss of what are effectively zone fares, something politically and financially unfeasible.

The TTC's cynicism regarding Queen's Park's talk of integration and refusal to commit to the Presto program was indicative of the broader political contestation and inertia over regional transport. While Metrolinx staff argued that the TTC was derailing regionally interconnected transit, the Commission adopted an expansionist posturing regarding their role in the GTHA. TTC leadership critiqued Queen's Park's policy rhetoric by suggesting it obfuscated the political and logistical challenges of regional transit integration. For the TTC, the central challenge of regional transit integration rested on service quality and the necessary provision of subsidies to cover the costs of operation rather than geographic integration of transit networks or fare collection systems. Citing the disproportionate size of the TTC relative to the other transit agencies signed up to Presto— and the difference in subsidies required per ride by the TTC (60¢) and *York Region Transit* (YRT, $4)—a former TTC Chair contended the Commission was a logical mass-transit provider for the region; especially since it could build on existing transit contracts to assume responsibility for transit operations across the GTHA (Chair, Toronto Transit Commission, interview, 2010).[5]

Queen's Park's solution to the inertia and territorial politics internalized within Metrolinx's institutional framework was to restructure its board of directors and reassert the province's authority over regional transportation. In March 2009, Premier McGuinty removed notable political figures, including Miller and Giambrone, from Metrolinx and replaced them with "corporate" board members with expertise in business, construction, finance, and customer service. At the same time, Ontario's Minister of Transportation assumed responsibility for developing transportation policy statements. But rather than depoliticizing Metrolinx, the shift from a "political" to a "corporate" board replaced the entrenched territorial politics with a new articulation of private political interest—in addition to resetting the balance of power between Queen's Park and local governmental units in the GTHA.[6] For a former Agency Chair, the board's reshuffling fundamentally redefined Metrolinx as a service delivery and coordination agency beholden to Queen's Park, rather than a body of regional governance: "Metrolinx had the possibility of being a governance body when it had politicians on its board. It could have evolved into something, which, for me, when you say governance … should have some ability to independently make policy which impacts on its territory. I think that is not what Metrolinx has evolved to.... My view is that the regional agent of governance for [the GTHA] is the Province. They have filled that role in themselves and that was a deliberate policy choice" (Chair, Metrolinx, interview, 2010).

Following the restructuring of the board and the transition to The Big Move's implementation phase, several municipal planners noted a decreasing level of involvement and conversation with Metrolinx, who were viewed as "working more as a private entity" compared to the concerted outreach during the RTP's formulation (Planner, Municipal Region of Durham, interview, 2010). Although several of the planning officials interviewed questioned the declining levels of information exchange between levels of government, they suggest that on a staff level, Metrolinx and the municipalities remained close, with progressive conversations continuing in most sectors. One success story here has been the Smart Commute network of transport management associations, who view their initial partnership with, and eventual incorporation into, Metrolinx as a vital step in fostering multi-stakeholder collaborations to promote sustainable transport across the GTHA (Program Manager, Smart Commute, interview, 2009). Municipal officials, however, remained wary of Metrolinx interjecting itself into local issues and the Agency has been criticized for a lack of transparency and public accountability (Krawchenko 2011). Local planners called for Metrolinx to play a strong role in local development, but as an institutional guide sharing their expertise on mobility hubs, etc., rather than exercising autocratic power. A problematic division between land use and transportation planning endures here: while transportation policy is predominantly formulated at the regional scale, land-use planning, even under the influence of Places to Grow, remains highly localized and only quasi-regional. As a consequence, concerns over a perceived de-prioritization of freight movement have persisted in response to the Big Move, especially in the municipal regions that now house much of the Toronto region's global transport and logistics infrastructure (Manager, Freight Haulage Firm, interview, 2009; Planner, Municipal Region of Durham, interview, 2010; Transportation Planner, Municipal Region of Peel, interview, 2010).

The tensions, contradictions, and synergies between localized territorial development strategies and the province's vision for a networked region are clearly evident in the region's emerging territorial "politics of collective provision" (Jonas et al. 2014). Investments in high-order transit infrastructure are deeply integrated in a program of material and symbolic post-suburban city-making throughout the region (Keil and Addie 2016).

Of particular note here is the proliferation of BRT systems, including the pioneering Viva network in the Municipal Region of York, that appeal to a more affluent suburban ridership. As a regional transit spokesperson suggested, the aim is "to reach the people, the business people, who are not going to look at riding transit as a step down. We've tried hard to put a distinguished, upscale, comfortable vehicle on the road" (Projects and Public Relations Coordinator, York Region Rapid Transit Corporation, interview, 2010). Stimulated by both the Places to Grow framework and monies made available through Queen's Park and Canada's Economic Action Plan (a federal response to the 2008–9 financial crisis), competing suburban downtowns in Mississauga, Brampton, Vaughan, and Markham present a challenge to the territorial primacy of Toronto and proffer a radical reorientation of the region's centre-periphery dynamics. Elsewhere in the GTHA, and in contrast to the wrangling over and eventual cancellation of Transit City, the City of Hamilton has pursued an LRT line from McMaster University to Queenston Circle that is slated to open by 2019. Additionally, a major new GO rail station in Hamilton's West End intends to greatly improve commuter rail service to Toronto (which currently operates one train per day) and eventually support commuter rail extensions into the Niagara region (see Figure 7.3). Indeed, the City of Toronto's struggles to identify a comprehensive agenda for future urban transit may ultimately serve to legitimize the political and planning authority of Metrolinx and embolden further provincial intervention to secure

Figure 7.3   The West Harbour GO station under construction in June 2015. The Canadian National Railroad mainline runs adjacent to the commuter rail track, indicating the centrality of freight rail to the economy of the Toronto region. Photo by author.

their vision for regional transportation and regional development in southern Ontario.

Conclusion

This chapter has highlighted the territorial and relational processes through which the Toronto region is being produced, rendered visible, and governed. The ongoing regionalization of urban transportation discloses the connection (and disconnection) of urban centres into new reticulated relationships while concomitantly interpolating new expressions, discourses, and technologies of state territoriality. The flows, circulations, connectivities, and interfaces facilitated by the GTHA's emergent regional transportation systems significantly challenge pre-existing localized territorial politics. Moreover, since all the political processes involved in the mobilization of the GTHA as a space of regionalism are not self-contained within its territorial boundaries, we are witnessing the region-in-becoming through complex, dynamic, and multiscalar mechanisms. Yet at the same time, the preceding analysis also illustrates the continuing significance of jurisdictionally defined political power structuring the emergent geographies and regulation of the regional space, as new logics of connectivity are overlaid upon, and reconfigure, established city–suburban and core–periphery dynamics. Perhaps most significantly, the techniques and discourses of regionalization are profoundly shaped by the provincial government, in line with the broad political organization of Canadian urban governance (Keil et al. 2015). But it is also important to note that the pressures of globalization and the necessity of grounding key economic flows in place have forwarded Toronto's surrounding municipalities as a pivotal economic space for southern Ontario, NAFTA, and the global economy. This shift is reflected in local officials' reoriented view of their position and importance within the region (Keil and Addie in this volume).

The formation of Metrolinx as a culmination of the province's smart growth program reveals a move toward new regionalism within southern Ontario. Although the product of top-down state reterritorialization, the current construction of the GTHA as a "space of regionalism" may allow Toronto to avoid the experiences of Montreal, which Tomàs (2012) argues remains hampered by the "metropolitan trap" and associated old regional conceptions. However, echoing Jonas and Pincetl's (2006) analysis of new regionalism in California, the reality of economic relations and power dynamics between the province and local governments has led to the fiscal and political disciplining of, in particular, the City of Toronto, rather than the extension of regional consensus and formation of collective agency. The GTHA as a "space of regionalism" has emerged as the spatial frame in which Toronto's infrastructural future is being decided, but Metrolinx embodies the top-down regionalized expression of Queen's Park's power, rather than constituting independent regional governance.

Southern Ontario as a "regional space" and site of everyday spatial practice, though, is experienced in a fragmented and partial manner that invokes challenges of access and transport justice for particular social groups and communities. Metrolinx is pursuing a development strategy intended to integrate the region's urban fabric, but enacts this vision through the establishment of privileged network components and growth nodes that concentrate capital and develops in uneven, disjointed spatial arrangements. Within the emerging geography of the globalizing region, the privileged infrastructures and spatial networks of The Big Move—which overlap local jurisdictional boundaries—will likely lead key centres to retain their dominant position in the GTHA, while new transportation technologies redefine and reinforce the dynamism of post-suburban hubs in its unfolding urbanized space-economy. If densification and regional connectivity offer an alternative urban imaginary for the GTHA, they do not provide equal access to urban mobility. This is particularly true for the communities bypassed in the establishment of premium regional transit service and for new immigrants who tend to face longer commutes within Greater Toronto (Axisa et al. 2012). As a result, questions of social equity and inclusion will need to be addressed moving forward if the region is to avoid crystallizing fragmented, uneven geographical development and processes of glocal bypass that lock in distinct power relations and struc-tural forms of discrimination (Hertel et al. 2015). As relational flows and urban networks are grounded, territorialized in place, it is therefore nec-essary to provide both innovative transportation solutions for new urban structures and establish adaptive political spaces through which a new politics of transport can be articulated. It remains to be seen if Metrolinx, as a regional institutional structure, has the capacity, adaptability, and governmental support to realize this end.

Notes

1 The concept of a regional transportation authority for the GTA gained traction in 2001 following a GTSB proposal for a separate region-wide body for their service area. The GTSB considered three existing agencies as potential models for a Greater Toronto transportation authority: the Regional Transportation Authority (Chicago), the Georgia Regional Transportation Authority (Atlanta), and Translink (Vancouver).
2 Queen's Park closed the Office for the Greater Toronto Area and transferred its staff to COSGP as part of this restructuring. With this, the GTA "essentially ceased to exist" as an entity in provincial policy (Frisken 2007: 288).
3 Metrolinx's initial board of directors comprised two appointees from the province, four from Toronto (including the mayor and chair of the TTC), one from Hamilton, and one from each of the municipal regions.
4 It is worth noting that such nodal development is not new to the Toronto region. The promotion of suburban sub-centres and controlled decentralization was a development priority articulated in Metropolitan Toronto's and the province's spatial Keynesian development state projects during the 1970s (see Government of Ontario 1970). The scale and spacing of Places to Grow and the province's mobility hubs, as well as the shifting regionalist discourses supporting them, however, mark them as a distinct articulation of regional growth in southern Ontario.
5 The TTC would ultimately announce plans for a system-wide adoption of Presto in 2014.
6 Metrolinx staff contested the idea that new "corporate" board members (including senior vice-presidents of the Four Seasons Hotel and the Bank of Montreal) brought their own political and economic agendas to the table, arguing they have brought a desire to incorporate advantageous private sector practices into a public sector organization "so that we get really the best of both worlds" (Executive Vice President, Metrolinx, interview, 2010).

References

Allen, J. and A. Cochrane. 2007. "Beyond the territorial fix: Regional assemblages, politics and power." *Regional Studies* 41(9): 1161–75.
Allmendinger, P. and G. Haughton. 2012. "Post-political spatial planning in England: A crisis of consensus?" *Transactions of the Institute of British Geographers* 37(1): 89–103.
Axisa, J. J., K. B. Newbold, and D. M. Scott. 2012. "Migration, urban growth and commuting distance in Toronto's commuter watershed." *Area* 44(3): 344–55.
Brenner, N. 2004. *New state spaces: Urban governance and the rescaling of statehood*. Oxford: Oxford University Press.
Chong, G. 2005. "Good ideas worth stealing." *Toronto Star*. April 6: A17.
Cidell, J. 2011. "Distribution centers among the rooftops: The global logistics network meets the suburban spatial imaginary." *International Journal of Urban and Regional Research* 35(4): 832–51.
Cidell, J. and D. Prytherch, eds. 2015. *Transport, mobility and the production of urban space*. New York: Routledge.
Courchene, T. 2001. "Ontario as a North American region-state, Toronto as a global city-region: Responding to the NAFTA challenge." In A. J. Scott, ed., *Global city-regions: Trends, theory, policy* (158–90). Oxford: Oxford University Press.

Ekers, M., P. Hamel and R. Keil. 2012. "Governing suburbia: Modalities and mechanisms of suburban governance." *Regional Studies* 46(3): 405–22.

Enright, T. 2015. "Contesting the networked metropolis: The Grand Paris regime of metromobility." In J. Cidell and D. Prytherch, eds., *Transport, mobility and the production of urban space* (172–86). New York: Routledge.

Frisken, F. 2007. *The public metropolis: The political dynamics of urban expansion in the Toronto region, 1924–2003.* Toronto: Canadian Scholars' Press.

Golden, A. 2012. *The case for regionalism revisited.* Speech to the Toronto Region Economic Summit, March 29, 2012. Toronto: Toronto Board of Trade.

Government of Ontario. 1970. *Design for development: The Toronto-centred region.* Toronto: Queen's Printers.

———. 2006. *Greater Toronto Transportation Authority Act, 2006.* Toronto: Government of Ontario.

Hertel, S., R. Keil, and M. Collens. 2015. *Switching tracks: Towards transit equity in the Greater Toronto and Hamilton Area.* Toronto: City Institute at York University.

Jonas, A. 2013. "City-regionalism as a contingent 'geopolitics of capitalism.'" *Geopolitics* 18(2): 284–98.

Jonas, A. 2012. "Region and place: Regionalism in question." *Progress in Human Geography* 36(2): 263–72.

Jonas, A., A. Goetz, and S. Bhattacharjee. 2014. "City-regionalism as a politics of collective provision: Regional transport infrastructure in Denver, USA." *Urban Studies* 51(11): 2444–65.

Jonas, A. and S. Pincetl. 2006. "Rescaling regions in the state: The new regionalism in California." *Political Geography* 25(5): 482–505.

Jonas, A. and K. Ward. 2007. "Introduction to a debate on city-regions: New geographies of governance, democracy and social reproduction." *International Journal of Urban and Regional Research* 31(1): 169–78.

Jones, M. and G. MacLeod. 2004. "Regional spaces, spaces of regionalism: Territory, insurgent politics and the English question." *Transactions of the Institute of British Geographers* 29(4): 433–52.

Kasarda, J. and G. Lindsay. 2011. *Aerotropolis: The way we'll live next.* New York: Farrar, Straus and Giroux.

Keil, R. and J.-P. D. Addie. 2016. "'It's not going to be suburban, it's going to be all urban': Assembling post-suburbia in the Toronto and Chicago regions." *International Journal of Urban and Regional Research* 39(5): 892–911.

Keil, R., P. Hamel, E. Chou, and K. Williams. 2015. "Modalities of suburban governance in Canada." In P. Hamel and R. Keil, eds., *Suburban governance: A global view* (80–109). Toronto: University of Toronto Press.

Keil, R. and D. Young. 2008. "Transportation: The bottleneck of regional competitiveness in Toronto." *Environment and Planning C: Government and Policy* 26(4): 728–51.

Kirkpatrick, L. O. and M. P. Smith. 2011. "The infrastructural limits to growth: Rethinking the urban growth machine in times of fiscal crisis." *International Journal of Urban and Regional Research* 35(5): 477–503.

Krawchenko, T. 2011. "Regional special purpose bodies for transportation and transit in Canada: Case studies of Translink and Metrolinx." *Canadian Journal of Regional Science* 34(1): 1–8.

MacLcod, G. and M. Jones. 2007. "Territorial, scalar, networked, connected: In what sense a 'regional world?'" *Regional Studies* 41(9): 1177–91.

McCann, E. and K. Ward. 2010. "Relationality/territoriality: Toward a conceptualization of cities in the world." *Geoforum* 41(2): 175–84.

———, eds. 2011. *Mobile urbanism: Cities and policymaking in the global age.* Minneapolis: University of Minnesota Press.

Metrolinx. 2008. *The Big Move: Transforming transportation in the Greater Toronto and Hamilton Area.* Toronto: Metrolinx.

Monsebraaten, L. 2003. "Hazel could start 'domino'; independence would kill Peel, major headache for McGuinty." *Toronto Star.* December 13: H01.

Morgan, K. 2007. "The polycentric state: New spaces of empowerment and engagement?" *Regional Studies* 41(9): 1237–51.

OECD. 2010. *Territorial reviews: Toronto, Canada.* Geneva: Organization for Economic Development and Co-operation.

Ontario Ministry of Transportation. 2007. *Transportation trends and outlooks for the Greater Toronto Area and Hamilton: Jurisdictional review of public transit systems.* Draft report, January 29, 2007. Toronto: Ontario Ministry of Transportation, IBI Group, and Greater Toronto Transportation Authority.

Phelps, N. A. and A. Wood. 2011. "The new post-suburban politics?" *Urban Studies* 48(12): 2591–610.

Siemiatycki, M. 2013. "The global production of transportation public–private partnerships." *International Journal of Urban and Regional Research* 37(4): 1254–72.

Soberman, R. M., D. Crowley, H. Dalkie, D. Peter, S. Karakatsanis, E. Levy, T. McCormack, and J. Vance. 2006. *Transportation challenges in the Greater Toronto Area.* Toronto: Residential and Civil Construction Alliance of Ontario.

Soja, E. 2015. "Accentuate the regional." *International Journal of Urban and Regional Research* 39(2): 372–81.

Tomàs, M. 2012. "Exploring the metropolitan trap: The case of Montreal." *International Journal of Urban and Regional Research* 36(3): 554–67.

———. 2015. "If urban regions are the answer, what is the question? Thoughts on the European experience." *International Journal of Urban and Regional Research* 39(2): 382–89.

Torrance, M. I. 2008. Forging global governance? Urban infrastructures as networked financial products." *International Journal of Urban and Regional Research* 32(1): 1–21.

Toronto Transit Commission. 2003. *Ridership growth strategy.* Toronto: Toronto Transit Commission.

Urry, J. 2003. *Global complexity.* Cambridge: Polity.

Wood, A. 2014. "The politics of policy circulation: Unpacking the relationship between South African and South American cities in the adoption of bus rapid transit." *Antipode,* advanced online publication: 1–18. DOI: 10.1111/anti.12135.

Interviews

Policy Director, Toronto Board of Trade, interview with J.-P. D. Addie, Toronto, November 3, 2009.

Program Manager, Smart Commute (North York and Vaughan), interview with J.-P. D. Addie, Toronto, November 4, 2009.

Manager, Freight Haulage Firm, phone interview with J.-P. D. Addie, November 11, 2009.

Chair, Toronto Transit Commission, interview with R. Keil and J.-P. D. Addie, Toronto, January 13, 2010.

Transportation Policy and Planning Advisor, Metrolinx, interview with R. Keil, Toronto, January 19, 2010.

Planner, Municipal Region of Durham, interview with J.-P. D. Addie, Whitby, February 4, 2010.

Chair, Metrolinx, interview with R. Keil, Toronto, February 12, 2010.

Executive Vice President, Metrolinx, interview with R. Keil, Toronto, February 12, 2010.

Transportation Planner, Municipal Region of Peel, interview with J.-P. D. Addie, Bramalea, February 22, 2010.

Director of Economic Development and Business Services, Municipal Region of Halton, interview with J.-P. D. Addie, Oakville, March 1, 2010.

Projects and Public Relations Coordinator, York Region Rapid Transit Corporation, interview by J.-P. D. Addie, Richmond Hill, May 5, 2010.

CHAPTER 8

"Build Toronto" (Not Social Housing)
Neglecting the Social Housing Question in a Competitive City Region

Teresa Abbruzzese

Introduction

IN THE LAST few decades, the neo-liberal project has altered irreversibly the Canadian welfare state. The scaling back of social welfare provisions and the increasing privatization of public utilities and institutions in the name of reducing government expenditure are among many of the changes neo-liberalism has wrought across the country. However, some forms of government withdrawal predate the current neo-liberal shift. The Canadian federal government's retrenchment in social housing programs is a notorious example. Canada is known not only today but also historically for being the only G8 country that does not have a national housing strategy. The devolution of jurisdictional authority and responsibility for housing from the federal government to the country's several provincial governments in the years from 1993 to 1995, and then to local municipalities following 2000, has augmented the current (and inevitable) housing crisis. The consequences have been damaging everywhere, but they can be seen and felt perhaps nowhere more obviously than in Canada's urban and suburban regions.

An examination of the continuing contradictions unleashed by a retreating state during the neo-liberal shift in Canadian cities shows how growing underinvestment in urban infrastructure, transit systems, and affordable housing is actually constraining rather than enhancing today's neo-liberal supporters' calls for "competitive growth." Public goods, such as social housing, are key urban policy areas that have suffered as a result of government devolution (Fowler and Layton 2002; Carroll 2002; Hulchanski 2004a, 2004b; Harris 2006; Walks 2006; Hackworth and Moriah 2006).

This chapter critically examines the sociospatial articulations and particular housing geographies that neo-liberalism has produced in the City of Toronto and its surrounding suburbs, a region known collectively as the Greater Toronto Area (GTA). It focuses, in particular, on the contradictions inherent in the neo-liberal practices, institutions, and policies that have been shaping the competitive GTA region at the global scale. I argue that recent priorities in urban policy-making fall short of producing the "quality of life" package that neo-liberal stakeholders constantly allude to and that, ultimately, hinges neither on neo-liberal discourses or competitive ideologies but on the production of an environmentally, economically, and socially sustainable region.

The GTA consists of the City of Toronto and its four outlying regions: York, Peel, Halton, and Durham. The location is a key site for investigating the major contradictions of global capitalism and the polarizing sociospatial impacts of neo-liberal urbanism, particularly in the housing sector. Current planning and policy debates in the City of Toronto focus on market approaches to delivering affordable housing options in the absence of any long-standing commitments from the federal and/or provincial governments for social housing provision or a regional body. This focus has been highlighted particularly with the election in 2014 of John Tory as mayor of Toronto. Tory's "Open Doors" initiative calls for streamlining the building and planning process as well as cutting red tape in the hopes of both freeing up more public and private land for development and finding more private partners who are interested in building affordable housing. In keeping with what has become a normalized neo-liberal trajectory in urban policy-making, Open Doors does not present any new strategies for the development of new, so-called affordable housing, or the repair of existing social housing stock in Toronto. Rather, the scheme is the typical prescriptive response—coming from yet another entrepreneurial mayor—to years of government disinvestment in the provision of public goods. Coating the prescription are Tory's discursive strategies. In his call to both the provincial and federal governments for committed fiscal investment toward what he and his regime refer to as affordable housing, he craftily intertwines morality and economics, thus glossing over the neo-liberal underpinnings of his Open Doors agenda.

A particular focus on social housing trends shows how an underlying neo-liberal ideology is shaping governance arrangements, fiscal priorities, and urban visions in the GTA. It also sheds light on how neo-liberal restructuring in the urban policy arena is relying increasingly on "the privatization fix"[1] of multi-scalar, public–private arrangements to address the growing shortage and disrepair of social housing. Such neo-liberal strategies of accumulation are couched within hegemonic competitive-oriented discourses promoting the Toronto region as a destination for business. The discourses themselves are legitimized through a broader discursive and ideological rhetoric that privileges home ownership as a way out of the supposed discomforts and shame of public housing.

To contextualize my study of Toronto's social housing crisis, I adopt a critical political economic lens, invoking, in particular, David Harvey's (2004) concept of "accumulation by dispossession." In Harvey's formulation, accumulation by dispossession is the destructive process whereby common goods and universal rights are taken away from vulnerable sectors and privatized in order to generate profit for the capitalist class. Thus the state's role in the provision of public goods is reconfigured if not removed. Following this Harveyian perspective, I argue that the ascendance of market logic in the provision of social housing in the City of Toronto and the GTA is not only exacerbating the uneven housing market and intensifying sociospatial polarization. The provision of housing through the market is also filtering social needs away from the public good, arguably making social housing a product of consumption and a key site for urban regeneration, thus facilitating capitalist accumulation processes (Hulchanski 2004b).

This chapter has two main sections. The first discusses the neo-liberal contradictions of competing regionalisms in the City of Toronto and its surrounding suburbs in what I label the "Four Rs" that characterize Toronto's entrepreneurial approach to metropolitan governance. The second section begins by setting the context of the Greater Toronto Area's (GTA) housing crisis through an examination of its structural underpinnings in housing policy at both the federal and provincial levels of government. I then examine the spatiality of housing affordability in Toronto and its inner and outer suburbs. My aim here is to uncover how the hegemonic logic of privatization, coupled with social engineering strategies to deconcentrate poverty, are territorial or place-based responses to wider systemic issues of increasing socio-economic inequality in the region. I point not only to the limitations of place-based policies in dealing with the structural roots of poverty at the regional level, but also the shortfalls in these policies when it comes to recognizing the destructive consequences of such territorial responses on communities and neighbourhoods.

Competing Regionalisms in the Greater Toronto Area (GTA)

At one time, Toronto was connected to a regional government, but this arrangement came to an end in 1975. While there is no longer any regional or metropolitan government in the Greater Toronto Area, there are various legislative regional planning frameworks to address the environmental, social, and economic consequences of unchecked suburban growth and the dominance of automobile culture in the last forty years. Since the demise of the regional government (Sancton 2002), land-use planning in the GTA has been fragmented and heavily shaped by private development and the real estate industry. As Pierre Filion and Trudi Bunting (2006: 20) observe with regard to Canadian cities in general, "Across the board, the planning of cities tends to have been fragmented, at a time when co-ordination was more than ever needed. Within the contemporary Canadian agglomeration, the attentive planning of individual subdivisions contrasts with poorly coordinated growth and infrastructure development at a metropolitan scale." In the GTA, leapfrog development and low-density suburban sprawl was subsidized by the Ontario provincial government (Sewell 2009). However, although such subsidization allowed for the building of water and sewage infrastructure over the years, little foresight was given to the unsustainable growth pattern being created.

Recent regional planning initiatives in Ontario and Toronto demonstrate that regionalism is not a coherent project. Rather, there are different forms and visions of regionalism that collide and compete with one another. By contextualizing these regional initiatives within the broader neo-liberal processes shaping the local state, we can see how planning has been instrumental in institutionalizing a neo-liberal ideology and in framing discourses on growth and sustainability. To some scholars, regionalism is nothing more than a sophisticated "packaged" politics of urban crisis management, which, as Brenner (2002) suggests, has become a typical response in an increasingly unstable post-Fordist and neo-liberal environment.

Within the last twelve years, three regional plans have been passed in Southern Ontario: the Oak Ridges Moraine Conservation Plan (2002), the Greenbelt Plan (2005), and the Places to Grow Plan (2006). All three plans represent the culmination of years of citizen mobilization in the GTA geared toward resisting unbridled development on ecologically sensitive lands, farmlands, and green space, and calling for development that is more environmentally and socially responsible/sustainable. Although contested by different groups—predominantly the development industry and pro-development local councils who were worried about the environmental restrictions these plans would place on them—the plans were eventually legislated by the Ontario provincial government.

The three regional plans are indicative of a new regional growth management regime which uses environmental and planning discourse to promote growth and regional competitiveness. It can, of course, be argued that there was a certain level of public participation (although streamlined and spectacle-oriented) in the drafting of the Oak Ridges Moraine Conservation Plan and the Greenbelt Plan through public meetings and the creation of a citizen advisory task force. However, there were no civic processes in place for the Places to Grow Plan, which was passed at the same time as the Greenbelt Plan (Wekerle et al. 2007). Thus within this interventionist regional growth regime, the province was crucial in passing legislative frameworks that, although they purported to encourage sustainable growth management, did not fundamentally deal with the roots of urban-regional unsustainability. Although the language of the Places to Grow Plan suggests controlled growth, the plan's call for "more trunk water and sewage mains and four new highways" (Wekerle et al. 2007), along with its emphasis on growth and productivity, reflects how capitalist interests are imbued with environmental legislation and large-scale infrastructure projects.

Thus, while current forms of regional governance in Toronto are provincially led, they are nevertheless operationalized through existing hierarchical local government structures in Ontario and existing territorial divides between the city and its suburbs.[2] These regionalisms do not address the new sociospatial politics and deepening consequences emerging from Toronto's regional development where social needs (i.e., social services, public transportation, affordable housing) typically associated with the city are increasingly needing further policy attention and intervention in the suburbs.

Governing the Entrepreneurial Toronto Region

The Toronto region is an important arena in analyzing what I see as the "Four Rs" of the contradictory nature of metropolitan governance in neo-liberal times, namely (1) rearranging institutional provisions and jurisdictional powers, (2) reforming policy regimes, (3) reconfiguring state and society relations, and (4) redefining the citizen as a consumer.[3]

R #1: Rearranging institutional provisions and jurisdictional powers

Neo-liberal logic defined Canada's Conservative government (2006–15) under Prime Minister Stephen Harper. Harper's restructuring mandate—

with its centralization of state power, decentralization of regulatory policies to facilitate privatization and the slashing of social programs, and regressive and austere policies—were all indications of this logic. However, this political framework is not particularly new. It has seeds in the Liberal Trudeau era (1968–79) and a first bloom during the Conservative Mulroney and Liberal Chrétien governments of the 1980s and 1990s (Evans and Albo 2008; Fanelli 2009). The approach also strongly echoes the Common Sense Revolution ushered into the Province of Ontario with the election in 1995 of Premier Mike Harris and his Progressive Conservative Party.

The neo-liberal political and economic shift reached a particular intensity in Ontario under Harris. Emphasizing and prioritizing devolution, Harris's Common Sense Revolution platform promoted a focus on "less government," "efficiency," privatization, aggressive cutbacks in social program funding, and deregulation. To some observers, the Harris government's aggressive restructuring of institutional provisions and its literal attack on the urban poor was evocative of Thatcherism and Reaganism (Boudreau, Keil, and Young 2009: 58). The double processes of centralization and decentralization, or what Peck and Tickell (2002) call "rollback" and "rollout" neo-liberalism, are the paradox through which this mode of regulation operates (Evans and Albo 2008).

From 1995 to 2003, the Harris regime managed to transform the political, economic, and social landscape of Ontario. This regime's hard and radical restructuring targeted the City of Toronto in particular, embedding Harris's notion of "commonsense" logic within Toronto's metropolitan government. Today, this logic continues to permeate provincial and local governance structures, public policy, and social-spatial relations, even though Harris's *Common Sense Revolution* has long ended.

A few of the lasting legacies of the Harris government in Toronto are the amalgamated city,[4] the dismantling of rent control, and the complete devolution of social housing programs to the municipalities with the passing of the *Social Housing Reform Act* (2000). Almost thirteen years later, the City of Toronto and its surrounding regions are still dealing with the Harris fiscal pinch. The responsibility among various city agencies to deliver social programs while tending to infrastructure repair and improvements at the same time continues to be a major and often overwhelming challenge.

R #2: Reforming policy regimes: from the Miller Years, to Ford Nation, to CivicAction John

The election of Mayor David Miller in 2003 carried the promise of progressive reform. Miller's supporters looked to him as someone who would replace not only Harris's harsh tactics but also former Mayor Mel Lastman's shallow boosterism and business-style politics. Voters saw in Miller a more critical leader who seemed to understand the economic, environmental, and social complexities of building a competitive global city for the twenty-first century.

At the time of Miller's election, the streamlined post-amalgamated City of Toronto was still experiencing the aftershocks of Harris's extreme restructuring. However, Miller's government did not entirely dismantle the neo-liberal project. Instead, it continued to work through a form of neo-liberal logic, albeit on a different terrain. The Miller government's approach was to promote the competitive city by building relationships with labour and civic groups and refocusing competitiveness through a cultural lens. The fact that Miller and his political executive were left-leaning reformists gave their policies and programs a certain progressive authenticity. Yet strong neo-liberal undertones emerge when we dig deeper into the political rhetoric of "the Miller Years."

David Miller's alliance with public sector unions and progressive social movements can be seen as having shaped what some analysts refer to as "Third Way" urbanism (Kipfer and Petrunia 2009; Fanelli 2009). This approach has not attempted to reverse urban neo-liberal rollbacks, but has forged ahead with this mode of regulation in marketing the city in an attempt to attract footloose capital and upper- and middle-income households. According to Kipfer and Petrunia (2009, 111),[5] the metropolitan mainstream is a "constellation of predominantly white, new middle-class gentrifiers, condominium dwellers, and edgy hipsters who define central city political culture." Miller tapped into this metropolitan mainstream by constructing Toronto as the "entrepreneurial city" through cultural-led strategies and place-making tools. In addition, in an attempt to advance the Toronto region's competitive creative city positioning in the global urban hierarchy, he catered to the business class with lower commercial property taxes.

Even with a centre-left mayor and council, neo-liberal urbanism became more entrenched during the Miller years. Toronto took on more entrepreneurial roles such as the role of the developer selling surplus city land (i.e., property that can be regenerated for profit) through the city-owned corporation, Build Toronto. Build Toronto was launched by Miller in 2009 to sell and/or develop underutilized land (e.g., parking lots, fields, and former industrial sites) and turn it into sites of accumulation through direct sales or by regenerating the value of assets by changing its zoning designation in order to pay for city debt (Dale 2011).

Under Miller's successor, Rob Ford (the right-wing populist who was elected mayor of Toronto in 2010), Build Toronto aggressively pursued this privatization fix to the city's debt load and operating budget costs by creating the political conditions to facilitate such transfers. Ford, born and raised in the Toronto suburb of Etobicoke, came to power with a strong following of supporters—the so-called "Ford Nation"—comprising in part fellow suburban dwellers with a deep dislike for "city people" and a mission to stop the "gravy train" of perceived excessive government spending.

One of Ford's mandates when elected was to sell off the Toronto Community Housing Corporation (TCHC), which would encompass $6 billion worth of housing stock that was, at the time, providing valuable housing for 164,000 tenants in the downtown and inner suburbs (Fanelli 2011). Whatever much-needed social housing stock remained in Toronto was under attack by the Ford regime, since it was regarded as fixed-capital that could be freed up and sold to the market for profit.

While Mayor Ford was unsuccessful in materializing his proposal to sell off more than 700 homes due to public outcry (voiced particularly loudly by the non-profit organization Tenants for Social Housing), and while the Ontario provincial policies in place limited his powers in governing social housing stock in the city, twenty-two properties were sold by the TCHC. The sales were arranged at the hands of former city councillor Case Ootes, appointed by Ford as an interim director to "clean up" the corporation after Ford fired its board amidst allegations of spending excesses (Day 2012).

Mayor John Tory (incumbent as of this writing) takes a more prudent and civic-oriented approach to city building—at least that is how he would like his approach to be seen. Yet this Former Chair of Toronto's Civic-Action (referred to by a least one prominent Toronto journalist by the nickname, "CivicAction John")[6] offers no clear break from Ford in this regard. Tory's current administration maintains the neo-liberal status quo, emphasizing privatization, public–private partnerships, low taxes, and a mobility politics that favours subways, shortened commute times for car drivers, and offering nothing beyond rhetoric to address the racialized and spatialized consequences of transit inequity in the city.

R #3: Reconfiguring state and society relations
The populist message behind "Ford Nation," as was constructed in the media, represented an ideological shift from David Miller's centre-left government and policies (Saberi and Kipfer 2010; Gordon 2013). The underlying sociospatial assumptions embedded in the discursive construction of Ford Nation pitted the "downtown elites" of central Toronto with the "narrow-minded" suburbanites of Toronto's inner-ring suburbs. This division may suggest that a populist message behind Ford Nation reveals a predominantly ignorant mass that absorbs the ideological attack on the public sector as wasteful and inefficient, and that the downtown is only a playground for city elites. However, according to Saberi and Kipfer (2010: 23) a deeper look at Ford's popularity reveals "much longer historical traditions of white-settler city Toronto: first, the tradition of a narrow, 'apolitical' and strictly property-oriented form of municipal politics that was consolidated a century ago and, second, the inward-looking, 'family-oriented' urban development model embodied by the mass-produced, resident-only, privately owned subdivisions of single-family bungalows that has defined the ideal of urban living since the 1950s." With no alternative progressive vision coming from the left, Ford's simple, working, "family man" message was the most convincing, not only to white conservative voters but to the working class as well. This was so particularly in wards where the majority of residents were (and still are) racialized immigrants and low-income residents (Saberi and Kipfer 2010; Gordon 2013).

Anti-elitist discourse was the kernel that helped Rob Ford gain city constituencies that have long suffered from stigmatization due to years of neglect and concentrated racialized poverty. His campaign focus on jobs and "stopping the gravy train" at City Hall also extended to his attack on the TCHC as inefficient, a position, which for many of the constituents living in derelict housing conditions, was far more reassuring than campaigns put forth by other contenders in the 2010 election focusing on building an inclusive Toronto (National Post Editorial Board 2011). For new immigrants trying to build a new life in Toronto, Ford's discourse of building Toronto's economy resonated. Such was the case even if his ideas of privatizing social housing and introducing a voucher system similar to the U.S. Section 8 "housing choice system" in order to "get people out of public housing" (Lorinc 2011; Kipfer and Saberi 2014) would further negatively impact the material realities of these constituents.

It appears Mayor Tory's "sensible" and "accountable" leadership is still trying to gain ground in the inner suburbs of Ford Nation. His recent positioning on key debates in the city, in which he supports populist policies, can be seen as political strategizing in an attempt to win over Ford's base. This manoeuvre will no doubt eventually distance him from the downtown elite, anti-Ford stance that helped him win the 2014 election.

R #4: Redefining the citizen as a consumer
The operating logic of urban neo-liberalism is to run the global city like a business in which citizens are seen as clients, customers, or consumers. Clearly, such an approach disrupts the state-society relations of the welfare state. Among the scalar contradictions of global city formation is the need to attract international capital, while at the same time working within municipal budgets and constraints in order to make this happen. Yet there is a vicious circle: as municipal budgets tighten, the city's dependence on global capital is fuelled. As a result, local governments cannot afford to keep services public.

Toronto's regional trajectory since the 1970s until now, i.e., from the period of deindustrialization to that of current global economic integration, demonstrates how urban policy has been reconfigured to create spaces for market-oriented growth and elite consumption practices (Brenner and Theodore 2002). The retrenchment of social welfare provisions has resulted in the privatization and outsourcing of municipal services, which has reduced public accountability. Citizens are now viewed as consumers, and public goods are no longer "public" but need to be purchased.

In the 1990s, the push toward privatization and neo-liberalization came from the suburbs. With Mayor Ford, it shifted to the City of Toronto proper. Mayor Ford altered the dominant construction of "the citizen as consumer" (even though that is what his agenda entailed) to the construction of "the citizen as taxpayer." The ideology of private property is heavily embedded in the idea of the taxpayer; thus property owners are privileged participants and maintain some influence in local participatory decision-making processes. Cuts in the public provision of social goods (e.g., social housing) coupled with an increase in private sector delivery of other public goods (e.g., garbage collection) was a strong mandate in Ford's regime (and it is now in Tory's as well), as he spent time convincing Torontonians that he was saving taxpayers money while increasing user fees.

Toronto's Social Housing Policy—A Broader and Longer History of Disinvestment

As mentioned in the introduction to this chapter, the erosion of social housing policy in Canada predates the neo-liberal transition of the country's federal policy. There are no legal or constitutional constraints imped-ing the federal (or provincial governments, for that matter) from interven-ing in social housing provision. Rather, Canada's current lack of a national housing vision reflects a historical continuity that prioritizes the private sector (Carroll 2002; Hulchanski 2004b; Harris 2006).

Federal housing policy privileging home ownership can be traced back to the Great Depression of the 1930s through the passing of the *Dominion Housing Act* in 1935. The Act sparked a program that attempted to stim-ulate a private housing market coming out of the slump of the Depression by facilitating mortgage lending. The process eventually transitioned into Canada's first national housing legislation, the 1938 *National Housing Act* (Harris 2006). This first piece of national housing legislation was the first step in regulating mortgage lending and borrowing. As a result, in 1946 the crown corporation called Central Mortgage and Housing (now known as the Canada Mortgage and Housing Corporation or CMHC) was created to administer joint loans and other federal housing initiatives under the *National Housing Act* (Hulchanski 2004b; Harris 2006). How-ever, up until 1963, when the federal government began to provide sub-sidized rental housing through joint provincial funding, most public funds from the CMHC prioritized home ownership.

In his analysis of the factors shaping Canadian housing policy, David Hulchanski (2004b: 223) notes: "Canada's housing system, in contrast to that of most Western nations, relies almost exclusively on the market mechanism for the provision, allocation, and maintenance of housing." Thus, it is important to recognize that although housing finance has become more widely accessible and flexible, the evolution of the Canadian housing market shows that once the building and financing of housing became more intertwined with the market, housing became understood as a commodity. It was no longer thought of as a common good and urban right.

Regressive housing policy trends, coupled with the increasing devolu-tion of housing provision from the federal government to the Ontario provincial government and eventually to municipalities in the GTA, have produced an uneven housing market that still privileges home ownership and neglects affordable and social housing. The fundamental danger of the supply-and-demand logic of the market is that it redefines the meaning of housing so that it cannot be identified as a social need (Hulchanski

2004b). The devolution of responsibility for housing did not come with increased ability and tools to improve social housing and thereby make it a viable alternative to home ownership in the province (Hackworth and Moriah 2006: 523).

Until recently, there had been virtually no new affordable housing construction in Toronto within the last fifteen years (Wellesley Institute 2006). Whatever affordable housing has been constructed has been piecemeal, and not very affordable for low- and moderate-income groups. According to the CMHC's definition of affordable housing, households should not have to pay more than 30% of their pre-tax income on rent. In Toronto's Official Plan, the definition of affordable rent is the average rent for a standard two-bedroom apartment in the private market, which is about $1,060 per month. Thus to be able to afford this rent, a household needs an annual income of $42,400, which does not match the reality of 40% of Toronto households that have annual incomes of less than $40,000 (Wellesley Institute 2006). According to Monsebraaten (2009: GT 01), "Some 647,000 Ontarians pay more than 30 per cent of their income on rent; more than 129,000 households are waiting up to 20 years for a social housing unit where rents are geared to income."

Most of the social housing stock in Ontario was built between the mid-1960s and the mid-1990s. Financing for social housing construction during this period was provided by a combination of federal, provincial, and joint federal-provincial cost-shared programs (Ontario Auditor-General Report 2009: 27). Community groups were also influential in building non-profit and co-operative housing during the 1980s and 1990s that shared market rate units and rent-geared-to-income (RGI) units (Ontario Auditor-General Report 2009). In the early 1990s, an average of 2,100 new affordable houses were built yearly (Wellesley Institute 2006). Public housing units built by governments during this thirty-year period were subsidized and administered by the CMHC and the Ontario Housing Corporation (OHC).

The winds of change that swept through Ontario under the neo-liberal regime of Premier Mike Harris began the process of devolution of social housing provision from the provinces to the municipalities. Harris explained this devolution as follows: "Government isn't in the business of putting up affordable housing and the feds backed out" (Bradley 2009).

During this transition period, while the downloading of social housing was occurring, the Ontario Ministry of Municipal Affairs and Housing continued administering social housing programs. In November 1999, the Canada–Ontario Social Housing Agreement was established, transferring responsibility for most Ontario social housing to the province. The transfer gave to Ontario (as well as to other provinces across Canada) the authority to download social housing programs to municipalities and to allocate federal funding for various housing programs (Ontario Auditor-General Report).

In December 2000, the process of downloading social housing was finally complete with the passing of the Ontario *Social Housing Reform Act* (SHRA). Under the Act, municipalities and private non-profits assumed the responsibility of social housing programs previously administered by the CMHC and the province. Forty-seven service managers now have the primary responsibility for funding and administering social housing programs (Ontario Auditor-General Report 2009). As Hackworth (2008: 13) notes, "If [Ontario Premier] Harris' initial cuts represented the 'roll-back' of the previous order, the SHRA surely marked the 'roll-out' of a set of institutions that would reproduce neo-liberalism in the sector long after the government's exit."

This particular neo-liberal "fix" involved the concomitant processes of deregulating private housing and downloading social housing, thus ensuring Ontario was officially "out of the housing business." The consequences of this fix, however, have been disastrous. With its implementation came the rapid loss of affordable rental housing, the deterioration of existing social housing stock, and virtually no new social housing construction. Whatever the number of social housing units built since 2000 by both the public and private sectors, they have not made up for the continuing loss of affordable housing units (Shapcott 2001).

With the responsibility of managing portfolios of rent-geared-to-income (RGI) units, managers working within an increasingly entrepreneurial framework of cost savings and service delivery efficiencies more aligned with the private housing market have accrued an enormous backlog of major capital repairs (Hackworth 2008; Lehrer, Keil, and Kipfer 2010; Côté and Tam 2013). The TCHC—the second-largest social housing provider in North America—is currently facing a $750 million capital repair backlog (Côté and Tam 2013). Under conditions of increasing rents and a dwindling affordable rental supply, the TCHC's situation reflects the neo-liberal austerity of the times. Increasingly, families with children, particularly single-parent families, are evicted and dispossessed of their homes (Lapointe and Novac 2004).

One strategy of such "accumulation by dispossession" included the City of Toronto's decision in 2012 (at the insistence of Mayor Rob Ford) to sell just some of the TCHC's single-family homes as a short-term funding fix. The right-wing Institute on Municipal Finance and Governance (2013: 4) argued this was a case of "radical thinking in desperate times."

This latest move by the city was a compromise from its initial approval to sell most of the TCHC's stock of single-family homes: 700 units out of the 58,000 rental housing units found in Toronto's high-rise towers in the inner suburbs. These 700 homes were prized assets, as they provided low-income tenants the opportunity to live in the city core close to amenities and crucial services that most of the dispossessed in the inner suburbs do not have access to.

Despite its devastating impacts—the loss of more affordable rental units, the further displacement of the poor, and the ongoing destruction of long-standing, mixed-income neighbourhoods in Toronto—this "privatization fix" through the sale of a percentage of TCHC stock was presented by the Ford regime as the only solution to deal with the TCHC's fiscal crisis (a crisis it had itself been responsible for constructing).

Even though a compromise had been reached on the number of TCHC units to be sold, recommendations put forth by a Special Housing Working Group (SHWG) reveal that the event marked a clear break from the state having a redistributive role in the provision of social housing. The SHWG's recommendations solidify "roll-with-it neoliberalization" (Keil 2009) tendencies, i.e., those that normalize market strategies and emphasize new partnership arrangements of private and non-profit actors to build affordable housing in the City of Toronto. In addition, an examination of SHWG discourse shows that home ownership continues to be emphasized as a way out of poverty. Thus, there is evidence of a continued hegemony of market logic in the provision of social services, along with a sharp indication of how social engineering operates through the devaluing of rental housing—an urban need for many vulnerable groups and a housing alternative for others.

The Regionalization of Housing in the Greater Toronto Area

A recent report from the Toronto Board of Trade states that in 2014 in its sixth annual Scorecard on Prosperity,[7] the board awarded the Toronto region an overall grade of B. The board ranked the region twelfth in the economy category and third for labour attractiveness (Toronto Board of Trade 2014). Overall, according to the board's report, Toronto has improved its position and now places third among twenty-four other global metropolises, with Paris being first and Calgary second.

The report concludes that Toronto can do better than "good enough" and that it has economic potential based on performance indicators, such as a strong banking sector, a strong housing market, and a livable environment (Toronto Board of Trade 2014: 49–50). The report even suggests that while housing affordability has improved since 2010, the region's weaknesses—transportation and climate—continue to disadvantage Toronto's overall performance and ranking.

What this report reveals is that Toronto has become a better and more affordable space in which to do business (Toronto Board of Trade 2014: 78). What it conceals, however, is Toronto's disturbing social housing trends. Toronto's affordable housing crisis is deepening, with 72,700 people on the affordable housing wait list (Monsebraaten 2013) and housing affordability intensifying across the region.

The deepening *social housing* crisis in Toronto is a reflection of broader economic growth trends and urban restructuring processes that are shaping its uneven social geography along class, race, and gender lines. The *affordable housing* crisis in the Toronto region is, on the other hand, a product of interrelated economic, urban, demographic, and political changes, and it is only intensifying in the absence of regional governance and investment from federal and provincial governments (Bunting, Walks, and Filion 2004; Bourne, Britton, and Leslie 2011). The socio-economic consequences of a retreating welfare state, regional and jurisdictional fragmentation, neo-liberal urban restructuring, and increasing privatization of public services in a high-growth competitive city-region, are spatially manifesting. Furthermore, they are creating what David Hulchanski (2010) refers to as "The Three Cities within Toronto."

Examining housing through a sociospatial lens reveals the intersectionality of housing with racialized and gendered poverty. In their work on the challenges of globalization and economic restructuring in the Toronto region, Bourne, Britton, and Leslie (2011: 237) argue that spatial processes of "suburbanization, inner suburban decline, and core area revitalization (gentrification)" are shaping the region's dispersed but concentrated development. These spatial processes, coupled with new immigrant settlement patterns and increasing segmentation and discrimination in the labour market, are contributing to a sociospatial inequality that can be defined by income polarization (Suttor 2006; Hulchanski 2010; Bourne, Britton, and Leslie 2011; Cowen and Parlette 2011).

Access to adequate and affordable housing in the GTA is thus an issue of regional inequity. Toronto's inner suburbs are manifesting conditions of decline and concentrated poverty similar to those found in inner cities in the U.S. On the other hand, the inner core and suburban municipalities together are experiencing high levels of economic development and population growth. The geography of employment is varied across the region, with particular jobs and activities concentrated in certain locations. While the downtown core specializes in "managerial occupations, business and finance, natural and social sciences, health, education and government services ... art, culture, recreation, and sport" (Bourne, Britton, and Leslie 2011: 248), manufacturing, shopping centres and office parks are concentrated in industrial nodes in the surrounding suburbs, particularly those of Vaughan, Mississauga, Brampton, and Oshawa.

In a recent interview, the Director of York Region's Housing and Residential Services highlighted the important relationship between housing affordability, transit, and lack of quality jobs when it comes to discussing increasing income disparities throughout the region:

> We have a saying around here, that transit is a housing issue, and housing is a transit issue. We talk to employers here that can't get employees to their work sites, who can't find the appropriate employees. I would suggest to you that it is a regional issue because if we don't have the ability for people to work and live in fairly close proximity, we are going to drive the economic viability of this city-region into the dumpster, and it's rapidly becoming a huge problem. It is hugely expensive to move around, especially if you're a lower income person. It's hugely difficult time-wise. It's hugely difficult to get childcare if your daycare centre, and your work, and your life are in different locations.... So I think it is a regional issue. I think, if we don't have a city-region where people of all income levels and all family make-ups can live wherever they need to, we're going to hurt our economic viability. (Interview with Roger Keil and Stefan Kipfer, Newmarket, ON, March 21, 2011)

The inner (postwar) suburbs of the GTA, have been steadily losing jobs. According to Bourne, Britton, and Leslie (2011: 251), "The inner suburbs of Etobicoke, North York, and Scarborough have experienced the greatest decline in income ... not surprisingly, suburban neighbourhoods characterized by falling relative incomes also tend to be areas of high unemployment and increasingly the home of many recent immigrants." With the concentration of low-to-moderate rental units in high-rise towers located in the inner suburbs, low-income households (particularly those of new immigrants, racialized minorities, and single-mothers) have little choice but to locate themselves in these areas. This is so even if members of these households have to travel further to find employment and have limited access to the Toronto Transit Commission's subway system (Hulchanski 2010).

The majority of this inner suburban, high-rise housing rental stock was built during the housing boom of the postwar years between 1945 and 1984. Intended for middle-class families (CUG+R 2010), such "tower in the park" suburban development was, at the time, considered progressive. Thus, nearly 2,000 high-rise modern apartment buildings were constructed throughout the region. Over the years, many if not most of these towers have suffered from neglect and disrepair at the hand of their (mainly) private owners. The situation has lead to severe disinvestment in these neighbourhoods, creating a dystopian reality that removes them far from the master-planned communities they once were and were supposed to be (CUG+R 2010).

Hulchanski's (2010) work on both the "Three Cities within Toronto" and the Centre for Urban Growth and Renewal (CUG+R)[8] shows how these clusters of apartment towers are now neighbourhoods of high social need. Supporting Hulchanski's assessment are the statistics provided by the Toronto Chapter of the United Way in its recent *Poverty by Postal Code 2: Vertical Poverty* report, which notes that by 2006, "nearly 40 percent of all families in high-rise buildings in the City of Toronto were 'poor'—up from 25% in 1981—giving proof to the idea of 'vertical poverty'" (United Way 2011: v). The concentration of poverty in Toronto's inner suburbs has been intensified by the lack of new affordable and social housing construction and the ongoing loss of rental stock due to gentrification and revitalization schemes.

Beginning in the Miller Years and continuing under the regime of the Ford Nation, Toronto's policy response to the spatialization of poverty has been shaped largely through a place-based approach. "Neighbourhood Improvement Areas" in the inner suburbs, consisting of twenty-two neighbourhoods but often lumped together as thirteen priority areas, were targeted specifically. In 2005, the Toronto Chapter of the United Way launched their Building Strong Neighbourhoods Strategy in response to earlier research findings contained in their first *Poverty by Postal Code* report (United Way 2004). These findings pointed to the growing concentration and isolation of low-income residents in Toronto's inner suburbs, and, additionally, to the steep rise in homicides during the summer months of that year, a phenomenon which came to be referred to as "the Summer of the Gun."

Strategies such as those represented by the creation of Neighbourhood Improvement Areas or the formation of the Building Strong Neighbourhoods Strategy involve targeting public resources to inner suburban, neglected areas. In addition, however, they also involve privatized revitalization schemes that attempt to regenerate these locations through the building of mixed-income units consisting of a diversification of housing tenures schemes and built forms. The underlying assumption is that the effects of revitalization will alleviate stigmatizations of violence associated with these neighbourhoods, reduce visible poverty, and make the neighbourhoods profitable and attractive to businesses and elites by changing their composition through deliberate social mixing.

While the economic elite has, by and large, adopted the language and progressive strands of social justice debates to promote redevelopment initiatives that espouse the benefits of "social mixing," "affordability," and "stability," it is important to not forget that these neighbourhoods are targeted because of their potential to create profit (Kipfer and Petrunia 2009). When looked at critically, it is not difficult to see how the redevelopment of priority improvement neighbourhoods—supported as they are by all the "right" planning language, including an emphasis on Jane Jacobs's neighbourhood philosophy[9]—effectively displaces the poor. This is because such redevelopment makes more room for more "valuable" citizens, in particular members of the so-called creative class (Boudreau, Keil, and Young 2009; Kipfer and Petrunia 2009; Lehrer, Keil, and Kipfer 2010).

One standout example is the five-phase project for Regent Park, one of Toronto's low-income neighbourhoods associated with concentrated poverty, public housing, crime, and decrepit buildings. With Jacobs's stamp of approval, the redevelopment of Regent Park, with its trendy arts and local business focus, aquatic centre, and new middle- and upper-class set of residents living in the market-rate condos and townhomes, has become celebrated and supported among neo-liberal elites and "creatives" as a successful model to deconcentrate poverty and make neglected neighbourhoods livable once again. What is not always known is that in order to make way for this particular venture in revitalization, a number of Regent Park residents were involuntarily relocated away from the community, often to areas where they found themselves isolated and in conditions of poverty worse than those they had experienced while living in the Park itself.

The strategy of social mixing, then, while purporting to embrace diversity, has actually ended up rendering the poor invisible. Redevelopment projects such as Regent Park (see Figure 8.1) create a homogenized urbanity where encounters with the city and difference are not spontaneous and genuine but are controlled and managed. Territorial power relations are embedded in these regeneration schemes such that they can be characterized as the recolonization of space. In the words of Lehrer, Keil, and Kipfer (2010: 87), "Recolonization is meant to turn a segregated public housing site into a 'normal,' 'successful' neighbourhood with a diversity of built forms, tenure types, income groups, and functions." However, as these authors illustrate, recolonizing territorial responses does not deal with the structural roots of poverty. They do not concern themselves with the

Figure 8.1   Juxtaposing realities of Regent Park (old and new). *Source*: Maju Tavera 2015.

devolution of social responsibilities from senior levels of government as a consequence of the retrenchment of the welfare state, nor do they worry about the scrapping of social housing construction, labour market segmentation, or systemic discrimination in both the labour and housing markets.

As the second phase of revitalization in Regent Park comes to an end, many of its relocated tenants are feeling uncertain. Even though they were promised the right to return, they are unsure whether or not they will be permitted to go back. If they are allowed to once again take up tenancy, they wonder if they will be able to restore their previous community social and support Networks, and they are concerned about how they will adjust with having to live with new upper-middle-class neighbours. Some of the tenants who have already gone back have expressed their surprise as well as feelings of having been duped when they found out that the units they would be reallocated to would be inside one of three buildings off-site. They had not realized or had not been told that reallocation to these buildings had been delineated by Regent Park's redevelopers as part of the plan to facilitate social mixing (Kelly 2014).

In March 2014, Toronto City Council approved a new ranking system based on an equity score. Under this new framework, sixteen new neighbourhoods were approved along with fifteen from the city's original priority neighbourhood strategy, while eight neighbourhoods were no longer eligible for funding, creating a total of thirty-one priority Neighbourhood Improvement Areas in the city. These place-based interventions, and the urban revitalization projects that have accompanied or are planned for them, can be seen as territorial expressions of accumulation by dispossession. The process of targeting neighbourhoods as "improvement areas" creates the necessary devaluation of capital fixed in land in order to "fix" it. As Marxist geographer David Harvey would likely explain it, the spatial-temporal fix (at the heart of the revitalization of Regent Park) is a territorial expression of the creative destruction forces inherent in capitalist accumulation processes. Urban regeneration is facilitated through the repossession of "valuable" land from the hands of low-income residents who live in these neighbourhoods and who have established community ties and support networks.

As a result of these processes, the Toronto region articulates an uneven geography of centrality and peripherality that is deepening the sociospatial divides between the gentrified inner core, the concentrated high-rise towers and apartments in the inner suburbs, and the sprawling mixed densities of suburban housing throughout Toronto's high-growth regions (York, Peel, Halton, and Durham). Housing tenure schemes throughout these three zones (the core, inner suburbs, and outer suburbs) of the region reflect the uneven housing market. The city's by now voracious appetite for condominium development indirectly creates an exclusionary inner core that caters to the consumption preferences of the upper-middle class, while processes of state-led gentrification continue to expel the working poor to outlying neighbourhoods in the inner and outer suburbs of the city-region. While the concentration of rental housing in the inner suburbs spatializes poverty vertically, the lack of social housing and rental units in the sprawling suburbs makes poverty and homelessness invisible in a sea of cookie-cutter subdivisions and illegal and/or substandard basement apartments.

The regionalization of housing in the GTA challenges the spatial thinking that associates social housing and social needs as exclusively City of Toronto problems. Amid the sprawling subdivisions north of Toronto's city limits—where automobile-dependent residential development reigns— is a landscape that reflects the cultural and economic proclivities of the "middle class,"[10] while veiling pockets of poverty. Deepening socioeconomic disparities are changing the dominant construction of the suburbs as a middle-class haven. A more accurate picture of Toronto's high-growth suburbs (particularly Richmond Hill, Markham, and Vaughan in York Region, and Mississauga and Brampton in Peel Region) would portray them as places where the most vulnerable—children, the elderly, single mothers, and recent immigrants—struggle to survive. As Hulchanski notes, "We have this image of suburbs as middle-income, but Brampton and Mississauga a long time ago stopped being a suburb. They are diverse municipalities on their own" (quoted in Mendleson 2013a).

The disparities I have been pointing to above and throughout this chapter are manifestations of growth, but it is growth without the appropriate social services to accommodate the diversity of needs of large numbers of the region's population who cannot or do not share the "middle-class" norm of home ownership. The contradictory challenges of housing affordability in high-growth suburbs, particularly for recent immigrants to York Region, is echoed by a long-time housing activist in that region:

Well, it [York Region] is a very expensive place to live. Housing is very expensive here. You know, a starter town house is $350,000. So we have that problem, and we also have an urban structure that is out of sync with need. We have very, very little rental housing. We have the lowest proportion of rental housing stock in the GTA. Toronto is over 50%. We're at 12%. What it's led to is that we have a lot of illegal basement apartments. Our municipalities of the lower tier are struggling with second suit policies. Most of them are talking about it, but they haven't quite got there yet.... We have a significant affordability problem. We also have a lot of new Canadians. We have a lot of families doubled, and tripled, and quadrupled up. So, a lot of those big houses, as we all know, are not single-family dwellings by a long stretch. (Director, Housing and Residential Services, York Region, in an interview with Roger Keil and Stefan Kipfer, Newmarket, ON, March 21, 2011)

Despite boasting the fifth-highest median family income in Canada, 14.8% of children under eighteen live in poverty in York Region (Aurora Banner 2012). York Region's recent census data reveals that two-thirds of its neighbourhoods are still considered middle-income (defined as individuals making close to the Toronto annual average of $44,271) and more than a fifth of neighbourhoods are considered high- to very-high-income (Mendleson 2013b). However, scattered throughout these pockets of wealth are very-low-income neighbourhoods constituting 14% of the region (Mendleson 2013b). Despite increased policy and planning attention in local municipal and regional Official Plans on smart growth, intensification, and walkable and healthy neighbourhoods, very little attention is being given to social housing in relation to jobs and precariousness in these discussions. Perhaps this tendency can be explained as part of the wider neglect of the sustainability question: the concept of sustainability clashes with underlying us-versus-them ethos coded in the suburban landscape.

Evidence from a recent housing study indicates that "more than 86 percent of all dwelling units in York Region are owner-occupied and only 13.7 percent of all dwelling units in the region are rental" (Preston et al. 2009: 296). According to this research, immigrants are more at risk of becoming homeless because they spend at least 50% of their income on housing, a practice that makes them asset rich but cash poor (Preston et al. 2009: 298). The main survival strategy of immigrants is to live with family and/or friends in crowded conditions, or to live in secondary suites.

In the Region of Peel, population growth and income polarization trends are similar to those found in York. Ongoing resistance to the legalization of basement suites in Brampton and increasing density in Mississauga point to class divisions between high-income earners and the working poor in these increasingly polarized municipalities. Recent data from the 2011 National Household Survey suggests that Peel "has the second highest prevalence of 'people living in low-income' at 12.6 percent, in which children less than 6 years old make up 10.2 percent of this figure" (Criscione 2013). While factors such as the lack of affordable housing and social housing, the erosion of manufacturing jobs, and the rise in precarious employment are fuelling these disparities, linguistic and cultural barriers to employment are also important forces heightening polarization as 80% of the population growth in Peel is from new immigrants (Mendleson 2013a). Similar to York Region, the Region of Peel is also exhibiting the polarizing trends of large cities (Hulchanski quoted in Mendleson 2013a). According to community workers and advocates, these trends are largely a result of provincial funding not being able to keep up with demands for social services.

What is missing from current regional initiatives is any attention to redistributive metropolitanism—a framework that emphasizes the need for regional policies to coordinate city and suburban economic development (Wekerle and Abbruzzese 2009; Swanstrom 2001). Political initiatives such as a regional housing justice movement seems to be even more idealistic with the phasing out of GTA pooling, colloquially referred to as the "Toronto tax." As the trends in York Region and the Region of Peel demonstrate, many high-growth suburbs are transitioning to municipalities that are beginning to exhibit social needs and challenges similar to those found in Toronto. The tendency politicizes any discussion on redistribution in the GTA, as suburbs are now competing with the city for funding from the Province of Ontario. Although most of the social housing in the GTA is concentrated in the core and inner suburbs of the city, redistribution in the Toronto context has focused recently on the suburbs getting back their pool dollars to pay for their own services. According to the director of the York Region Alliance to End Homelessness—a coalition group that no longer exists due to lack of funding—it is still unclear whether much of the money that is now being saved from the phasing out of the Toronto tax is going back to fund social services.

> We were quite outspoken about that because at the time when pooling happened, there was an effort made in the region to get all kinds of community organizations signed on to say, "We need those pooling dollars to come back to York Region. We have our own needs here. We need to those dollars back." And so, finally, when they decided to end pooling, the community is going, "Okay, so where's the money going?" And it went into the regional budget, and so less pressure on the budget—$13.2 million a year reduced pressure on the budget. And the community is going, "Hold on a minute. You've got us all to sign on and say that this money should come back and it could be invested in the community." And so we deputed at a regional council workshop around GTA pooling. We were quite involved in it and, I'd say, one of the things that has emerged over the last while has been a multi-year plan for the community and health services that is looking at a more strategic way about how that department is working and how they're framing their work and how money is being invested, and where it is going and how the community is going to be consulted in that. (Interview with Roger Keil and Stefan Kipfer, Newmarket, ON, March 21, 2011)

Thus, as the politics of housing provision transcends the urban-suburban divide, the regionalization of housing in the GTA grows ever more uneven and complex. With much of the population and job growth occurring in the outer ring of the city, the suburbs are increasingly urbanizing and exhibiting the polarizing trends of many large Canadian cities (Walks 2011). To date, there has been no mobilization around housing in the GTA connecting the displaced and marginalized from the redevelopment public housing projects in the city with the neglected populations in the high-rises of the inner suburbs and the invisible populations in the outer suburbs. However, a housing movement that attempts to make the necessary connections to other transit and social, ecological, and economic justice movements in the city would be vital in order to normalize the housing question so that public debate does not focus merely on property values and profit margins, but on the very real social need of housing and its importance in the overall sustainability of the region.

Conclusion

As this chapter has indicated, urban neo-liberalism has created a scenario in which its stakeholders see the private sector as the only viable solution for affordable housing construction in the City of Toronto and the GTA. However, as I have aimed to make clear, the private sector will only get into the business of building affordable housing with the support of the state, which will have to facilitate development by reducing the risk involved for private developers through incentives, such as waiving municipal development costs. As the Toronto Board of Trade's (2014) Scorecard on Prosperity suggests, providing affordable housing choices creates the illusion that Toronto is a livable city, which is key to its remaining competitive globally.

The danger of relying on the market for affordable housing provision is that home ownership becomes the privileged form of housing tenure, touted as the surest and fastest way for low- and middle-income groups to get out of poverty. Such a limited and narrowly focused economic conception of housing divorces this public good from the commons at the same time as it preempts any alternative vision or lifestyle choices that challenge capitalist relations. But even more disconcerting perhaps is the fact that the real housing needs of the working poor and of vulnerable groups are becoming increasingly dependent on the whims of developers and their myopic dedication to creating profit margins.

An examination of the materiality of the housing trends that have shaped the Toronto region's uneven geography reflects a combination of elements from different historical periods from the early industrial city to the post-Fordist metropolis. Moreover, it underscores the spatialized consequences of disinvestment, governmental downloading of social housing, and the reliance on market mechanisms for housing supply. Current planning and policy initiatives focus on renewal as a way to regenerate capital value in the high-rise towers and priority neighbourhoods of Toronto that have witnessed years of decline and disinvestment. However, there is a question that planners, civic groups, and builders coordinating these renewal schemes continue to neglect: how can we find legacies and progressive remnants of regional coordination from Toronto's past, from the time when it used to be known as "a city that worked"? Place-based initiatives to deal with concentrated poverty that lack a regional vision risk becoming another mechanism for state-led gentrification.

Governing the region in the absence of any regional coordination between the inner city and the inner and outer suburbs, or of policies dealing with the systemic issues of racialized poverty and rising income polarization, is creating a city that, unfortunately, no longer works. The result is a homogenized and discompassionate urbanity that, while catering to business elites and knowledge-workers deemed valuable for sharpening the region's competitive edge, increasingly dispossesses its working poor and vulnerable populations.

Notes

1 A central tenet of David Harvey's (2004) theorizations on the "privatization fix" is the privatizing of public assets and the contracting out of essential services as an overall strategy to "fix" or restore capitalist accumulation processes during periods of crisis.

2 See Roger Keil and Jean-Paul D. Addie in this volume for a more in-depth discussion of existing city–suburban divides in the City of Toronto.

3 In-depth historical analyses of the neo-liberalization of Toronto can be found in Boudreau, Keil, and Young (2009) and in Kipfer and Keil (2002).

4 Amalgamation occurred in 1998 when Metro Toronto was formally integrated into a megacity complex with its six surrounding municipalities of East York, Etobicoke, North York, Scarborough, and York.

5 See also Schmid and Weiss (2004) and McLean (2005).

6 CivicAction is a non-profit group consisting of senior executives and business leaders throughout the GTA interested in influencing public policy debates focusing on the social, economic, and environmental challenges that hinder the region's economic prosperity. The nickname CivicAction John can be found in *Toronto Star* columnist Edward Keenan's June 15, 2015 piece, "Why is John Tory playing to Rob Ford's base?"

7 This scorecard provides an overview of the "region's performance" among twenty-four international city-regions based on various measures of economic performance and livability. Funding of this research is largely provided by Certified Professional Accountants of Ontario.

8 The Centre for Urban Growth and Renewal (CUG+R) is a non-profit research organization founded in 2009 that consists of two planning, architecture, and design firms E.R.A Architects and planningAlliance (pA), and the Cities Centre at the University of Toronto.

9 Jane Jacobs's—often associated with the monikers as urban guru or high priestess of planning—alternative vision of the master-planned community emphasized mixed-use development and high-density as stimulators of social and economic vitality at the neighbourhood scale.

10 I use quotation marks around this term to emphasize that it is a social construction based on perceptions and assumptions associated with the term.

References

Aurora Banner. 2012. "12.7% of York residents live in poverty: Study." *York Region*, November 14. Accessed on August 15, 2014. www.yorkregion.com/news-story/1456570-12-7-of-york-residents-live-in-poverty-study/.

Boudreau, J.-A., R. Keil, and D. Young. 2009. *Changing Toronto: Governing urban neoliberalism*. Toronto: University of Toronto Press.

Bourne, L., J. N. H. Britton, and D. Leslie. 2011. "The Greater Toronto Region: The challenges of economic restructuring, social diversity, and globalization."

In L. S. Bourne, T. Hutton, R. G. Shearmur, and J. Simmons, eds., *Canadian urban regions: Trajectories of growth and change* (236–68). Don Mills: Oxford University Press.

Bradley, L. 2009. "Easing housing crisis." *Sudbury Star.* December 5. Accessed on May 18, 2014. www.thesudburystar.com/2009/12/05/easing -housing-crisis.

Brenner, N. 2002. "Decoding the newest 'metropolitan regionalism' in the USA: A critical overview." *International Journal of Urban and Regional Research* 23: 3–21.

Brenner, N. and N. Theodore. 2002. "Cities and the geographies of 'actually existing neoliberalism.'" *Antipode* 34(3): 349–79.

Bunting, T., A. R. Walks, and P. Filion. 2007. "The uneven geography of housing affordability stress in Canadian metropolitan areas." *Housing Studies* 19(3): 361–93.

Carroll, B. W. 2002. "Housing policy in the new millennium: The uncompassionate landscape." In E. P. Fowler and D. Siegel, eds., *Urban policy issues: Canadian perspectives* (69–89). Oxford: Oxford University Press.

Centre for Urban Growth and Renewal (CUG+R). 2010. "Tower neighbourhood renewal in the Greater Golden Horseshoe: An analysis of high-rise apartment tower neighbourhoods developed in the post-war boom (1945–1984)." Accessed on October 5, 2014. Toronto: Queen's Printer. www.cugr.ca/tnrggh.

Côté, A., and H. Tam. 2013. "Affordable housing in Ontario: Mobilizing private capital in an era of public constraint." *IMFG Perspectives. Munk School of Global Affairs, University of Toronto* 3: 1–14. Accessed August 17, 2014. http://munkschool.utoronto.ca/imfg/uploads/238/1409affordablehousing proofr2.pdf.

Criscione, P. 2013. "Stats show high number of Peel children live in poverty." *Brampton Guardian.com.* September 27. Accessed August 8, 2014. www .bramptonguardian.com/news-story/4129668-stats-show-high-number-of -peel-children-live-in-poverty/.

Dale, D. 2011. "Fords want to speed up land sales to ease debt." *Toronto Star.* August 2. Accessed August 14, 2014. www.thestar.com/news/gta/2011/08/02/ fords_want_to_speed_up_land_sales_to_ease_debt.html.

Day, N. 2012. "An in-depth look at the fight to save social housing in Toronto." *Rabble.ca.* February 13. Accessed August 17, 2014. http://rabble.ca/news/ 2012/02/depth-look-fight-save-social-housing-toronto.

Evans, B. and G. Albo. 2008. "Harper's bunker: The state, neoliberalism and the election." *The Bullet* 139. September 25. Accessed March 25, 2014. www .socialistproject.ca/bullet/bullet139.html.

Fanelli, C. 2009. "Managing the crisis in Toronto: Class power and striking city workers." *The Bullet* 237. July 10. Accessed May 18, 2014. www .socialistproject.ca/bullet/bullet237.html.

———. 2011. "Selling the city: Rob Ford's Toronto." *The Bullet* 533. August 8. Accessed May 18, 2014. www.socialistproject.ca/bullet/533.php.

Filion, P. and T. Bunting. 2006. "Understanding twenty-first century urban structure: Sustainability, unevenness, and uncertainty." In T. Bunting and P. Filion, eds., *Canadian cities in Transition* (1–23). Don Mills: Oxford University Press.

Fowler, E. P. and J. Layton. 2002. "Transportation policy in Canadian cities." In E. P. Fowler and D. Siegel, eds., *Urban policy issues: Canadian perspectives* (155–71). Oxford: Oxford University Press.

Gordon, T. 2013. "Rob Ford, Ford Nation and the suburbs: What's going on?" *New Socialist*, November 25. Accessed on May 13, 2014. www.newsocialist .org/729-rob-ford-ford-nation-and-the-suburbs-what-s-going-on.

Hackworth, J. 2008. "The durability of roll-out neoliberalism under centre-left governance: The case of Ontario's social housing sector." *Studies in Political Economy* 81: 7–26.

Hackworth, J. and A. Moriah. 2006. "Neoliberalism, contingency and urban policy: The case of social housing in Ontario." *International Journal of Urban and Regional Research* 30(3): 510–27.

Harris, R. 2006. "Housing dreams, responsibilities, and consequences." In T. Bunting and P. Filion, eds., *Canadian cities in transition* (272–86). Don Mills: Oxford University Press.

Harvey, D. 2006. *Spaces of global capitalism*. London and New York: Verso.

———. 2004. "The 'new' imperialism: Accumulation by dispossession." *Socialist Register* 40: 63–87. Accessed May 18, 2014. http://socialistregister.com/index .php/srv/article/view/5811#.U3j6Vy9BzNs.

Hulchanski, D. J. 2004a. "How did we get here? The evolution of Canada's 'exclusionary' housing policy system." In J. D. Hulchanski and M. Shapcott, eds., *Finding room: Policy options for a Canadian rental housing strategy* (179–94).Toronto: Cities Centre Press, University of Toronto.

———. 2004b. "What factors shape Canadian housing policy? The intergovernmental role in Canada's housing system." In R. Young and C. Leuprecht, eds., *Canada: The state of the federation, 2004—Municipal-federal-provincial relations in Canada* (221–47). Montreal and Kingston: McGill-Queen's University Press.

———. 2010. "The three cities within Toronto: Income polarization among Toronto's neighbourhoods, 1970–2000." Toronto: Cities Centre Press, University of Toronto.

Keil, R. 2002. "'Common-sense' neoliberalism: Progressive conservative urbanism in Toronto, Canada." *Antipode* 3: 578–601.

———. 2009. "The urban politics of roll-with-it neoliberalization." *CITY* 13(2–3): 231–45.

Keil, R. and D. Young. 2008. "Transportation: The bottleneck of regional competitiveness in Toronto." *Environment and Planning C: Government and Policy* 26: 728–51.

Kelly, S. 2014. "Happy but not happy." *TVO: The inside agenda* (blog). April 9. http://theagenda.tvo.org/blog/agenda-blogs/happy-not-happy-regent-park.

Kipfer, S. 1998. "Urban politics in the 1990s: Notes on Toronto." In R. Wolff, A. Schneider, C. Schmid, P. Klaus, A. Hofer, and H. Hitz, eds., *Possible urban worlds: Urban strategies at the end of the 20th century* (172–79). Basel: Birkhaeuser.

Kipfer, S. and R. Keil. 2002. "Toronto Inc? Planning the competitive city in the new Toronto. *Antipode* 34(2): 227–64.

Kipfer, S. and J. Petrunia. 2009. "'Recolonization' and public housing: A Toronto case study." *Studies in Political Economy* 83: 111–39.

Kipfer, S. and P. Saberi. 2014. "From "revolution" to farce? Hard-right populism in the making of Toronto." *Studies in Political Economy* 93: 127–51.

Lehrer, U., R. Keil, and S. Kipfer. 2010. "Reurbanization in Toronto: Condominium boom and social housing revitalization." *disP* 180(1): 81–90.

Lorinc, J. 2011. "The Toronto community housing conundrum." *Spacing: Toronto*, March 7. Accessed on August 17, 2014. http://spacing.ca/toronto/2011/03/07/lorinc-the-toronto-community-housing-conundrum/.

McLean, H. 2005. "Go west, young hipster: The gentrification of Queen Street West." In J. McBride and A. Wilcox, eds., *Utopia: Towards a new Toronto?* (156–62). Toronto: Coach House Books.

Mendleson, R. 2013a. "Peel transformed from middle-class suburbia to income extremes." *Toronto Star*. April 6. Accessed on August 8, 2014 www.thestar.com/news/gta/2013/04/06/peel_transformed_from_middleclass_suburbia_to_income_extremes.html.

———. 2013b. "York Region's poverty rises along with wealth: More residents struggling amid private clubs, estates." *Toronto Star*. June 29. Accessed on August 8, 2014. www.thestar.com/news/gta/2013/06/28/york_region_seeing_rising_affluence_and_deepening_poverty.html.

Metrolinx Board. 2014. *The Big Move: Transforming transportation in the Greater Toronto and Hamilton Area*. Greater Toronto Transportation Authority, 2008. Accessed on May 13, 2014. www.metrolinx.com/thebigmove/Docs/big_move/TheBigMove_020109.pdf.

Monsebraaten, L. 2009. "'Nearly homeless' struggle to hang on." *Toronto Star*. November 16. Accessed on May 18, 2014.www.thestar.com/news/gta/2009/11/16/nearly_homeless_struggle_to_hang_on.html.

———. 2013. "Updated Ontario affordable housing waiting lists still climbing." *Toronto Star*. November 12. Accessed on May 18, 2014.www.thestar.com/news/queenspark/2013/11/12/ontario_affordable_housing_waiting_lists_still_climbing.html.

National Post Editorial Board. 2011. "Toronto's angry (non-white) voters." *National Post*. October 27. Accessed on August 15, 2014. http://fullcomment.nationalpost.com/2010/10/27/national-post-editorial-board-torontos-angry-non-white-voters/.

Ontario Ministry of Infrastructure. 2006. *Growth plan for the Greater Golden Horseshoe*. Toronto: Queen's Printer.

Ontario Ministry of Transportation. 2007. *MoveOntario 2020*. Toronto: Queen's Printer.

Ontario Ministry of Municipal Affairs and Housing. 2000. *Social Housing Reform Act*. Toronto: Ministry of Municipal Affairs and Housing.

———. 2002. *Oak Ridges Moraine conservation plan*. Toronto: Ministry of Municipal Affairs and Housing.

———. 2005. *Greenbelt protection plan*. Toronto: Queen's Printer.

Peck, J. and A. Tickell. 2002. "Neoliberalizing space." *Antipode* 34: 381–404.

Preston, V., et al. 2009. "Immigrants and homelessness—At risk in Canada's outer suburbs." *Canadian Geographer* 53(3): 288–304.

Saberi, P., and S. Kipfer. 2010. "Rob Ford in Toronto: Why the ascendancy of hard-right populism in the 2010 mayoral election?" *New Socialist*. November 24. Accessed March 15, 2014.www.newsocialist.org/webzine/analysis/314-rob-ford-in-toronto-why-the-ascendancy-of-hard-right-populism-in-the-2010-mayoral-election.

Sancton, A. 2002. "Metropolitan and regional governance." In E. P. Fowler and D. Siegel, eds., *Urban policy issues: Canadian perspectives* (54–68). Oxford: Oxford University Press.

Schmid, C. and Daniel Weiss. 2004. "The new metropolitan mainstream." In INURA and R. Palosicia, eds., *The contested metropolis: Six cities at the beginning of the twenty-first century (252–60)*. Basel: Birkhäuser.

Sewell, J. 2009. *The shape of the suburbs: Understanding Toronto's sprawl.* Toronto: University of Toronto Press.

Shapcott, M. 2001. "Made-in-Ontario housing crisis." *Canadian Centre for Policy Alternatives* Technical Paper #12. Accessed on May 2, 2014. www.policyalternatives.ca/sites/default/files/uploads/publications/Ontario_Office_Pubs/housing_crisis.pdf.

Toronto Board of Trade. 2014. "Toronto as a global city: Scorecard on prosperity 2014." Accessed on October 1, 2014. www.bot.com/advocacy/reports/Pages/Scorecard-on-Prosperity.aspx.

United Way of Greater Toronto. 2004. "Poverty by postal code: The geography of neighbourhood poverty (1981–2001)." Toronto: United Way. Accessed on October 1, 2014. www.unitedwaytoronto.com/document.doc?id=59.

———. 2005. *Strong neighbourhoods: A call to action.* Toronto: United Way of Toronto. Accessed on February 5, 2014. www.unitedwaytoronto.com/whatWeDo/reports/strongNeighbourhoods.php.

———. 2011. Poverty by postal code2: Vertical poverty. "Declining income, housing quality and community life in Toronto's inner suburban high-rise apartments." Toronto: United Way. www.unitedwaytoronto.com/document.doc?id=89.

Swanstrom, T. 2001. "What we argue about when we argue about regionalism." *Journal of Urban Affairs* 23(5): 479–96.

Walks, R. A. 2006. "Homeless, housing affordability, and the new poverty." In T. Bunting and P. Filion, eds., *Canadian cities in transition* (419–37). Don Mills: Oxford University Press.

———. 2011. "Economic restructuring and trajectories of sociospatial polarization in the twenty-first-century Canadian city." In L. S. Bourne, T. Hutton, R. G. Shearmur, and J. Simmons, eds., *Canadian urban regions: Trajectories of growth and change* (125–59). Don Mills: Oxford University Press.

Walks, R. A. and L. S. Bourne. 2006. "Ghettos in Canada's cities? Racial segregation, ethnic enclaves and poverty concentration in Canadian urban areas." *Canadian Geographer* 50(3): 273–98.

Wekerle, G. R., and T. Abbruzzese. 2010. "Producing regionalism: Regional movements, ecosystems and equity in a fast and slow growth region." *Geo-Journal* 75(6): 581–94.

Wekerle, G. R., L. A. Sanberg, L. Gilbert, and M. Binstock. 2007. "Nature as a cornerstone of growth: Regional and ecosystems planning in the Greater Golden Horseshoe." *Canadian Journal of Urban Research* 16(1): 20–38.

Wellesley Institute. 2006. *The blueprint to end homelessness in Toronto: A two-part action plan.* Toronto: Wellesley Institute.

Interviews

Director, York Region Alliance to End Homelessness, Newmarket, March 21, 2011.
Director Housing and Residential Services, York Region, Newmarket, March 21, 2011.

CHAPTER 9

Shortcomings and Promises of Governing City-Regions in the Canadian Federal Context
The Example of Montreal

Pierre Hamel

IN RELATION TO GOVERNANCE, processes of decision-making in city-regions are strongly influenced both by globalizing trends and local culture dynamism. This is not to say that innovation in regards to economic activity is unimportant. Economical factors, global, and local, remain structurally decisive in many ways. Nevertheless, I will consider city-region and metropolitan governance in reference to cultural life, cultural behaviour, and cultural meaning, not with the intention of subordinating economy to culture, but to underline that, in some respect, culture is overwhelming in regards to governing and/or governance issues.

For that matter, I am relying on a specific sociological understanding of culture. Going with post-structural and post-colonial visions of the world, this cultural sociological perspective insists on the importance of significations embedded in or generated from social practices. Interpretations of meanings coming from those practices and their experiences are necessary to assess social life. As Isaac Reed (Reed 2007: 11) underlines, critical reading and normative transformative orientation of action are necessarily linked:

> from a cultural sociological perspective, it should be clear that ideas about knowledge and the social that originate from a structural situation of oppression, and the social experiences such a situation entails, are not destined to stay there. The act of criticism—of speaking truth to power, representing the underrepresented, speaking in the voice of the other—is

not *determined* by a position in the social structure but rather *enabled* by certain positions in the social structure, then made available to many through various forms of communication and thus *codified* into a cultural context of action. Like many cultural forms, these amendments to 'democratic thought' have followed a Durkheimian path, according to which symbolic formations that originate from certain points in the social structure ... take on a life of their own.

Along with this perspective of cultural sociology, actors are never completely in command of their actions. Speech acts produce connotations that actors cannot predict: "This is why Ricoeur compared action to a text, since acts, once committed, escaped the interpretation of their authors.... In tracking down these unintended meanings and showing how as a background for and an environment of action, they explain the flow of social life, cultural sociology denaturalizes the social. The application of these techniques of denaturalization to the processes that enable or prohibit democratic practice, therefore, always suggests how social life *could be otherwise*" (2007: 12).

Keeping this in mind and referring to the case of Montreal, one may recall that over the last thirty years, globalizing trends and local culture were dealt with by economic and political actors—and in many occasions by social actors of civil society—in different ways according to the capacity of urban regimes in place to challenge both intense economic restructuring processes at play and the dominant political landscape prevailing at the regional and national levels.

My argument in this chapter proceeds in three steps. First, I sketch the current issue of metropolitan governance in Montreal. It is impossible to understand the challenges of that governance without considering the nature of coalitions that are active at the city-regional scale, in addition to taking into account the role of the central city that, up until now, remains unstable and difficult to predict, but continues to play a major role in defining these coalitions. Second, I provide an overview of some of the major highlights of Montreal's urban and regional development in order to better define the main challenges ahead. Third, I address these challenges through a consideration of the specificity of the Canadian federal context that is necessarily involved but usually underestimated in urban studies.

The Issue of Metropolitan Governance

The modern Montreal city-region must deal with a series of challenges that other North American city-regions are facing as well. These challenges concern economic and social integration of immigrants, the reduction of social and economic inequalities, public efforts to address climate change, the funding of local social and health services, and infrastructures of the central city, but also support to social and economic innovation in order to cope with the structural forces of globalization. Can one speak of a stable hierarchy or combination between these challenges? Is there a priority? I can at least mention that these challenges are not mutually exclusive. More importantly, even if such challenges are similar to those found elsewhere, these are no less indebted to the culture and history of a specific place marked by constraints and opportunities of their own. Otherwise, how would it be possible to understand and explain the rise and fall of Montreal over the nineteenth and twentieth centuries?

This is certainly not the place to recall the numerous factors at work in this process, not to mention that extensive research has already highlighted these elements (Higgins 1986; Levine 1990). Once without any doubt Canada's metropolis (Léveillée 1987), Montreal is nowadays struggling to reduce its slide compared to the economic dynamism of the main North American city-regions (OECD 2004). The agglomeration is currently engaged in a repositioning process, even though the strategy for such a restructuring is far from being established with certainty.

However, one must remember that at the turn of the twenty-first century, through an ambitious reform, the Quebec State has transformed the governing urban system of the whole metropolitan region by implementing a new governing body while also revising the status and powers of existing ones. Resulting in a new division of power between municipal bodies, the reform was implemented with great frustration among local elected representatives. It was imposed from above and, for that matter, received very little support from the mayors of municipalities of the region, with the exception of the current mayor of the City of Montreal.

Thus, at the metropolitan scale, a new tier of planning and coordination was implemented: the Montreal Metropolitan Community (MMC). The territory covered by this new institution corresponds more or less to the Montreal census metropolitan area (CMA) as defined by Statistics Canada. Eighty-two municipalities were included in that territory established for planning and management purposes. In a way, this third level of planning and decision-making for dealing with social, economic, and urban development at a regional scale was the first step of the reform. The second step was to create a megacity by imposing a merger of the municipalities on the Island of Montreal. But in order to make this amalgamation acceptable to the mayors of suburban municipalities on the island, the creation of the megacity was accompanied by a decentralizing process at the level of boroughs—newly established by the reform—following, to delimit their boundaries, the limits of the previous suburban municipalities or those of the neighbourhoods of the former City of Montréal. This decentralization can be considered as the third step of the reform. All told, at the end of a complicated process, the new megacity comprises nineteen boroughs, to which one should add the fourteen suburban cities that have decided to be de-merged—becoming reconstituted municipalities—and be part of the agglomeration council representing all the municipalities of the island of Montreal.

This is not the place to detail and assess this huge institutional reform and its shortcomings, as it has already been done (see Hamel 2005; Hamel 2006; Hamel and Rouseau 2006; Boudreau et al. 2006). Suffice it to say that the reform did not help social, economic, and political actors face the deconstruction and reconstruction processes they were coping with in order to overcome Montreal's relative economic decline. Neither did it contribute to solving the problems of corruption that blight the management of the City of Montreal, a situation that goes back at least to the end

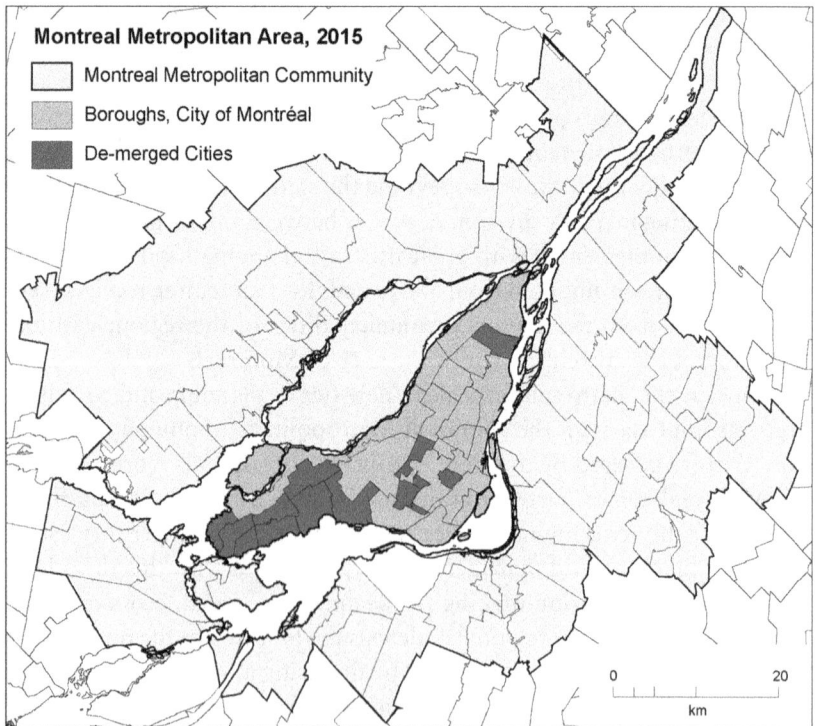

Map 9.1   Montreal Metropolitan Area, 2015. *Source:* Université de Montréal.

of the 1990s (Pratte 2013). On the positive side, however, the reform succeeded for one of the first times in decades in introducing political concerns about urban challenges framed at a metropolitan scale. This was particularly expressed in a planning proposal concerning metropolitan land use and development released by the MMC (*Un grand Montréal attractif, compétitif et durable. Projet de Plan métropolitain d'aménagement et de développement* 2011). This planning document clearly stated that issues of urban development were convergent with environmental concerns. In that respect, while addressing such issues, public action should necessarily be conceived and organized at the metropolitan scale.

At the same time one must be aware that discussing the requirements of defining urban planning at the metropolitan scale is far from implementing them effectively. It seems there is still a distance to travel before this point is reached. Many barriers would need to be overcome before building a social representation of the metropolitan space as a viable political and cultural reference for everyone. The MMC that is driving the planning discourse at a city-regional scale does not have the legitimacy to convince other social, economic, and political actors that the regional tier is pertinent and reliable to address urban issues. For example, to what extent are municipalities of the Northern Shore—which were strongly opposed to the creation of the MMC under the rationale that the municipalities of the periphery do not have to pay for the mismanagement by the central city—ready to effectively support the orientation of urban development at the metropolitan scale as elaborated by the MMC in its planning document based on Transit Oriented Development (TOD)?

Uncertainty about planning at the regional scale, due to the low level of enthusiasm by suburban municipalities of the periphery in sharing the costs and orientation of urban development brought forward by the MMC, is not the only point of contention regarding the future of Montreal. At the central-city level, a lot of opposition to sharing a mutual project with the suburbs also prevails. As it is the case in other North American urban agglomerations, over the last decades middle-class households have preferred the periphery to the central city, bringing with them resources that are no longer available to pay for maintaining and renewing the infrastructures and/or proximity services provided by the central city. In that respect, a bit of resentment is palpable among some citizens living within the limits of the central city. Local democracy at the neighbourhood or borough levels is not easily compatible with metropolitan democracy (Booth and Jouve 2005). If the intent is to define the governability of city-regions, one of the conditions remains to construct these regional spaces as political territories (Lefèvre 2013). Such a requirement necessarily raises a definitional element: what is a political territory? The elements brought in by Lefèvre refer to the involvement of economic, social, and political actors and their capacity to build a "legitimate collective action" (Lefèvre 2013: 237) that relies on five specific conditions: "presence of a collective decision system; common interests perceived as such; integration mechanisms; internal and external of representation of the collective actor; capacity for innovation" (ibid.). In the case of metropolises, these elements need to be produced at the metropolitan scale, which is particularly difficult due to the multiplicity of actors involved.

Added to this is the fact that the notion of collective action as defined here raises theoretical problems. In its sociological acceptation—especially in the literature on social movements (Snow, Soule, and Kriesi 2004)—the notion is used above all in connection with a contentious dimension related either to the conflict of class interests or the incompatibility of identity values characterizing diverse social groups. In other words, if the presence of multiple actors makes the building of collective action difficult, thus far, within a sociology of social movements—in contrast to the generally accepted definition by the sociology of organizations—this has been conceived exclusively in a conflict-ridden situation, where the clash of interests must be taken seriously into account. Beyond the efforts to define common interests and other incentives for sharing a common representation, the divisions between those actors are structural and should be seen in this light. Thus, more attention to the configuration of actors involved and to the nature of conflicts defining them must prevail.

Montreal's Urban and Regional Development

City-regions nowadays are in constant processes of adapting their built environment to ever-changing requirements for competing in the market place. This observation is anything but new: this has certainly always been the case. Processes of adapting cities and city-regions to internal and external causes are inherent to the relations inhabitants maintain with their built environment. However, what is specific to the current era of globalization is that the interconnection between internal and external factors is more intense than it has been experienced until recently. For that matter, local economic, social, and political actors have to rethink their strategies and models of action if they wish to improve their control over urban development.

From the middle of the nineteenth century to the 1930s, Montreal was the economic hub of Canada. But that gilded period is nothing more than a distant memory of little help nowadays in getting by in an era of service economy and global competition. Several geographical, historical, and political factors can explain the favourable position attained by Montreal's metropolis during that era. These factors started to change dramatically during the great depression of the 1930s—if not a decade or two earlier— as suggested by Léveillée (1978), with other geographical locations being favoured, especially Toronto. As mentioned by Linteau et al. (1989: 544), at the beginning of the twentieth century, American businesses preferred to establish their branches in Ontario. In 1936, for example, 66% of these in the manufacturing sector were settled there, compare to 16% in Quebec.

It is a well-known fact that Montreal in the early 2000s ranked in the bottom quintile in the hierarchy of North American cities. This observation is congruent with the data gathered by the OECD through a survey based on standard criteria (CDP per person, percentage of the population having attained higher education, job creation, business productivity) (OECD 2004). Among Canadian cities with population above 500,000 inhabitants, Montreal has the highest rate of individuals with lower incomes (29%) (Sgro 2002). Other indicators are not too encouraging either. One may evoke the innovative capacity of businesses, the dynamism of entrepreneurship, or the amount of headquarters of major North American and international companies. For each one, Montreal was lagging behind North American regions with a similar demographic weight.

Such a diagnosis must be highlighted by two series of comments. First, as underlined by Mario Polèse (2012), it is unusual—if not exceptional— that a country's primary city be displaced over time by another. But this is what happened in Canada, as revealed by the 1981 census, when the Toronto metropolitan region officially exceeded in demographic terms the metropolitan region of Montreal. The argument made by Polèse is fairly straightforward: a French-speaking city cannot be the financial and commercial centre of a predominantly anglophone country. From then on, one has to bear in mind that the *francisation* (refrenching or refrenchifying) of Montreal—at the outset, during the first half of the seventeenth century, Montreal had been established under the French regime—could not be done without incurring some expenses. However, despite these sizeable expenses, for the French-speaking population the "Reconquest of Montreal"—to borrow Marc V. Levine's well-known book title (1990)—was a vital move. It was somehow required for breaking down the relationships of colonial domination by the anglophone economic elites as structured in class and ethnic terms over the years (Guindon 1990). In other words, the linguistic battles over the defence and protection of the French language in Montreal were symptomatic of profound economic and social inequalities as experienced by the francophone working class and by the francophone community in Quebec at large. These struggles were reinforced through political commitment in the direction of a national movement during the period of the Quiet Revolution at the beginning of the 1960s.

The language issue—and with it ethnic and class conflicts—was not the only one to be taken into account in explaining the reversal of the Canadian urban hierarchy. Other elements were also at play, such as technological changes and the fact that a major restructuring of industrial activities was under way from the 1960s onward. The transition from a manufacturing economy to a service economy established for businesses new conditions of development and new technological requirements. The adaptation process was particularly difficult for Montreal businesses struggling with modernization and technological innovations. As it is the higher service sector activities in this context that define the economic basis of cities, it appears that language was revealed to be a major asset (Polèse 2012). Such was the case for the areas of finance, management, and communication, three sectors among those crucial for adjusting to the service sector economy, and where the position of the Montreal francophone business elite has been ambivalent, as it promoted the French language and culture while adjusting to an English-speaking environment.

The second series of comments is related to a political economy approach to urban development in a post-industrial context. In the global economic situation, while the international market is introducing new constraints to investments and job creation, city governments can still make "urban strategic choices" (Savitch and Kantor 2002: 23). In other words, the pathway of development is not completely determined by structural factors. Nonetheless, market conditions—defined as "circumstances or forces that make cities more or less appealing to private capital" (Savitch and Kantor 2002: 43)—remain "driving variables" impossible to avoid when it comes to highlighting the orientation taken by local actors. But these conditions are not developed in a void. Bad or adverse conditions can always be moderated or changed by other driving variables, such as the intergovernmental support that a city can benefit from in order to compensate or alleviate bad market conditions. In other words, and even if there is very little leeway, cities can act "strategically."

These remarks generate more questions than answers. Nonetheless, they bring to the fore the fact that choices should be made and action taken even though results remain uncertain. However, one must recognize that all decisions or actions do not have the same value. The cultural context and the targeted or expected outcomes are central in defining the course of action. And as normative solutions are of little use, this should be considered from an empirical standpoint defined in relation to a cultural sociological perspective.

Let us return to Montreal. Keeping in mind our previous comments, it is a well-known fact that over the last decades, economic and political leaders of the city—their composition coinciding at least in part with those of the city-region—"have been unable to restore the city's past vitality" (Hamel and Jouve 2008: 19). Their task has certainly been made difficult by the context of economic uncertainty at the continental and global scale, but also by the lack of resources for improving the built environment, supporting economic entrepreneurship, and attracting investments in cutting-edge sectors where Montreal could benefit from leading businesses or possibly have, in the coming years, an advantageous position.

For the city, the change of scale in territorial frame—through adding two tiers of governance at the turn of the new millennium—is also part of the equation. New possibilities of interaction between social, economic, and political actors following the reforms did not generate a more stable urban management system, however (Bherer and Hamel 2012). In addition, a corruption scandal that had been going on for several years was disclosed at City Hall in June 2013,[1] not to mention that a similar type of fraud was also discovered in suburban municipalities such as Laval.[2] The scandal included elected officials, civil servants—public managers as well as professionals—and private contractors involved in schemes of collusion between businesses, bribes to civil servants, and illegal financing of political parties by construction and building contractors. All these tricks were disclosed by the Commission of Inquiry on the Awarding and Management of Public Contracts in the Construction Industry—the Charbonneau Commission—set up in October 2011 by the former Liberal government of Jean Charest. The disclosure of these misappropriations clearly did not help to increase citizen confidence in the functioning of democracy at the local and/or metropolitan scale. In addition, these behaviours have contributed to breeding cynicism in the public, fostering in citizens an inward turn. They have only increased the sense of helplessness that Montreal's citizens already felt toward politics.

In short, with the scandals and corruption came greater doubts about the capacity of political strategies, and political initiatives generally, to contribute to Montreal's economic recovery. At the same time, the main challenges the city and its citizens have to face are not going to vanish overnight. The political scene remains one of the main grounds where public action can be initiated. For that matter, one must recall that within the framework of Canadian federalism, it remains difficult to bring together the various levels of government to cope with urban development issues. This is particularly true in the case of Montreal, due at the outset to historical reasons, even though other concerns, such as the lack of public resources coming from the federal government, have also been mentioned (Sgro 2002).

Urban Politics in the Canadian Federal Context

According to the separation of powers established in the 1867 Canadian constitution, municipalities fall exclusively within provincial jurisdiction. From the outset, one can speak of a true federal disengagement toward urban issues, with the exception of a short period that led to the creation of the Ministry of State for Urban Affairs, which existed between 1971 and 1979 under the Trudeau government. For the first time in Canadian history, urban advocacy groups had succeeded placing "urban affairs on the public agenda" (Spicer 2011: 117).

Here it is necessary to recall why the Liberals in power decided to discontinue the Ministry of State for Urban Affairs. The Parti Québécois (PQ) came to power in Quebec in 1976 and made claims to "limit federal intrusion into provincial jurisdiction by opposing various federal pro- grams" (Spicer 2011: 124). This test of strength initiated by the PQ gov- ernment was followed by support from other provinces for the same cause. Largely, Canadian provinces were thinking that they should manage urban affairs themselves. In 1976 the provincial municipal affairs ministers agreed to cancel further meetings with their federal counterparts (Sancton 2012; Spicer 2008: 124). Following this confrontation, the federal gov- ernment never reoccupied the arena of urban affairs. This does not mean that through its spending power, on different occasions, the federal gov- ernment did not influence important decisions taken at the local level in regards to transport or other urban infrastructures. But most of the time, these interventions were made on behalf of ad hoc programs or in relation to federal properties constructed within city boundaries. In other words, there was no longer political will at the federal level for building a com- prehensive stance in regards to the urban question. While there was a short focus on urban issues under the Chrétien Liberals with the Prime Minis- ter's Task Force on Urban Issues, chaired by Judy Sgro, and subsequently in the NDP-supported Paul Martin Liberal government, the push toward more federal involvement was halted by the Harper Conservatives, who have not had a power base in Canada's large cities. Only more recently did the official opposition (the federal NDP) make urban issues a major plank of the party's platform under their Urban Affairs Critic Matthew Kellway.

This standpoint is anything but awkward to the observers of the urban scene (Andrew 2013), as Canadians are increasingly living in cities and have never been more concentrated in city-regions (Hiller 2014). As Luc Turgeon (2006) underlines, Canadian cities are struggling with three important deficits threatening their future. The first is a fiscal deficit. If federal government and provincial revenues increased significantly over the years, those of cities grew at a slower pace than the rate of inflation. The second deficit—largely a consequence of the first—concerns the decay of urban infrastructures. This problem is even more acute in metropolitan regions where the majority of Canadians are living. It is also found in metropolitan regions where the third deficit is a growing concern: since the 1970s, poverty rates have risen dramatically. This is even more troubling in areas where poverty is concentrated, showing a multi-dimensional and intergenerational character.

These flaws in the federal planning and management of urban issues are the same all over the country. Nonetheless, their consequences are necessarily more devastating in city-regions facing weak market conditions or struggling to obtain redress for a situation that was unfavourable to local and global investments, as has been the case in Montreal during several decades. As a result, when we think in political terms, the role of the federal government and its responsibility cannot be ignored. This is even more crucial as seen from a Quebec national perspective, where the tension with the federal government was often defined in strategic terms.

It is not because the Ministry of State for Urban Affairs has been abandoned by the federal government that urban affairs are not on the policy agenda (Andrew, Graham, and Phillips 2003; Young 2012). The formal absence of the federal government in those matters does not prevent (as mentioned previously) on some occasion its presence as a partner and sometimes as a major political actor (Horak 2012). Beyond the limits of its financial commitment, the local state defined as an actor and institution necessarily includes the federal government (Magnusson 1985). Here it seems unavoidable to think in terms of multilevel governance for better understanding the arrangements between the main tiers of the state, as we are in presence of a dynamic process in the making (Piattoni 2010). With this in mind, I now turn to the coalitions involved in metropolitan governance, with reference to culture and cultural life.

Governance and Urban Regime in Montreal

Over the last fifty years, even if urban regimes in Montreal were largely orientated toward adjusting local policies to market requirements for promoting economic and urban development, more than anything else, it is hybridism that has characterized those coalitions (Hamel and Jouve 2008). Until the 1980s, Montreal's urban regimes were based on a mix of conservatism and entrepreneurialism, dependent on the public sector. Under pressure from both business milieux and social movements, those regimes ultimately opened up to processes of modernization.

However, the strategies suggested by economic and political elites were unable to solve the restructuring issues brought in by the Fordist crisis. This failure can explain the emergence of a new strategy in the 1990s based on the internationalization of Montreal through an aggressive marketing approach in the sectors of the new economy. This strategy was already defined at the metropolitan scale, albeit limited to the Island of Montreal. A regional mobilization of resources was needed toward the end of the same decade to support the creation of new institutional actors such as Montréal International, a public-private agency in charge of attracting headquarters of international corporations involved in biotechnology, new information and communication technologies, and aeronautics.

A few years later the provincial government carried out its ambitious urban and metropolitan reform, creating, among other things, the MMC (Tomàs 2012). One of the objectives of that reform was to stop the intense competition for investments among the cities on the Island and between the City of Montreal and the suburbs in the Northern and Southern Shore of the agglomeration. But has the cooperation between cities at the metropolitan scale, as intended by the urban and metropolitan reforms, been successful in consolidating the urban regime in the making? To what extent were the institutions and projects implemented on behalf of the reform able to create compromises necessary for returning to Montreal an economic dynamism similar to the one that prevailed during the industrial era? In order to answer these questions, let us take a quick look at the issue of image-building.

Image-building has always been related to urban planning and policies. Images play a key and active role in political discourse (Lehrer 2000 and 2006; Harvey and Young 2012). Since 2002, different groups associated with a variety of professional and economic domains—culture, tourism, design, technological innovation, knowledge—have tried to convince everyone of the superiority of their representation for promoting Montreal on the market and the international stage. Supported by several public and private institutions, these groups promoted their vision with great enthusiasm.

Without going into all the controversies around image-building in Montreal, for the time being it is possible to conclude that "no single actor is currently strong enough to convince the others to adhere to a particular vision. The result is, if not a perpetual state of confrontation, a least a series of parallel endeavours with no sign of convergence in the medium term" (Bherer and Hamel 2012: 118). I would reiterate the same conclusion when looking at recent events. But how could one understand such a situation? Why is it so difficult to find common ground? This can be explained not only by the hybrid character of Montreal's urban regime or by the fragmentation of interests in the established multi-governance system, but by the nature of governance itself, especially at the metropolitan scale and more specifically due to the difficulty of creating a collective actor that so far seems unavoidable in order to promote cooperation in such a context. According to Christian Lefèvre (2013: 238), two requirements would thus be necessary:

1) The definition of a metropolitan identity—that image-building in one way or another can contribute to.

2) The production of a territorial leadership at the metropolitan scale. Such requirements are profoundly enmeshed with culture, as defined previously, emphasizing its sociological perspective. Without a consideration of cultural aspects, it will be difficult to build a common or shared identity for the city-region and define the hegemonic discourse required for producing leadership.

The cultural dimension of civic and urban life introduces constraints and opportunities for action. Antonio Gramsci well understood the slowness of cultural transformations (Piotte 1970: 221). For him, social and political changes were related to the capacity of organic intellectuals to adapt cultural representation to material infrastructure. Culture is a component of day-to-day conduct that conveys values and meanings required by social life.

I do not claim to be able to summarize the local culture of Montreal and its transformation in a snapshot. Nonetheless, we must go back to the cultural dimension of civic urban life to highlight the issue of governance in its attempt at economic recovery. At first, the notion of diversity is striking as the main characteristic in defining local culture, and although there are several aspects to it beyond history, history should eventually also be taken into account.

Since the 1980s, diversity in local culture has been expressed among the representations of urban development as promoted by different categories of social and economic actors. Diversity and multiculturalism are certainly major characteristics of Montreal's culture, as it is for all city-regions of the world. However, the division, conflict, and the mix and cooperation between anglophone and francophone cultures remain peculiar or specific to Montreal's past and present. This configuration has a long history, with direct consequences in terms of adaptation for the incoming diverse ethnic communities that have been taking part in the building of the city over the years, and this needs to be considered when defining the urban and metropolitan identity of the city-region and/or supporting a territorial leadership for its revival.

We can go back to the 1960s to see francophone middle-class households leaving, significantly, the central city for the suburban periphery. From then on, the social face of Montreal would never be the same. This shift in territorial occupancy of inhabitants was accompanied by a process of metropolitanization that has profoundly transformed Montreal's urban and social reality. The electoral weight of the francophone voters has been decreasing in the territory of the City of Montreal, as has their daily presence in inner-city neighbourhoods. In addition, these households were replaced—at least partially—by new waves of immigrants, transforming the image of our two solitudes (to use the title of Hugh MacLennan's novel often mentioned to describe Montreal's historic social reality) into one of a multicultural city (Germain and Rose, 2000). Such representation of multiculturalism as a specific trait of the inner city's cultural mosaic is also reinforced by the fact that anglo Montrealers have increasingly left Montreal since the coming to power of the Parti Québécois in 1976, lessening the importance of the traditional spatial divide between east and west upon which the image of a divided city is built.

The imprint given to the city by anglo Montrealers is ingrained in the urban fabric and profoundly contributes to the definition of its local culture. However, at the city-region scale, some francophone enclaves of the urban fringe, such as those in Laval and Longueuil, or within cities of lesser importance in demographic terms of the Northern and Southern Shores, have introduced a new balance between central city and urban fringe, gradually transforming the representation of Montreal as a metropolis.

But one should keep in mind that this is above all a process in the making. As in other North American cities, outward migration to suburbia—even if it is was done at a slower pace than elsewhere—has been part of a "metropolitan revolution" giving access "to a variety of lifestyle entrées to suit the tastes and predilections of a broad range of [inhabitants]" (Teaford 2006: 167). At the metropolitan scale, the urban way of life in Montreal is rebalancing and re-interpreting the old anglo–franco division with new influences coming from different sources: the affirmation of a stronger identity by French-speaking Montrealers within the central city and within the urban fringe; the diversification of immigration favouring the emergence of multi-ethnic neighbourhoods in different parts of the city-region; the increased presence of international students; and the emergence of globalizing trends redefining access to the anglophone culture and/or reinforcing its presence.

The new challenges Montreal has been facing over the last few decades in relation to lifestyle and culture have compelled the economic and political elites to revise past alliances and build new compromises. The success of these configurations can only be assessed through the test of time and taking into account what brought the agglomeration as a whole to its current condition. Nonetheless, an examination of specific urban issues, such as housing and transportation, can give us an overview of what is going on in the strategic field of urban governance.

Montreal has always been characterized by a higher proportion of tenants than homeowners. Even though, starting in the 1990s, the percentage of homeowners increased, this figure remains relatively low compared to standard North American metropolises. For example, in 1996, within the city limits, we find a relatively small percentage of homeowners, 34% (Ville de Montréal 2001: 4), in comparison to most North American cities. And although this percentage has slightly increased—due mainly to processes of gentrification in inner-city neighbourhoods—it remains relatively low.

This characteristic of Montreal residential real estate is related at least to two factors:

1) By the mid-nineteenth century, Montreal had become a major industrial metropolis; this was achieved through bringing in, during a short period of time, thousands of workers' families from the countryside to provide cheap labour for industrial factories; as these households did not have the resources to access home ownership, no other option was available to them other than to become tenants.

2) Starting in the 1970s, de-industrialization hit the industrial basis hard; thus, Montreal's economic restructuring has been slow, while a large portion of the population lacked the resources to access home ownership; in addition, the "reconquest" of the city by

francophones (Levine, 1990) took its toll on the renewal of business networks; this must also be taken into account when assessing the city's capacity to adjust to the new external global economic environment by giving inhabitants new opportunities in terms of improving their economic condition. In other words, Montreal's economic adaptation to its new social, political, and economic reality has been slow, and this explains the fact that in regards to the housing market, Montrealers were less inclined than other North Americans to become homeowners.

This said, gentrification is traceable to the back-to-the-city movement of the 1980s has also been active in Montreal, but at a slower pace than elsewhere. Gentrification has changed the social composition of home ownership in several neighbourhoods adjacent to the city centre and even in others neighbourhoods located farther away, such as Maisonneuve or Villeray, a process currently in progress.

These transformations in dwellings occupancy are necessarily related to two interconnected processes: the flight of middle-class households to the outer suburbs and the arrival of new immigrants. In that respect, one should know that in the Province of Quebec, almost nine immigrants out of ten choose the Montreal area upon arrival. Actually, almost one person in four living in Montreal is foreign-born, and by 2031 it is estimated that this proportion could rise to nearly one in three (Communauté métropolitaine de Montréal 2013). The main factor of demographic increase in the Montreal city-region—including Laval and Longueuil—is clearly international immigration.[3] The pattern of immigration in Montreal can be associated to similar patterns found in other Canadian cities. As such, we do not find in Montreal the hyper segregation prevalent in major U.S. urban areas (Leloup 2008). However, this does not mean that immigrants and especially newcomers do not have major obstacles to overcome in order to successfully realize their social and professional integration.

In comparing the situation of visible minorities in Montreal to that of Vancouver and Toronto, one finds that the territorial concentration of those minorities is higher in Montreal (Société d'habitation du Québec, 2008). In addition, the proportion of households of low-income visible minorities living in underprivileged neighbourhoods is also higher in Montréal: 54% in Montreal, 19% in Toronto, and 10% in Vancouver. In other words, in Montreal social space is further characterized by a social hierarchy bringing together ethnic and class factors (Leloup 2008). Newcomers are also relying more on private housing, as social housing accounts for only 9.4% of the overall rental stock on the territory of the Montreal Metropolitan Community (Poitras 2008). Finally—and again in comparson with Vancouver and Toronto—newcomers are less likely to become homeowners in Montreal during the first four years after their arrival (Poitras 2008).

Access to housing relative to a project of building a "just city" (Soja 2010) remains subordinated to the availability of resources that households can devote to it. In addition, this access in terms of value in use remains subordinated to the main urban infrastructures that give housing its functional, economic, social, and cultural dimensions. In other words, housing location—within a specific neighbourhood or metropolitan area—in terms of access to work and other activities, is crucial. This stems from several constraints and is dependent upon policies and political choices that determine the configuration and development of main urban infrastructures, starting with planning mobility and transportation over the metropolitan area.

Historically, due to its favourable geographical location on the St. Lawrence River during the French regime, Montreal had all it needed to become a successful trading post. This was a determining factor for the future of what was going to be Canada's metropolis and one of the main ports in North America. Historically, transportation and the role played by the port were crucial issues for regional development. It remains so nowadays, even if Montreal has lost ground since the heyday of the industrial era. In the second half of the twentieth century, the Port of Montreal became an important international container port and keeps on being an active economic actor in the region.

In the current post-industrial context, Montreal continues to depend on transport to support its creativity and growth. But even if part of its economic activity continues to rely on port activities, they are no longer the central factor of the transport system in the city-region. Since the mid-twentieth century, the car has been revealed as an important mode of transport in Montreal. Nonetheless, transport, and above all public transport, is proving to be a central issue. Over the years, the dominance of the automobile has proved both advantageous (in terms of mobility, comfort, and speed) and disadvantageous (in terms of congestion, pollution, waste of public space dedicated to cars, and parking). Transport regulation is thus confronted with the issue of implementing compromises. And in that respect, during the last decades, political choices—with more or less success—were made to improve the general public transport system of the Montreal city-region.

Even though the incidence of car use remains high, active transportation is increasingly playing a greater role. And to a large extent, the governance of the public transport system reflects what is going on with the governance of the whole territory of the city-region. In other words, the difficulty of building alliances and making public and political choices regarding public transport is similar to the one met by the instances of territorial governance, generally speaking, in their planning approaches.

Thus in 1999 Quebec created a public agency—the Agence métropolitaine de transport (AMT)—aimed at developing public transport services in relation to improving commuting efficiency at the metropolitan scale. AMT activities are numerous and so coordination with the institutions in charge of transport in municipalities is unavoidable. The main activities of the AMT are described on its web site as follows: "AMT's mandate includes the management of reserved bus lanes as well as Highway Occupancy Vehicles (HOVs) on the A-15 north of the A-40, metropolitan terminuses, park-and-ride lots, and a budget of $163 million, which is shared among the transit corporations and inter-municipal public transit organizations. Apart from these essential services, AMT is also responsible for Montreal's commuter rail service, which links the downtown core with communities as far west as Hudson, as far east as Mont-Saint-Hilaire, and as far north as Saint-Jérôme" (AMT 2014). Although independent as a public organization, this agency is accountable to the Quebec Transport minister. Since its establishment, tensions with municipalities of the city-region have not been long to emerge. The mayors of several municipalities, starting with Montreal, found that the agency was encroaching on their jurisdiction.

A recent example is the legal proceedings initiated by the City of Montreal against AMT in the Supreme Court. Following the subway extension at Laval, Montreal asked for a compensation payment from AMT because, during the construction of the subway, which lasted from 2003 to 2006, the Agency used the Jeanne-Sauvé Park in the Ahuntsic-Cartierville borough and two adjacent streets as access ramps to the underground site (Normandin 2014). To this example, one may add that since 2013, the MMC has been in charge of planning the metropolitan arterial network of transport, while AMT is responsible for "improving commuting efficiency at a metropolitan scale," as mentioned previously. One can imagine that occasions for conflict between these two functions are difficult to avoid.

Concluding Remarks

In what city do we wish to live in? The issue of urban and metropolitan development and governance must be examined in reference to the recent globalizing tendencies in the world economy, as well as in connection to the quality of life urban dwellers aspire to in reference to local culture. There is no predefined or universal solution to the problem of improving urban living, especially at the metropolitan scale, where divisions between social groups are easily replicated through territorial divisions.

From the 1950s to the 1980s, Montreal's urban regime was character-ized above all by hybridity. It "rested upon a mix of conservatism, largely dependent upon the public sector, and entrepreneurialism, also dependent on the public sector" (Hamel and Jouve 2002: 31). This regime was severely challenged by the Fordist crisis of the end of the 1970s and the beginning of the 1980s, and slowly replaced by the mid-1980s with a new regime, also relying on the public sector, with an active participation by representatives of the business elite milieu. However, from then on, the international promotion of Montreal would no longer rely mainly on the organization of major international events but, instead, on a marketing strategy to better position the agglomeration in selected sectors of the new economy.

With the new regime, a consensus prevailed among its promoters that the mobilization of resources required for the international promotion of Montreal should be carried out at the metropolitan scale. This change in perspective was based on the acknowledgement of the fact that for many years the economic promotion of Montreal was compromised by the com-petition between the City of Montreal and the suburban centres of the Northern and Southern Shores. Even if the cooperation between these diverse components of the agglomeration seems nowadays largely accepted by the majority—bringing new alliances between economic and political actors—conflicts of interests and tensions among those partners still pre-vail. As it has been expressed through the difficulty of image-building around creating a new identity for Montreal, the division among social, economic, and political actors needs to be better understood.

Over the last decade, at the metropolitan scale, Montreal's urban regime did not succeed in finding a viable compromise between the main stakeholders, despite the fact that a consensus is in the making around the necessity of implementing new forms of cooperation. At the same time, the requirement to improve the social and economic dynamism of the agglomeration—underlying the international promotion of Montreal—is far from being based on shared social and cultural values. In that respect, urban and environmental movements have introduced concerns about social inequalities and about improving the living conditions of the whole population that are not shared by economic elites.

Beyond conflicting interests and the clash of values, stable and/or viable arrangements in metropolitan governance necessarily raise the question of local culture. Governance does not evolve in a void. Its capacity to define innovative and efficient political forms of cooperation is based on the cultural environment of action. In respect to urban and suburban living, what elements deserve to be retained if not promoted in relation to the fundamental, distinctive character of the city-region? What are the major characteristics defining the social cultural system of Montrealers? How is the presence of recent immigrants and the bilingual attitude of new generations reshaping the city's "patchwork of clashing cultures" (Semley 2014: R10)? And how should we interpret the recent upheavals in Montreal and Laval—with their political consequences—following the recent collusion and corruption scandals? Will the new alliances within the political class be able to meet the social and political expectations of Montrealers?

These questions are on the political agenda and can be added to several traditional ones regarding economic innovation and dynamism that have gone unresolved until now. Montreal is undoubtedly confronted with new issues, but past problems have lost none of their relevance today: What support can Montreal expect, on one hand, from the provincial government, and on the other hand from the federal government? In the light of the last provincial elections—and faced with what can be interpreted as a relative decline of the Quebec independence movement—what public resources are going to be available for the future of the city-region in the name of the two superior levels of government? How is it possible to improve living conditions for the majority of inhabitants in the Canadian federalist context if public resources for infrastructures and public services are diminished? This question is not exclusive to the Montreal city-region. It can be applied to several other Canadian metropolitan areas. But in the case of Montreal, due to its recent past and the special nature of the catching-up process involved, lack of state support could prove critical over the next few years. This is certainly a story to follow.

Notes

1 "It doesn't seem to want to get better, does it? Montreal has been making headlines lately—and for all the wrong reasons. First 'Pastagate,' then 'Turbangate,' and then, just before the Charbonneau Commission (and all its shocking revelations) took a little summer break, we watched our interim mayor (the one placed in power because the previous one resigned after allegations of corruption) hauled off in handcuffs this past Tuesday morning, facing 14 corruption-related charges himself" (Drimonis 2013).

2 "In one memorable, scandal-plagued week, no less than one-quarter of Quebecers have seen their mayor resign under a cloud of suspicion. The head of the province's third-largest city, Laval, announced his resignation Friday, just a few days after his Montreal counterpart tiptoed down the same political plank" (Panetta and Banerjee 2012).

3 Within the Montreal metropolitan area, in 2011, 33.2% of immigrants chose Montreal, while 17.8% settled in Longueuil and 24.6% in Laval, the rest opting for the other municipalities of the North and the South Shore (Communauté métropolitaine de Montréal 2013).

References

AMT (Agence Métropolitaine de Transport). 2014. Website of the Agency: www .amt.qc.ca/.

Andrew, C. 2013. "Les métropoles dans le système politique canadien." In P. Hamel and J.-M. Lacroix, eds., *Les relations Québec-Canada.Arrêter le dialogue de sourds?* (105–12). Bruxelles: P. I. E. Peter Lang.

Andrew, C., K. A. Graham, and S. D. Phillips, eds. 2003. *Urban affairs back on the policy agenda*. Montreal and Kingston: McGill-Queen's University Press.

Bherer L. and P. Hamel. 2012. "Overcoming adversity, or public action in the face of new urban problems: The example of Montreal." In M. Horak and R. Young, eds., *Sites of governance: Multilevel governance and policy making in Canada's big cities* (104–35). Montreal and Kingston: McGill-Queen's University Press.

Booth P. and B. Jouve, eds. 2005. *Metropolitan democracies*. Aldershot: Ashgate.

Boudreau, J.-A., et al. 2006. "Comparing metropolitan governance: The cases of Montreal and Toronto." *Progress in Planning* 66(2): 1–54.

Communauté Métropolitaine de Montréal. 2011. *Un grand Montréal attractif, compétitif et durable*. Projet de Plan métropolitain d'aménagement et de développement, Montréal: Communauté Métropolitaine de Montréal.

———. 2013. *Perspective Grand Montréal*: Bulletin de la Communauté Métropolitaine de Montréal (décembre). Montréal: Communauté Métropolitaine de Montréal.

Drimonis, T. 2013. "We all have a responsibility to fight corruption." *Huff Post, Politics*. Accessed July 13, 2015, at www.huffingtonpost.ca/toula-foscolos/ montreal-corruption_b_3491089.html.

Germain, A. and D. Rose. 2000. *Montréal: The quest for a metropolis*. Chichester: John Wiley.

Guindon, H. 1990. *Tradition, modernité et aspiration nationale de la société québécoise*. Montréal: Éditions Saint-Martin.

Hamel, P. 2005. "Municipal reform in Quebec: The trade-off between centralization and decentralization." In J. Garcea and E. C. LeSage, Jr., eds., *Municipal reform in Canada: Reconfiguration, re-empowerment, and rebalancing* (149–73). Don Mills: Oxford University Press.

———. 2006. "Institutional changes and metropolitan governance: Can de-amalgamation be amalgamation? The case of Montreal." In E. Razin and P. J. Smith, eds., *Metropolitan Governing: Canadian Cases, Comparative Lessons* (95–120). Jerusalem: Magnes Press.

Hamel, P. and B. Jouve. 2002. "In search of a stable urban regime for Montreal: issues and challenges in metropolitan development." *Urban Research & Practice* 1(1): 18–35.

Hamel, P. and J. Rousseau. 2006. "Revisiting municipal reforms in Quebec and the new responsibilities of local actors in a globalizing world." In B. Young and C. Leupretch, eds., *Canada: The state of the federation 2004: Municipal–federal provincial relations in Canada* (139–60). Montreal and Kingston: McGill-Queen's University Press.

Harvey, J. and R. Young, eds. 2012. *Image-building in Canadian municipalities.* Montreal and Kingston: McGill-Queen's University Press.

Higgins, B. 1986. *The rise and fall of Montreal?* Moncton: Institut canadien pour le développement régional.

Hiller, H. H. 2014 "Canadian urbanization in historic and global perspective." In H. H. Hiller, ed., *Urban Canada* (3–19). Don Mills: Oxford University Press.

Horak, M. 2012. "Conclusion: understanding multilevel governance in Canada's cities." In M. Horak and R. Young, eds., *Sites of governance: Multilevel governance and policy making in Canada's big cities* (340–70). Montreal and Kingston: McGill-Queen's University Press.

Lefèvre, C. 2013. "Gouverner les métropoles: l'improbable gouvernement métropolitain." *Sociologie et sociétés* 45(2): 223–42.

Lehrer, U. 2000. "Reality or image? Place selling at Postdamer Platz." In *The contested metropolis: Six cities at the beginning of the 21st century* (44–52). Basel, Berlin, Boston: Birkhaüser.

———. 2006 "Replacing Canadian cities: The challenge of landscapes of 'desire' and 'despair.'" In T. Bunting and P. Filion, eds., *The Canadian city in transition*, 3rd ed. (438–49). Don Mills: Oxford University Press.

Leloup, X. 2008. "La Géographie résidentielle: Bilan et approche critique sur les questions de concentration, ségrégation, 'ghettoïsation'." In *L'Habitation comme vecteur d'Intégration dans la ville: Quoi de neuf?* (14–23). Québec: Société d'Habitation du Québec.

Léveillée, J. 1978. *Développement urbain et politiques gouvernementales urbaines dans l'agglomération montréalaise, 1945–1975.* Montréal: Société canadienne de science politique.

———. 1987. "L'action économique de la ville de Montréal." In J. Bouinot, ed., *L'action économique des grandes villes en France et à l'étranger* (7–31). Paris: Economica.

Levine, M. V. 1990. *The reconquest of Montreal: Language, policy and social change in a bilingual city.* Philadelphia: Temple University Press.

Linteau, P.-A., R. Durocher, J.-C. Robert, and F. Ricard. 1989. *Histoire du Québec contemporain. Le Québec depuis 1930 (Tome 2).* Montreal: Boréal.

Magnusson, W. 1985. "Urban politics and the local state." *Studies in Political Economy* 16: 111–42.

Montreal Metropolitan Community, 2011. *Un grand Montréal attractif, compétitif et durable.* Montréal: Communauté métropolitaine de Montréal.

Normandin, P.-A. 2014. "La Ville de Montréal en cour Suprême contre l'AMT." *La Presse.* March 22.

OECD. 2004. *Examens territoriaux de l'OCDE: Montréal, Canada.* Paris: Éditions de l'OCDE.

Panetta, A. and S. Banerjee. 2012. "Gilles Vaillancourt quits: Mayor of Laval resigns amid Quebec corruption scandal." *Huff Post, Politics*. Accessed July 13, 2015 at www.huffingtonpost.ca/2012/11/09/gilles-vaillancourt-quits-mayor-laval_n_2101603.html.

Piattoni, S. 2010. *The theory of multi-level governance: Conceptual, empirical, and normative challenges*. Oxford: Oxford University Press.

Piotte, J.-M. 1970. *La pensée politique de Gramsci*. Montréal: Parti Pris.

Poitras, L. 2008. "Synthèse." In *L'Habitation comme vecteur d'Intégration dans la ville: Quoi de neuf?* (56–57). Québec: Société d'Habitation du Québec.

Polèse, M. 2012. "Montreal économique: de 1930 à nos jours. Récit d'une transition inachevée" In D. Fougères, ed., *Histoire de Montréal et de sa région (Tome 2: De 1930 à nos jours)* (959, 1004). Québec: Presses de l'Université Laval.

Pratte, A. 2013. "Un cancer bien connu." *La Presse*. March 21: A12.

Reed, I. 2007. "Cultural dociology and the democratic imperative." In I. Reed and J. C. Alexander, eds., *Culture, society and democracy: The interpretive approach* (1–18). Boulder, CO: Paradigm.

Sancton, A. 2012. "The urban agenda." In H. Bakvis and G. Skogstad, eds., *Canadian federalism: Performance, effectiveness and legitimacy*, 3rd ed. Toronto: Oxford University Press.

Savitch, H. V. and P. Kantor 2002. *Cities in the international marketplace*. Princeton: Princeton University Press.

Semley, J. 2014. "Vive la différence!" *Globe and Mail*. August 2: R10.

Sgro, J. 2002. *La stratégie urbaine du Canada: une vision pour le XXIe siècle*. Ottawa: Publications du Gouvernement Fédéral.

Snow, D. A., S. A. Soule, and H. Kriesi, eds. 2004. *The Blackwell companion to social movements*. Malden: Blackwell.

Soja, E. W. 2010. *Seeking spatial justice*. Minneapolis: University of Minnesota Press.

Spicer, Z. D. 2011. "The rise and fall of the Ministry of State for Urban Affairs: A re-evaluation." *Canadian Political Science Review* 5(2): 117–26.

Teaford, J. C. 2006. *The metropolitan revolution: The rise of post-urban America*. New York: Columbia University Press.

Tomàs, M. 2012. *Penser métropolitain? La bataille politique du Grand Montréal*. Québec: Presses de l'Université du Québec.

Turgeon, L. 2006. "Les villes dans le système intergouvernemental canadien." In A.-G. Gagnon, ed., *Le fédéralisme canadien contemporain. Fondements, traditions, institutions* (403–33). Montréal: Presses de l'Université de Montréal.

Ville de Montréal 2001. *Profil socio-économique de la Ville de Montréal*. Montréal: Ville de Montréal.

Young, R. 2012. "Introduction: Multilevel governance and its central research question in Canadian cities." In M. Horak and R. Young, eds., *Sites of governance: Multilevel governance and policy making in Canada's big cities* (3–25). Montreal and Kingston: McGill-Queen's University Press.

CHAPTER 10

Winnipeg
Aspirational Planning, Chaotic Development

Christopher Leo

Introduction

URBAN SPRAWL HAS long been a major preoccupation of the literature on North American urban development. Within that literature, a distressing amount of attention has been devoted to definitional discussions, but in these pages we will skirt that terrain. We will instead proceed by diktat, defining sprawl as low-density, single-use development: neighbourhoods or sections of cities marked by exclusivity, not only of residential, commercial, industrial, or agricultural land uses, but also of low, medium, and high densities, and light and heavy commercial and industrial development. In the world of sprawl, these multiple exclusivities are further multiplied by the definition of particular design types, residential wealth gradations, and other specificities of land use.

Much of the literature on sprawl is critical of many of these varieties of exclusivity, maintaining that they kill urbanity, choke off street life, and mandate environmentally harmful dependence on automobiles. Thomas Sieverts intervenes in this long-running debate with an observation and a proposition. The observation is that the definition of sprawl advanced here no longer describes an important proportion of newer development. Instead, Sieverts describes current built forms as taking the form of the Zwischenstadt, which is characterized by "increasingly fractured ... boundaries between urban fabric and open space and nature; the gradual disappearance of the traditional hierarchical pattern; and the mutual penetration of built forms and landscapes" (Sieverts 2003: x; Keil et al. 2009; Young et al. 2010).

The observation contained in the word Zwischenstadt, therefore, is that what was once a comprehensible cityscape, with both centre and periphery well defined, and marked by a clear hierarchy of high-, medium-, and low-density uses, seems to be becoming a thing of the past. A clear contrast between city and countryside is dissolving into an amorphous landscape of workplaces, residences, and places of business, connected by fast means of transportation, but interspersed with the countryside in a way that is no longer clearly identifiable as either urban or rural. It lacks either an identifiable centre or a clear hierarchy of central, intermediate, and peripheral places.

In other words, sprawl's fragmented but still orderly arrangement of mutually exclusive land uses has fragmented further, to the point where, in many places, there is no longer such a thing as an identifiable city, despite the presence of traditionally urban land uses. While such fragmentation and dispersal clashes with a conventional planner's idea of what constitutes an orderly distribution of land uses, Sieverts sees nothing to be alarmed about. He argues, on the contrary, that not only are Zwischenstadt development patterns not objectionable, they are beneficial: they open up new possibilities for agriculture and provide, literally and figuratively, a field for potentially groundbreaking advances in design.

Sieverts's observation is unlikely to generate serious debate. It describes land-use patterns that are familiar to both Europeans and North Americans. His proposition—that Zwischenstadt patterns need not pose problems, and may well open exciting possibilities—is a different matter. Zwischenstadt, which Sieverts translates as "in-between cities," could be less ambiguously translated as "urban land uses between cities."[1] In a European context, he can make a reasonable case that a scattered development of urban land uses across the countryside is not necessarily a cause for alarm, and may open up new possibilities, precisely because Europe already has cities with high concentrations of population and jobs.

In Europe, urban job and population concentrations are high enough

- to ensure the viability of rapid, convenient, relatively affordable city and intercity public transportation;
- to make both city and intercity transportation by private automobile less convenient than it is in North America; therefore,
- to avoid the additional harm to the environment that is inevitable if public transportation is reduced to the status of a last resort for

those in poverty, while private transportation becomes virtually everyone else's transportation of choice; and

- to make it feasible to provide a high level of urban public services.

Whatever its merits in a European context, in many North American regions the amorphous landscape of workplaces, residences, and places of business—which Sieverts sees as a praiseworthy characteristic of the spaces between cities—becomes an ongoing threat to the environment if it characterizes cities themselves. This is because it either places obstacles in the way of efficient provision of public transportation and other public services, or indeed makes public transportation entirely unfeasible. As a consequence, it multiplies the burden imposed on the environment through the discharge of hydrocarbons. Moreover, an amorphous landscape of workplaces, residences, and commerce, if it is found in cities, courts the risk that the extension of infrastructure needed to accommodate wide-spread or universal use of private vehicles will escalate the cost of service provision beyond the limit of viability.

This chapter examines land-use practices in Winnipeg, a typical example of a sprawling North American metropolitan area, in order to gain a more detailed view of how North America's amorphous urban landscapes are created and what problems they produce. Although sprawl is ubiquitous across urban North America, Winnipeg's situation is in other ways strikingly different from that of the four city-regions that are the primary focus of this volume. Although like all twenty-first-century cities, it is integrated "into a ... globalized urban network" (Allahwala's and Keil's characterization, in the introduction to this volume, of the four city-regions), its primary connections are more limited.

A metropolitan area with a 2015 population of 793,400 (City of Winnipeg 2016), Winnipeg is a stand-alone city some 1,300 km from Calgary, the nearest comparably sized city. Located near the geographical centre of North America, it is integrated into a continental transportation network that extends south into Mexico and beyond, as well as to the Atlantic, Pacific, and Arctic coasts. Its global connections are far more limited than those of Frankfurt, Paris, Montreal, and Toronto. Its population is growing slowly and its economy is relatively stable. It boasts a lively and varied arts scene, but, unlike Toronto, it does not claim cultural vanguard status.

Nevertheless, Winnipeg has been buffeted by the global winds that have blown through cities across Europe and North America, producing accelerated competitive pressure on local businesses in the wake of the North American Free Trade Agreement and other globalizing initiatives.

Consequently, Winnipeg has lost traditional manufacturing jobs and seen a growth of cheap-labour production and services, in addition to fiscal austerity, the effects of which have been accentuated by the disappearance of regional equalization programs previously sponsored by the federal government.

The focus of the present chapter is not global competitive pressures, but the regional competition over land development that determines metropolitan growth patterns. Like many North American municipalities, Winnipeg (and other rural districts, urbanizing areas, and cities in the metropolitan area) publish planning documents that purport to show how a local or provincial planning process that ensures the efficient and effective delivery of public transportation and other public services guides the growth of the metropolitan area.

For those who follow the politics and administration of growth day to day, these documents fail to conceal the fact that planning is, in reality, a cleanup operation designed to legitimize decisions that are driven primarily by developers. The process prioritizes the interests of those developers, and of the residents of their new neighbourhoods, over the interest of the city as a whole. A brief look at the city's early growth and three development case studies will provide evidence for this statement and demonstrate how the development process works in practice.

Winnipeg's Politics of Urban Growth

From the beginning, city planning in Winnipeg has been an aspiration, struggling to catch up with reality. A pair of artists' aerial views of Winnipeg from 1880–81 nicely illustrates this point. The first (Figure 10.1) shows a wide, unpaved street flanked on either side by buildings. In the background we see scattered housing, apparently located, oriented, and spaced to suit the convenience of the individual property owner, rather than to conform to any set pattern.

Figure 10.2 provides an overview of the city as it was then, and, superimposed on the same scattering of buildings seemingly located at random, an extensive street grid, likely someone's aspirational view of the city as it might develop. From a distance, it appears that the locations of buildings are uninfluenced by the grid.

The two pictures aptly foreshadow the future of planning in Winnipeg. The Department of Planning, Property and Development produces a wealth of planning documents, filled with statements that represent planning correctness,[2] but the actual directions for the growth and development of the city are driven by development proposals. Planning documents

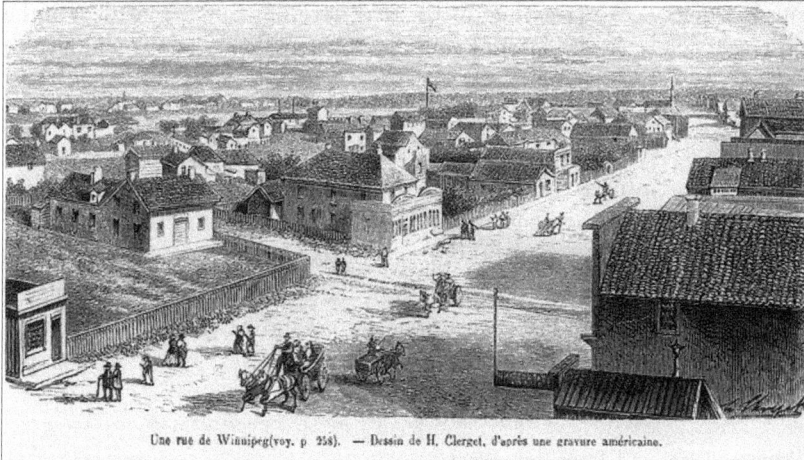

Figure 10.1   Winnipeg, circa 1880.

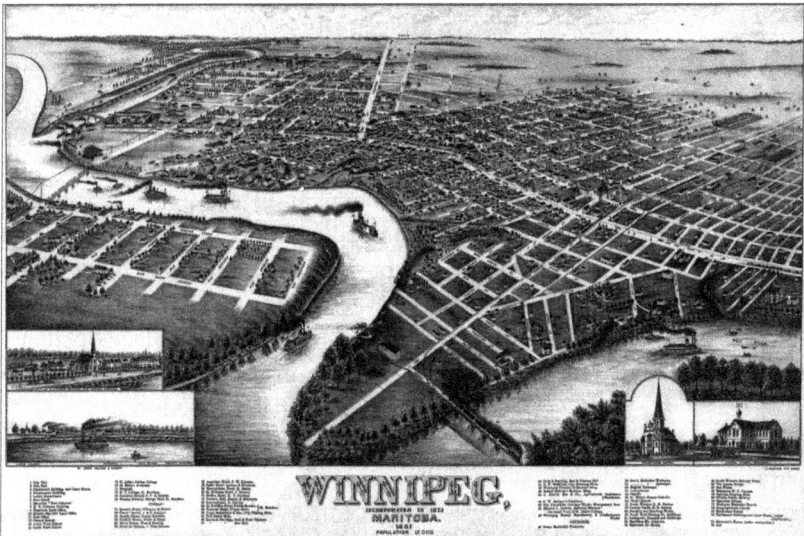

Figure 10.2   Bird's-eye view of Winnipeg, 1881. Virtual Heritage Winnipeg, photo gallery, Achives of Manitoba, Stoval Advocate Collection, Item 25, accessible at http://virtual.heritage winnipeg.com/windowsPhotoPan.php?fileNum=%2009-027.

ratify, and do the best their writers can to justify, what has been decided by developers.

Meanwhile, developers cherry-pick the areas that are the easiest, the most convenient, or the most profitable to develop, and bypass others, secure in the knowledge that the city will extend roads and other municipal services as required by the new developments, regardless of the expenses incurred ultimately by Winnipeg taxpayers. That includes not only roads, sewerage, and water lines, but also transit service.

These expensive services have to be extended across lands that generate the low levels of taxation typical of farmland or unoccupied tracts, rather than the much higher taxes that come from urban development. Once occupied, new developments beyond the empty tracts require conveniently located community centres and library branches, and the same response times for fire fighters, police, and paramedics that more densely populated areas of the city enjoy. Street cleaning, snow removal, grass cutting, insect control, and everything else the municipality provides, has to serve empty parcels of land as well as full ones.

Waverley West and Transcona West

We will examine some of the many examples of land that earns minimal revenues, served and/or bypassed by the full range of municipal services; but first, the context. In 2006, Winnipeg city council was debating how it should respond to developer demands to make a vast new tract of land available for development. The tract, known as Waverley West, contained enough land for decades of future development, but developers, drawing on an analysis produced by the Department of Property, Planning and Development (Winnipeg, Property, Planning and Development 2004: 13, 18), argued that it must be opened immediately because, without it, the supply of lots available for development would last only eight to ten years. City council acceded to the developers' demands.

At this writing, ten years later, Waverley West is partly developed and developing rapidly, though the bulk of it remains undeveloped—substantial areas nearer the centre of the city, and areas bypassed or serviced by older infrastructure and services. A particularly clear example—a comparison of Waverley West (10.9 km from the city centre) with an area called Transcona West (7.6 km from the centre)—comes close to capturing the magnitude of the problem.

Winnipeg's planning practices are standard issue in North American city planning. A critical assessment of the growth practices of most North American cities would likely produce results not unlike those described in these pages, although Winnipeg may well be a particularly egregious case. The egregiousness is visible in the fact that, while the city's infrastructure budget is lavished on first-class roads, sewers, and water lines serving new subdivisions, older infrastructure is allowed to deteriorate radically. News reports in both Winnipeg newspapers, the *Winnipeg Free Press* and the

Winnipeg Sun, confirm earlier studies (Leo and Brown 2000: 201–5; Leo and Anderson 2006: 181–83).

The *Sun* (Turenne 2011) reported that, by the city's own reckoning, more than 20% of the city's streets are rated in poor condition (the lowest rating), meaning that the street must be completely rebuilt or at least undergo major rehabilitation. A few days later, the *Free Press* (Skerritt 2011) added some figures to show that the roads are continually getting worse and that the city has nowhere near the resources it needs to repair the streets quickly enough to keep pace with their deterioration (see Figures 10.3 and 10.4).

Instead, the city has, in effect, given up on attempts to solve the problem. A public works official admitted to the *Sun* that the city's priorities are shifting away from streets in poor condition to those that have not yet reached that state, on the premise that it is better to maintain what is viable than to salvage what is not. Since the streets in worst condition tend to be those in the poorest neighbourhoods, the neglect of downtown streets is tantamount to the ghettoization and decay so distressingly familiar in American cities.

Anyone who observes these conditions and then reads Plan Winnipeg 2020 Vision (Winnipeg 2000) will suffer an attack of cognitive dissonance. The plan, read in isolation from on-the-ground observation, leaves no doubt that it is resolved to apply planning profession's best practices.

Figure 10.3   Potholes in an inner-city street. Photo by Christopher Leo.

Figure 10.4   Potholes in an inner-city street. Photo by Christopher Leo.

Using mandatory language, the plan (Winnipeg 2000: 29) promises that

> The city shall promote compact urban form in support of sustainability by
>   i) approving new residential, commercial, and industrial sub-divisions only when ... a full range of municipal infrastructure can be provided in an environmentally sound, economical, and timely manner;
>   ii) evaluating residential, commercial development proposals using benefit–cost analysis to measure long-term revenues, expenditures, and impacts on existing developments within a life-cycle costing framework;
> iii)   meeting transportation demand in ways that reduce reliance on the automobile, improve integration of transportation modes, and improve effectiveness of the existing transportation system;
>   iv) encouraging infilling of vacant lands and the revitalization of existing neighbourhoods to maximize the use of existing infrastructure;
>   v) supporting new development which is adjacent to, and compatible with, existing development and which is designed to minimize the spatial use of land.

It is evident that there is little correspondence between the thought processes that went into the writing of the plan and those that govern actual development. To be sure, point i, the promise to provide "a full range of municipal infrastructure ... in [a] ... timely manner" is kept, but if there were any serious consideration of either environmental soundness or economy, as promised in point i), the idea of ensuring that new development be adjacent to existing development would have suggested itself immediately.

Point ii, the use of benefit–cost analysis, in the conceptions of the Department of Planning, Property and Development, is very straightforward. When a new development is proposed, costs to the city are calculated in three categories: the building or development of roads, parks, and underground municipal services. These costs are totalled and charged to the developer. The developer is then deemed to have covered "all the costs" of the development. Not counted in the calculation are other costs referred to above: The provision of fire, police, and paramedic response times comparable to those that more densely populated areas of the city enjoy; street cleaning, snow removal, grass cutting, insect control, and everything else the municipality provides. In short, the benefit–cost analysis, in effect, counts all the benefits but overlooks many of the costs (Leo 2002: 219–21).

The reference to reducing "reliance on the automobile, improv[ing] integration of transportation modes, and improv[ing] effectiveness of the existing transportation system"—point iii—is largely humbug. Until recently, the only public transportation Winnipeg offered was an

Figure 10.5 Transcona West and developed land to the east that must be served by infrastructure and service traversing empty land. *Source*: Google Maps, Earth view.

old-fashioned bus system, which—though its officials do an impressive job of making a virtue of their limitations—reduces reliance on automobiles only for that minority of commuters willing to put up with the discomfort and inconvenience of buses. The only other gesture toward improved public transportation has been the recent completion of the first half of a single bus rapid transit line (the first of six that have been in the plan for some forty years).

A glance at Figure 10.5 is enough to expose the chicanery in the suggestion, in point iv, that city policy encourages the infilling of vacant lands, maximizes "the use of existing infrastructure," or minimizes the "spatial use of land." The only truth in that statement is that the city has been impressively successful in a series of initiatives to revitalize the homes—but not the streets—in older, inner-city neighbourhoods. Point v essentially repeats the falsehoods in point iv, and they gain no veracity in the retelling.

In short, the development of new neighbourhoods—Plan Winnipeg 2020 Vision to the contrary—has been guided not by the theoretical invocation of good planning practice but by the demands of different developers to develop pieces of land on their own, in their own time, and at their own pace. The city has followed their lead obediently, constructing the infrastructure necessary to give them whatever they have asked, largely regardless of cost. The appearance of planning is constructed retrospectively, to conceal a reality that looks orderly, but lacks the coherence needed to permit the development of a viable and affordable network of services and system of public transportation.

Springfield Municipality: A Classic Zwischenstadt, Rationalized by Planning Jargon

Most of the population of the Winnipeg metropolitan area is located in the central municipality of Winnipeg, in which there remains ample space for further development. Surrounding Winnipeg are a small city, Selkirk, a town, Stonewall, and thirteen rural municipalities. Most of these municipalities compete with Winnipeg to attract residential and other development. In this section, we look at the development plan for one of those municipalities, Springfield, and contrast it with the reality of the way the municipality is developing.

In their discussion of planning principles, the Winnipeg planners were content to invoke such uncontroversial planning principles as environmental sustainability and spatial compactness, and claim, in defiance of the facts, that these motherhood statements constituted Winnipeg's guiding principles.

Springfield's planners work harder. The plan (Springfield Rural Municipality 2011) sets out a convincing analysis of Springfield's landforms:

- Red River Valley
- Birds Hill Kame Deposit
- Eastern Lake Terrace
- Brokenhead River Basin

This categorization is followed by some sensible general principles, such as:

- preservation of agricultural viability and natural resources
- separation of heavy industry from other uses
- concentration of commercial and light industrial uses in urban centres
- prevention of proliferation of residential development, especially along highways

The four landforms include:

- two high-potential agricultural areas, the Red River Valley and the Brokenhead River Basin;
- the Eastern Lake Terrace, which is defined as having lower agricultural potential; and
- the Birds Hill Kame Deposit, near a provincial park, that is the prime source of ground water for the municipality.

A substantial scholarly literature cites a variety of ways that residential development in farming areas damages the viability of agriculture: complaints from residents about smells, heavy machinery on roads and other perceived nuisances resulting from agriculture, as well as impacts of the presence of urban residents that interfere with farming operations, such as commuter traffic, harassment of farm animals by pets, and escalation of land prices that inflate the cost of farming (Leo et al. 1998).

The proposed Springfield official plan itself states that the growth potential of livestock husbandry has already been limited by past residential development (Springfield Rural Municipality 2011: 28). To this point in the plan, therefore, an analysis of landforms has indicated the location of good agricultural areas and important water resources, while statements of objectives have stressed the determination to preserve these assets in the face of urbanization.

However, when we turn to the part of the plan in which proposed zoning categories are set out, it appears that we are reading a different plan. Most of the residential development is in the larger of the two prime agricultural areas and in the area where the major resource of ground water is located. All the residential development on top of the prime water resource relies on septic tanks for sewage disposal, which invariably pose a greater risk to ground water than a community sewage system. Furthermore, there is a cluster of residential development planned in the community of Anola, which is located in the low-potential agricultural area and would therefore seem to be the preferable area for urban development if harm to agriculture were to be minimized. However, this community can only accommodate a limited amount of development because it has not been provided with the water and sewage services needed for higher concentrations of development.

Nor are there any plans for providing Anola with services, even though the plan states that there is a demand for residential development in the area. Meanwhile, two urban communities in the middle of the prime agricultural area, Oakbank and Dugald, have been provided with the services required for higher concentrations of urban development. In short, everything possible is done to encourage urban development in those areas that the plan claims a determination to protect, and almost nothing done to encourage development in the area that the plan designates as unsuitable for other purposes.

Attendance at two hearings of the municipal board panel (May 17 and 24, 2000) provided insights into this incongruity. From a variety of statements that were made, it became clear that, in the past, numerous residents of the municipality had been able to improve their fortunes by subdividing farmland in order to sell it for residential development, and that others wished—at the time of the hearings—to follow suit. When witnesses at the hearing called attention to the gap in the plan between objectives and proposed outcomes,[3] the argument was repeatedly made that, since some had been allowed to subdivide their land, it was not fair to restrict others from doing so.

In short, the municipality was meeting its legal obligations by providing something that resembled a plan, but political pressures from constituents in a community small enough to allow almost anyone to have a personal relationship with her or his representative on council prevented the municipality from adhering to the principles stated in the plan. In a community as small as this one, it is not necessary to imagine overt corruption of decision-makers through the offer of inducements to neglect their duties in order to understand what is happening. In the absence of

clear provincial planning guidelines, pressures on council are too immediate and too personal to permit genuine planning. It is those who stand
to gain from development that largely determine the way the community
will develop. The political realities of the planning process defeat aspirations to sound urban planning.

Conclusion

Although many of the details of Winnipeg's politics of urban planning
differ from those in Springfield Rural Municipality, the fundamental problem is the same in both jurisdictions: The decision-makers are too close
to those who will be affected by decisions to allow for a reasonable expec-
tation that development practice will be governed by planning principles.
When developers and individual citizens are well-placed to offer or with-
hold financial or other inducements—including friendship in the case of
Springfield—it is unreasonable to expect that good planning practice will
trump individual interest. As long as local politicians remain responsible
for both the formulation of planning principles, and their implementation,
planning aspirations will continue to be trumped, and chaotic development will remain the inevitable outcome.

Notes

1 Keil and Young offer a different interpretation. They characterize Canada's "in-
between cities" as follows: "In-between the old downtowns and the new suburbs
of urban Canada, a hitherto underexposed and under-researched mix of residential, commercial, industrial, educational, agricultural and ecologically protected
areas and land uses has become the home and workplace, and increasingly also
the playspace of most people in Canada." Their primary concern is with the risk
of disaster in these improperly planned regions (2009: 488ff.).

2 See the entries, under References below, entitled *Sustainable Water and Waste: An
Our Winnipeg Direction Strategy*; *Sustainable Transportation: An Our Winnipeg
Direction Strategy*; *Our Winnipeg: It's Our City, It's Our Plan, It's Our Time*;
Complete Communities: An Our Winnipeg Direction Strategy; *Plan Winnipeg
2020 Vision: A Long-range Plan for City Council*.

3 I was present at the hearing as a witness, invited to testify as an expert, and was
one of several there who pointed to the gap.

References

Bourne, L. S., T. Hutton, R. G. Shearmur, and J. Simmons. 2011. *Canadian urban
regions: Trajectories of growth and change*. Don Mills: Oxford University
Press.

Galston, R. 2009. "The failures of Waverley West." *Winnipeg Free Press*. February 23.

Keil, R. and D. Young. 2009. "Fringe explosions: Risk and vulnerability in Canada's
new in-between landscape." *Canadian Geographer* 53(4): 488–99.

Leo, C. 2002. "Urban development: Planning aspirations and political realities." In *Urban Policy Issues*, 2nd ed., ed. E. P. Fowler and D. Siegel. Toronto: Oxford University Press.

Leo, C. and K. Anderson. 2006. "Being realistic about urban growth." *Journal of Urban Affairs* 28(2): 169–89.

Leo, C. and W. Brown. 2000. "Slow growth and urban development policy." *Journal of Urban Affairs* 22(2): 193–213.

Leo, C. with M. A. Beavis, A. Carver, and R. Turner. 1998. "Is urban sprawl back on the political agenda? Local growth control, regional growth management and politics." *Urban Affairs Review* 34(2): 179–212.

Manitoba, Agriculture, Food and Rural Initiatives, Soil and Landscape Management Section. 2011. *Soils of the Municipality of Springfield*. Winnipeg: Author.

Manitoba Local Government. 2012. *Welcome to Manitoba's capital region*. Winnipeg: Author. www.gov.mb.ca/ia/capreg/index.html.

Polèse, M. 2009. *The wealth and poverty of regions: Why cities matter*. Chicago: University of Chicago Press.

Sieverts, T. 2003. *Cities without cities: An interpretation of the Zwischenstadt*. London and New York: Spon Press.

———. 2003. "Urbanität und Zwischenstadt." In Forschungsgruppe Bodenseestadt (Hrsg.): Vision Bodenseestadt. Städtebauforschung zwischen Utopie und Machbarkeitsstudie (138–49). Weimar: VDG.

———. 2000. Zwischenstadt, zum Stand der Dinge. In *archithese*, Sondernummer, November 2000, S. 6–11.

Skerritt, J. 2011. "City streets rougher, data show." *Winnipeg Free Press*. November 21.

Springfield Rural Municipality. 2011. *Development Plan By-Law No. 98–22*. Winnipeg: Author.

———. 2012. *Planning Department*. Winnipeg: Author. www.rmofspringfield.ca/pdf/page%2014%20-%20figure%202%20major%20landforms.pdf.

Turenne, P. 2011. Winnipeg's roads to ruin. *Winnipeg Sun*. November 13.

Winnipeg. 2000. *Plan Winnipeg 2020 Vision: A long-range plan for City Council*. Winnipeg: Author.

———. 2012. *Community trends report: Selected demographic and economic information*. Winnipeg: Author.

———. 2013. *Population of Winnipeg*. Author. May 2013. http://winnipeg.ca/cao/pdfs/population.pdf.

———. n.d. *A Sustainable Winnipeg: An Our Winnipeg direction strategy*. Winnipeg: Author.

———. n.d. *Complete communities: An Our Winnipeg direction strategy*. Winnipeg: Author.

———. n.d. *Our Winnipeg: It's our city, it's our plan, it's our time*. Winnipeg: Author.

———. n.d. *Sustainable transportation: An Our Winnipeg direction strategy*. Winnipeg: Author.

———. n.d. *Sustainable water and waste: An Our Winnipeg direction strategy*. Winnipeg: Author.

Winnipeg, Planning, Property and Development. 2004. *City of Winnipeg residential land supply.* Winnipeg: Author.

Young, D., P. B. Wood, and R. Keil. 2010. *In-between infrastructure: Urban connectivity in an age of vulnerability.* Kelowna: Praxis (e)Press.

CHAPTER 11

Sustainability Fix Meets Growth Machine
Attempting to Govern the Calgary Metropolitan Region

Byron Miller

[There are many] questions about how environmental management is being incorporated into urban governance in different urban contexts, not least in terms of how local territorial structures associated with ecological modernization are situated in relation to those concerned with promoting urban development, managing territorial redistribution, and the like.

—*While, Jonas, and Gibbs, 2004: 549–50*

The problem of metropolitan governance [is] an expression of the politics of scale.... Emphatically, however, questions about the politics of scale are derivative of more fundamental ones having to do with the politics of space.

—*Cox, 2010: 216*

WHILE QUESTIONS of urban governance remain strongly grounded in the politics of growth, development, and competition (Molotch 1976; Logan and Molotch 1987; Harvey 1989; Stone 1989; Leitner 1990; Cox 1993; Jonas and Wilson 1999), the politics of sustainability, metabolism, and political ecology (Swyngedouw 1996; Harvey 1996; Heynen, Kaika and Swyngedouw 2006; Bulkeley et al. 2012) are becoming increasingly significant. Drawing from both these themes, an emergent literature on "critical sustainabilities" is beginning to examine the relationships between the politics of environmental and social sustainability on one hand, and issues of growth and development on the other (While, Jonas, and Gibbs 2004, 2010; Krueger and Gibbs 2007; Rosol 2013; Tretter 2013).

Increasingly the notion of growth as an overriding and uncontestable imperative is being challenged. Especially significant is the relationship between urban sustainability and carbon control, on one hand, and urban growth politics on the other (Gibbs and Jonas 2000; While et al. 2004, 2010; Jonas et al. 2011; Gibbs et al. 2013). With increasing frequency, sustainability and carbon control initiatives are producing a "new environmental politics of urban development" (Jonas et al. 2011) in which the qualities of the urban living place, use values, and sustainability place-marketing begin to supplement or displace traditional forms of interurban competition and entrepreneurialism.

While the literature addressing this phenomenon is producing important insights, it does so largely (but not exclusively) from the perspective of a localist ontology (MacLeod and Jones 2011), or what Angelo and Wachsmuth (2014) call "methodological cityism." Much can be learned from studying the dynamics of individual cities, but the processes of "nature" do not stop at city boundaries, and the politics and policies of urban growth and development are certainly not confined within city boundaries (McCann and Ward 2011; Miller and Nicholls 2013). Important power relations and causal dynamics are omitted when we limit our analytical vision to a particular geographical "container."

A more robust understanding of urban growth and development dynamics is afforded by a perspective that recognizes the diverse spatialities through which the politics and policies of urban growth and development are constituted (Jessop, Brenner, and Jones 2008; Cox 2010; Miller 2013) and, indeed, how the constitution of spatial relationships is itself a matter of political power and struggle. These themes play a more prominent role in the growing literature on the politics of metropolitan and regional governance, a literature that often deals with multiple collective actors competing and cooperating in multiple territorial jurisdictions, all within a relational, contested, scalar state (e.g., Allen and Cochrane 2007; Brenner 2002, 2004; Boudreau 2003, 2007; Boudreau, Keil and Young 2007; Cox 2010, 2011; Jonas and Ward 2007; Jones and MacLeod 2004; Jones 2013; MacLeod and Jones 2007; Niedt and Weir 2010; Ward and Jonas 2004; Young and Keil 2010; Macdonald and Keil 2012; Jonas et al. 2014). Cox (2010, 2011), for example, stresses the importance of the state's differentiated and malleable territorial and scalar form. The territorial and scalar constitution of the state is a fundamentally relational and dynamic matter (Jonas 2012), shaped by collective actors seeking to alter the amalgamation of material interests, access to resources, allocative and authoritative capacities, flows of capital investment, territorially specific tax bases, spatial divisions of consumption (both collective and private), land values, and territorial identities and alliances. As interest groups seek advantage, they often attempt to restructure the territorial and scalar structure of the state to their advantage.

The territorial and scalar relations of the state are not the only spatial relationships that come into play when examining issues of metropolitan and regional governance. While a geographically differentiated state structures interests and political action, collective actors strategically seek to alter state structures. Collective action is pursued in a variety of forms as economically motivated special-interest groups, localist, and regionalist movements, NIMBY groups, and other collective actors build and mobilize their networks, form alliances, and promote place-based identities to further solidarity or rationalize exclusion (Jones and MacLeod 2004; Ward and Jonas 2004; MacLeod and Jones 2007; Allen and Cochrane 2007; Pastor et al. 2009; Niedt and Weir 2010; Jones 2013). These networked and place-based relationships are critical to understanding the scalar and territorial constitution and reconstitution of metropolitan governance structures.

Despite the contentious nature of metropolitan politics, much of the literature on metropolitan governance and politics focuses on the broad structural forces of post-Fordist neo-liberal capitalism that have been associated with a radical rescaling of state power, capacity, and responsibility (Peck and Tickell 1994; Brenner 2004). Rescaling has had profound effects, particularly for metropolitan regions, where the downloading of responsibilities and the pitting of city against city in competition for capital investment has fundamentally altered the nature of urban governance, exerting strong pressure on cities to amalgamate and/or form metropolitan governments (Brenner 2004; Boudreau 2003, 2007; Boudreau et al. 2007; Sancton 2000). Yet the actual causal mechanisms and processes for such rescaling—including the creation of metropolitan governance structures—are often neglected. Frequently capital-logic arguments are invoked or implied in which "the rescaling of state functions and the assembling of institutions around city-regions (or metropolitan areas) is seen as a deliberate orchestration on the part of the national state (or local, regional, and national actors selectively empowered by the state) as it seeks to adjust its territoriality to the changing geographical imperatives of late capitalism" (Ward and Jonas 2004: 2125). What is missing in these accounts are the actual "conflict[s], divisions, struggles, and strategies [that] develop around the distribution of the social product—a separate politics of economic development and collective provision as well as their interconnections—as [well as] the geography of state structures and powers implicated in such ... politics" (Ward and Jonas 2004: 2127). Indeed, while the move toward various forms of metropolitan governance has been widespread, it has been neither uniform nor universal. Very significant differences in state structures, capacities, and struggles exist among, as well as within, countries, affecting the dynamics through which metropolitan-scale "new state spaces" are—or are not—constructed.

The history of metropolitan governance in the Calgary metropolitan region provides a particularly instructive case in the complexity, contingency, and contention through which institutions of metropolitan governance can be forged—and dismantled. The Calgary metropolitan region is extremely complex, marked by conflicts over tax base, collective provision, private consumption, environmental and fiscal sustainability, water allocations, geographically based divisions of material interests and identities, disputes over state authority and the nature of democratic governance, and an intense politics of scale involving actors and interests at the provincial, metropolitan, municipal, and sub-municipal scales. Perhaps most surprisingly, the Calgary metropolitan region has seen a retreat from a strong system of regional planning and regulation operating from the 1950s to the 1990s, to the present weak system of "voluntary cooperation" (lacking institutions of metropolitan government and absent a provincially approved metropolitan plan), during the very era in which the pressures of globalization, neo-liberalism, and increasing inter-metropolitan competition are supposed to have produced cohesive metropolitan institutions, strategies, and plans.

In the absence of any overarching framework of metropolitan governance, the Calgary metropolitan region has seen different municipalities adopt very different visions and strategies for the future, often fundamentally at odds with each other. First and foremost, the lines of conflict are drawn between the City of Calgary,[1] which is attempting to remake itself on the basis of sustainability principles incorporated in its 2009 Master Development Plan and Transportation Plan ("Plan-It"), and the County of Rocky View, which is attempting to attract as much growth and investment as possible, with a minimum of regulation. The central conflict, in other words, is between a central city seeking a "sustainability fix" (While, Jonas, and Gibbs 2004) to its fiscal, environmental, and quality of life problems, and a growing suburban county characterized by "growth machine" politics (Molotch 1976; Logan and Molotch 1987; Jonas and Wilson 1999). These fundamentally incompatible approaches to growth and development have led to a seemingly intractable standstill over the approval of the proposed "Calgary Metropolitan Plan." To understand how the governance of the Calgary metropolitan region became so contentious, one must begin by examining the geographical constitution and capacities of the state system in which the region is embedded.

Geographies of State Systems and Metropolitan Governance in Canada

The geographical constitution of the Canadian state system exhibits certain similarities to, but also important differences from, the American state system with which it is frequently compared. While the American state (i.e., the United States as a state) is often treated as the unspoken norm, it is in fact highly federal (decentralized) and fragmented compared to most advanced capitalist-democratic states. European states exhibit structural characteristics running the gamut from highly federal, e.g., Switzerland and Germany, to highly centralized, e.g., the Netherlands and the United Kingdom. Canada represents another highly federal system, albeit with a twist: the central state has no ministry of urban affairs and the national government has neither coherent urban policies nor significant funding programs for municipalities, yet municipalities themselves have very limited fiscal and authoritative capacity (Horak and Young 2012). Instead, Canadian urban policy is controlled first and foremost by the provinces (Garber and Imbroscio 1996). These differences in scalar state structure and capacity are critically important because they circumscribe the ability of Canadian municipalities to both compete and cooperate with each other, as well as chart their own independent trajectories. This is not to say that municipalities have no powers: they plan land use, transportation, water and sewer infrastructure; they provide standard municipal services. But they perform all these functions relying on miniscule federal transfers, modest provincial transfers, and just a few local revenue generation mechanisms, first and foremost property taxes and user fees.

As a result of highly constrained fiscal capacity and inadequate federal and provincial fiscal transfers, Canadian municipalities have accumulated huge infrastructure deficits. The Federation of Canadian Municipalities (FCM) estimates the Canadian municipal infrastructure deficit to be $171.8 billion—addressing only drinking water systems, waste-water and stormwater networks, and municipal roads (Federation of Canadian Municipalities 2012). Addressing public transportation systems, social housing, schools (typically a provincial responsibility), energy-efficiency retrofits and other essential infrastructure would push that number several times higher. The net result is that Canadian municipalities face severe and ongoing budgetary problems related to pressing infrastructure needs, municipal service demands, and highly constrained means of revenue generation, with few tools to incentivize capital investment. As a result much

Canadian urban planning, policy, and politics centres on finding efficiencies in the planning and operation of cities, and on capturing new sources
of revenue by exerting political pressure on "higher" levels of the state
(typically the provinces) and by attracting taxable development that might
otherwise locate in neighbouring municipalities. These imperatives are not
particularly conducive to inter-municipal cooperation on a metropolitan
scale.

A further consequence of Canada's highly federal multi-scalar governance system is that the sustainability and more narrowly focused carbon
control pressures, opportunities, and resources that typically emanate
from the central states of other less federal countries simply aren't encoun-
tered by Canadian municipalities. Sustainability and carbon control policy
initiatives often originate in international and national arenas—e.g., the
United Nations Agenda 21 Program, the Kyoto Protocol, the European
Union 20-20-20 targets, various national programs to regulate carbon
emissions and incentivize carbon reduction—while implementation is
often delegated to local and regional scales of the state (Gibbs and Jonas
2000). That such policies would originate at international and national
scales is not surprising, given the global and unbounded nature of these
problems. But what happens when the "upper level" state architecture
pertaining to sustainability and carbon control is weak or absent? Canada
is a case in point: (1) Canada's Liberal government signed the Kyoto
Protocol in 1997 and ratified it in 2002, but did very little to achieve its
greenhouse gas reduction targets. In the face of significantly rising greenhouse gas emissions, the Conservative government of Canada withdrew
from the protocol in 2011. (2) Agenda 21 was never taken up in a meaningful way in Canada. (3) There is no coherent NAFTA policy on greenhouse gas emissions and some critics link NAFTA to the accelerated
development of the Alberta oil sands, as well as increased deforestation.
(4) Carbon markets and other market-based mechanisms designed to
reduce greenhouse gas emissions are still in their infancy in Canada and
not strongly promoted. For example, Alberta's "Climate Change Central,"
an agency established in 2000 to administer Alberta's modest carbon offset
and energy efficiency programs, was defunded in 2012 and its doors closed
in 2014. (5) There is no coherent Canadian multi-scalar structure to coordinate and administer greenhouse gas reduction programs. Indeed, a recent
comprehensive analysis of Canada's greenhouse gas emissions reduction
policies identifies "the weakness of the intergovernmental system used to
develop co-ordinated federal-provincial policy" as one of the most significant impediments to meaningful greenhouse gas reductions in Canada
(MacDonald et al. 2013: v).

This is *not* to say that sustainability policies and politics have not been taken up in Canadian cities. On the contrary, sustainability and carbon control agendas have been strongly embraced by most major Canadian cities, including Calgary. But the cities that have adopted these policies have done so for their own place-specific reasons that frequently fail to translate to other municipalities in the same metropolitan region, municipalities that face different problems and have different priorities. National programs promoting sustainability and carbon control have not been a basis for incentivizing metropolitan cooperation and planning in Canadian metropolitan regions.

So, on what basis might institutions of metropolitan governance be constructed in Canada? They can, of course, be imposed from the top down, and this is indeed what occurred in the Toronto and Montreal metropolitan areas as the Ontario (1954–2006) and Quebec (2000–2006) provincial governments imposed a series of mergers, amalgamations, metropolitan federations, and regional growth plans, all with the aim of improving the coordination of infrastructure provision and achieving cost savings. These metropolitan governance measures, while highly contentious, have generally held up in the face of political opposition, albeit with periodic reform and revision.

But this is not the Calgary story. The history of metropolitan governance in Alberta has been virtually the inversion of the Ontario and Quebec stories. In 1995, Alberta abolished its renowned regional planning system and any pretence to coherent and coordinated metropolitan growth. Since 1995 municipalities have made growth and development decisions without oversight or coordination from metropolitan or regional planning commissions. In the place of regional planning commissions has been an ad hoc system of voluntary inter-municipal coordination, which has been limited at best. To understand how the governance of the Calgary metropolitan region came to be laissez-faire in the extreme (to put the most non-judgmental spin possible on the current state of affairs), it is important to recount the contentious history of regional planning in Alberta.

Contentious Metropolitan Governance: A Brief History of Regional Planning in Alberta

Regional planning in Alberta has to be understood in the context of Alberta's twentieth-century propensity for economic booms and busts and, in particular, the problems created by rapid and inadequately regulated growth during boom times. Alberta's first planning act, the 1913 *Town*

Planning Act, was introduced during Alberta's first major economic boom to regulate the process of land subdivision and minimize rampant land speculation, much of it occurring outside established municipalities. The province's first regional planning act, the 1929 *Town Planning and the Preservation of the Natural Beauty Act*, was intended to regulate land use and development along Alberta's rural highways by introducing zoning and other regulatory powers; it also provided for the creation of municipal and regional planning commissions, but regional commissions were not created due to the onset of the Great Depression and concomitant downturn in growth (Climenhaga 1997). With the discovery of oil in Leduc in 1947, however, Alberta's economy began to take off once again, bringing new waves of immigrants to the province and stimulating significant growth in urban centres, especially Calgary and Edmonton.

In the wake of the Leduc oil boom the provincial legislature passed the *Town and Rural Planning Act of 1950*, establishing district planning commissions, albeit with weak enforcement powers, to deal with rapidly growing exurban development characterized by poor or non-existent infrastructure and service provision as well as inadequate revenue to address even the basic needs of residential settlement. In 1954, to assess the increasingly problematic and controversial settlements on the fringes of Edmonton and Calgary, the province created the "Royal Commission on Metropolitan Development in Edmonton and Calgary," also called the McNally Commission. The McNally Commission released its recommendations in 1956, advocating a strong system of regional (metropolitan) planning commissions in which municipalities would be required to join their region's planning commission, and regional plans would be enforced. In 1957, the Commission's recommendations were made law, ushering in what many consider to be the strongest system of metropolitan planning ever introduced in North America.

Underlying the McNally Commission's recommendations were four basic principles (Parker 2005; Ghitter 2010): (1) There should be one unified social and economic entity in each metropolitan area, ensuring tax base equity. (2) Where business tax base is developed just outside an urban municipality, the tax revenue generated should accrue to the municipality that provides municipal services to the business's workers. (3) Urban municipalities are entitled to grow and expand into rural areas. (4) Where areas adjacent to a city take on urban characteristics, these areas are best planned and governed by one central municipality. These four principles underlay what came to be known as the "uni-city" concept: a governance and planning notion based on the proposition that equity and efficiency are best served by subsuming virtually all growth and development in a metropolitan area within a single municipality. The ability to bring growth and development under the control of one central municipality was achieved through two principal mechanisms: (1) urban municipalities' ability to annex adjacent rural land as needed to accommodate urban growth, and (2) the ability to regulate development—including authority over land subdivision—within a buffer zone surrounding the central urban municipality; the buffer was initially set at eight kilometres, later revised to five. The mechanisms by which growth on the urban fringe was regulated proved to be very effective: at the time of the dismantling of Alberta's regional planning system in 1995, over 90% of the population of the Calgary metropolitan region was located within the City of Calgary.

While the uni-city framework was highly effective from the standpoint of promoting contiguous urban growth and relative equity in infrastructure and service provision (including in rural municipalities where subdivision was approved) in the Calgary metropolitan area, it clearly favoured urban municipalities over rural municipalities and rural landowners. Rural municipalities typically had an even more deficient tax base, relative to need, than urban municipalities, yet the uni-city framework made significant expansion of rural tax bases within the buffer zones of urban municipalities virtually impossible, and inadequate water provision constrained development beyond the buffer zones. This situation was especially problematic in a province where provincial transfers have long been inadequate. Additionally, constraints on the expansion of rural employment, commercial activity, and infrastructure served to suppress rural land values. The autonomy of rural municipalities, particularly Rocky View and Foothills, which border Calgary, was significantly constrained.

Not surprisingly, the Calgary Regional Planning Commission's very success was cause for resistance and resentment among many rural interests and their political representatives. While planners and urban analysts praised the effectiveness of the commission in managing growth from a regional perspective, its effectiveness did not sit well with the rural power base of Alberta's ruling Progressive Conservative Party. When the free-market, anti-regulation, neo-liberal government of Ralph Klein came to power in 1992, the handwriting was on the wall. By 1994, Klein's Minister of Municipal Affairs, Stephen West, had defunded and shut down Alberta's regional planning commissions. A new *Municipal Government Act*, passed in 1995, eliminated mandatory and binding regional planning and empowered all municipalities to set their own growth and development agendas. To the extent that there was to be regional planning it was to be entirely voluntary, giving each municipality the ability the withdraw from any plan or agreement not entirely to its liking.

Alberta had suddenly flipped from having the strongest regional planning regime in North America to having none at all. In the ensuing years a variety of forms of low density development—sprawl—began to spring up in rural areas surrounding the City of Calgary, particularly to the west of the city in Rocky View. By the late 1990s, Calgary was experiencing its own ever-greater fiscal strain as provincial transfers to cities were cut, more growth occurred outside the city—utilizing Calgary's infrastructure and services but not contributing to its tax revenue, and Calgary's own practice of subsidizing relatively low-density residential development within its borders became an ever greater burden. To add to the fiscal strain, the quality of life in Calgary seemed to be steadily declining. Increasing traffic congestion, crowded schools, declining air quality, and a host of other environmental as well as economic problems gave rise to the perception that the city and its surrounding metropolitan region were on the wrong path. By the end of the decade there was recognition that some form of regional coordination was needed, but rural municipalities had no appetite to create new institutions of regional planning. Nonetheless, in 1999, through the instigation of Calgary mayor Al Duerr, representatives of fifteen municipalities began to meet to discuss issues of common concern and build interpersonal relationships, eventually forming the Calgary Regional Partnership (CRP). Participation in the CRP was and remains entirely voluntary and, in the first several years after its founding, the organization did not address land-use and transportation issues and did not seek to become a governmental body. The early years of the CRP represented a very tepid first step toward recognizing and discussing the regional nature of many issues faced by the (eventually eighteen) municipalities. The real action toward addressing issues of growth and sustainability began in the City of Calgary in the first decade of the twenty-first century as citizens began to question the wisdom of Calgary's growth trajectory and policies.

Calgary Moves toward a Sustainability Agenda

Calgary has long been known as a pro-growth, anti-regulation city, dominated by the suburban development industry. Its growth, while planned and orderly, has nonetheless been based (until recently) on low-density residential subdivision, segregated land uses, and automobile dependence, hence the city's reputation as a poster-city for urban sprawl. This pattern of growth seemed to work reasonably well until the late 1990s, when a new oil-driven economic boom suddenly put many more cars on the road, overburdened infrastructure generally, and called into question the wisdom of building a generally unwalkable, automobile-dependent city. It was increasingly recognized as expensive, too. In 2001, Calgary elected a new mayor, Dave Bronconnier, who ran on the slogan "Moving Calgary Forward," but was more frequently associated with the unofficial slogan, "roads, roads, roads," and denials that Calgary had a sprawl problem. In the early days of the Bronconnier era, emphasis was placed on building and widening roads, but over time broadened to include a greater emphasis on public transportation and, eventually, a willingness to rethink the direction of the city.

A turning point came in 2004, when city council, under Mayor Bronconnier's leadership, initiated a city-visioning project dubbed "imagineCalgary." The imagineCalgary visioning process ultimately engaged over 18,000 citizens and, based on the work of five working groups addressing governance, the built environment, the natural environment, social conditions, and the economy, laid out a vision for a very different future, one that would be far more equitable, socially and economically secure, environmentally sound, and participatory. In 2006, the citizen-driven imagineCalgary *Long Range Urban Sustainability Plan for Calgary* was accepted by city council as an advisory document, laying the foundation for the development of a new municipal development and transportation plan. That same year Mayor Bronconnier gave the keynote address at the Sustainable Cities PLUS Network conference in Vancouver, which was held in conjunction with the World Urban Forum; the topic of his address was imagineCalgary.

From 2006 to 2009, Calgary city planners worked on the development of a new plan to guide the growth and development of the city, Plan-It, which explicitly integrated land-use and transportation planning, including public transit and active modes of transportation. Indeed, the central premise behind Plan-It was that cities must be understood as innately interconnected systems, rather than as collections of discrete stand-alone entities. An extensive public hearing process guided the development of the new sixty-year plan, with planners eventually laying out three very different scenarios for consideration by the public and city council: (1) "Dispersed"—essentially business as usual, with 69% of Calgary's housing stock being single-family detached and the automobile remaining the dominant mode of transportation; (2) "Compact"—a complete about-face focusing on intensification, public transit, and walkability, with virtually all new growth taking place within the built footprint of the city and only 15% of the housing stock in single family detached dwellings; (3) "Hybrid"—the compromise scenario, splitting future growth evenly between greenfield suburban development and intensification within the built footprint of the city, with 31% of the housing stock in single family detached dwellings; this scenario was adopted by city council. In addition to radically redirecting the city's growth patterns—previously virtually all growth occurred in greenfield suburban locations on the fringe of the city, which was the principal reason Calgary needed to coordinate with surrounding rural municipalities—Plan-It called for the construction of "complete" communities in which all daily needs could be met locally, a significant shift toward public transit with 25% of all trips on public transit, and a much greater emphasis on walking and bicycling.

Not surprisingly, the plan was controversial. The Urban Development Institute (UDI) (the Calgary development industry lobby) argued that the existing pattern of suburban-focused development represented consumer choice and that Plan-It was a "social engineering" document that would force consumers to make choices they didn't want. Many conservative members of city council were inclined to agree with UDI and were initially prepared to vote against Plan-It. But citizens mobilized in favour of Plan-It and presented a variety of critiques of the UDI position. Undoubtedly the argument that was most persuasive with conservative members of Council was the economic one. An independent analysis, commissioned by the city and performed by the IBI Group, demonstrated that the City of Calgary would save $11.2 billion in infrastructure costs and $130 million annually in operating costs with the recommended Hybrid version of Plan-It, compared to the continuation of the status quo (City of Calgary 2009)—a point strongly stressed by citizen groups.

Ultimately, Plan-It was unanimously passed by Calgary city council and, coupled with subsequent decisions to raise suburban development levies, represented a major defeat for the suburban development industry. Plan-It constituted a sustainability fix to the city's increasingly problematic fiscal situation, not to mention a strategy for reversing the city's declining quality of life. Angry developers, however, threatened a range of responses, from backing a slate of development-industry candidates in the upcoming election to taking their business outside the city. While never realizable on a massive scale due to significant constraints on water provision outside the city, this latter threat did contain elements of plausibility. Indeed, planners working on Plan-It understood the importance of coordinating with adjacent municipalities as Plan-It was being developed, bringing the story full circle to the issue of metropolitan governance.

The Calgary Regional Partnership and the Calgary Metropolitan Plan: Controversy, Chaos, and Limbo

The ongoing discussions of regional growth issues among members of the Calgary Regional Partnership led, in 2004, to the realization that the CRP needed to become a formal organization. That year it incorporated as a not-for-profit organization, began hiring staff, and started to undertake research on economic development and public transit issues, funded by provincial grants and municipal membership fees. By 2006, in the face of rapid regional growth and Calgary's own work to develop a new master development and transportation plan, the CRP decided it would address issues of land use and transportation after all, and established the terms of reference for a Calgary Regional Plan (later renamed the Calgary Metropolitan Plan). Between 2007 and 2009, planners focused on the drafting of the Calgary Metropolitan Plan (CMP), with the help of extensive citizen input from across the then eighteen participating municipal jurisdictions. City of Calgary planners working on Plan-It were also engaged to ensure the two plans would be compatible.

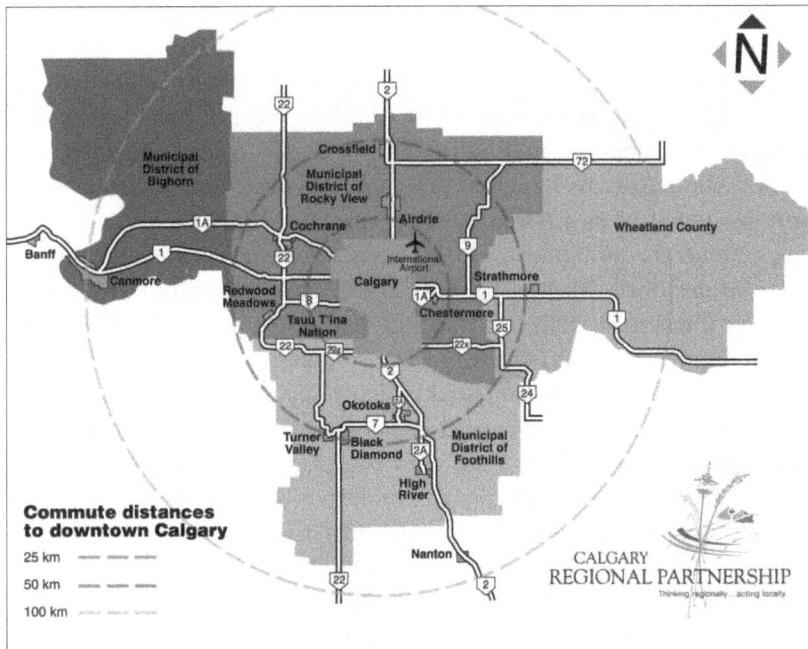

Figure 11.1   Calgary Region: Where Opportunity Drives Prosperity. Cochrane, AB: Calgary Regional Partnership (2008).

The need for coordinated regional planning had become especially clear after the infamous 2004–6 Rancher's Beef slaughterhouse location and servicing debacle (Ghitter and Smart 2009), an episode in regional anti-planning that almost defies belief. In the wake of the BSE crisis the Rancher's Beef consortium sought, in 2004, to locate a state-of-the-art slaughterhouse in an industrial area of northeast Calgary, near the Calgary airport and existing residential neighbourhoods. When residents succeeded in blocking its approval, Rancher's Beef sought approval to build at a new location approximately one kilometre from the original proposed site, just outside the City of Calgary in the Municipal District of Rocky View. Under the old regional planning system Calgary could have easily vetoed the proposal, but in the absence of regional planning Rocky View quickly approved the Rancher's Beef proposal as a step in its plans to boost its tax base. There was just one problem: Rocky View had no infrastructure to service the slaughterhouse and Calgary refused to extend water and sewer to it. Moreover, not only was the construction of the slaughterhouse in danger, Rocky View also lacked the means to provide sufficient water and sewer to a major regional mall project—Cross Iron Mills—under way in an undeveloped area near the hamlet of Balzac. After several failed attempts to secure water—and under threat of legal action—Rocky View was finally able to purchase water rights from the Western Irrigation District for $15 million (Calgary Herald 2007) and build a new fifty-three-km waste-water pipeline from Balzac, north of Calgary, to an upgraded waste-water treatment plant in the hamlet of Langdon, east of Calgary, incurring $25 million in debt to finance construction (Massot 2014). The Balzac to Langdon pipeline and waste-water system "was promoted in 2005 as a system capable to service 16,000 acres of residential, commercial and industrial development with capacity equivalent to 100,000 persons" (Massot 2013: 1). The Rocky View Council voted to approve the system, believing that it would attract a significant amount of development and that levies on development would bring in about $10 million per year, allowing Rocky View to pay off the debt quickly and expand its property tax revenue stream (Massot 2013: 2). Those revenues never materialized. In 2006 the province placed a moratorium on any further water licences from the over-allocated Bow River—the principal source of fresh water for the Calgary metropolitan area. "From that moment, Rocky View's dreams of developing 16,000 acres and a 100,000 equal [sic] in residential, commercial, and industrial development were dead in the water (pun intended)" (Massot 2013: 2).[2]

Without new water supplies very little new development is possible in Rocky View. Limited development along the fifty-three-kilometre pipeline, combined with very low waste-water levies, has meant that in some years Rocky View has "had to obtain holidays on debt payments, which [has] increased the debt even more, to a peak $75 million" (Massot 2013: 3). Simply put, Rocky View's go-it-alone build-anywhere growth strategy has been a massive failure, increasing debt instead of revenue. Under these circumstances one might expect Rocky View to have embraced the Calgary Metropolitan Plan when it was presented for approval, a plan that would have required more efficient patterns of development to which the City of Calgary would extend water (utilizing its water licence) and sewer services.

When the Calgary Metropolitan Plan came before the CRP Executive Committee for approval in June 2009, the vote was fourteen to three in favour—the fourteen votes in favour were all urban municipalities, representing 94% of the region's population,[3] as Calgary mayor Naheed Nenshi (elected in 2010) points out (Nenshi 2013). The three dissenting votes were all rural municipalities: Rocky View and Foothills—the two municipalities surrounding Calgary (Figure 11.1)—and Wheatland. A fourth rural municipal district, Big Horn, withdrew from the CRP before the Executive Committee vote. Although the margin of support was lopsided, it was not sufficient. Regional plans do not become official in Alberta until provincial approval is granted and, despite the Minister of Municipal Affairs' strong words of support, the province insisted, under pressure from rural municipalities, that there be unanimous agreement on the Plan. The three rural municipalities, in essence, vetoed the Plan. All members of the CRP were strongly encouraged by the province to enter a mediation process to attempt to resolve their differences.

At first glance the lines of conflict were clear. The rural municipalities demanded the CMP "scrap the density rules, alter planned growth areas and conditions for water sharing." They also objected to the voting structure for revising the plan. Urban municipalities contended such changes "would render meaningless the long-awaited plan to concentrate future growth without building over too much farmland" (Markusoff 2009: 1).

The CMP was clearly constructed with the same sustainability principles as Plan-It in mind. According to the *Calgary Metropolitan Plan*, under the heading "Our Future Is Sustainable," "One conclusion stands out in our planning thus far—the status quo is not acceptable. If development continued with no regional plan and no regional collaboration, our region's footprint would increase by approximately 125,000 hectares and costs of infrastructure would be unsustainable. With regional planning, our development can be more compact and would only increase by 45,000 hectares with infrastructure costs, both above and below ground, decreasing proportionately" (Calgary Regional Partnership 2009: 2). These principles were not the ones guiding the rural opposition, however. Instead, rural interests argued that the CMP represented an infringement of property rights (by guiding growth into corridors, landowners outside the corridors would be deprived of the ability to reap speculative profits from land sales), that higher densities in designated corridors represented urban development that was incompatible with a "rural lifestyle," and that the proposed voting structure for future amendments ostensibly gave Calgary a "veto" over changes to the Plan. Based on these objections all four rural municipalities ultimately withdrew from the CRP, leaving the entire rural fringe around Calgary outside the jurisdiction of the Plan.

The voting structure, in particular, would prove to be an especially intractable issue. To understand this issue, it is important to distinguish between the voting rules for approval of the Plan—the province decided to require unanimous assent for initial approval—and the proposed rules for future changes to the Plan. Under the Plan, a double-majority would be required for future changes: (1) municipalities representing, at a minimum, a majority of the region's population would need to vote in favour, and (2) at least two-thirds of the municipalities comprising the CRP would need to vote in favour. This formula would ensure that neither Calgary nor a minority population block could impose change and that either Calgary or a two-thirds block of smaller municipalities could veto any proposed change. In other words, the formula would require a broad consensus, including both Calgary and many smaller municipalities, before any changes could be made.

The objections presented by municipal representatives on the CRP Executive Committee do not, however, tell the full story of rural attitudes toward the Calgary Metropolitan Plan. In the municipal district of Foothills, to the south of Calgary, objections to the Plan were rooted primarily in concerns over unwanted development. The CMP included a growth corridor extending south from Calgary in the direction of Okotoks, a town that for several years had operated under a self-imposed cap on growth. Foothills itself is strongly oriented toward ranching and few in the area want that to change. Foothills's objections to the Plan, in other words, had less to do with desire for rapid growth than with a desire not to grow.

Rocky View is a very different story. The population of the western part of Rocky View County is generally very wealthy: median household income in the Springbank/Elbow Valley part of Rocky View County stood at $174,363 in 2006, more than double the median household income of Calgary (cited in Gondek 2013). The Springbank, Elbow Valley, and

Bearspaw areas of western Rocky View County are characterized by large lot "acreage" development with stunning vistas west to the Rocky Mountains. Residents of this part of Rocky View are generally opposed to further development and are particularly concerned about a proposal to build a planned 1,750-acre development called "Harmony" that would add 10,000 people to the area. Development discourse in the western part of the County is extremely unharmonious and has given rise to a strong secessionist movement, with many in the area seeking to leave Rocky View and join further-west rural Bighorn County. The eastern part of the County, by contrast, lacks spectacular scenery, has a much lower median household income, and contains the major growth corridor between the northern edge of Calgary and the City of Airdrie, including the Cross Iron Mills regional shopping mall, the Rancher's Beef plant (reopened in 2014 as Harmony Beef), and the fifty-three-kilometre pipeline from Balzac to Langdon. It is here that Rocky View has pinned its hopes of expanding its tax base to raise the revenue it needs to fund a variety of projects and gain meaningful fiscal and political autonomy from Calgary.

Indeed, it is difficult to overestimate the importance of the autonomy issue. Resentment of Calgary's historical control of development on its border under the old regional planning system remains strong, with some rural actors likening it to colonialism. Many officials and residents explicitly analyze regional planning issues in terms of "the rurals" versus "the urbans." Among some Rocky View officials the assertion of municipal autonomy, coupled with strategies to expand the tax base, trump all other concerns. As one Rocky View County councillor, describing the process that led to the development of Cross Iron Mills, put it: "Cross Iron Mills is the County thumbing its nose at Calgary and declaring war. Anyone who wants cheap land and a low tax rate should come to Rocky View County.... We are no longer that cute county that did everything off the cuff. Cross Iron Mills blew that world apart" (cited in Gondek 2013: 254). Or, as another analyst of Calgary metropolitan politics, Geoff Ghitter (himself a Rocky View County resident), describes the situation: "What Rocky View has now is not a growth management strategy; it is instead a growth mismanagement strategy that champions development while ignoring its costs. It is based on a misguided belief that more development enhances its fiscal position and by a venal attitude that sees development being approved as revenge for regional planning. Infrastructure spending has been rushed without due consideration or vision. Yet here we are. What will we do about it?" (cited in *Canadian Guerilla News* 2010).

Dysfunction and the Search for Common Ground

So what *is* being done about the Calgary metropolitan regions governance impasse? The Calgary Regional Partnership remains active and intact, but missing all of its former rural members. In their absence the Calgary Metropolitan Plan has no real regulatory impact, not only because it has not been approved by the province but because it does not address the rural areas surrounding the region's urban municipalities where the most pressing growth management issues lie. In the first three years following the failed 2009 attempt to have the plan approved, the remaining urban members of the CRP continued to revise the Plan and seek common ground with the rural municipalities. While progress was made, it was not sufficient to entice the rural municipalities back into the CRP. In 2012, the by then twelve members of the CRP unanimously re-approved an updated version of the CMP, still without the participation of Rocky View, Foothills, or any other rural municipality. By February 2013, the City of Calgary's frustration with negotiations over the CMP reached a full boil. Calgary mayor Naheed Nenshi published an opinion piece in the *Calgary Herald* accusing the provincial government of doing nothing to move approval of the Plan forward, sending mixed and contradictory messages to different constituencies, and treating the City of Calgary as a "farm team" in negotiations over inter-municipal and scalar governance arrangements. In a follow-up interview, Nenshi exclaimed: "I'm very frustrated.... When I hear the minister and the premier start talking about items we thought we were negotiating, and laying down the laws so the city is the farm team, and to be told what it's going to be, this is a big problem.... we need a little more political leadership from the province on this—and that's me choosing my words carefully" (Nenshi, cited in Huffington Post Alberta 2013).

The provincial Minister of Municipal Affairs, Doug Griffiths, responded by calling the Mayor a "peacock," but hired a mediator and told the urban and rural municipalities to undergo mediation. A Calgary Metropolitan Plan Mediation Working Group was formed and was able to resolve several points of conflict: the priority growth areas in the Municipal District of Rocky View were removed from the Plan, the regional water and waste-water servicing agreement was reworded to explicitly specify that the City of Calgary is willing to provide water and waste-water services to members of the CRP to support growth in areas specified by the CMP, clarification that membership in the CRP is voluntary and that different municipalities can take different approaches to achieving the goals of the CMP was added, and a dispute resolution procedure was agreed upon. There was no agreement, however, on voting rules for future changes to the Plan (Calgary Regional Partnership 2013) and, as a result, unanimous endorsement of the Plan was not achieved.

Nonetheless, in April 2014, the members of the CRP relented and added a veto over changes to the Plan for any individual municipality, no matter how small, that believes it might be adversely affected by a proposed change. All the demands made by the rural municipalities made during mediation were met and in May 2014 the new (acting) Minister of Municipal Affairs, Greg Weadick, wrote to the chair of the CRP, declaring, "The Calgary Metropolitan Plan represents a proactive and responsible vision for the region, and all municipalities in the region are to be commended for working to bring this plan to a point where all parties can support it" (Weadick 2014: 1). As of April 2016 the rural former members of the CRP still had not rejoined the CRP and the Calgary Metropolitan Plan still had not been approved by the province.

Conclusion: Sustainability Fix versus Growth Machine and the Politics of Space

The dysfunctional governance of the Calgary metropolitan region underscores the fact that "regionalisation is not neutral with respect to wider interests, structures and processes operating inside the competition state. The question, then, is whether the process is driven 'from below' or happens in response to pressures 'from above'; therefore, the form of territorial politics does matter" (Jonas et al. 2014: 2459). Indeed, the form of territorial—and scalar—politics matters greatly.

Governance of the Calgary metropolitan region has been fraught with conflict since its very inception in 1957 (Almujhairy 2014). Under a planning process that was driven "from above," the Calgary Regional Planning Commission could veto development proposals in its adjacent buffer zone, compromising not only neighbouring rural municipalities' sovereignty over development within their borders, but also their ability to build an adequate tax base to meet collective consumption needs. As a result, rural municipalities frequently appealed to the provincial government to override CRPC decisions—a scalar strategy made possible by a rural-friendly political opportunity structure at the provincial scale, based in the provincial government's desire to maintain its rural power base. While the CRPC had the power to make and implement decisions that strongly affected the course of regional growth and development, such decisions rarely represented a regional consensus and often provoked conflict and provincial intervention over specific development proposals. Even more significantly, the CRPC provoked intense resentment from rural municipalities and rural development interests that foreclosed any possibility of genuine collaboration.

When regional planning commissions were abolished in Alberta, metropolitan governance became a "flat" and voluntary process of building consensus among ostensibly equal parties. But in this new laissez-faire era, municipalities can simply opt out of metropolitan coordination and planning—or, again, lobby the province—when decisions are not to their liking. The opportunities for building effective plans based in regional consensus are scarcely better under this "collaborative" approach. Indeed, twenty years after the abolition of the CRPC, there is still no operational Calgary Metropolitan Plan. Given municipalities' dramatically different political dynamics and diametrically opposed development logics—e.g., Calgary's pursuit of a cost-containment sustainability fix versus Rocky View's pursuit of economic growth and a vastly expanded tax base—it is no surprise that it has been extremely difficult to build consensus for the Calgary Metropolitan Plan. A diversity of needs, interests, identities, ideologies, and logics makes building metropolitan governance "from below" extremely difficult, particularly when neither the provincial nor federal government has coherent urban policies to establish a context and common ground for negotiations; there is no clear framework for regional or multi-scalar decision-making; membership in the CRP is optional, allowing easy exit from negotiations; there are few incentives for collaboration from "higher" levels of the state; and municipalities are largely left to their own insufficient devices to generate the revenue required to meet residents' needs. And if these hurdles to building a regional approach to growth and development were not enough, the Province of Alberta requires unanimous support from all municipal governments before it will approve a metropolitan plan.

In this quasi-anarchic situation the politics of municipal-territorial interests reign supreme, and these interests vary by municipality. Too often, each municipality pursues the revenue generation and/or cost-containment strategy its elected officials believe will serve it best, with relatively little consideration for the broader implications beyond the municipality's borders. The politics of collective consumption—and increasingly the politics of private consumption—are displaced from broad societal questions of how to divide the social surplus, to a competitive inter-spatial growth politics pursued by individual municipalities—hardly the sort of politics conducive to thinking about metropolitan regions as innately intertwined social, economic, and environmental systems.

There are alternatives. If revenue generation and distribution questions were "upscaled" (Macdonald and Keil 2012) to a regional, provincial, or even national scale and addressed through a needs-based framework, inter-municipal competition for revenue generating development[4] could be dramatically dampened, opening up space for a broader, deeper, and less parochial social, economic, and environmental discussion. Such an approach to municipal funding, which is utilized in the Netherlands and several other countries with strong central states, might seem inconceivable in Alberta. And yet Alberta has adopted exactly such an approach, on the provincial scale, for the funding of primary and secondary schools: local education property taxes are pooled at the provincial scale, added to provincial general revenues, and redistributed to local school districts on a needs basis. Alberta's primary and secondary school system is underfunded, but its distributional inequities are minimal, leading to broad and spirited discussions about the funding parameters of the system itself, as opposed to leaving individual school districts to pursue go-it-alone revenue generation strategies.

Uncooperative beggar-thy-neighbour approaches to urban development can produce a variety of undesirable outcomes, from sprawl and its associated energy, environmental, and commuting costs, to unnecessary and expensive duplication of infrastructure, to inefficient service provision. The inter-spatial competition that represents a major impediment to cooperative regional governance is not a natural phenomenon, but rather a function of territorial and scalar politics (and structures). The Calgary metropolitan region's governance politics is itself a politics of territorial and scalar structures of the state, as both the abolition of Alberta's regional planning system in the 1990s, and more recent attempts to create new regional planning mechanisms, attest. The way forward through the region's current governance impasse will undoubtedly entail further changes in territorial and scalar relations.

For now, this much is certain: Alberta's population continues to grow. Alberta generated 87% of Canada's new jobs between February 2013 and February 2014, according to Statistics Canada, producing a steady stream of migration to Alberta. Even in the context of 2015's low oil prices, in-migration continued to exceed out-migration. Much of Alberta's growth has occurred in the Calgary metropolitan region, placing the region's infrastructure, environment, and quality of life under ever-growing pressure. The impacts of rapid growth are affecting the entire metropolitan region, and regional solutions and governance mechanisms must be found. The competitive pressures of neo-liberal globalization have not produced effective metropolitan governance in the Calgary metropolitan region: effective forms of governance clearly do not automatically manifest from functionalist logic. Rather, they are always political achievements. The struggle for effective, fair, and equitable governance of the Calgary metropolitan region continues.

Acknowledgements

I am grateful to Geoff Ghitter, Pierre Hamel, Andy Jonas, Roger Keil, Bob Miller, Alan Smart, and Eliot Tretter for comments provided on an earlier draft of this chapter. The final version does not necessarily reflect their views, and I am, of course, responsible for any errors.

Notes

1 It should be noted that the City of Calgary and many of the smaller municipalities of the Calgary metropolitan region share a common vision of the growth and development of the Calgary metropolitan region.
2 Adding to the fiasco, the Rancher's Beef plant closed in 2007.
3 According to 2011 Statistics Canada data, Calgary's 2011 population was 1,096,833, while the population of the entire Calgary Region was 1,278,976. The two rural municipalities surrounding Calgary, Rocky View, and Foothills, had populations of 36,461 and 21,258, respectively. Wheatland County, which is not considered part of the Calgary Region for statistical purposes, had a 2011 population of 8,285.
4 While this discussion focuses on the counter-productive effects of municipalities' competition for revenue generating development, a similar case could be made for non-state actors promoting questionable development, such as landowners in inaccessible, environmentally sensitive, and expensive-to-service locations. Given that much of the motivation for farmers' and ranchers' land sales to land developers is to provide for their well-being in retirement or the well-being of their children, an alternative to quasi-anarchic and unsound land development practices could be more comprehensive and robust social welfare policies.

References

Allen, J. and A. Cochrane. 2007. "Beyond the territorial fix: Regional assemblages, politics and power." *Regional Studies* 41(9): 1161–75.
Almujhairy, A. 2014. *The central role of collaborative planning in shaping the future of the metropolis: An evaluation of collective decision-making in the Calgary metropolitan region*. Unpublished doctoral dissertation, Faculty of Environmental Design, University of Calgary. 169 pages.
Angelo, H. and D. Wachsmuth. 2014. "Urbanizing political ecology: A critique of methodological cityism." *International Journal of Urban and Regional Research*, 1–14.
Brenner, N. 2002. "Decoding the newest 'metropolitan regionalism' in the USA: A critical overview." *Cities* 19(1): 3–21.
———. 2004. *New state spaces: Urban governance and the rescaling of statehood*. Oxford: Oxford University Press.
Boudreau, J. 2003. "The politics of territorialization: Regionalism, localism and other isms … The case of Montreal." *Journal of Urban Affairs* 25(2): 179–99.

———. 2007. "Making new political spaces: Mobilizing spatial imaginaries, instrumentalizing spatial practices, and strategically using spatial tools." *Environment and Planning A* 39(11): 2593–611.

Boudreau, J., R. Keil, and D. Young. 2007. *Changing Toronto: Governing the in-between, the global and the local.* Peterborough: Broadview Press.

Bulkeley, H., V. Broto, M. Hodson, and S. Marvin, eds. 2012. *Cities and low carbon transitions.* New York and Oxon: Routledge.

Calgary Herald. 2007. "Tapped out: Water woes, part 2." *Calgary Herald.* December 1. www.canada.com/story_print.html?id=0967acd9-5c73-4fde -94e7-84ee685bf51d.

Calgary Regional Partnership. 2009. *Calgary Metropolitan Plan,* June 19.

———. 2013. Calgary Metropolitan Plan Mediation Working Group: Final Report, July 18.

Canadian Guerilla News. 2010. 3 Things, July 3, at www.canadianguerilla.com/ News/Entries/2010/7/3_CGN_6_3_Things.html.

City of Calgary. 2009. *The implications of alternative growth patterns on infrastructure costs.* Report prepared by the IBI Group, April 2. 58 pages.

Climenhaga, D. 1997. *The death and life of regional planning in the Calgary area.* Unpublished Master of Journalism thesis, Carleton University. 166 pages.

Cox, K. 1993. "The local and the global in the new urban politics: A critical view." *Environment and Planning D: Society and Space* 11: 433–48.

———. 2010. "The problem of metropolitan governance and the politics of scale." *Regional Studies* 44(2): 215–27.

———. 2011. "From the new urban politics to the 'new' metropolitan politics." *Urban Studies* 48(12): 2661–71.

Federation of Canadian Municipalities. 2012. *Canadian infrastructure report card 2012.* www.canadainfrastructure.ca/downloads/Canadian _Infrastructure_Report_Card_EN.pdf.

Foran, M. 2009. *Expansive discourses: Urban sprawl in Calgary, 1945–1978.* Athabasca: Athabasca University Press.

Garber, J. and D. Imbroscio. 1996. "The myth of the North American city reconsidered: Local constitutional regimes in Canada and in the United States." *Urban Affairs Review* 31(5): 595–624.

Ghitter, G. 2010. *Sustainability, complexity and the city: An evolutionary geography of path dependence in the Calgary metropolitan region.* Unpublished doctoral dissertation, Department of Geography, University of Calgary. 392 pages.

Ghitter, G. and A. Smart. 2009. "Mad cows, regional governance, and urban sprawl: Path dependence and consequences in the Calgary region." *Urban Affairs Review* 44(5): 617–44.

Gibbs, D. and A. Jonas. 2000. "Governance and regulation in local environmental policy: The utility of a regime approach." *Geoforum* (31): 299–313.

Gibbs, D., A. Jonas, and A. While. 2002. "Changing governance structures and the environment: Economy–environment relations at the local and regional scales." *Journal of Environmental Policy and Planning* 4: 123–38.

Gibbs, D., R. Krueger, and G. MacLeod. 2013. "Grappling with smart city politics in an era of market triumphalism." *Urban Studies* 50(11): 2151–57.

Gondek, P. 2013. *Pressures of hybridity: An analysis of the urban–rural nexus.* Unpublished doctoral dissertation, Department of Sociology, University of Calgary. 317 pages.

Harvey, D. 1989. "From managerialism to entrepreneurialism: The transformation in urban governance in late capitalism." *Geografiska Annaler, Series B: Human Geography* 71(1): 3–17.

———. 1996. *Justice, nature and the geography of difference.* Oxford: Wiley-Blackwell.

Heynen, N., M. Kaika, and E. Swyngedouw, eds. 2006. *In the nature of cities: Urban political ecology and the politics of urban metabolism.* New York and Oxford: Routledge.

Horak, M. and R. Young, eds. 2012. *Sites of governance: Multilevel governance and policy making in Canada's big cities.* Montreal and Kingston: McGill-Queen's University Press.

Huffington Post Alberta. 2013. "Nenshi accuses province of treating Calgary like 'farm team,' Minister Doug Griffiths fights back." *Huffington Post Alberta.* February 11. www.huffingtonpost.ca/2013/02/11/mayor-naheed-nenshi-farm-team-minister-doug-griffiths_n_2662494.html.

Jessop, B., N. Brenner, and M. Jones. 2008. "Theorizing sociospatial relations." *Environment and Planning D: Society and Space* 26: 389–401.

Jonas, A. 2012. "Region and place: Regionalism in question." *Progress in Human Geography* 36(2): 263–72.

Jonas, A. and E. Goetz. 2014. "City-regionalism as a politics of collective provision: Regional transport infrastructure in Denver, USA." *Urban Studies* 51(11): 2444–65.

Jonas, A. and D. Wilson, eds. 1999. *The urban growth machine: Critical perspectives two decades later.* Albany: SUNY Press.

Jonas, A. and K. Ward. 2007. "Introduction to a debate on city-regions: New geographies of governance, democracy and social reproduction." *International Journal of Urban and Regional Research* 31(1): 169–78.

Jonas, A., D. Gibbs, and A. While. 2011. "The new urban politics as a politics of carbon control." *Urban Studies* 48(12): 2537–54.

Jones, M. 2013. "Polymorphic spatial politics: Tales from a grassroots regional movement." In W. Nicholls, B. Miller, and J. Beaumont, eds., *Spaces of contention: Spatialities and social movement* (103–20). Surrey, UK, and Burlington, VT: Ashgate.

Jones, M. and G. MacLeod. 2004. "Regional spaces, spaces of regionalism: Territory, insurgent politics and the English question." *Transactions of the Institute of British Geographers* 29: 433–52.

Krueger, R. and D. Gibbs, eds. 2007. *The sustainable development paradox.* New York and London: Guilford Press.

Leitner, H. 1990. "Cities in pursuit of economic growth: The local state as entrepreneur." *Political Geography Quarterly* 9(2): 146–70.

Logan, J. and H. Molotch. 1987. *Urban fortunes: The political economy of place.* Berkeley: University of California Press.

MacDonald, D., J. Monstadt, and K. Kern. 2013. *Allocating Canadian greenhouse gas emission reductions amongst sources and provinces: Learning from the European Union, Australia and Germany.* University of Toronto, Darmstadt

University, and Wageningen University. www.environment.utoronto.ca/AllocatingGHGReductions2013/docs/AllocatingGHGReductions2013.pdf.

Macdonald, S. and R. Keil. 2012. "The Ontario greenbelt: Shifting the scales of the sustainability fix?" *Professional Geographer* 64(1): 125–45.

MacLeod, G. and M. Jones. 2007. "Territorial, scalar, networked, connected: In what sense a regional world?" *Regional Studies* 41(9): 1177–91.

———. 2011. "Renewing urban politics." *Urban Studies* 48(12): 2443–72.

Markusoff, J. 2009. "No agreement over growth plan." *Calgary Herald*. June 13. http://forum.skyscraperpage.com/showthread.php?t=170246.

Massot, E. 2013. "Rocky View's debt still needs investigation." *County News*. October 14. www.countynewsonline.ca/2013/10/14/opinion-18/.

———. 2014. "Wastewater system not financially sustainable: Official." *County News*. February 17. www.countynewsonline.ca/2014/02/17/news-26/.

McCann, E. and K. Ward, eds. 2011. *Mobile urbanism*. Minneapolis: University of Minnesota Press.

Miller, B. 2013. "Spatialities of mobilization: Building and breaking relationships." In W. Nicholls, B. Miller, and J. Beaumont, eds., *Spaces of contention: Spatialities and social movements* (285–98). Surrey, UK, and Burlington, VT: Ashgate.

Miller, B. and A. Smart. 2011. "'Heart of the new west?' Oil and gas, rapid growth, and consequences in Calgary." In T. Hutton, L. Bourne, and J. Simmons, eds., *Canadian urban regions: Trajectories of growth and change* (269–90). Oxford: Oxford University Press.

———. 2012. "Ascending the main stage? Calgary in the multilevel governance drama." In R. Young and M. Horak, eds., *Multilevel governance of Canadian cities* (26–52). Montreal and Kingston: McGill-Queen's University Press.

Miller, B. and W. Nicholls. 2013. "Social movements in urban society: The city as a space of politicization." *Urban Geography* 34(6): 1–22.

Molotch, H. 1976. "The city as a growth machine: Toward a political economy of place." *American Journal of Sociology* 82(2): 309–32.

Nenshi, N. 2013. "Calgary is being treated like a farm team by Premier Redford." *Calgary Herald*. February 11. www2.canada.com/story.html?id=7947052.

Nicol, L. 2013. *Water and city-regionalism: Discourse, power and hidden dynamics*. Unpublished doctoral dissertation, Department of Biosystems and Biodiversity, University of Lethbridge. 283 pages.

Niedt, C. and M. Weir. 2010. "Property rights, taxpayer rights, and the multiscalar attack on the state: Consequences for regionalism in the United States." *Regional Studies* 44(2): 153–65.

Parker, R. 2005. "Calgary: A uni-city at 50 years." *Plan Canada* 45 (autumn): 29–31.

Pastor, M., C. Benner, and M. Matsuoka. 2009. *This could be the start of something big: How social movements for regional equity are reshaping metropolitan America*. Ithaca: Cornell University Press.

Peck, J. and A. Tickell. 1994. "Searching for a new institutional fix: The after-fordist crisis and the global-local disorder." In A. Amin, ed., *Post-Fordism* (280–315). Oxford: Blackwell.

Phelps, N. and A. Wood. 2011. "The new post-suburban politics? *Urban Studies* 48(12): 2591–610.

Rosol, M. 2013. "Vancouver's "eco-density" planning initiative: A struggle over hegemony?" *Urban Studies* 50(11): 2238–55.

Sancton, A. 2000. *Merger mania: The assault on local government.* Montreal and Kingston: McGill-Queen's University Press.

Stone, C. 1989. *Regime politics: Governing Atlanta, 1946–1988.* Lawrence: University Press of Kansas.

Swyngedouw, E. 1996. "The city as hybrid: On nature, society and cyborg urbanisation." *Capitalism, Nature, Socialism* 7(2): 65–80.

Tretter, E. 2013. "Contesting sustainability: 'SMART' growth and the redevelopment of Austin's Eastside." *International Journal of Urban and Regional Research* 37(1): 297–310.

Ward, K. and A. Jonas. 2004. "Competitive city-regionalism as a politics of space: A critical reinterpretation of the new regionalism." *Environment and Planning A* 36(12): 2119–39.

Weadick, G. 2014. "Letter from the Minister of Municipal Affairs to Barry Williamson, Chair, Calgary Regional Partnership." May 14. www.calgaryregion .ca/crp/calgary-regional-partnership0/Newsroom/overview.html.

While, A., A. Jonas, and D. Gibbs. 2004. "The environment and the entrepreneurial city: Searching for the 'urban sustainability fix' in Manchester and Leeds." *International Journal of Urban and Regional Research* 28(3): 549–69.

———. 2010. "From sustainable development to carbon control: Eco-state restructuring and the politics of urban and regional development." *Transactions of the Institute of British Geographers* 35(1): 76–93.

Young, D. and R. Keil. 2010. "Reconnecting the disconnected: The politics of infrastructure in the in-between city." *Cities* 27(1): 87–95.

CHAPTER 12

Provincial Distrust Weighs on Vancouver's Regional Governance

Emmanuel Brunet-Jailly and Ève Arcand[1]

Introduction

THE GLOBALIZATION of trade has brought an irreversible change in urban regions. For the last twenty years, they have been understood as areas of production and wealth creation, which in turn has driven a worldwide process of increased urbanization and concurrent labour migration. Although urban regions take varied forms in different countries, the literature points to similar sets of issues: the loss of natural areas, the increase of motorized transportation networks, the increase in social inequity. These challenges contribute to a debate regarding the best modes of municipal and regional government.

Some scholars point to the importance of region-wide cooperation and collaboration to foster sustainable forms of social and economic growth, while others argue that region-wide municipal competition serves best worldwide regional economic competitiveness.

Over the last century a number of views have informed the discussion on the form of government an urban region should take. The Old Regionalism defended elected and effective government, which the public choice criticized by arguing that larger government is inefficient, and that small is beautiful and efficient.

Since the 1990s, metropolitan discussions have raised ideas of regionalisms associated with the emergence of a new wave of studies and public policy ideas, sometimes referred to as the "new regionalism." These discussions emerged in the context of questioning the welfare state and its ability to meet the needs of society (Delorme 2005; Keating 1991; Sassen 1996).

In Canada, the works of Andrew Sancton and Robert Young (2009) point to the "foundational" system that forms Canadian governance: they argue that what is foundational is made up of provincial-municipal governance systems where municipalities and local governments implement provincial policies. Particularly interesting is the work of Smith and Stewart (2009), who detail how British Columbia has traditionally favoured the efficiency side of the efficiency-accountability equation (as described in chapter eight of Peter Self's 1977 work). They note that since 2001 the provincial government, with its *Community Charter* (2004) and *Local Government Act* (2008), has persisted in discouraging local democratic practices in a province that traditionally discounts democratic accountability (electoral finance controls, ward systems, result reporting, and oversight) in favour of structural mechanisms that promote efficiencies in governance and policy-making and implementation (Berger 2004). The view, however, that municipalities were "democratically elected, autonomous, responsible and accountable level of government," as stated in the Community Charter (2003), is balanced with the view that the province cannot allow one large "municipality to hold up the provincial interest" (UBCM 2008).

All in all, the literature discusses the rise of urban regions as spaces of increased democracy, civil engagement, and solidarity; however, in the specific case of Vancouver, British Columbia, there is one singular issue that needs notice: the important role of the relationship between urban[2] and provincial governments, and, the clear distrust of the superior provincial government. This is illustrated in this chapter, which, drawing on both secondary sources as well as semi-structured elite interviews with stakeholders in planning, public transportation, and housing, details how, over the last fifteen years, the distrust of the provincial government has undermined local pan-regional attempts of coordination and collaboration in the area of transportation. This in turn allowed the province to influence fundamentally the regional governance of planning and housing. Although it led to strong protests, and to the rise of regional political awareness, local policy choices and democracy were undermined at the regional level. While citizen groups and community and municipal officials ended up having little political clout, the power of key provincial political and economic players, on the contrary, swelled despite local political protests.

This chapter first reviews briefly the national, provincial, and regional contexts before discussing ideas of new regionalism as applied to the Vancouver region.

Canadian, Provincial, and Regional Context of Metro Vancouver

In Metro Vancouver, as is documented in this section of the chapter, region-wide issues face two related fundamental weaknesses: (1) the mechanism of democratic representation at the regional level is indirect; municipally elected and regionally appointed officials represent their constituencies on a regional board, not a council, hence weakening the regional level, which in turn (2) undermines the political and financial capacity of the regional level. This system limits the power of the regional level in favour of the fragmented local and provincial levels asymmetrically, while strengthening the influence of provincial choices over those of a structurally divided region. Following a presentation of the regional district system of British Columbia, the next two sections focus on Metro Vancouver's planning, transportation, and housing, detailing the above argument.

British Columbia is one of ten Canadian provinces (and three territories) that have exclusive authority regarding the organization of their local government systems. Today, the federal level of government has great interest in local government affairs and has been active, in particular over the last twenty years, in areas such as local environmental, energy, sustainability, and transportation issues that affect cities and rural communities. However, while the federal government does not have *direct* constitutional authority, provinces do.

Despite this constitutional fragmentation of federal authority, however, a broad overview across Canadian provinces and territories indicates that municipalities in particular provide similar core services to their communities. These vary marginally, but most municipalities provide services such as policing, fire protection, planning and building regulation, waste collection, and water distribution. Most also fund transportation services. But in some provinces municipal services include health, social, and education services. For instance, in Ontario, municipalities administer health services and manage social housing.

In British Columbia, a province of about 4.5 million people, 160 municipalities provide the bulk of local services, and interestingly, in many instances, since 1967, have federated themselves into regional districts (RDs)—a form of regional government that is at the core of this chapter. However, these regional districts have not been designed by provincial edicts. Indeed, municipalities in British Columbia came into being because of what Brian Walisser (2010: 20), a provincial official, calls an "empty vessel."

These "empty vessels" were de facto legal frameworks. Originally these stated nothing about who should partner with whom and did not decide which services the resulting bottom-up federated regional government would provide. The primary characteristic of all "empty vessels" or RDs was that their size and functions would result from negotiations between neighbouring municipalities. Negotiators had to decide collectively to work together across the territories of their municipal boundaries and according to a variable geometry of functions or services that were also negotiated and that varied according to local needs. These two fundamental axes of negotiations organized both territorial and service partnerships across federated municipal systems.

Today all twenty-seven RDs stem from such federations of municipalities. The RDs provide the structure for mechanisms of inter-municipal service provisions. They also offer a forum where rising issues can be discussed on a region-wide basis, and in the least populated areas they provide democratic forms of representation: local elections. These are areas with no formally established municipalities. The districts vary significantly in size, population, and function: The smallest one is less than 2000 square kilometres in size, whereas the largest one is 120,000 square kilometres (i.e., four times the size of Belgium). Similarly, the largest in population serves 2.4 million people, while the ten smallest ones in population serve no more than 40,000 people combined. Yet, all in all, these twenty-seven federated urban and rural regions administer well over 3,000 municipal service agreements.

It is because of this rather singular background that the Vancouver region is particularly interesting: it is the most populous of all the federated agreements and it has been in place for nearly a half century. It is large enough to overshadow provincial politics when issues pertaining to the region of Vancouver are front-and-centre in the media. The latest such example would be the 2010 Olympic Games, which grew from being a local initiative to being a provincial affair (Brunet-Jailly 2014).

Yet it is also a complex system of governance where municipally elected and appointed officials meet to discuss region-wide issues. Regional District officials are not directly or even indirectly elected, but chosen to represent their municipalities according to the issue at stake on the RD board. Indeed for Walisser, Paget, and Dann, regional districts are an *ideal* mechanism to "cope with complex, divisive issues at a regional scale" where mutual interests conflict with particular interests, and where scale is also never set because it varies and is in flux, depending on interests and functions or services at stake (transportation or water provision having vastly different scales than police or health service provisions, for instance). And, because most traditional forms of government or governance simply do not match the reality of urban and rural regions, RDs, according to Walisser et al., are the best possible answer because they marry successfully scale and efficiency of service delivery, hence providing the best level of services at the lowest possible price, while providing regional communities with effective forms of political representations. For instance, they point to the Vancouver region, also called the Low Mainland of British Columbia, as a typical example where there are "75 relatively autonomous bodies contributing to the governance of two regions,"[3] and thus suggest that regional districts are the best system of regional governance worldwide.

Planning and housing policies across the Vancouver region have been contentious for many years, particularly over the last ten years due to tensions between provincial and municipal levels of government that have greatly affected local transportation choices (detailed in the second part of this chapter) and are now affecting relationships between municipalities across the Vancouver region and lower mainland and with the provincial government. Local commentators have argued that Metro had to submit to provincial choices through the use of transportation policy choices to bend local/municipal choices to both provincial and business preferences (Shaw 2008; Murphy 2009, 2010).

Metro Vancouver, which used to be called Greater Vancouver or the "Greater Vancouver Regional District" (GVRD), is a service provider district. Historically, it took care of major policy issues, such as the drainage of the Fraser River to prevent flooding in the lower part of the Fraser Valley. In Vancouver, districts were in charge of a few clear policy areas on behalf of a few municipalities that had agreed to federate their resources to address issues too large to handle alone.

Today, Metro Vancouver (officially since 2007) federates three districts and one corporation: the Greater Vancouver Regional District (GVRD, created in 1967), the Greater Vancouver Sewerage & Drainage District (GVS&DD, set in 1914), the Greater Vancouver Water District (GVWD, founded in 1924), and the Metro Vancouver Housing Corporation (MVHC); these are also managed by their specific boards. There are other similar districts in the region, for instance, the Lower Mainland Region, the Westminster Land District, and the Fraser Valley Health Authority that manages large health infrastructures. School districts, although distinct, manage the primary, middle, and high schools.

Metro Vancouver is in charge of a much larger number of policy arenas: water, liquid waste, and solid waste remain, but newer responsibilities are taking more political importance. These include housing, regional planning, air quality, Regional Park, and the district corporation. In all, it is a large area spanning nearly 2,800 square kilometres (1,120 square miles), the most densely populated region in British Columbia and the third largest urban region in Canada. Ultimately, Metro Vancouver is a federation of municipal-district-utilities and their constituent municipalities. The role of the federal level, therefore, is to see that the regional level produces and distributes the services necessary across all member municipalities; its history is important in this regard because without floods and other waste issues the very existence of the districts could be in question. The GVRD charter sets a few key roles: to ensure financial sustainability, to align local and regional priorities, and to be particularly inclusive by increasing region-wide citizen awareness of the services provided by Metro, but also to lobby all other governments likely to partner with Metro; hence, to communicate effectively.

In 2014, the decision-making authority of Metro, still legally called the Greater Vancouver Regional District, is a board of forty representative members representing twenty-four local authorities (twenty-two local municipalities, one township, and one First Nation) but each member's power is proportional to the population they represent. The formula is one vote per 20,000 inhabitants up to five votes. In total, the board shares 136 votes to work together and to provide a number of services, and also provide park services for a twenty-fifth local government, the municipality of Abbotsford.

The municipality of Vancouver remains the largest of all with about 610,000 inhabitants, while both Burnaby (250,000) and Surrey (470,000) are also important. The smallest are the villages of Lions Bay and Belcarra, and the First Nation of Tsawwassen. The fastest growing may be Richmond in the Greater Vancouver Airport area, with a population of nearly 200,000. Interestingly, there are seventeen First Nations, or about 7,600 First Nations people, that are within the district boundaries but do not take part in the district policies, yet are likely to be affected by its decisions. There are a few areas that are not part of Metro Vancouver but work with the district tourism promotion policies despite being part of the Fraser Valley district: Abbotsford, Chilliwack, Mission.

Metro Vancouver is a relatively small bureaucracy, located in Burnaby, of about 1,300 staff headed by a chief administrative officer. It spends 84% of its resources on water, and on liquid and solid waste. Metro Vancouver has eight key departments that develop policy in the following areas: communication and external outreach, human resources, corporate services, finance and housing, liquid waste and solid services, water services and planning, policy and environment. These also include managing the 9-1-1 emergency service across the region and the electoral area as well. In brief, Metro provides region-wide services, and also a number of local services in specific areas of the region that are not incorporated into municipalities.

As for water, Metro Vancouver controls the Cleveland dam and manages the Capilano, Seymour, and Coquitlam reservoirs, and is able to deliver efficient, sustainable drinking water to a 2,600-kilometre-square area. Regarding waste, Metro Vancouver administers the sewers and pump stations that drain refuse waters from around the region as well as all the solid wastes, which go to the Ashcroft Manor Ranch landfill. Another more recent but very important part of its activities includes managing the Vancouver Housing Corporation, whose goals are to develop policy to address housing issues in the region, in particular for homeless and low-income individuals.

Other areas of policy include (1) the promotion of a regional agricultural strategy to produce sustainable and affordable food in the region; (2) the implementation of a regional Ecological Heath Action Plan; (3) the improvement of air quality in the region, and the limiting of the region's contribution to climate change in particular with the implementation of the Integrated Air Quality and Greenhouse Gas Management Plan; and (4) the preservation and conservation of twenty-two parks and nature reserves that primarily focus on maintaining their native plant population and the original ecosystems found, for instance, in regional rainforests and bogs. Metro Vancouver is also implementing a Corporate Climate Action Plan, for which the ultimate goal is "carbon neutrality" and "resiliency" across all its infrastructures, by increasing usage of renewable energy and lowering energy consumption (Metro Vancouver 2011a).

Metro Vancouver also has expertise in regional planning. As such, it is responsible for developing the regional growth strategy (Regional Growth Strategy), a function that has developed progressively since 1914, was prominent in the 1970s, was partially lost in the 1980s, and reasserted in the 1990s when the GVRD managed the emergence of a Livable Region Plan called Choosing Our Future. At the time it was perceived as a "real achievement to have reached such a regional 'policy consensus'" (Oberlander and Smith 1993: 365). The latest version is nearing region-wide adoption, a process that started with rolling ten-year plans in 2009 and has continued yearly since then. Today, Langley Township is the only RD member that does not have agreement for its "Regional Context Statement," a requirement to get its official community plan and then zoning bylaw development permits approved. A court ruling in favour of Langley Township argued that Metro did not have the right to dictate land use to a municipality, but Metro appealed. It seems the regional growth strategy process has been burdened with legal reservations because many landowners and other stakeholders are concerned at some of the predicted outcomes.

The regional plan assumes a population growth of 600,000 and concurrently about 550,000 new homes, but Metro Vancouver's strategy is seeking to limit sprawl regionally with the implementation of urban containment boundaries and a goal to have 55% of region-wide residents living within walking distance of transit. Indeed, this current exercise is controversial but includes interesting key elements: to develop a compact urban area, sustainable transportation system, and regional economy while developing complete communities and environmental and climate change policies.

Historically, this is the most ambitious planning exercise and regional growth strategy, its goal being to coordinate all its members' plans and to replace the "Livable Region Strategic Plan" with "Metro Vancouver 2040—Regional Growth Strategy" and "Transport 2040: A Transportation Strategy for Metro Vancouver—Now and In the Future." The coupling of both plans drew criticisms because of the imbalanced relationship these imply at a time when Metro municipalities have lost control over TransLink, the body that plans and implements public transportation across the region. Some of the criticisms include the following: (1) Both plans were drafted in parallel but with transportation heavily influenced by the provincial view that it should be funded by private sector real estate investments—following Hong Kong's model. (2) The role of Metro regarding green zones would be lessened. (3) Metro would have historically higher levels of control over municipal Official Community Plans. (4) Concurrently, TransLink would see its influence over land use increase through its review of (a) the Regional Growth Strategy and Regional Context Statements, and its primary role in Frequent Transit Development Corridors. (5) A Translink mandate to funnel real estate development funds. (6) The "Renewable Energy Generation" is deemed unsustainable (Murphy 2010).

In conclusion, it is clear that there are backlashes in Vancouver in areas that would be the most affected by the plan: Grandview-Woodland, Downtown Eastside, or Marpole, and across some municipalities such as Burnaby, Coquitlam, Delta, Langley Township, or Surrey. Yet very few groups were able to agree on a process that is primarily driven by provincial views of what Metro Vancouver should look like, as our review of Metro transportation planning demonstrates.

Public Transportation Planning in Metro Vancouver

For the last twenty years, a central goal of Metro Vancouver has been to ensure development and transportation while favouring car reduction. One public policy instrument for the management of all transportation networks was Translink, a multi-modal agency that managed flows across the Metro region thanks to a comprehensive strategy (TransLink 2008). Recently, as detailed below, the local-regional-provincial partnership that sustained Translink, however, resulted in the seizure of the mass-transit project by the provincial government. Indeed, it is the South Coast British Columbia Transportation Authority (SCBCTA), also known as TransLink, that provides public transportation services to the region. Founded in 1999, it is a regional body that covers the Metro Vancouver area. It mandates that regional plans must be established over twenty years and must be renewed every ten years. TransLink implement a multi-modal transportation strategy because it has the responsibility to plan and manage all modes of public transportation: The transportation system "core" is a light rail, called SkyTrain, a technology developed by Bombardier. In addition, there is a large network of buses, a commuter train serving the metropolitan area, and a sea shuttle service, called SeaBus, that crosses the Burrard Inlet and connects downtown Vancouver with its North Shores.

Across Metro Vancouver, the coordination between land use and planning of public transportation takes a Transit-Oriented Development (TOD) planning form along the corridors and around SkyTrain stations. Indeed, it is enough to ride the SkyTrain to witness how much the implementation of the rapid light rail system has impacted the location of new office, housing, and business projects. Several high-density residential towers are located along and around SkyTrain stations and many are still under way, and despite an increasingly significant supply, demand does not seem to have run out. It is noteworthy that these efforts seem to have begun to reduce car use, in particular home-to-job commutes. Indeed, according to one interviewee, since 2007 there has been a marked increase in the occupancy rate of office space along the SkyTrain corridor, while areas less well served by public transportation show slower growth rates.

TransLink has also created a division dedicated to improving the linkages between planning and transportation. Because municipal planning is required to acknowledge Metro's Regional Growth Strategy, TransLink produced a good practice guide outlining the principles of Transit Oriented Communities (TOC), a variant of the TOD. The zoning plans of municipalities are subject to their recommendations as outlined in the guide (TransLink 2011).

Interviews suggest that the limited number of stakeholders in development planning, and planning of public transportation, facilitates the coordination of development and transportation policies across Metro. For example, in public transportation matters, the limited number of organizations facilitates the standardization of user fees across the region. In addition, the multi-modal responsibility of TransLink promotes a holistic approach to the mobility of people and goods across the region. In addition, the small number of organizations reduces issues of overlapping jurisdictions, such as those found between TransLink and BC Transit, the agency responsible for public transit in British Columbia outside the Metro area.

Where good relations between the players at the metropolitan level appear to facilitate a local-regional-territorial integration of development and transportation processes, relations between the metropolitan and provincial levels, however, have not been simple in recent years. One illustration of their difficulties is found in the conflict that arose before and during the construction of the Canada-line, the most recent SkyTrain line, which connects the city of Richmond, Vancouver International Airport, and the City of Vancouver (RAV). This project began in the early 2000s.

In the context of increased traffic congestion, development of environmental awareness, and the competitive bid to hold the 2010 Winter Olympic Games, Vancouver mayor Larry Campbell's campaign platform included plans to strengthen transit between the municipalities of Vancouver and Richmond. At that time, several projects to improve the network were being looked at by TransLink, such as the "Broadway Corridor" or the "Coquitlam line." However, thanks to specific funding sources the RAV line took priority. Indeed, the project, estimated at $1.9 billon, was made possible through a partnership between the federal government, the provincial government, the Greater Vancouver Regional District, and Vancouver International Airport. These stakeholders, however, bypassed local-municipal and pan-regional views in this process.

The project divided municipal officials within Metro. On one hand, several elected officials considered other SkyTrain extension projects much more important and profitable. For instance, according to an analysis based on potential traffic, Coquitlam (a suburb east of the city of Vancouver) was deemed more profitable. Others suggested that the increasing role of the private sector in public transportation was affecting Translink's decision-making, and feared its interference in TransLink affairs. Moreover, other elected officials encouraged the use of public–private partnerships and suggested that TransLink be managed "like a business" (Siemiatycki 2005). The "pros RAV" and "against RAV" then engaged in a struggle that confronted political municipal, provincial, and federal officials, or private sector and technical/engineering points of views. For instance, some underscored that the conditions set by the private sector contractor guided the entire project toward a SkyTrain technology, while other, less expensive options already subjected to TransLink reviews were not successful (Siemiatycki 2006).

Following months of negotiations on the role and responsibilities of the parties involved, the project was finally submitted to Metro Vancouver (the GVRD board) in May 2003. After the longest and most heated council meeting in its thirty-seven years of existence, the project was approved by a single vote (Siemiatycki 2005). The RAV was then submitted again for funding approval to TransLink's board. That board, comprising mayors of municipalities, rejected the project seven votes to five.

Transportation Minister Kevin Falcon, the most ardent defender of the RAV line, then agreed to increase the funding responsibility of both the province and the private sector. The project was then submitted less than a month later for a second time to TransLink, which rejected it again because elected officials considered the project too expensive. Furious with the directors of TransLink, Falcon nevertheless agreed to again raise the provincial contribution to sixty-five million dollars. "The final offer" of the RAV project was then submitted for a third time to the TransLink board in December 2004 and accepted by a majority of eight to four.

The debate about the RAV line considerably weakened TransLink's image and greatly damaged relations between its managers and the Ministry of Transportation. In March 2006, Minister Falcon punished TransLink with the implementation of a "TransLink Governance Review Panel." This was hardly a veiled response to TransLink's second negative vote. Indeed, Falcon declared that the directors of TransLink should have to live with the consequences of their actions (Mickleburgh 2004).

The three persons on the TransLink Governance Review Panel were to undertake a review of TransLink's governance model. More specifically, they were to consider in detail (1) the division of responsibility and control between the province and TransLink transportation issues in the metropolitan region; (2) the size, composition, and appointment process to the TransLink board; (3) the responsibilities, authority, and powers of the GVRD within the *Greater Vancouver Transportation Authority Act*;

(4) the responsibilities, authority, and powers of TransLink to set up income levels for all service provision and capital usage; and (5) how to ensure that the government would effectively contribute to the oversight of TransLink in case decisions affected provincial interests.

According to their report, submitted in January 2007, the Working Group believed that the current governance of TransLink did not exceed the vision of local elected officials (TransLink Governance Review Panel 2007). Thus it made three main recommendations: first, the group recommended the transfer of day-to-day management of TransLink to a board of directors composed of non-elected members; second, it recommended the creation of a council of mayors that would be responsible for approving the budget, for selecting the members of the board of directors, and for approving the transportation plan; third, it recommended the establishment of an independent commissioner to review TransLink's business conduct. The commissioner would be appointed by the Council of Mayors and be responsible for approving fee increases and ensuring the transparency of the organization to the public.

An informal appropriation of public transit by the provincial government followed. The new form of governance, as proposed by the Working Group, received provincial approval in the form of Bill 43. Since the review and implementation of Act 43, stakeholders have raised concerns, arguing that the law marked a steep increase in the influence of the private sector in transportation and was a major blow to democracy (Luba 2007; Kadota 2010; Brunet-Jailly 2014). In fact, Act 43 breaks both accountability and transparency linkages that elected officials provided. As one interviewee told us, "This means that we now have a situation where we have local and regional legislation and no representation ... the link to the people that we elect and the way the money is being spent has been broken ... it is clearly taxation without representation."

The majority of stakeholders interviewed argued that TransLink decisions were now made behind closed doors. Indeed, local officials have little control over how money is spent by TransLink, but they must comply. For example, they are forced to accept increases in property taxes to fund TransLink projects.

As a result of the review of TransLink, technical coordination between TransLink and municipalities has become much more difficult. Traditionally, coordination was partly provided by the Major Road and Transportation Committee, a metro scale committee of municipal engineers that met on a monthly basis. In the past, this committee made recommendations on decisions before they were presented to TransLink board of directors. However, since the implementation of the new governance, the Major

Road and Transportation Committee has received clear instructions that it will now be informed of decisions and be asked to provide feedback that is thought to have little impact on final decisions.

To sum up, in the Greater Vancouver area there was a will to ensure the integration of both development and transportation mechanisms that would favour the reduction of car usage. Because of the relatively small number of organizations involved in the area, coordination seemed effective. During the late 1990s, an important success factor was the establishment of TransLink, a multi-modal agency aimed at providing the metropolitan area with a strong body able to significantly improve transportation flow thanks to a comprehensive strategy bringing together both planning and transportation requirements for the Metro region (TransLink 2008). Elected mayors sat on the TransLink board and brokered integrated planning and transportation decisions regionally. However, a major difference between local, municipal, and provincial officials about the pre-2010 Olympic Games construction of the Canada Line (RAV) resulted in an informal appropriation by the province of the mass-transit project.

Conclusion

The metropolitan experience in the lower mainland of British Columbia documents how Metro Vancouver struggles with provincial distrust. The provincial government's balanced policies of recognition of the role of municipalities in the intergovernmental architecture of Canada do not extend to the ability to work with the municipalities of the Vancouver region and Metro Vancouver. This distrust runs so deep as to make provincial politicians well aware of the political cost that the city of Vancouver and the Metro region holds for provincial politics. It results in a weakened metropolitan scale (Kübler and Tomas 2010), which has important negative effects on regional democracy and region-wide planning, housing, and transportation coordination.

Although there is a clear sense that pan-regional coordination is strong and reduces intra-regional economic competition while also increasing environmental and sustainable concerns, for the provincial government, policies that are seen as critical and as driving economic competitiveness also dictate urban transportation and planning decisions. Because cities are the basic unit of the global production system, in British Columbia the provincial government has become the regulatory hand that leads the way, alongside the private sector.

Metro Vancouver is a striking example of North American urban regions where network governance and coordination has not transformed into a space of increased democracy, civic engagement, and solidarity, but remains a space where the regional scale is organized to provide a forum of collaboration for municipalities struggling with issues, and wherever working across the region adds value and is cost effective.

To return to our governance conundrum regarding the form regional governance takes in Vancouver; what our study underscores is that in British Columbia, the continuum of integration is *not* local-regional-horizontal and territorial, but is regional-vertical-intergovernmental and networked. The provincial government's regulatory superiority strengthens both a weak *territorial-but-networked* form of governance, where coordination and partnerships are intergovernmental and networked with a strong presence of the private sector—which is crucial to strengthening the financial and technical views of primary investors.

Notes

1 This chapter is part of the research project "Vancouver World Cities," which began in 2008 with a conference, "Making Vancouver a World City?," and was followed with two workshops in 2010 and 2011 held in Grenoble, France, and Vancouver, BC. A number of publications share in part the data and analyses discussed here. For instance, a chapter in French in Arcand (2016); Brunet-Jailly (2016) reviews the post–2010 Olympic Games' Campbell legacy; Brunet-Jailly (2014) underscores the lack of political representation of poor and street people in Vancouver.
2 This chapter differentiates urban from local and municipal governments. Urban refers to what is not rural. A local government is a generic term that defines an organization servicing an area or territory. Local governments include municipalities and districts. Municipalities are incorporated and elected bodies that democratically represent and provide a multitude of services to that population and territory. Districts are not elected bodies; they are understood as utilities or functional local governments often providing one, at most two, services to their members. In British Columbia districts federate municipalities that agree to share a service.
3 Walisser et al. cite thirty municipalities, twelve first nation governments, three regional districts, and thirty-six functional regional and subregional entities such as hospitals, economic development bodies, school districts, and others.

References

Agence métropolitaine de transport. 2012. *L'Agence métropolitaine de transport.* Accessed April 10, 2013. http://www.amt.qc.ca/agence/.
Arcand, E. and E. Brunet-Jailly. 2016. "Planification et participation à Vancouver." In M. Gariepy et O. R. Baillargeon, eds., *Gouvernance et Planification Collaborative.* Montréal: Presses de l'Université de Montréal.
Bish, R. L. 1971. *The public economy of metropolitan areas.* Chicago: Markham/Rand McNally.
Brenner, N. 2002. "Decoding the newest 'metropolitan regionalism' in the USA: A critical overview." *Cities* 19(1): 3–21.

Berger, T. 2004. "A city of neighbourhoods: Report of the 2004 Vancouver Electoral Reform Commission." *City of Vancouver.* Accessed July 2013. www .city.vancouver.bc.ca/erc/.

Burdett, R. and P. Rode. 2007. *The endless city.* London: Phaidon.

Burdett, R. and D. Sudjic. 2011. *Living in the endless city.* London: Phaidon.

Brunet-Jailly, E. and J. Martin, eds. 2010. *Local government in a global world.* Toronto: University of Toronto Press.

Brunet-Jailly, E. 2011. "Metropolitan cooperation, theory and practice." *Regions & Cohesion* 1(1): 78–100.

———. 2014. "Participation of the urban poor in Vancouver, Canada." In A. Sancton and C. Zhenming, eds., *Citizen Participation at the Local Level in Canada and China.* London: CRC Press.

———. 2016. "Vancouver—the 2010 Olympic Games: A mitigated success for Premier Campbell." In T. Summerville and J. Lacharite, eds., *The Campbell Revolution: Power and Politics in British Columbia from 2001 to 2011.* Vancouver: McGill-Queen's University Press.

Champagne, É. 2002a. "L'émergence du nouveau régionalisme aux États-Unis et sa portée sur la réorganisation des pratiques métropolitaines: une étude de cas du nouveau régionalisme dans la région métropolitaine de Baltimore." Études urbaines, Institut national de la recherche scientifique-Urbanisation Culture Société.

———. 2002b. "Le nouveau régionalisme métropolitain aux États-Unis." *Organisations et territoires* 11(3): 111–18.

Collin, J.-P. and M. Tomàs. 2004. "Metropolitan governance in Canada or the persistence of institutional reforms." *Urban Public Economics Review* 2: 13–39.

Delorme, P. 2005. "De L'école de Chicago à l'imaginaire urbain." In P. Delorme, ed., *La ville autrement.* Québec: Presses de l'Université du Québec à Montréal. 9–27.

Dente, B. 1990. "Metropolitan governance reconsidered, or how to avoid errors of the third type." *Governance* 3(1): 55–74.

Florida, R. 2002. *The rise of the creative class.* New York City: Basic Books.

Gilbert, R. and A. Pearl. 2010. *Transport revolutions: Moving people and freight without oil.* Gabriola Island, BC: New Society Publishers.

Gray, A. and B. Jenkins. 1995. "From public administration to public management: Reassessing a revolution?" *Public Administration* 73(73): 85–99.

Gruening, G. 2001. "Origin and theoretical basis of new public management." *International Public Management Journal* 4: 1–25.

Hall, P. 2014. *Good cities, better lives—How Europe discovered the lost art of urbanism.* Oxford: Routledge.

Kadota, P. 2010. *Evolution of regional governance in British Columbia with special focus on the Metro Vancouver Area.* Victoria: University of Victoria.

Keating, M. 1995. "Size, efficiency and democracy: Consolidation, fragmentation and public choice." In D. Judge, G. Stocker, and H. Wollmann, *Theories of Urban Politics* (117–34). London: Sage.

Keil, R, J.-H. Boudreau, P. Hamel, and B. Jouve. 2007. "New state spaces in Canada: Metropolitanization in Montreal and Toronto compared." *Urban Geography* 28(1): 30–53.

Lapsley, I. 2009. "New public management: The cruellest invention of the human spirit?" *ABACUS* 45(1): 1–21.

Luba, F. 2007. "New TransLink board seen as 'erosion of democracy': Power to raise property taxes." *The Province*. November 1.

Metro Vancouver. 2011a. *Metro Vancouver 2040: Creating our future*: Metro Vancouver.

———. 2011b. *Metro Vancouver. About us. FAQ*. Accessed April 12, 2013.www .metrovancouver.org/about/Pages/faqs.aspx.

Mickleburgh, R. 2004. "Vancouver airport link voted down." *Globe and Mail*. June 19. Accessed March 28, 2013.

Ministère des Affaires Municipales et de la Métropole. 2000. *La réorganisation municipale: Changer les façons de faire, pour mieux servir les citoyens*. Montréal: Gouvernement du Québec.

Mintzberg, H. 1996. *Managing government, governing management*. Cambridge, MA: Harvard Business Review.

Mouritzen, P. E. 1989. "City size and citizen's satisfaction: two competing theories revisited." *European Journal of Political Research* 17: 661–88.

Murphy, E. 2009. "Say 'no' to Translink and Metro's Hong Kong model for funding transit." *Straight.com Vancouver's Online Source*. August 9. www.straight .com/news/say-no-translink-and-metros-hong-kong-model-funding-transit.

———. 2010. "Metro Vancouver's new draft regional growth strategy raises concerns." *Georgia Straight.com—Vancouver's Online Source*. January 10. www.straight.com/news/metro-vancouvers-new-draft-regional-growth -strategy-raises-concerns.

Norris, D. 2001. "Prospects for regional governance under the new regionalism: Economic imperatives versus political impediments." *Journal of Urban Affairs* 23(5): 557–71.

Oberlander, P. and P. Smith. 1993. "Governing Metropolitan Vancouver: Regional intergovernmental relations in British Columbia." In D. Rothblatt and A. Sancton, eds., *Metropolitan governance: American/Canadian intergovernmental perspectives*. Berkeley, CA: Institute of Governmental Studies Press.

Ostrom, V., C.M. Tiebout, and R. Warren. 1961. "The organizations of government in metropolitan areas: A theoretical inquiry." *American Political Science Review* 55: 831–42.

Ouellet, M. 2012. "Évaluation de l'intégration 'forme urbaine – transports durables' dans les trois grandes régions métropolitaines canadiennes: nouvelle approche exploratoire." Montréal: Faculté de l'aménagement, Université de Montréal.

Parks, R. B. and R. J. Oakerson. 2000. "Regionalism, localism, and metropolitan governance: Suggestions from the research program on local public economies." *State & Local Government Review* 32(3): 169–79.

Pineault, S. 2000. "Rapports de pouvoir et enjeux métropolitains dans l'agglomération montréalaise, 1920–1961: Les problèmes de l'organisation institutionnelle, de la planification du territoire et du transport des personnes." Quebec City: Institut national de la recherche scientifique.

Sancton, A. 2000. *Merger mania*. Kingston and Montreal: McGill-Queen's University Press.

Sancton, A. 2000. *La frénésie des fusion: une attaque à la démocratie locale.* Westmount: Price-Patterson.

Sassen, S. 1990. *The mobility of labor and capital.* Cambridge: Cambridge University Press.

Sassen, S. 1996. *Losing control? Sovereignty in an age of globalization.* New York: Columbia University Press.

Saunders, D. 2010. *The arrival city: The final migration and our next world.* Toronto: Knopf Canada.

Savitch, H. V and R. K. Vogel. 2000. "Introduction: Paths to new regionalism." *State & Local Government Review* 32(3): 158–68.

Shaw, C. 2008. *Five ring circus: Myths and realities of the Olympic Games.* Gabriola Island, BC: New Society Publishers.

Siemiatycki, M. 2005. "The making of a mega project in the neoliberal city." *CITY* 9(1): 67–83.

———. 2006. "Implications of private–public partnerships on the development of urban public transit infrastructure: The case of Vancouver, Canada." *Journal of Planning Education and Research* 26(26): 151.

Statistiques Canada. 2013. *Municipalités (subdivisions de recensement) les plus populeuses, par province et territoire, 2011.* Accessed April 12, 2013. www12 .statcan.gc.ca/census-recensement/2011/as-sa/98-310-x/2011001/tbl/tbl5-fra .cfm.

Stephens, G. and N. Wikstrom. 2000. *Metropolitan government and governance: Theoretical perspectives, empirical analysis, and the future.* New York: Oxford University Press.

Swanstrom, T. 2001. "What we argue about when we argue about regionalism." *Journal of Urban Affairs* 23(5): 479–96.

Swyngedouw, E. 2004. *Social power and the urbanization of water: Flows of power.* Oxford: Oxford University Press.

Tiebout, C. 1956. "A pure theory of local public expenditure." *Journal of Political Economy* (64): 416–24.

TransLink. 2008. *The road less travelled: TransLink's improbable journey from 1999 to 2008.* Vancouver: TransLink.

———. 2011. *Transit oriented communities: A primer on key concepts.* Vancouver: TransLink.

TransLink Governance Review Panel. 2007. *TransLink governance review: An independent review of the Greater Vancouver Transportation Authority.* Vancouver: Translink.

UBCM (Union of British Columbia Municipalities). 2006. *The first century.* Granville Island: Granville Island Publishing.

———. 2008. *Local government in British Columbia.* Vancouver: UBCM.

Vogel, R. K. and N. Nezelkewicz. 2002. "Metropolitan planning organizations and the new regionalism: The case of Louisville." *Journal of Federalism* 3 (1): 107–29.

Wallis, A.D. 1994. "The third wave: Current trends in regional governance." *National Civic Review* 83(3): 290–310.

Walisser, B. Gary Paget and Michelle Dann. 2013. "New pathways to effective regional governance: Canadian reflections." In G. Sansom and P. McKinley, eds., *New century local government: Commonwealth perspectives.* London: Commonwealth Secretariat.

Wallisser, B. 2010. *Adapting B.C. approach to regional government*. Region #279: 20–23. Accessed July 2014. www.academia.edu/6665146/Adapting _British_Columbias_Approach_to_Regional_Government_Strategies_for _Peripheral_Regions.

Interviews

Simon Fraser University
University of British Columbia
Translink
City of Surrey
City of Burnaby
Better Environmentally Sound Transportation
MetroVancouver
Concert Properties

European Regions

CHAPTER 13

The Global City Comes Home
Internalized Globalization in Frankfurt Rhine-Main

Roger Keil and Christoph Siegl

Introduction

WHILE COMPETITIVENESS is often associated with the creative economy of urban cores, the focus of this chapter is the Frankfurt *urban region* with its growing web of metropolitan governance. Three methodological assumptions anchor our argument: first, uneven and contested economic and demographic growth has characterized many urban regions at least until the onset of the recent global economic crisis; second, this growth takes shape in a new morphological, spatial, scalar, and topological manner which Europeans have begun to recognize as *Zwischenstadt* or In-Between City (Sieverts 2003); and third, the institutional changes triggered by these growth (and shrinkage) dynamics are characterized by intense political conflict and sometimes social struggles over territorial, cultural, and political space. This begs the central question this chapter wants to address: Does the Frankfurt region get established as a political space in which a collective actor forms, or does the region act collectively? By extension, we are asking, is such collective agency well analyzed through the concepts of urban regime and urban growth machine once regionalized? Furthermore, has the politicization that characterized an earlier form of globally oriented growth machine politics in Frankfurt been replaced by an internally recalibrated regionalism that is naturally global and silently depoliticized?

We assess how elite conceptions and actions in Frankfurt are changing with regard to the felt pressures of global competition. The chapter is guided by the hypothesis that after more than three decades of intensive appeals for the globalization of the Frankfurt urban region, there has been a discursive shift in which policy- and decision-makers abandon the global for the regional. Based on a series of interviews with decision-makers in Frankfurt, we argue that today's regional regime in Frankfurt-Rhine-Main has in many ways turned its attention inward. At the same time, the region, while increasingly important as a point or reference and territorial space for the structured coherence of the global city, has been depoliticized. Politically problematic issues tend to be sectoralized and cast in technological terms.

Urban Politics in Frankfurt

In the 1980s, the Frankfurt region was subject to analyses that foregrounded a regime and growth machine approach. "New urban politics" in the 1980s coincided largely with a process of intense restructuring and globalization. In hindsight, it is also clear that the onset of the more-than-public politics of urban entrepreneurialism pioneered at that time carried the seed of neo-liberalization into the "communal" (*kommunal* is "municipal" in German) domain of urban politics. The Wallmann regime in Frankfurt during the 1980s was one of the first neo-liberal urban regimes which, we now understand, played on the entire register between image politics and social exclusion, and predated the iconic urban neo-liberalism of Rudy Giuliani by a decade (Keil and Lieser 1992: 53). This laid the groundwork for a long-term continuity of entrepreneurial governmentalities in the Frankfurt regime (Schipper 2012).

When we speak of a regime in the context of Frankfurt, we have in mind a combination of state-centred actors in the city and the region: regional, industrial, and economic actors, many operating at the global scale; elite organizations at the regional level, such as the chambers of commerce; the special government institutions and committees that run the fairgrounds and airport; and civic organizations, such as the trade unions, the environmental movement organizations, and advocacy associations dealing with immigrant and foreigner issues. These regimes or growth coalitions are different from those found in the United States or even in Canada, as they do not rely to the same degree on a mobilization of private sector actors in pursuit of growth, but more on the institutionalized, or corporatist networks of power in the organized and state-centred capitalism found in Germany, where state strategies have historically played a more central role at all levels of government.

Centred on a core ideological project of global city formation under Christian Democrat mayor Walter Wallmann in Frankfurt—high-rise buildings, investments into the built environment of culture (Museum-sufer) linked to populism and xenophobia—axial master planning under Albert Speer, Jr., the financial industry and the fairgrounds (which pursued spectacular architectural projects with starchitects such as Ungers, Jahn, KPF, and others), and regional economic expansion based on aggressive airport extension, a "growth machine" laid the groundwork for Frank-furt's "maturation" from a national centre of the German economic mir-acle to becoming a central hub of the global financial and producer service industries. The lessons learned from the Wallmann regime were these:

> First, integration of the local, national and global levels of analysis is a pre-condition for an understanding of current processes of world-city for-mation [in Frankfurt].... Second, even though the conservative Wallmann regime helped propel the city into the global age, the mode of political regulation that the conservative regime represented is by no means the only possible one. Both modest and radical reform might be able to modify the "inevitability" of growth, economic development, racism and selective exclusion, local powerlessness, and the fetishism of the urban image.... Thirdly, ... any given system of local regulation, any structured coherence is indeed only a temporary arrangement suffering from a chronic instabil-ity.... Its spatial borders, its class structure, and its economic base are constantly redefined. Local political struggles, moreover, are crucial to this process. Their capacity to impact the formation of the structured coherence of a world-city ranges from the power of transitory or more stable political projects to open attacks on the structures in formation. (Keil and Lieser, 1992: 59–60)

The sweepingly neo-liberal Wallmann regime was replaced by a regime of socio-ecological reform during the 1990s. A social democratic and green municipal government replaced the conservative one in 1989, which was interpreted, at the time, as a shift from the regime of "selective exclu-sion" to a regime of "selective integration" represented by the new "red-green" coalition of social democrats and greens (Keil and Lieser 1992; Ronneberger and Keil 1993; Keil and Ronneberger 1994; Keil and Ron-neberger 2000). While it continued to accept the necessity of globally oriented growth in Frankfurt, there were some significant changes in direc-tion for the local regime. The new red-green government, in particular, embarked on an ambitious project to re-regulate the city's relationships with its regional environment. The core project in this regard was the Frankfurt GreenBelt, which established a real and discursive space of nature conservation around the city and at the border of the booming municipalities in the region (Keil and Ronneberger 1991). During that time, a host of conflicts arose between the inner city and the exurbs, in particular around controversial land-use decisions and "urban" encroachments on the semi-rural periphery (Keil and Ronneberger 1994).

The red-green experiment was replaced in 1995 by yet another regime, one of the first black-green coalitions in a German city between the reascendant Christian Democrats and the Green Party. Mayor Petra Roth, the first directly elected female mayor of any big city in Germany, led a conservative-liberal-green coalition which returned to the traditions of multiparty, not quite non-partisan governance, in Frankfurt that existed before Wallmann's ideological regime in the 1980s. Roth, a politician from the urban fringe of Frankfurt, was successful in playing up her non-elite, peripheral origins and merged populist politics with strong direction in supporting the continuing expansion of Frankfurt's global city ambitions. During her tenure as Mayor, Frankfurt consolidated its position as the leading continental banking centre and as the financial capital of the Eurozone. In 2012, the long mayoral reign of the Christian Democratic Party ended in Frankfurt. Mayor Roth, who had played an active role in regional politics, was succeeded by Social Democrat Peter Feldmann. While Feldmann's new *Magistrat* took a number of steps to differentiate their policies from their conservative predecessors, this was not the case in terms of regional integration.

The political regime transition in Frankfurt since the 1980s sketched in the preceding paragraphs is represented in Table 13.1. It attempts to provide, at a glance, an overview of the political forces that have driven the regime formation. It is, at its core, a political perspective onto complex economic, spatial, and social processes, driven by a dense mesh of social and political agency and situated in the particular historico-geographical constraints of the structured coherence of the Frankfurt region as it responds to and co-produces the globalization processes that have contextualized urban politics everywhere in recent times.

Frankfurt's Global City Status: Not Quite London

Frankfurt's status as one of the major global cities has been noted since the late 1980s both by hyperbolic boosters in the Wallmann regime and by critical researchers who began to apply, first anecdotally and then systematically, the emerging world city paradigm to the German financial capital (see Keil and Ronneberger 2000 for a summary). In recent years, the literature on Frankfurt's global status has concentrated on Frankfurt's status in a network of major international service firms. One of the main issues in global city research has been to explain the relationship of the global network and local concentration. Does one beget the other? For

Table 13.1 Political succession in Frankfurt

Frankfurt Regimes	Mayors	Parties	Discourse	Regime actors	Social struggles
1977–1989	Wallmann-Brück (SPD politicians Hofmann (culture) and Wentz (planning)	CDU (SPD)	Political splits of *Heimat* and World city; Culture and urbanity; High-rise starchitecture; Selective exclusion; neo-liberalism; populism	Global capital, airport, fairgrounds, Local and regional conservatives	Airport expansion; squatting; Deindustrialization, Anti-fascist politics;
1989–1995	Hauff-Schöler (Wentz) (green politicians Cohn-Bendit, Fischer, Koenigs)	SPD-Greens (red-green)	Global city; Selective integration (Office for Multicultural Affairs); Ecological modernization (greenbelt, green high-rise); Administrative reform; Global city goes regional	Social democratic modernizers Social movements; Environmentalists	Struggles over regional expansion; "slaughterhouse" conflict
1995–2012	Roth (Wentz)	CDU-Greens (black-green)	Global city region; Rescaling of planning; Transportation; Housing	Globalized paternalism; Euro-capital	Airport expansion
2012–	Feldmann	SPD (city council majority black-green)	Social equalization, housing, infrastructure development	Reevaluation of scalar relationships of Land, region and city	Airport expansion; Housing, Blockupy, new poverty

Frankfurt, this has been a particularly important question, as the reality of its less than extensive integration into the global city network of firms (compared with competitors such as London or Paris) is compounded by its underdog status in terms of lifestyle and attractiveness advantages.

Frankfurt's global city economy benefits from its multi-layered connectivity globally but also nationally and regionally: the region's polycentricity is clearly a positive locational factor: "Frankfurt's ability to attract globally operating service firms depends not least on the region's capacity to provide a wide range of supportive services that are themselves well embedded within Germany. From this functional service perspective, polycentricity works well for Rhine-Main—but its relational character defies confinement to a territorially bounded space, however fuzzy the delimitations" (Freytag et al. 2006: 170).

Frankfurt Rhine-Main's economic profile suggests that there are at least two interlocking economies at work that feed off each other but are scaled rather differently. There is at one end the globally oriented service industry including, at its centre, finance. And there is, at the other end, a regional economy based on logistics, machine building, the chemical industry, and a service sector that is calibrated to regional and national needs (various interviews with regional planners). Clearly there is much overlap between these two economies, perhaps most obviously in the case of logistics that services and is dependent on the airport, as the most globalized transportation hub of the region, but that also caters to regional and national needs not directly linked to the globalized part of the economy. The *Leitbild* (guiding image) for the regional land-use plan is explicit about what the valued sectors of the economy are: "biotechnology, finance, communication technologies and media, logistics, material technology (*Materialtechnik*), as well as management consulting" (Planungsverband 2005: 5).

A Short History of Regional Governance in Frankfurt Rhine-Main

Metropolitan governance has received increasing attention as cities spill over their traditional political and bioregional boundaries and as urban regions have been structured increasingly as amorphous "in-between cities" (Sieverts 2003) without clear morphological and density delineations that used to be typical of the older separations of suburbs and inner cities. Frankfurt is an important region where to study the governance of the in-between city (Sieverts, 2003). Frankfurt's regional composition makes it a prime example of post-Fordist landscape before the name; old village cores grow out into successful cities and communities of a flexible and suburban age: Eschborn, Kronberg, Oberursel, etc. In another part of the region, old village cores get adorned with a ring of social housing in traditional tower blocs where "ghettos" of immigrants and refugees emerge (Dietzenbach) (Keil and Ronneberger 1994).

Frankfurt Rhine-Main, like most urban regions, has gone through a series of dynamic redefinitions during the past generation (Bördlein 1999). At present, and although most continue to think of the region as a Frankfurt-centric, Hessian metropolitan area, a rather expansive definition has taken hold among policy-makers and planners, which covers a spatial area of more than 13,000 square kilometres and a population of 5.3 million people and which covers territory that extends into Rhineland-Palatinate and Bavaria (Hoyler et al. 2006: 127; based on the Planungsverband 2005). One of the few regions in Germany that has seen continuous economic growth despite large-scale industrial restructuring, Frankfurt Rhine-Main has been under particular pressure to rethink and redo its governance and planning mechanisms. This was enhanced by the perceived and real articulation of the region with the global economy that has often been used as a rationalization for change to the system of territorial and institutional governance. In the 1980s, the City of Frankfurt was tied into a relatively unique system of regional governance through the Umlandverband Frankfurt (ULV), an association of municipal governments in which the central city—with the lion's share of inhabitants and jobs—only had one vote. While the city was the elephant in the room, it was also hampered by that arrangement, which stood in the way of using the ULV as an instrument of its own interests.

During the past two decades, the regional identity and the definition of collective agency in the Frankfurt region went through a series of rescalings. The city-central obsession and the centre–periphery dichotomy of the 1980s were increasingly reframed by the notion of a polycentric metropolitan area wherein Frankfurt was but one (albeit large) and not the only centre of the Rhein-Main region. This characteristic of the Frankfurt region had been recognized in the early global city literature that noted Frankfurt's reliance on regional assets (Lieser and Keil 1988; Keil and Lieser 1992; Keil and Ronneberger 1994; Keil and Ronneberger 2000). The global city went "up the country" (Keil and Ronneberger 1994) and the centre of the city had perhaps moved from the financial core of the CBD to the airport around which a global city economy of a new (flexibilized, post-Fordist, internationalized) type had taken shape.

In the beginning of the 1990s, the chambers of commerce (Industrie- und Handelskammern, or IHKs) of the Frankfurt region coordinated efforts to place Frankfurt/Rhein-Main in an advantageous position in the international interregional competition. In 1991, the IHKs of the region joined together to establish the "IHK-Forum Rhein-Main as an economically oriented regional alliance" (Blatter 2005: 144). At least discursively, this association was successful in upscaling Frankfurt by deploying a "large-scale demarcation of the region ... which transcends boundaries of the *Land* and encompasses next to all of southern Hesse also the regions of Mainz and Worms in Rhineland-Palatinate as well as the Aschaffenburg region in Bavaria" (Blatter 2005: 144–45). This upscaled definition of the region is shared by most powerful actors. It came with a distinctive ideological split in between the central city social democratic position (stressing regional inequities) and the regional elite position (stressing locational competition). Blatter (2005: 145) notes that an association for economic development, Wirtschaftsförderung Region Frankfurt/Rhein-Main e.V., was founded in 1995 as a social democratic counterweight to the conservative IHK-Forum. It remained the only institutional innovation in this area during the decade and ultimately became an attractive instrument of regional economic marketing, although conflicts between local and regional interests remained. The new conservative government at the level of the *Land* after 1999 favoured a "use-centred form of regional cooperation." After 2000, the government introduced legislation to create a regional council (Rat der Region) consisting of members of the cities, communes, and counties that remained politically insignificant. And it established the planning agency Planungsverband Ballungsraum Frankfurt/Rhein-Main out of the disbanded Umlandverband Frankfurt. While geographically expanded, the new entity's portfolio was actually cut, as it was reduced to two spatial planning tasks: regional land-use planning and landscape planning (Blatter 2005: 146; Regional Planning Official, interview with author). The Planungsverband was an institution with limited power, which had to share planning authority with other bodies and did not extend beyond the boundaries of the *Land* Hesse (Hoyler et al. 2006: 128). The Planungsverband Ballungsraum had to be seen in the context of federal and *Land* policy directives such as the Hessian Ballungsraumgesetz of 2001, which was meant to put a temporary end to the regional debate. It was set up to address intermetropolitan competition, to deal with financial equalization between cities and surrounding counties (*Kreise*), and to bring existing administrative structures more in line with emerging problems and challenges of urban and regional governance (interview with former commissioner of regional planning association).

At the same time, the Mayor of Frankfurt conceived the *Regionalkonferenz* of big cities and counties in the region with the stated goal of sharpening the focus of the region's identity and regional agency. These activities by the regional and local states are accompanied by a flurry of "civic initiatives" (Blatter 2005: 146) such as the Wirtschaftsinitative Frankfurt Rhein-Main," which are really attempts by the economic elite, somewhat motivated by a fuzzy form of regional patriotism and philanthropy, to establish a positive image of the region. These initiatives (like for example Metropolitana and regional workshop) aimed at creating a regional identity through iconic projects (*Leuchtturmprojekte*) such as the "tower project," which would symbolically link the region's tall buildings by a laser beam (Blatter 2005: 147; see also Langenhagen-Rohrbach, 2003; Langenhagen-Rohrbach 2005).

In addition to these "civic" activities, "much of the cooperation between Frankfurt and its neighbours [is left to] voluntary inter-municipal arrangements" (Hoyler et al. 2006: 128–29). Partly under pressure of the Hesse *Land* government—which can force communes and cities into partnerships to deal with practical issues such as waste, sewage, water, sports and culture, infrastructure, green space management, marketing and economic development—these arrangements have been more or less institutionalized formally (interviews with former commissioner of regional planning association; associate director, regional planning association). Among those that have created an infrastructure are the Frankfurt Rhein-Main GmbH – International Marketing of the Region and the Kulturregion Frankfurt-Rhein-Main-gGmbH; among those that have been initiated are an agency for transportation management and Regionalpark Rhine-Main. In sum, "the emerging picture is one of a downscaling of political responsibilities from the regional to the municipal level and the reluctant creation of purpose-specific cooperative arrangements with variable membership and only partly overlapping geographies" (Hoyler et al. 2006: 129). There are ongoing attempts to create strategic documents and policies that are directed both at outside effect (identity, marketing, economic development, locational attractiveness) and internal planning coordination among governments and other actors in the region (land-use planning, transportation, green spaces, housing, etc.). One such document is the Strategic Vision for the Regional Land Use Plan and for the *Regionalplan Südhessen*, published in 2005 and used as a discursive bridge between the Planungsverband and the plan-sanctioning Regional Assembly Südhessen of the Regierungsbezirk Darmstadt (Hoyler et al. 2006: 131–32; various interviews with regional planning experts).[1]

Governance in Frankfurt was considered distinct from most other urban regions, as it deals with the consequences of continued growth, which appears both as a metropolitan and central dynamics. Blatter (2005: 143) has used the phrase "paradox and paralyzed forms of governance in globalized urban regions" to describe Frankfurt (and Munich). He is skeptical as to whether the various regional institutions created since the 1990s add up to a powerful set of tools for regional governance and submits that "the situation in the Frankfurt region is characterized by political blockades" (Blatter 2005: 146). He notes that the massive politicization of regional initiatives in Frankfurt-Rhein-Main has led to a flurry of activities but not to a working institution of regional governance. The role of Frankfurt remains critical to all activities and has sometimes regressively recycled notions of regional imperialism more in line with the politics of the early twentieth than the early twenty-first century, when, for example, Frankfurt's Chief Financial Officer floated the idea in 2002 to annex rich suburban cities as a solution to regional governance conundrums (Blatter 2005: 148).

In 2011, the Planungsverband was dissolved, as it was felt that its competencies were too limited and fragmented. It was reborn as the Regionalverband (Regional Authority), a regional institution "responsible for the development of common regional image" (www.region-frankfurt .de). The new authority carried over landscape planning and land-use planning from its predecessor. In contrast to the Planungsverband, it also took on recreation, sports, culture, and place marketing. The financing of cultural institutions and activities remained a central challenge in the work of the new authority. Economic development, planning, and transportation planning were put under the auspices of the Regional Authority. In line with the general trend toward internalized globalization, the new authority was meant to pool "the strengths of the entire region ... to vie with the other metropolitan regions" (www.region-frankfurt.de).

In terms of the changing national planning context for these recent developments in regional governance in Frankfurt, federal spatial planning policy in Germany "moves away from the traditional focus on inter-regional equality and places greater emphasis on strengthening key metropolitan regions." On the basis of this general policy framework, they contend, "political and economic actors in the administratively fragmented polycentric region have produced various contested and geographically divergent regionalizations of Rhine-Main" (Hoyler et al. 2006: 124). And importantly, "the functional diversity and multiplicity of perspectives in Rhine-Main have been reimagined as positive assets in the latest regional strategic policy documents and initiatives" (Hoyler et al. 2006: 124–25). This latter point in particular deserves emphasizing, as it supports the idea that regional political actors can act strategically and collectively despite and even on the basis of a divided or even contradictory set of tactics employed internally or externally. Promotion of polycentricity, then, may

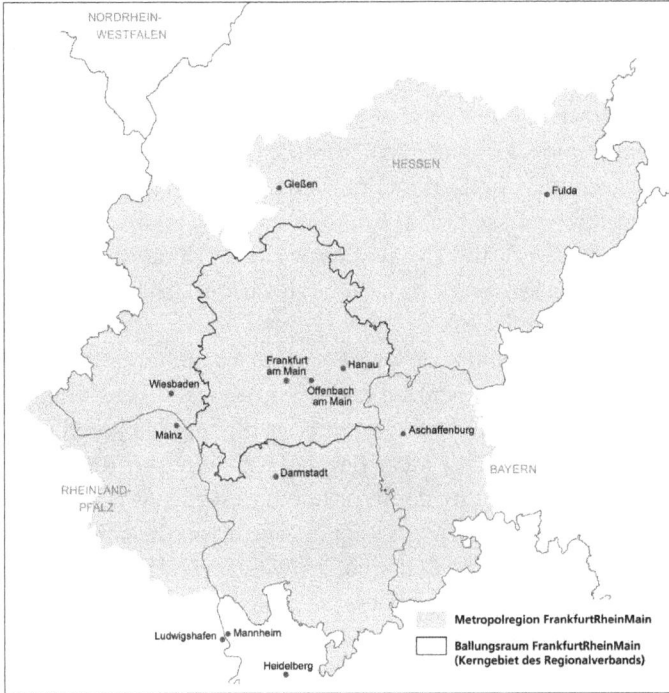

Figure 13.1 Frankfurt. *Source*: https://upload.wikimedia.org/wikipedia/de/0/0eMetropolregion_FRM.jpg. Reproduced with permission.

be a ideal way of driving the interests of Frankfurt Rhine-Main as a region: "Despite its high international visibility, the region remains internally fragmented both politically and administratively and lacks a clear regional identity" (Hoyler et al. 2006: 133). Now regional actors have begun to discontinue their purely externally oriented strategies aimed at world market and global flow integration, and have instead looked at regional diversity as an asset for the structured coherence of the region. The polycentricity of the Frankfurt region (as of any region) is not just visible in the political and planning structures and institutions, but other dimensions and criteria need to be deployed to understand the nature of polycentricity (Fischer et al. 2005: 440). Connectivity between firms and labour markets (commuter streams) are other forms that express the real life of an urban region. The knowledge industry connectivity of cities in the Rhine-Main region is a case in point (Fischer et al. 2005: 445). This characteristic is seen to have mixed results for regional governance that "prevented the development of integrated policies across the [megacity-region]" (Freytag et al. 2006: 170).

At some level, the new regional regime in Frankfurt Rhine-Main constitutes itself as an upscaled machine for boosterism. At another level, it rescales the regional welfare state and system of collective consumption (housing, infrastructure). It also simply acknowledges the expanding regional constitution of the "structured coherence" of the metropolis exactly because the insertion of Frankfurt Rhine-Main into the various streams and flows of the global economy has necessitated and delivered institutional, material, and social infrastructures at the scale of an imagined region (which remains a mixed-bag of various definitions: state, ecology, culture, economy, etc.).

The internal consolidation of the region has its own constitutional effects: the region gets recognized and previously *imagined* boundaries of the growth regime become *firm* boundaries that are anchored in a set of institutions as well as public identities. In fact, Frankfurt Rhine-Main (or whoever might speak for it, claim, or boost it) wants to be recognized as a region in multiple senses: a city-region centred on the core city; an economic region—one seen as dynamic, growing, wealthy, modern, global, etc.; and ecological region—with a set of policies of conservation in place; a cultured region with a distinct "rhine-mainish" identity; and a political and planning region, which has been through a serious of more or less successful attempts—initiated in turn by central, regional or local states and business, civic and environmental groups—to make the region hold together through political reform that creates jurisdictional boundaries and responsibilities that coincide with this or the other economic, social, or environmental need for regulation. The rescaling—regionalization and globalization—of the urban regime was not uncontested, but the basis for intense social, spatial, and political conflict and strong ideological debate. In this sense, Frankfurt Rhine-Main is not much different from other regions (see Painter 2008: 344).

A Regional Politics of Polycentricity: How Far Does the Regime Reach?

Regions have historically answered this question in praxis in very different ways. One central question here is, of course, the very reach, range, and size of the territory that is imagined as the one that needs regulation and governance. The question of how large the Frankfurt region is, for example, has often been posed (Hoyler 2005). But the question does, of course, not just extend to the territorial area that is associated with the region, but also to the relationships through networks and across space in which the region is constituted. In order to secure economic gain sustainably in a "learning region," for example, the guardians of regional governance need to be tied in with higher and lower level decision-makers and need to understand the interlaced relationships of the region as territory with the region as relational construct. At all times, the regime was a multi-scalar arrangement with the federal state (airport) and the *Land* heavily involved in the major decisions affecting the city and the region.

Inside the region, polycentricity is an often-acknowledged condition of governance (Hall and Pain 2006). In the Frankfurt case, polycentricity is official policy and stated objective of almost every published document. In reality, such public doctrine belies the existing dissimilarity of the city of Frankfurt with all other cities and communities in the region, a dissimilarity which has often plagued political institutionalization of regionalism as discussed above. In practical terms, the region has been built from the inside out through the networking of social service provision and economic development as well as political institutions across the always-oscillating territorial image of where Frankfurt Rhine-Main begins and ends.

The consolidation of the regional regime has taken place around a set of infrastructure and service issues. In order to limit the influence of Frankfurt but also to introduce a sense of efficiency into the process of public service provision, the Christian Democratic *Land* government of Hesse with its *Ballungsraumgesetz* introduced a system of organized fragmentation by encouraging communities into voluntarily founding specialized service bodies through which to collaborate on the provision of hard services such as waste removal but even cultural policy (interview with city commissioner finance). The subtext is not just governance reform through technical efficiencies but also neo-liberal state retrenchment in areas that are costly to government. There has been a tradition since the 1970s, but recently supported by *Land* policies, to deal with technical issues of the region through task-specific functional associations (*aufgabenspezifische Zweckverbände*), which since the 1990s have been corporations (Ltd. – GmbH) at arms length from the various levels of the state. Among those have been the Rhein Main transportation authority (RMV), the waste removal agency (Abfall GmbH), and the locational marketing corporation (Standortmarketing GmbH). This has led, in the eyes of one observer, to a "confusing netting of regional and partially regional 'limited companies' with their governing boards and executives" (interview with former commissioner, regional planning association). A Frankfurt politician also reminds us that "the region is not the sum of Ltd. Corporations" (interview with city commissioner, finance). While this is in line with the agglomeration law (*Ballungsraumgesetz*) passed by the *Land*, the law gives no indication of how trans-agency coordination is supposed to be handled. While the *Ballungsraumgesetz* created the conditions for a certain pacification of the highly politicized regional debate in the Frankfurt region, it did not lay to rest issues of intra-regional coordination of service agencies, cost equalization, and social redistribution. In some cases, it actually hid or increased tendencies for socio-economic segregation and differentiation among cities and communities in terms of their ability to sustain required service levels for their populations (schools, eldercare, etc.) (Former commissioner, Regional Planning Association, interview with the author).

All Frankfurt regime politics have been heavily politicized with ideological and tactical consideration front and centre in any definition, conceptualization, and implementation of region and regional policy. In fact, the entire last twenty years are the product of heavily politicized cross-scale manoeuvres, as political parties have moved in and out of local, regional, and federal governments in Frankfurt as well as other cities, Hesse, and Germany.

In the recent round of regionalization, though, political strife has been lower in intensity, as more pragmatic attempts at using the region to "internalize globalization" have been made. As this happens, though, the traditional tension between the tunnel-visioned local politics and the regional problematics in housing, transportation, and environmental protection (e.g., waste) have persisted and even become more pronounced as Frankfurt continues to play its role as the biggest kid in the schoolyard—albeit less aggressively (interview with city commissioner, environment and health).

Regionalism as Internal(ized) Globalization

Today, globalization as a concept or keyword works neither as an unassailable war cry of city boosters, nor as a general stand-in to explain urban change in the critical literature. In the case of Frankfurt, it can be shown that the global has ceased to be a self-explanatory, overarching concept for urban development, and that urban politics has regrouped as a set of functionalist specialty discourses such as that of the creative city. As city politics in the Frankfurt region have increasingly been re-localized, they also became largely devoid of traditional political conflict. Instead, questions of social justice and diversity were partly integrated into the formal and bureaucratic political process in that city. This, of course, did not keep the highly alter-globalization-oriented movement of Blockupy from springing up in the aftermath of the continuing financial and economic crisis in Europe after 2008.

We can characterize Frankfurt Rhine-Main's current philosophy and praxis of regionalism as "internalized globalization." This means in the first place that globalization as a process has been taken for granted, and has been internalized and largely accepted by actors in the regional political process. This is different from the "glocalization" (Swyngedouw 1997) processes of the 1980s and 1990s, when the global had to be first established as a discursive and real space in which cities and communities in the region were operating. But the concept also entails that when globalization is accepted as the general condition of existence for jurisdictions today, the work of globalization is done in and by the local and regional regimes. This is a departure from the frantic attempts of previous years to dress the region up for regional competition (based on the—questionable—assumption that such competition is decided in circuits external to the region). There is now a certain resigned, or relaxed, *Gelassenheit* (equanimity) in the discourse of regionalism in Frankfurt. This shift has been supported by institutional, ideological, and political moves on the regional stage. And it can be traced through political, economic, social, and environmental processes where it has taken hold. It must be added, though, that just as there can never be a fully settled "structured coherence," but rather just a tendency toward structured coherence, inter-municipal and inter-regional competition both at home and in the world never entirely gives way to cooperation. It always exists latently beneath attempts to create a more horizontal and cooperative form of governance in the region.

"Internalized globalization" relies on a few preconditions that were created earlier. During the 1980s and 1990s, the Frankfurt global city region experienced a double opening that facilitates the "internalized globalization" of the region today:

1) the central city economy opened toward the region: the global city went to "the countryside," as its infrastructural functions (airport, water, transportation) extended beyond the political boundaries of the core municipality. In a strange and somewhat unpredictable recent point in that development, even the Frankfurt Stock Exchange, long almost synonymous with the city's financial prowess, moved its main operations to the edge city of Eschborn (Belina 2013; Belina and Lehrer in this volume); and

2) the (generally spoken) global economy: world city formation in Frankfurt was to a large degree a deliberate process set in train by an aggressively internationally oriented regime which intended and went to work integrating Frankfurt into the extant flows of international investment, capital, and service delivery. A recent "think piece" produced for the mayor expresses this well: "The idea of a

NetworkCity Frankfurt Rhine-Main is based on the essential core of the small German *Global City*, which draws its significance in the first place from its integration into international, national, and regional nets. One peculiarity of Frankfurt is that Frankfurt more than other German cities reflects the idea of networking in its built, functional and ideational constitution. The vision of a Network-City concentrates on the positive opportunities for development of Frankfurt in the context of a polycentrally structured region" (AS&P 2009: 15). Frankfurt has long been imagined by both local decision-makers and external analysts as a place of natural conflu-ence of the flows of global network society. In a recent exemplary statement, Hans Joachim Kujath has explained:

> Transaction-networks between select large cities, a global urban network, where knowledge is exchanged in digi-tized form but also in personal contacts during meetings, events and fairs. In these cities, this type of knowledge economy creates for itself high performance *"business districts."* In Germany, above all the *City* of Frankfurt stands for this, which has developed into a globally net-worked transaction centre with the banks, the stock exchange, the Messe and multiple *"business services."* The *City* is marked to a high degree by finance capital, the banks and the great corona of partly globally active service companies. And the city defines itself as a *"trans-action metropolis,"* or as a node in a *"space of flows,"* as Castells has described it. Frankfurt gains its particular image from this unique role (in Germany) as global city in the *"space of flows."* (Kujath 2008: 18, authors' translation)

Municipal and regional politics have been seen as either supportive of or even generative of developments that would facilitate the integration of Frankfurt into those (not always well defined) networks. Some network aspects are taken for granted (the airport, the international fairground, the financial industry, the famous *"Finanzplatz"* Frankfurt), clearly but-tressed by the decision to make the Main metropolis the seat of the Euro-pean Central Bank, which has made the city the core of the Euro financial economy. Interestingly, though, the Bank chose a location quite some distance from the actual financial centre downtown to show its indepen-dence from the commercial banking and financial sector to which Frank-furt has been home.

The multiplicity of Frankfurt Rhine-Main, of its cities and communi-ties, is considered a major strength in the international competition of regions, and regional planning is geared toward supporting the networked division of labour and the "cooperation (*Zusammenspiel*) of all actors" in the region (Planungsverband 2005: 5). The focus is clearly on segmented integration of land uses and people. The region "has always been interesting for people of many nations" and has been "open to the world and liberal." But it is also "family friendly" and strives to present a high quality of life: "culture, urban spaces, recreational areas" (Planungsverband 2005: 5). This and other planning documents play down Frankfurt's centrality. Like the global competition in which the region allegedly finds itself, the core functions of Frankfurt are taken for granted and remain unchallenged. This points to a recalibration of the regime toward an internal process of dialogue and conversation—as well as dispute and conflict—among the 200 cities and communities, and countless civic groups and enterprises, that make up the region's polity. The appeal for unity amidst diversity is the predominant programmatic thread that can be seen throughout documents that deal with regional planning and policy. It can also be heard in the statements, public and private, of regional actors, such as the ones interviewed for this project.

In the area of economic development, which still deals predominantly with the chasing of growth sectors in the regional economy, the perennial discussions of an International Building Exhibition (*Internationale Bauausstellung IBA*) has demonstrated a certain degree of willingness of disparate and often competitive actors in the region to work together in an attempt to create joint projects.[2] An idea floated at the end of 2008, for example, to create a university campus location in the harbour area that connects neighbouring Frankfurt and Offenbach was interpreted by at least one commentator as a sign that the "jealous competitions" among cities and communities from previous years might be overcome to create a new period, when "in the moment of global competition, the times of local rivalries have passed" (Arning 2009: F4). Praising the idea of a "network of knowledge, which unfolds its threads from the harbour between Frankfurt and Offenbach" (ibid.), a local pundit noted at the time the opportunities for regional cooperation which would produce regional cohesion—at least symbolically—first, and global incorporation second. A small caveat is necessary here: While it can be argued that the new Frankfurt regional regime has used the polycentric and diverse structure of the region to forge new alliances, the Offenbach example demonstrates that if one such instance of cooperation sours—as it subsequently did in the Hafen Offenbach case—a rather hierarchical power structure is revealed, with Frankfurt (blaming the Offenbach government for being unprofessional) re-establishing itself plainly as the self-appointed regional leader.

Also, as long as there is no administratively unified region, the competition for taxes remains a main driver in regional conversations, and the long-debated equalization of financing culture in the region between Frankfurt and communities in the periphery remains unresolved. At issue has been the equalization of cultural services. Frankfurt is the sole source of financing for the public theatre (Schauspiel) and the Opera, which are also used to a large extent by people from suburban municipalities. One result has been the creation of the *Kulturfonds* in 2007, which aims at bundling regional cultural and financial resources and to enable cultural megaprojects. This is ostensibly geared toward better positioning Frankfurt in global interurban competition and to increase quality of life in the region (www.kulturfonds-frm.de/).

Some of the reasons for the more relaxed attitude around regionalization are that "internalized globalization" comes with a "natural" division of labour that increases the weight of the centre in Frankfurt Rhine-Main. As elsewhere, the "popular refrain" (*Gassenhauer*) of the creative class determines much of the discourse of regional economic growth in the city and in the region. But the services that support such a class (such as flexible daycare facilities) cannot be found in the small villages and towns of the region, and force this workforce into a central location for work and housing (interview with former commissioner, regional planning association). Moreover, artists and other creatives would not consider moving into the periphery; quite the contrary is true, as Frankfurt suffers a constant exodus of home-bred creatives who move to Berlin when they have the chance (interview with manager, municipal arts project). Similarly, the much-trumpeted "renaissance of the central cities" may be mostly to the benefit of Frankfurt, which sees a resurgence of its inner-city housing areas and re-urbanization of older and wealthier populations (interview with commissioner, regional planning association).

Frankfurt continues to emphasize its place in the globalized region as embedded and localized: "Both the economic orientation and the social reality of the region Frankfurt Rhine-Main are clearly marked as global. At the regional scale, it is even more important what is also true for Frankfurt to a lesser degree: the strength of the internationality must be grounded in place, tied in also into a regionally-oriented ecnmic and service structure, into an old cultural landscape. City and region become liveable (*"lebenswert"*) not predominantly through their international networking but through qualities in situ. This balance between external orientation and inner strength can only be found in the region in a joint effort and in fair cooperation" (AS&P 2009: 14; see also Reiss-Schmitt 2003).

Conclusion

What lessons can be learned from this case study of "internalized global-ization" in Frankfurt Rhine-Main in the context of this book on collective agency? The first finding we can isolate from this particular narrative is that, while there are similar overall conditions (globalization, neo-liberal-ization) under which the problems of regional governance are approached in Germany or elsewhere, there is considerable difference in process and outcome (Blatter 2005; Hoyler et al. 2006). The specific set of political actors and institutions in the Frankfurt region has guided Rhine-Main's insertion into global streams under the guidance of their own ideological, territorial idiosyncrasies. This chapter treated the actors that pursue "internalized globalization" in Frankfurt Rhine-Main as a regionalized growth machine or regional regime. They include state, economic, and civic actors, and they are contested by oppositional forces in and outside the ruling elite alliance. While it will be impossible to derive from the Frankfurt case alone a more general tendency, on the basis of the argument put forth above, it will be possible to ask similar kinds of questions in other local and regional circumstances, especially around institutional innovation, reach of local and regional agency, and actor-interaction in sectoral and territorial governance.

Second, this means we can think differently about the *politics* of glo-balization. While actors in the process of urban governance, as much as those who analyze this process, think of articulation into systems of interurban competition (global cities) as a constraint (*Sachzwang*) under which they have to submit their policies and institutions, we may just invert this thinking and accept that what is rather the case is that global-ization and neo-liberalization are processes that are determined by the constraints set for them by collective actors at the urban and regional scale. This point takes up and expands the observation made *inter alios* by Andy Jonas and Kevin Ward (2007: 170), and by extension by Ananya Roy (2007), that to think of urban regions simply as more or less success-ful "building blocs" of the global economy and to forget about how they are constituted "politically and reproduced through everyday acts and struggles around consumption and social reproduction" would be mis-leading. In fact, the Frankfurt example even provides evidence for the internalization of certain modes of thought and practice, of a certain governmentality that has been found to come with "roll-with-it neoliber-alization" (Keil 2009; Schipper 2012).

Third, we can use this case study to illustrate that globalization is not a linear process. It is not a steady expansion of an urban region's aggressive and programmatic deterritorialized insertion into the flows and institutions of global capitalism. Quite the opposite is happening in Frankfurt right now. After three decades of aggressive globalization chasing, the regional elites—regime, growth machine—have relaxed their attempts to become global at all costs and have partly used Frankfurt's already achieved status as a global centre to refocus economic, social, and environmental policies around questions of quality of life (housing, transit, culture). It is clear that this refocusing has had its own problems, as internal differentiation/globalization has ceased to be recognized as a challenge and has become the basis for a classed and racialized segregation of the region in which privileges and disadvantages are distributed at a regional scale.

Fourth, the Frankfurt example, due to the underlying research design of interviewing largely established decision-makers in the region, underplays the potential for contestation and qualification of internalized globalization. It is clear that the new forms of governance that will emerge from this current period will be under scrutiny of a regional polity that has gotten used to appellations of globalism and regional cohesion alike, while jobs have vanished, public services have been compromised, and promises not kept. The subsequent potential of that constellation for future democratic and social justice demands to be reinserted into the regime is great. The political game played by Frankfurt regimes that dropped into and out of globalization and neo-liberalization discourses over the past twenty years has only temporarily appeared immune to large-scale contestation. From this experience, it is possible to draw larger questions on the permeability of elite politics to resistance and critique "from below."

One ongoing political initiative from below is Blockupy, a network of multiple leftist organizations and groups that rose from the international Occupy movement in 2011. Blockupy refers to a combination of blockade and occupation. The network called for Days of Action in both 2012 and 2013 in Frankfurt. The goal of these events was the targeted disturbance of the everyday affairs of the financial sector, especially of the European Central Bank, as well as the bundled protest against European Union financial and (implicitly) social policy. In both years, massive demonstrations were accompanied by street violence. The police was criticized for excessive force and the local state was accused of limiting the right to protest. This, in turn, led to ongoing media coverage and growing attention to and sympathies with the causes of Blockupy.

Together with such protests as the citizens movement Stuttgart 21, Blockupy initiated a revival of protest movements in Germany during the

2010s. This new wave of protest ostensibly uses the theatrical nature of urban spaces by using media spectacle as a counterweight to elitist, and allegedly depoliticized and cliquish, urban and regional politics. The protests have not yet led to a noticeable change in direction of those politics, but had two important consequences: First, the urban protest movement was shown to be a useful means of political expression to a broader public and, second, the vulnerability of urban and regional decision-making structures became visible. Previously dominant elitist politics were confronted with a broad critique "from below." Especially in the case of Blockupy, the almost apathetic performance of the local and regional governments escalated the conflict. Blockupy events also took place in 2014 und 2015, focusing on the opening of the new building of the European Central Bank. They were the source of heavy mobilization of anti-capitalist forces and led to violent confrontations between demonstrators and security forces.

In conclusion, then, in terms of the overall framework set by the new urban politics, we can observe that such politics can be guided by a wide variety of regimes. As illustrated, inter alia, by the regime transition illustrated in Table 13.1, we can conclude that it is possible for urban regimes to tread various, and often radically different, pathways to establishing a temporarily sustainable interface between local and regional conditions and the ever changing demands of a globalized economy and society. What the Frankfurt example shows is that the topological unboundedness of urban regions today (Amin 2004) and the dramatic rescaling of regional politics (Brenner 2004) create a dynamic field of action for local policymakers, activists, and regional decision-makers.

Notes

1 The Land of Hesse is divided into three Regierungsbezirke or governmental districts. The Darmstadt district is responsible for Frankfurt and much of its region (various interviews).

2 The idea of an IBA was first seriously floated in 2008 but then put to rest. More recently, in the autumn of 2013, the issue got renewed attention. The Chamber of Commerce demands an IBA with a focus on housing, while the Social Democrats want the focus on transportation. The new Land government has not made its position known at the time of writing (www.faz.net/aktuell/rhein-main/ihk-moechte-internationale-bauausstellung-identitaet-durch-innovatives-wohnen-12643474.html).

References

AS&P (Albert Speer und Partner). 2009. "Frankfurt für Alle: Handlungsperspektiven für die internationale Bürgerstadt Frankfurt am Main." www.frankfurt -fuer-alle.de/.

Amin, A. 2004. "Regions unbound: Towards a new politics of place." *Geografiska Annaler* 86B(1): 33–44.

Arning, M. 2009. "Die Macht der Idee: Mit dem Gedanken eines Wissensnetzes, das seine Fäden von Frankfurt und Offenbach aus entfaltet, lässt sich vieles anfangen." *Frankfurter Rundschau* F4. www.fr-online.de/frankfurt _und_hessen/nachrichten/frankfurt/1645247_Die-Macht-der-Idee .html?sid=bc39cd5621769b6844a3895372ae9cc3.

Belina, B. 2013. "Region, Strukturierte Kohärenz und Continuously Emergent Scalar Fix. Zu Kooperation und Konkurrenz in der Global City Region Frankfurt Rhein-Main." In *Die konflikthafte Konstitution der Region. Kultur, Politik, Ökonomie* (140–61). Münster: Westfälisches Dampfboot, ed. Ortrun Brand, Steffen Dörhöfer and Patrick Eser.

Belina, B. and U. Lehrer. This volume.

Blatter, J. 2005. "Metropolitan governance in Deutschland: Normative, utilitaristische, Kommunikative und Dramaturgische Steuerungsansätze." *Swiss Political Science Review* 11(1): 119–55.

Bördlein, R. 1999. "'Region Rhein-Main': Rahmenbedinungen und Konzepte im Institutionalisierungsprozess einer Region." *DISP* 136/137: 63–69.

Brenner, N. 2004. *New state spaces: Urban governance and the rescaling of statehood*. Oxford: Oxford University Press.

Fischer, C., T. Freytag, M. Hoyler, and C. Mager. 2005. "Rhein-Main als polyzentrische Metropolregion. Zur Geographie der Standortnetze von wissensintensiven Dienstleistungsunternehmen." *Informationen zur Raumentwicklung*, Heft 7, 439–46.

Freytag, T., M. Hoyler, C. Mager, and C. Fischer. 2006. "Rhine-Main: Making polycentricity work?" In P. Hall and K. Pain, eds., *The polycentric metropolis: Learning from mega-city regions in Europe* (163–71). London: Earthscan.

Glückler, J. 2004. "Geographien der Vernetzung und Skalen der Globalisierung – Das Beispiel der Unternehmensberatung in Frankfurt." *Petermanns Geographische Mitteilungen* 148(4): 28–37.

Hall, P. and Kathy Pain, eds. 2006. *The polycentric metropolis: Learning from mega-city regions in Europe*. London and Sterling, Virginia: Earthscan.

Harding, A. 1995. "Elite theory and growth machines." In D. Judge, G. Stoker, and H. Wolman, eds., *Theories of urban politics* (35–53). London: Sage.

Hitz, H., R. Keil, U. Lehrer, C. Schmid, K. Ronneberger, and R. Wolff, eds. 1995. *Capitales Fatales: Urbanisierung und Politik in den Finanzmetropolen Zürich und Frankfurt*. Zürich: Rotpunkt-Verlag.

Hoyler, M. 2005. *Where does Frankfurt end?* GLA Seminar "Measuring World Cities," London, September 22. www.london.gov.uk/mayor/economic_unit/ docs/michael_hoyler.pdf; accessed March 11, 2009.

Hoyler, M., T. Freytag, and C. Mager. 2006. "Advantageous fragmentation? Reimagining metropolitan governance and spatial planning in Rhine-Main." *Built Environment* 32(2): 124–36.

Jonas, A. E. G. and K. Ward. 2007. "Introduction to a debate on city-regions: New geographies of governance, democracy and social reproduction." *International Journal of Urban and Regional Research* 31(1): 169–78.

Keil, R. 2009. "The Urban politics of roll-with-it neoliberalization." *CITY* 13(2–3) (June-September): 231–45.

———. 2002. "'Common sense' neoliberalism: Progressive conservative urbanism in Toronto, Canada." *Antipode* 34(3): 578–601.

Keil, R. and P. Lieser. 1992. "Frankfurt: Global city – local politics." *Comparative Urban and Community Research. An Annual Review* 4: 39–69.

Keil, R. and K. Ronneberger. 1991. "Arkadien Postmodern: Stadtlandschaft Zwischen Streuobst und Gewerbepark." In T. Koenigs, ed., *Vision Offener Grünräume: GrünGürtel Frankfurt* (196–208). Frankfurt: Campus.

———. 1994. "Going up the country: Internationalization and urbanization on Frankfurt's northern ridge." *Environment and Planning D: Society and Space* 12(2): 137–66.

———. 2000. "The globalization of Frankfurt am Main: Core, periphery and social conflict." In P. Marcuse and R. van Kempen, eds., *Globalizing cities: A new spatial order* (228–48). Oxford: Blackwell.

Kujath, H. J. 2008. "Die Städte der Wissensökonomie." In H.-B. Stiftung, ed., *Kreativen:Wirkung Urbane Kultur, Wissensökonomie und Stadtpolitik* (16–20). Berlin: Heinrich-Böll-Stiftung.

Langhagen-Rohrbach, C. 2003. "Stadtplanung in Frankfurt am Main und in Zürich. Wer macht die Stadt?" *Rhein-Mainische Forschungen* 124: 181–206.

Langhagen-Rohrbach, C. and R. Fischer. 2005. "Regionalwerkstatt Frankfurt-Rhein-Main. Region als Prozeß?" *Standort* 29(2): 76–80.

Lieser, P. and R. Keil. 1988a. "Frankfurt. Die Stadt GmbH & Co.KG." *Stadtbauwelt* 79(48): 2122–27.

———. 1988b. "Zitadelle und Getto: Modell Weltstadt." In W. Prigge and H. P. Schwarz, eds., *Das Neue Frankfurt: Städtebau und Architektur im Modernisierungsprozess 1925-1988* (183–208). Frankfurt: Vervuert Verlag.

Painter, J. 2008. "Cartographic anxiety and the search for regionality." *Environment and Planning A* 40(2): 342–61.

Planungsverband Ballungsraum Frankfurt/Rhein-Main. 2005. *Frankfurt/ Rhein-Main 2020 – die europäische Metropolregion. Leitbild für den Regionalen Flächennutzungsplan und den Regionalplan Hessen.* Frankfurt: Planungsverband. (published together with Regierungspräsidium Darmstadt – Regionalversammlung)

Reiss-Schmidt, S. 2003 "Zwischen Heimatgefühl und Weltstadtanspruch: Die Region Frankfurt/Rhein-Main." *DISP* 152(1): 80–86.

Ronneberger, K. and R. Keil. 1993. "Riding the tiger of modernization: Red green municipal reform politics in Frankfurt am Main." *Capitalism Nature Socialism* 4(2): 19–50.

Roy, A. 2007. "The 21st-century metropolis: New geographies of theory." *Regional Studies* 43(6): 819–30.

Schipper, S. 2012. *Genealogie und Gegenwart der 'unternehmerischen Stadt'. Neoliberales Regieren in Frankfurt am Main zwischen 1960 und 2010.* Münster: Westfälisches Dampfboot.

Sieverts, T. 2003. *Cities without cities: An interpretation of the Zwischenstadt.* London and New York: Spon Press.

Swyngedouw, E. 1997. "Neither global nor local. 'Glocalization' and the politics of scale." in *Spaces of globalization: Reasserting the power of the local*, ed. K. R. Cox. New York: Guilford Press.

CHAPTER 14

Grand Paris
The Bumpy Road toward Metropolitan Governance

Stefan Kipfer, Julie-Anne Boudreau, Pierre Hamel, and Antoine Noubouwo

Introduction

IN MAY 2010, the French Senate approved the *Projet de Loi relatif au Grand Paris*, the first law to implement the vision of the former administration under President Nicolas Sarkozy for the Paris urban region. The law contains provisions to build new transit routes (most notably a new automatic subway ring linking various strategic points in the Paris region), to create a new agency (*la Société du Grand Paris*) responsible for planning the new rail infrastructure and urban development in the vicinity of the new subway stops, and to set up a public authority (*l'Établissement public de Paris-Saclay*) to develop an extensive research and development cluster on the Saclay plateau in the southwestern periphery of the region (République Française 2010). After months of negotiation and consultation, an agreement was reached in January 2011 between the national government and the regional authority (the *Région Ile-de-France*) on the route of the automatic subway. This followed a separate government decree in late 2010 that created an integrated police authority for the four central *départements* of the region. The ambitious, transit-centred regional development project was presented as a competitive response to other global cities, particularly London. In the official vision, shiny, securitized automated transit will link economic clusters to each other and the world market while "unlocking" land rent at strategic sites.

The Institutional Architecture of the Paris Region

The 1982 decentralization law (and its companion laws voted throughout the 1980s and 1990s) stipulates that executive power should be transferred from the prefect to elected officials in the departments and regions. In 2003, the decentralization principle was reinforced when the region *Ile-de-France* became a fully autonomous level government with legislative powers (equal to departments and communes). Nevertheless, as a younger institution, the region remains relatively weak, with a budget of 7 billion euros in 2007 (Dallier 2008: 187).

In 2007, most, but not all of the Paris region (le *bassin parisien*) was governed by 1,281 *communes*, the region *Ile-de-France* (created during the decentralization reforms since 1982), the eight *départements* (created in 1968), numerous intercommunal agreements, and many special-purpose bodies responsible for transit, electricity, natural gas, water, etc. Appointed representatives of the central state (such as the *préfet*) also play an important role, often in competition with the elected officials in communes, departments, and the region.

The region *Ile-de-France* produced in 1994 a *Schéma directeur de la region Ile-de-France* (SDRIF), in compliance with the 1995 *loi Pasqua* stating that regions are responsible for the elaboration of the master plan, subject to final approval by the state (as well as at six strategic points during the elaboration process). But even after final approval, the state can still approve development projects that are contrary to the master plan with general interest projects (*projet d'intérêt général*, PIG) and national interest operations (*operations d'intérêt national*, OIN).

A new *SDRIF* was approved by the regional council in September 2008. The national government refused to approve the plan until June 2010, when it transmitted it to the State Council for final approval. In November 2010, the *Conseil d'État* gave negative advice, due to the discrepancies between the regional plan and the government project for the *Grand Paris*. The central state objected not only to the region's transit plan but also to provisions in the *SDRIF* that restrict night flights at Charles-de-Gaulle, limit highway development, and set residential housing targets at *La Défense*. Also, the SDRIF continues to infringe on the turf of the state's famous engineering corporation—*Ponts et Chaussées*—and its Ministry of infrastructure (interview with representative of the SDRIF, July 17, 2008).

In 2006, the Socialist mayor of Paris, Bertrand Delanoë, and his Communist deputy Pierre Mansat, in charge of relations with the *banlieues*, created the *Conférence métropolitaine* to bring together elected officials in Paris and the first two rings of suburbs.

In 2007, President Sarkozy announced an international architectural competition for Greater Paris. In 2008, he set up a new Secretary of State for the capital region headed by Christian Blanc. In 2008, Philippe Dallier, UMP Senator of Seine-St-Denis, proposed to merge the City of Paris and the three surrounding *départements*, abolish intercommunal agreements, and create an entity for transportation, housing, economic development, and security. The Balladur report of 2009 made similar proposals. In 2009, the Sarkozy government introduced the *Grand Paris* law, creating the *Société du Grand Paris*, and created the *Atelier international du Grand Paris* to write a charter for the Greater Paris.

In December 2013, the French Assembly passed a law to create by 2016, the *Métropole du Grand Paris*, a giant inter-municipal institution (*intercommunalité*) governed by a combination of appointed and elected politicians with their own fiscal resources and planning powers for housing and shelters (but not transportation). The *Métropole* covers the City of Paris and its three surrounding *départements*, 124 municipalities and 6.5 million Parisians. Supported by some fractions of the Socialist Party over others, this initiative follows various pink-green-red suggestions to complement regional transit with a mechanism to steer housing intensification in the region. In contrast to earlier discussions under François Hollande, it does so, however, separately from the *Région Ile-de-France* and its transportation authority. It also comes at the expense of the existing inter-municipal districts that were at the heart of the flexible, semiformal *Paris Métropole* project championed by reform Communists and Delanoë, mayor of Paris. Without going as far as amalgamation, *Métropole du Grand Paris* weakens the *départements* and follows broadly the conceptual vision of Senator Dallier, from which Blanc and Sarkozy shied away (Vincendon 2013b; Braouezec 2013; Subra 2013; Jérôme 2014).

As a result, the initiative was opposed not only by the right but also the Communist Party. More broadly speaking, the *Métropole du Grand Paris* is one component in the decentralization reforms pursued by Hollande. And it is part of a series of adjustments in French urban policy, including a re-regulation of tenant–landlord relations, planning reforms to strengthen compact urban development, changes in the terminology and spatial focus of place-based urban intervention (*politique de la ville*), the prohibition of discrimination by residential address in hiring processes, a selective amalgamation of regional governments outside *Ile-de-France*, and further efforts to territorialize security and policing (the *zones de sécurité prioritaires*). This broader context, and the shift to a regional focus in housing policy in Paris, has led some to call for a formal integration of urban renewal and public housing redevelopment (*rénovation urbaine*) with *Grand Paris* regional governance (Ledoux 2013). However, the clear victory of the right in the 2014 municipal elections and the subsequent right turn of the Hollande government have dampened the prospects for some of these projects.

Inspired by Henri Lefebvre's critique of the 1965 regional plan, Jean-Pierre Garnier (2012) argues that, just as its Gaullist predecessor, *Grand Paris* represents a "techno-bureaucratic" urban strategy to homogenize, fragment, and hierarchize social space. According to Garnier, the project helps naturalize urbanization insofar as it rests on a cross-partisan compromise and depoliticizes development through procedural governance talk and architectural spectacle. Followed by a high-profile architectural competition in 2009 and the creation of a State Secretariat for Greater Paris (headed by Christian Blanc) in 2008, the *Grand Paris* law was indeed one of several others—including the national housing renovation policy (since 2003), the abolition of the *taxe professionnelle* (in 2009), and nation-wide reform of subnational government (in 2010)[1]—that signalled a selective market- and security-focused re-centralization of urban politics under Chirac and Sarkozy. However, significant work was required to produce the cross-partisan compromise that now undergirds the *Grand Paris* law. The latter was tabled after a period of trial and error between 2006 and 2009 and was followed by negotiations through which institutional constraints and political resistance were attenuated. Not a comprehensive governance reform, but a project-driven attempt to rejig the balance of forces in the Paris region, *Grand Paris* speaks to the difficulties of governing metropolitan regions against the odds of uneven development, territorial conflict and multi-layered institutional contradictions.

We proceed as follows. In the first section, we provide the theoretical and historical context to the *Grand Paris* initiative. Broadening Garnier's Lefebvrean insights, we introduce the major lines of contradiction that shape metropolitan politics in Euro-America: economic restructuring, socio-political conflict, and the materiality of the state. We do this in part by revisiting the two main historical precursors of the current regional initiatives of the French state: Haussmannian interventions in the Second Empire and the Third Republic, and the Gaullist strategies early in the Fifth Republic. Second, we zero in on the way in which contemporary regional interventions have tried to negotiate the limitations and contradictions of late Fordist regional planning. We revisit the major visions for Greater Paris that were floated prior to 2009. Undertaken in 2008, our primary research shows that these competing visions revealed cross-cutting forms of disagreement among institutional actors about the partisan orientations, policy objectives, institutional forms, and scales of intervention.

Then we discuss the way in which the *Grand Paris* proposal responded to opposition inside and outside the governmental right and managed to push the pink (Socialist), green (Green), and red (Communist) majorities in the Paris region into something resembling a state-induced territorial compromise. We conclude with comments about the comparative implications of our study and the ongoing uncertainties of governing urban regions.

The Challenges of Regional Governance

Effective and comprehensive ways of governing urban regions in the modern capitalist world are rare. Why? As we know from Henri Lefebvre (1978), the role of the state in producing space—including the shifting terrains of metropolitan regions—is caught between the role of coordinating the chaotic flux of capitalist space-time and the task of instituting political domination by means of territorial relations between central and peripheral spaces. Developing and redirecting Lefebvre, David Harvey (1989) has pointed out that to make urban regions "cohere" as real estate investment frontiers, infrastructure complexes, and sites of (re-)production is difficult, not the least because investments in the built environment are tied to other circuits of accumulation through temporal crisis and geographical unevenness. As Lefebvre insists, more so than Harvey, the uneven and crisis-ridden landscapes of metropolitan regions are also sources for conflicts between socio-political forces over issues ranging from land use, democracy, surplus appropriation, and modes of life that states can organize territorially, but not eliminate (Schmid 2003). The difficulties of coordinating the flux of accumulation and organizing territorial relations are compounded and refracted by contradictions inherent in the institutional matrices of state-space, notably those between different—and historically shifting—scalar configurations of state intervention (Brenner 2004). These three-fold, economic, socio-political, and institutional contradictions explain why regional governance arrangements—be they understood as regional class alliances (Harvey 1989), regimes or growth coalitions (Logan and Molotch 1987; Stone 1993), territorial compromises (Schmid 2003), or state-scalar fixes (Brenner 2004)[2]—remain partial, temporary, and with uncertain effects on future rounds of urban-regional development.

Paris is a highly pertinent case to illustrate these points, not the least because of the exceptional role the central state and revolutionary politics have historically played in shaping regional development and forming a territorialized political pattern pitting working class against bourgeois social spaces. The extended Haussmann era (from 1853 into the period of the Third Republic that followed the demise of Bonaparte) and the second part of the postwar period (from 1958 into the early 1970s) were the most formative examples of de facto regional planning and governance in Paris. The term *Grand Paris* was widely used between the 1910s and the 1930s when politicians, planners, and housing reformers from the reformist left, such as Henri Sellier, proposed annexations, metropolitan-wide institutions, and comprehensive plans in order to address infrastructure, transportation, and housing shortages, particularly in the haphazardly expanding industrial zones and working-class districts outside the central city. But these initiatives, including the famous Prost regional plan of the 1930s, remained either unrealized or ineffective at the time (Subra 2009a: 51–54; Marchand 1993: 226–45, 258–61; Gilli and Offner 2008: 24–27). Like Sarkozy's *Grand Paris*, Haussmann's and Delouvrier's projects emanated from the statist right, leaving profound marks on the socio-political and institutional landscape of greater Paris. Both projects intervened in the restructuring of Paris's regional space economy. They reorganized relations among political forces territorially, and with distinct national and international implications. They helped recast the institutional form of France's (post-)imperial state.

The strategies of Baron Haussmann and his successors to annex the ring of growing "villages" inside the Thiers fortifications, build overlapping layers of modern infrastructure (train stations, rail lines, parks, water, electricity), and facilitate speculative real estate development on major boulevards and squares with public debt instruments and new expropriation tools, helped shaped the second industrial revolution. They leveraged new credit for large-scale and longer-term investments shrank the circulation time of capital and built the material foundation for a much more encompassing, and culturally enthralling, modern commodity culture (Harvey 2003; Benevolo 1993; Chevalier 1994; Subra 2009b; Marchand 1993: 95–97). Politically, Haussmann responded to the 1848 revolution in various ways, also by borrowing from warfare techniques against civilian populations developed during the conquest of Algeria (Bugeaud 1997). Cutting boulevards through dense, rebellious quarters, and annexing Paris's rapidly industrializing "villages" beyond the inner *faubourgs*, was meant to turn Paris into a pacified centre of the French empire. The rationalization of urban administration embodied in a homogenized landscape of *arrondissements* was part of the process through which France formed a modern imperial-capitalist state (Cooper 2005; Mooers 1991; Weber 1979). Haussmann's regime was brought to a halt by rising public debt levels, the real estate slump in the late 1860s and the subsequent long depression, the Franco-Prussian war, and the Commune of 1871. But Haussmanism continued to inform urban strategies in the Third Republic and helped enshrine the distinction between *beaux quartiers* and *Paris populaire* that shaped Paris politics long into the twentieth century (Hazan 2002; Pinçon and Pinçon-Charlot 2004, 2007; Marchand 1993: 88–90, 101–2, 134–42).

The second moment in metropolitan reform was Paul Delouvrier's 1965 regional plan (the *Schéma directeur d'aménagement et d'urbanisme de la région de Paris*) to link urban renewal in central Paris to a system of new towns, regional suburban train lines, and expressways. A case of neo-Haussmannian, Gaullist technocratic development (Marchand 1993: 306–14), Delouvrier's plan aimed to inject a technologically optimistic and growth-oriented dynamism into French Fordism. Responding to urban growth that had started to outpace the first ring of suburbs (*la petite couronne*), it intended to turn a revitalized central Paris and existing post-war suburbs (notably the large housing estates, *Grands Ensembles*) into pillars of a broader, pluri-functional and polycentric urban region (Subra 2009a-b; Giacone 2010; Chevalier 1994; Merlin 1991; Dagnaud 1983). Having failed to save French Algeria with the Constantine Plan, Delouvrier also tried to modernize the French state with entrepreneurial and voluntarist planning capacities centred on inter-bureaucratic collaboration and a series of instruments to intervene in property markets (Harari 2005; Fredenucci 2003; Subra 2009b: 33–38 Marchand 1993: 312–14, 326–35; Merlin 1991: 35–43, 66–82; Dagnaud 1983). Most importantly, Delouvrier reshaped regional relations of force, which since the early twentieth century had crystallized into an opposition between the Bonapartist, then Gaullist, right in central Paris (Nivet and Combeau 2000) and the "red" belt of working-class *banlieues* (Fourcaut 1996; Stovall 1990; Pinçon and Pinçon-Charlot 2004; Marchand 1993: 194–205, 257). Creating a temporary region-wide governmental district (*District de la région de Paris*) in 1961 and replacing the existing three *départements* with eight smaller ones in 1968 were attempts to contain the Communists in one: *Seine-Saint-Denis*. Not successful in this regard—*Val de Marne* turned Communist also—the Delouvrier plan to expand transit, hospitals, and universities to working-class suburbs nonetheless consolidated the Gaullist-Communist territorial compromise of the postwar era (Giacone 2010; Marchand 1993; Donzel 2010).

The manifold limitations of Gaullist regional planning—and the transformations of the region since the 1980s—set the stage for the *Grand Paris* debates in the early twenty-first century. As a framework for unlimited growth, the 1965 regional plan was stopped in its tracks by the economic crisis of the mid-1970s and superseded by subsequent rounds of regional restructuring. First, the socio-spatial form of late Fordist Paris—central Paris, the first ring suburbs (*la petite couronne*) and the new towns—was remade by processes of deindustrialization, gentrification, and exurbanization. These transformed the social composition of central Paris and the inner suburbs, expanded the industrial and residential patchwork in the new towns, exurbs, villages, and historic towns of the *grande couronne*, and greatly complicated the links between employment, residence, and transport in the region (Panerai 2008; Berger 2004, 2006; Dodier 2007; Le Goix 2006; Pernet 2001; Gilli 2007, 2008; Offner 2007). Second, the Gaullo-Communist compromise survived 1968 but was undermined by the end of Gaullist rule in central Paris in 2001 and the decline of Communist influence in the red suburbs (Blet 2001; Jeanne 2009). Since the 1980s, social struggles by migrant workers and their offspring superseded the left–right divide; the political meaning of *banlieue* changed from red bastion to racialized "ghetto" (Masclet 2006; Subra 2004; Stovall 2003). Segregation along class and race intensified in complex, not dualist ways (Préteceille 2006, 2009). Third, technocratic *dirigisme* not only failed to overcome the institutional divide between central Paris and the surrounding suburbs, a Haussmannian legacy (Ronai 2004; Pinçon and Pinçon-Charlot 2004; Fourcaut et al. 2007), but was also undercut by the pro-market shifts under Giscard and the decentralization reforms begun under Mitterrand. Overlaid with ascending neo-liberalism, these reforms gave rise to "the era of governance," accentuating the difficulties of policy implementation (Lascoumes and Le Galès 2005) and multiplying disjunctures between central and subnational state scales (Lefèvre 2009).

Grand Paris: The Work of Governing (2006–9)

In hindsight, one may be tempted to see the *Grand Paris* project as a seamless and rational response to the structural contradictions shaping the Paris urban region, an attempt to (1) adjust to the perceived competitive pressures facing global city Paris with a transit-linked series of export platforms in a multi-polar urban region; (2) supersede with a bold initiative the piecemeal metropolitan reform strategies chosen by the red-pink-green alliances (which control the majority of local, *départemental*, and regional bodies in region); and (3) "clean up" regional governance to create an institutional environment less cumbersome than the current *mille-feuille* of overlapping jurisdictions. Certainly, *Grand Paris* continues the deeper shift from postwar territorial equalization to competitive metropolitanization in France, and the socio-spatial polarities this shift entails (Veltz 2009).[3] Sarkozy's Secretary of State for Paris, Christian Blanc, never tired to present his government's initiative as a strategy to deal with the competitive challenges of Paris coherent enough to be compared to its Haussmannian and Gaullist antecedents. However, such a self-serving representation of *Grand Paris* overlooks not only the degree to which the initiative was itself the result of a period of trial and error preceding the legislative process, but also ignores the fact that the ongoing implementation of *Grand Paris* has helped forge a fragile territorial compromise between the Sarkozy regime and the territorial bases of the opposition.

In 2007, President Sarkozy announced an international architectural competition for Greater Paris. In 2008, he set up a new Secretary of State for the capital region headed by Christian Blanc and commissioned former Prime Minister Édouard Balladur to revise local governance in general and in Paris. By that time, the debate on the future of the region was already under way. Initially, this debate was led by two left initiatives. In 2006, the Socialist mayor of Paris, Bertrand Delanoë, and his Communist deputy Pierre Mansat, in charge of relations with the *banlieues,* created the *Conférence métropolitaine* to bring together elected officials in Paris and the first two rings of suburbs. The election of Delanoë in 2001 ended almost a century of right-wing rule in the capital and ushered in a new era of project-based cooperation between Paris and surrounding Communist and Socialist municipalities (Mairie de Paris 2008; Ronai 2004). The resulting conferences and reports began to shape the debate on the future of the region (Chemetov and Gilli 2007; Fourcault et al. 2007; Offner 2007). In 2009, the *Conférence métropole* morphed into *Paris Métropole*, a loose entity of special purpose districts and civil society actors (*syndicat mixte et ouvert*) to pool resources and facilitate inter-municipal and inter-departmental cooperation.[4] Meanwhile, in 2007, the region *Ile-de-France*, under Socialist president Jean-Paul Huchon, launched consultations on the new master plan (*Schéma directeur de la region Ile-de-France*, SDRIF). The rise of the region had created conflict with the central state ever since it was charged with master planning in 1995. Huchon and his pink-green majority on the regional council asserted its role in transportation, housing, and economic development, proposing to strengthen its transit agency, the *Syndicat des transports d'Ile-de-France* (STIF), and create a new housing district, *Syndicat du logement d'Ile-de-France* (SLIF).

The debate on the future of *Grand Paris* was shaped by these three constellations of actors and institutions that gravitated around the Sarkozy government, the regional government *Ile-de-France*, and the City of Paris with its surrounding municipalities. In our interviews with politicians, advisors, academics, intellectuals, urban professionals, lobbyists, bureaucrats, and administrators in 2008, we identified four lines of conflict: (1) conflicts entrenched in partisan politics, (2) conflicts about the objectives of metropolitan governance, (3) conflicts about the instruments of intervention, and (4) conflicts about state decentralization. At the most general level, the *Grand Paris* debate pitted the socio-ecological reform project of the region, the city of Paris, and the *Conférence métropole* against the competitiveness project of Sarkozy and Blanc. This overall divide followed partisan lines in the respective local and regional strongholds of the right (in the municipalities and departments of the wealthy west and south of the agglomeration) and the left (concentrated in the north and east with pockets in the south and west of the region). These partisan divides were underscored by the fact that the local and regional Socialists, Greens, and Communists were also primary opponents of Sarkozy's nation-wide projects to reorganize the institutional and financial jurisdictions of the sub-national levels of the state: municipalities, *départements*, regions.

Partisan distinctions translated into different policy objectives. While for the proponents of the regional plan and the leaders of *Paris Métropole* the main priorities were ecological sustainability and territorial solidarity (to equalize social expenditures and fiscal resources), to paraphrase an advisor to an UMP politician with great influence in regional debates (interview, July 1, 2008), the Sarkozy government foregrounded economic competitiveness and the capacity of Parisians to "enrich themselves" through private and propertied urban development. Although clearly present in public discourse, these ideological and policy differences were not absolute. The Socialist, Green, and Red proponents of regional planning and inter-municipal dialogue, for example, are not opposed to "maintaining Paris in the select club of global cities" (Estèbe and Le Galès 2007: 64). Rather, they insist on combining private economic and real estate development with social and ecological reforms. Also, neither of the three camps is homogenous but riddled with various factional, scalar, and institutional divides. The Sarkozy government had to contend with exponents of the right most active in the regional council, the departments, and the municipalities, where NIMBYisms of all stripes are most pronounced. The voice of capital was splintered between the Chamber of Commerce and Industry of Paris (CCIP), which shares the "technical" perspective of some regional planners despite its ideological critique of the regional plan (interview, July 11, 2008), and the competing Chambers of Commerce in other departments. Finally, both the left and right had to deal with the public corporations and the representatives of the central state in the *préfectures*, which weigh heavily on and cut across the *mille-feuille* of state scales. If partisan divisions and disagreements on policy goals were fraught with cross-cutting fissures, they were also complicated—partly reinforced, partly attenuated—by conflicting views about the proper policy instruments. Tensions were clear between those who argued for region-wide institutional reforms and those who favour working through urban projects (place-making initiatives). On the one side, the region pushed strongly for the use of a new master plan (SDRIF) as a tool to systematize urban development, "clean up" multiple layers of policies in housing, transportation, and economic development, and override opposition against densification. On the other side, both the central government and *Paris Métropole* ended up defending less-than-comprehensive approaches to regional governance. *Paris Métropole* was conceived as an open-ended political space of deliberation and piecemeal cooperation between elected officials, professionals, and bureaucrats. After the Sarkozy regime abandoned comprehensive governance reform (see below), it zeroed in on the automated subway-ring proposal with a highly specific territorial focus: a network of districts close to train stations but decoupled from local, departmental, and regional territories and planned by the state-appointed *Société du Grand Paris* (SGP) (interview, June 27, 2008). While technocratic instead of deliberative, this approach also leaves the perimeter of the metropolitan region "deliberately unclear," focused neither on Paris nor the *Ile-de-France*, but on the "direct economic impact zone of Paris and its dense area" (interview with a representative of Christian Blanc, July 18, 2008).

The final line of conflict was about state rescaling and ran through all the others. Most local-regional actors saw the *Grand Paris* project as a recentralization of power in urban policy, particularly because the project joined other reforms that weakened the electoral weight and financial resources of the *départements* and the regions. Indeed, Sarkozy's initiative questioned the leadership capacity of the region in matters of competitiveness. It also capitalized on the fact that decentralization reforms had remained ambivalent, with representatives of the central state playing ongoing, if not always visible, roles in local-regional decision-making (interview, July 16, 2008). In transit, for example, jurisdictions are divided between the regional planning agency (STIF) and the major operators SNCF (*Société national des chemins de fer français*), RFF (*Réseau ferré de France*), and RATP (*Régie autonome de transports parisiens*). The role of the state in the transit companies makes it difficult for the STIF to exercise control (interview, July 2, 2008). Also, the fact that the central state retained jurisdiction in regional planning allowed it to block adoption of the regional plan, which contradicted various national priorities. Sarkozy's recentralizing approach also ran into obstacles, however. The transit-centred, engineering-heavy *Grand Paris* project has not meshed clearly with the results of the 2009 architecture competition because they were developed by ministries with different bureaucratic cultures: The Ministry of Culture in the case of the architectural competition, the Ministry of Ecology (formerly Equipment) in the case of the *Grand Paris* project. As we will see, the implementation of *Grand Paris* re-qualified the role of the central state.

Toward a Territorial Compromise? (2009–12)[5]

When the Sarkozy government introduced the *Grand Paris* law in late 2009, it had already abandoned the idea of pursuing comprehensive governance reform, as UMP senator Phillippe Dallier had suggested and as Sarkozy himself contemplated as late as 2007. Yet, the original plans for comprehensive governance reforms quickly ran into opposition internal to the government camp, as the local and regional representatives of the governmental majority were confronted by the realities of electoral defeat in the 2008 municipal elections (*Le Monde*, May 29, 2008; February 24, 2009). This defeat dashed any hope of sustaining a comprehensive institutional reform with right-wing electoral power. Given this unfavourable balance of forces, the Sarkozy government proceeded in 2009 to counter the Socialist, Green, and Communist forces in the region indirectly, with a project-based approach linking transit infrastructure with private real estate expansion and a partial re-appropriation of local, departmental, and regional planning powers by the state-appointed *Société du Grand Paris*. In addition, the government recast the governance of *La Défense* to overcome local opposition to expanding the financial district (Subra 2009a: 76–78; Pinçon and Pinçon-Charlot 2010: 118–21, 135–52; Donzel 2010; *Le Monde*, July 21, 2009).

Adopting the *Grand Paris* law in 2010 was not the end of the story, however. Shortly before the law was passed, the regional elections resulted in another resounding defeat of the UMP. After the final vote on the law, Christian Blanc resigned over a corruption scandal. The *Grand Paris* file was handed over to ministers more open to compromise with the region, while the UMP allowed its local representatives to join *Paris Métropole* (Ramnoux 2010). In this context, implementation further modified the project. First, negotiations over the transit route resulted in an agreement between the government and the region. Originally, the distinctions between national and regional transit priorities were clear enough for the *Conseil d'État* to advise against signing the region's plan into law. Blanc's *Grand Huit* underground subway emphasized long-range intra-regional mobility to link employment zones to each other and to the European high-speed network while opening up undeveloped zones in the south and south-western parts. Key among these was the greenfield project of Saclay, touted as a French Silicon Valley (*Humanité*, November 7, 2010). The *Arc-Express* subway of the STIF and the SDRIF prioritized labour-market access for workers and proposed a more finely spun transit web between existing, unevenly serviced suburban zones (Offner 2007: 108–10; Ile-de-France 2008). In the new political context, the government agreed to merge elements of the regional plan with its scheme and route the renamed *Grand Paris Express* in a Y shape through the heart of the left-dominated east, from the tertiary employment zone *Plaine-St-Denis* to the belt of stigmatized suburbs in *Seine-St.-Denis* and *Val-de-Marne* (Subra 2009b: 104–5; 2012: 224–29). Although the Greens and local farmers continued to oppose the Saclay project, which they think will spur leapfrog development and worsen the employment imbalance between eastern and western suburbs, negotiations led to an agreement between the government and the region.

Second, the housing and development side of the *Grand Paris* legislation was also modified after the spring of 2010, even though on this front the contrast between the *Grand Paris* initiative and the regional plan was unmistakable. The latter was committed not only to private-sector urban development but also to inter-municipal fiscal equalization and a greater institutional capacity to spread public housing provision across the region, with a 30% target per municipality and the proposed regional housing district (SLIF). The former is focused narrowly on "unlocking" real estate potential in districts around future regional subway stations, which are to be governed by the state-controlled *Société du Grand Paris* and thus exempt from sub-national planning approval. This strategy of area-specific land valorization embodied in the SDG was only a part of the government's neo-liberal housing strategy, which was framed as a vision of France as a "society of property owners" (*une France de propriétaires*). Ranging from permitting low-interest mortgages to squeezing state subsidies to social housing providers, Sarkozy's housing policies remained for the most part outside the purview of regional planning, but they are brought into clear focus in local-regional conflicts like those at *La Défense*, where the left-leaning municipality Nanterre continues to be embroiled in ongoing conflict with the right over the aggressive expansion of office space and luxury housing into working-class Nanterre (Donzel 2010; interview, June 30, 2008).

During the implementation of the *Grand Paris* law, the governance of transit-oriented development has shifted. Even as it began to include right-wing municipalities in the region, *Paris Métropole* succeeded in inserting itself as a broker between the *Société du Grand Paris* on one hand, and the local and departmental authorities on the other. Instead of simply a top-down agency of the state, SDG's role in development is subject to the kind of multi-scalar partnership contracts (*contrats de développement territorial*) so characteristic of the era of governance brought about by the twin forces of decentralization and neo-liberalization (Subra 2012: 200–213). Overseen by boards (*comités de pilotage*) comprising SDG members, local councillors, prefectoral representatives, and transit officials, plans for the lands around the seventy-two future transit stations are hoped to accelerate ongoing development projects (*Urbanisme* 2012).[6] In Clichy-Montfermeil, for example, the automatic subway station will be located right in the middle of the high-rise district that was the epicentre of the 2005 riots. It will be at the heart of the comprehensive housing renovation project pursued by the Conservative Montfermeil and the Socialist Clichy-sous-Bois as a response to those riots. Placed next to a high-rise building slated to be a cultural hub co-financed by the Ministry of Culture (Frayet 2012), the transit link is meant to achieve the goals of redevelopment: breaking up the stigmatized housing project by securitizing space, pushing entrepreneurialism, and blending racialized populations with newcomers.

Beneath and beyond regional governance, one can thus detect points of cross-partisan agreement on housing and development. Since 2003, public housing renovation has become the centrepiece of territorialized urban policy—the famous *politique de la ville* with which the French state has responded to urban rioting since the 1980s (Tissot 2007; Dikeç 2007). Under the auspices of a national agency (*L'Agence Nationale de la Réno-vation Urbaine*), public housing demolition efforts are now more coherently coordinated through the central state (Epstein 2013). Yet they allow municipalities such as Clichy-sous-Bois and Montfermeil leeway to pursue their priorities of shrinking, blocking, or revalorizing public housing (Lelévrier 2010). Like the *Grand Paris* initiative, public housing governance in the Paris region has undergone selective upward rescaling after years of ambiguous institutional devolution. This selective recentralization is based on an assumption shared by most political forces: spatial concentrations of public housing tenants (particularly tenants of colour) represent

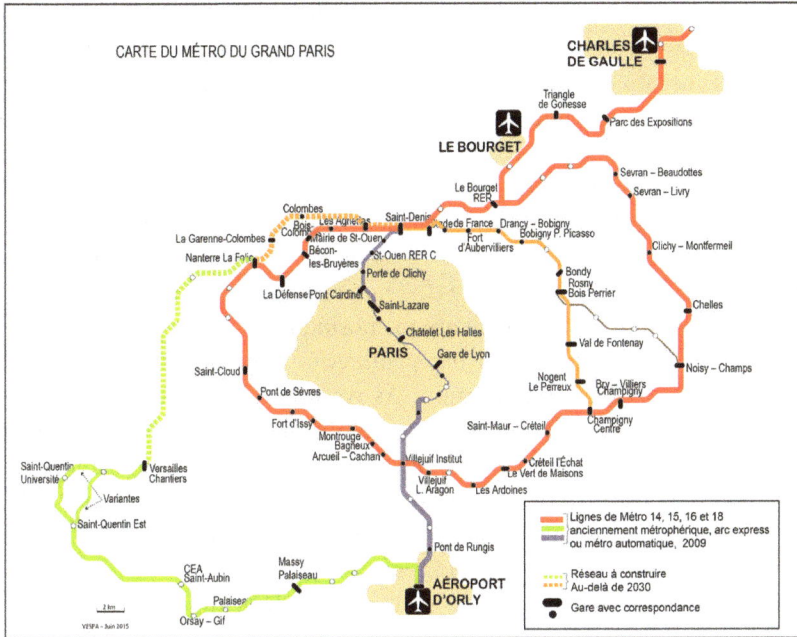

Figure 14.1   System map, Paris regional subway. *Source*: Société du Grand Paris.

a politically dangerous pathology that can be neutralized only by destructuring housing estates with "social mixity" (Belmessous 2006; Kirszbaum 2008). These cross-partisan assumptions indicate why most actors involved in the *Grand Paris* debates treated the racialized problematic of the *banlieue* as an unspoken subtext. They were one factor in the decision by housing and anti-racist activists to stay away from the *Grand Paris* debates (interviews, July 7, 2008; October 2, 2008). They also help us understand why one aspect of regional governance reform, the region-wide police district with a focus on policing public housing estates (*Grand Paris sécuritaire*), was created in late 2010 without debate (Mandraud 2009; Belmessous 2010: 85–89).

Conclusion

What are the comparative lessons to be learned from the *Grand Paris* debates? As in other urban regions, regional governance in Paris is fraught with contradictions related to the centrifugal forces of uneven development, territorialized socio-political tensions, and intra- and inter-institutional blockages. These suggest that dreams for a neatly bounded, institutionally seamless, and cooperative state to govern the multi-polar capitalist metropolis is a pipe dream. In contrast to some cities (including at least two of our comparison cases, Toronto and Montreal), however, *Grand Paris* has been subject to a political debate between two competing regional visions: on one hand, the statist neo-liberal project for regional competitiveness, land valorization, and "security" developed by the Sarkozy government; on the other, the red-pink-green regional reform projects of the regional government of *Ile-de-France* and the inter-municipal structure of *Paris Métropole*, which are proposing to embed neo-liberal competitiveness with social housing production, ecological reform, and inter-municipal fiscal equalization. As we have shown, the distinction between these two visions was not at all absolute and was shot through with various cross-cutting divergences over policy instruments and state rescaling. But it was significant enough to transform what are often "technical" deliberations over regional governance into significant political controversy. This is not surprising, given that for the French state as a whole, the stakes of governing Paris remain high (Jeanne 2009).

How has the stalemate between Sarkozy's *Grand Paris* project and the two "left" alternatives by *Ile-de-France* and *Paris Métropole* been overcome? Here, too, the Paris case is comparatively revealing. For Sarkozy's project did not come about as a result of a new regionalist class alliance or region-wide growth regime, as some North American literatures expect us to believe. It also was not the outcome of a piece-meal process of institutional adjustment to the "functional" complexities of the new urban region, as some institutionalist arguments would predict. To deal with the overlapping institutional complexities of the Paris region (including the legacy of three decades of ambiguous decentralization) and the electoral dominance of the red-pink-green block in the region, the Sarkozy regime chose a concerted, project-based form of central state intervention. In self-proclaimed continuity with Haussmann and Delouvrier, this intervention signaled not only a selective "return of the state" to the Paris region. It also allowed Sarkozy to bypass cross-partisan resistance to general governance reform in the region while attenuating left and green opposition with concessions on regional transit and development (Subra 2009b: 94–99). In March 2013, the Socialist government under François Hollande and Jean-Marc Ayrault in fact affirmed its commitment to *Grand Paris Express* even as it proceeded to rearticulate the project of competitiveness by regional transit with a vague discourse of solidarity, closer links to the existing transit networks and regional governance reform aimed at coordinating housing intensification in the central suburbs (Ayrault 2013;

Subra 2013; Gilli 2013). The broad continuities between the Socialist and the Conservative administrations are not only a function of President Hollande's much-touted pragmatic neo-liberalism. They also suggest that the work of governing between 2006 and 2011 has yielded something resembling a territorial compromise between the post-Gaullist hard right and the governmental left.

If history is any indication, the state-induced territorial compromise of *Grand Paris* is tenuous. Haussmann's and Delouvrier's projects ran into multiple limitations: fiscal crisis, uneven development, territorialized social conflict, and institutional blockages. In this light, several factors will decide if *Grand Paris* will be more than a "fantastic account" (Léonhardt 2011) built on symbolic unity (Enright 2013).

First, the grandiose, neo-Keynesian project will likely face ongoing financial uncertainties. While formally underwritten by the Hollande government, the thirty-one-billion-euro project will have to survive future rounds of austerity (to which the Socialist government is committed) as well as political shifts between now and its expected completion in 2030. The first of these shifts took place in the 2014 municipal elections, which tipped the balance of forces in the Paris region to the right. Second, despite its ambition to facilitate inter-suburban connectivity, the plan itself cannot tackle car-dependent sprawl in *Ile-de-France* and the larger *bassin parisien*. *Grand Paris* may in fact further spatial disarticulation by encouraging land-rent inflation in central suburbs, overdeveloping *La Défense*, and promoting greenfield development in the Saclay district. This has been highlighted recently by a coalition that has called for a moratorium by *Grand Paris Express* to stop real estate speculation, the destruction of green space and agricultural land, the centralization of decision-making, and the competitive logic of regional transportation (Constif 2013). Third, instead of simplifying the institutional *mille-feuille* of Greater Paris, the *Société du Grand Paris*—and now the *Métropole du Grand Paris*—have added yet more layers of institutions and deal-making to the existing cake of overlapping state scales.

Finally, the compromise that sustains the project sits on thin ice. The *Grand Paris* saga underscores that regional governance tends to solidify networks among institutional actors instead of dealing with the "object of governance"—inhabitants and everyday life in the metropole (Gilli and Offner 2008: 108). There is a divide between the state and the political class, on one hand, and various working-class social spaces in Greater Paris, on the other. Since the world-economic crisis, this divide has deepened, particularly for the most precarious and racialized segments of the Parisian working class (Onzus 2013). Consent over *Grand Paris* may be solid in the extended state, but, haunted by the spectre of revolt (last invoked in Trappes in July 2013), it cannot dissolve deeper sources of political danger.

Notes

We wish to acknowledge the research assistance of Claire Pillet.

1 The abolition of the *taxe professionnelle*, a payroll tax, deprived sub-national governments of a further 7 to 8 billion euros in revenue (Laurent 2010). The territorial reform law was passed in November 2010 after nation-wide mass demonstrations. The law was criticized as a central state attack on local democracy and the welfare state. The law shrinks competencies and undermines proportional representation at two levels of government that still deliver significant levels of redistributive services and are most open to left-green electoral success: the *départements* and the *régions* (Mongin 2010; Giblin 2009; *Le Monde*, October 12, 2010).
2 We distinguish governance as a normative-managerial project in policy discourses and academic literatures from critical analyses of the contradictory constellations of socio-political forces, territorial relations, and institutional forms that rule urban regions. See the introduction to this volume as well as Jessop (1997), Walters (2004), and Davies (2011).
3 This shift is encapsulated in the mandate of DIACT (*Délégation interministérielle à l'aménagement et à la compétitivité des territories*), an agency charged with positioning Paris in relation to the world economy instead of "tempering" national disequilibria, which had been the case with its predecessor DATAR (*Délégation à l'aménagement du territoire et à l'action régionale*) created in 1963.
4 A district (*syndicat*) is legally different from a community (*collectivité*). It is not a level of government with fixed territorial limits and directly elected officials.
5 See Schmid 2003.
6 According to JP Morgan, the main beneficiaries of this approach will be the large real estate firms and institutional investors with holdings close to the subway stations (Vincendon 2013a).

References

Ayrault, J.-M. 2013. "Le Nouveau Grand Paris: pour une région compétitive et solidaire." www.gouvernement.fr/print/premier-ministre/le-nouveau-grand-paris-pour-une-region-competitive-et-solidaire. Accessed December 18, 2013.
Belmessous, H. 2006. *Mixité Sociale: Une Imposture*. Nantes: Atalante.
———. 2010. *Opérations Banlieues*. Paris: La Découverte.
Benevolo, L. 1993. *The European city*. Oxford: Blackwell.
Berger, M. 2004. *Les Périurbains de Paris: De la ville à la métropole éclatée*. Paris: CNRS.
———. 2006. "Périurbanisation et accentuation des logiques ségrégatives en Ile-de-France." *Hérodote* 122: 198–211.
Blet, J.-F. 2001. "Qu'est-ce que le système RPR? Entretien." *Mouvements* 13: 25–31.
Braouezec, P. 2013. "Il faut une réforme plus proche des territoires." *L'Humanité*. 17 April. www.humaite.fr/print/politique/patrick-braouezec-il-faut-une-reforme-plus-proche-520467.

Brenner, N. 2004. *New state spaces.* Oxford: Oxford University Press.

Bugeaud, M. 1997. *La Guerre des rues et des maisons.* Paris: Jean-Paul Rocher.

Chemetov, P. and F. Gilli 2007. "Paris, ville mondiale." In J.-M. Offner, ed., *Le Grand Paris: Problèmes politiques et sociaux* 942 (46–47). Paris: La documentation française.

Chevalier, L. 1994/1977. *The assassination of Paris.* Chicago: University of Chicago Press.

Cooper, F. 2005. *Colonialism in question: Theory, knowledge, history.* Berkeley: University of California Press.

Costif (Coordination pour la Solidarité d'Ile de France et contre le Grand Paris). 2013. "Stop au Grand Paris." http://costif.parla.fr. Accessed October 24, 2013.

Dallier, M.-P. 2008. *"Le Grand Paris: Un vrai projet pour un enjeu capital."* No. 262, session ordinaire de 2007–8 du Sénat. Annexe au procès-verbal de la séance du 8 avril 2008. Rapport d'information fait au nom de l'Observatoire de la décentralisation sur les perspectives d'évolution institutionnelle du *Grand Paris.*

Davies, J. S. 2011. *Challenging governance theory: From networks to hegemony.* Bristol: Policy Press.

Dikeç, M. 2007. *Badlands of the republic.* London: Blackwell.

Dodier, D., ed. 2007. "Vivre les espaces périurbains." Special Issue. *Norois* 205(4): 7–136.

Donzel, S. 2010. "Le pôle de *la défense* vu de nanterre." *Esprit* 363: 132–44.

Enright, T. E. 2013. "Mass transportation in the neoliberal city: The mobilizing myths of the Grand Paris Express." *Environment and Planning D* 45: 797–813.

Epstein, R. 2013. *La rénovation urbaine. Démolition-reconstruction de l'État.* Paris: Presses de Sciences Po.

Estèbe, P. and P. Le Galès. 2007. "La mosaïque des pouvoirs." In J.-M. Offner, ed., *Le Grand Paris: Problèmes politiques et sociaux* 942 (60–64). Paris: La documentation française.

Fourcaut, A., ed. 1996. *La Ville divisée: Les Ségrégations urbaines en question.* Paris: Créaphis.

Fourcaut, A., E. Bellanger, and M. Flonneau, eds. 2007. *Paris/Banlieues: Conflits et Solidarités 1788–2006.* Paris: Créaphis.

Frayet, A. 2012. "Deux ans après, la 'tour Médicis' enfin sur des rails." *Le Monde.* February 3. www.lemonde.fr/culture/article/2012/02/02/deux-ans-apres-la-tour-medicis-enfin-sur-des-rails_1637947_3246.html.

Fredenucci, J.-C. 2003. "L'urbanisme d'État: nouvelles pratiques, nouvelles acteurs." *Ethnologie Française* 37: 13–20.

Garnier, J.-P. 2014. "'Greater Paris': Urbanization but no urbanity – How Lefebvre predicted our metropolitan future." In L. Stanek, C. Schmid, and Á. Moravánksy, eds., *Urban revolution now: Henri Lefebvre in social research and architecture* (133–56). London: Ashgate.

Giacone, A. 2010. *Les Grands Paris de Paul Delouvrier.* Paris: Descartes.

Giblin, B. 2009. "Attention, un train de réformes territoriales peut en cacher un autre." *Hérodote* 135: 3–24.

Gilli, F. 2007. "Une nouvelle géographie de l'emploi." In J.-M. Offner, ed., *Le Grand Paris: Problèmes politiques et sociaux* 942 (36–38). Paris: La documentation française.

———. "Paris: ville, capitale et métropole internationale." *La Vie des idées*. October 29. www.laviedesidees.fr/Paris-ville-capitale-et-metropole.html.

———. 2013. Nos métropoles doivent pouvoir réduire les inégalités sociales. *Le Monde*. March 15. www.lemonder.fr/journalelectronique/donnees/protege/20130315/html/901684.html.

Gilli, F. and J.-M. Offner. 2008. *Paris, Métropole hors les murs: aménager et gouverner un Grand Paris*. Paris: Presses de Sciences Po.

Harari, J. 2005. "Ségrégation territoriale: L'effet des politiques foncières et des stratégies d'aménagement." *Hérodote* 13: 103–21.

Harvey, D. 1989. *The urban experience*. Baltimore: Johns Hopkins University Press.

———. 2003. *Paris, capital of modernity*. New York and London: Routledge.

Hazan, E. 2002. *L'invention de Paris*. Paris: Seuil.

Ile-de-France. 2008. *Schéma directeur de la région Ile-de-France*. www.sdrif.com/fileadmin/unloud_file/doc_accueil/SDRIF.PDF.

Jeanne, M. 2009. "Paris, un enjeu capital." *Hérodote* 135: 80–109.

Jérôme, B. 2014. "L'alliance tactique entre Paris et la Seine-Saint-Denis." *Le Monde*. January 23. www.lemonde.fr/politique/article/2013/01/23/departements-l-alliance-tactique-entre-paris-et-la-seine-saint-denis_1821039_823448.html.

Jessop, B. 1997. "A neo-gramscian approach to the regulation of urban regimes: Accumulation strategies, hegemonic projects, and governance." In M. Lauria, ed., *Reconstructing urban regime theory* (51–73). Thousand Oaks, CA: Sage.

Kirszbaum, T. 2008. *Mixité Sociale dans l'Habitat*. Paris: La documentation française.

Lascoumes, P. and P. Le Galès. 2005. *Gouverner par les Instruments*. Paris: Presses de Sciences Po.

Ledoux, N. 2013. "Pour un Grand Paris de la rénovation urbaine." *Métropolitiques*. November 6. www.metropolitiques.eu/spip.php?page=print&id_article=578.

Le Goix, R. 2006. "Les gated communities aux Etats-Unis et en France: Une innovation dans le développement périurbain?" *Hérodote* 122: 107–37.

Lefebvre, H. 1978. *De L'Etat 4*. Paris: Union Générale des Éditions.

Lefèvre, C. 2009. *Gouverner les Métropoles*. Paris: Lextenso.

Lelévrier, C. 2010. *Action publique et trajectoires résidentielles: Un autre regard sur la politique de la ville*. Habilitation: Université de Paris-Est.

Léonhardt, F. 2011. "The fantastical account of Grand Paris." *Métropolitiques*. September 28. www.metropoliques.eu/The-Fantastical-Accounts-of-Grand.html.

Mairie de Paris. 2008. *No limit: Étude prospective de l'insertion urbaine du périphérique de Paris*. Paris: Éditions du Pavillon de l'Arsenal.

Mandraud, I. 2009. "Le *Grand Paris* sera d'abord celui de la sécurité." *Le Monde*. September 16. www.lemonde.fr/politique/article/2009/06/16/le-grand-paris-sera-d-abord-celui-de-la-securite_1207462_823448.html.

Marchand, B. 1993. *Paris: Histoire d'une ville*. Paris: Seuil.

Masclet, O. 2006. *La Gauche et les cités: Enquête sur un rendez-vous manqué*. 2nd ed. Paris: La Dispute.

Merlin, P. 1991. *Les Villes nouvelles en France*. 2nd ed. Paris: Presses Universitaires de France.

Mongin, O. 2010. "Le *Grand Paris* et la réforme des collectivités territoriales. Quel retour de l'État?" *Esprit* 363: 120–31.

Mooers, C. 1991. *The making of bourgeois Europe: Absolutism, revolution and the rise of capitalism in England, France, and Germany*. London: Verso.

Offner, J.-M., ed. 2007. *Le Grand Paris: Problèmes politiques et sociaux* 942. Paris: La documentation française.

———. 2007. "Les déplacements." In J.-M. Offner, ed., *Le Grand Paris: Problèmes politiques et sociaux* 942 (108–10). Paris: La documentation française.

Onzus (Observatoire nationale des zones urbaines sensibles). 2013. *Rapport 2013*. www.onzus.fr/uploads/media_items/rapport-de-l-onzus-2013.original.pdf. Accessed December 20, 2013.

Nivet, P. and Y. Combeau. 2000. *Histoire politique de Paris au XXᵉ siècle*. Paris: Presses Universitaires de France.

Panerai, P. 2008. *Paris métropole: Formes et échelles du Grand Paris*. Paris: Éditions de la Villette.

Pernet, C. 2001. "Déplacements en Ile-de-France: Vivre la ville sans détruire la Planète." *Mouvements* 13: 59–68.

Pinçon, M. and M. Pinçon-Charlot. 2004. *Sociologie de Paris*. Paris: La Découverte.

———. 2007. *Les Ghettos du Gotha: Comment la bourgeoisie défend ses espaces*. Paris: Seuil.

———. 2010. *Le président des riches*. Paris: La Découverte.

Préteceille, E. 2006. "La ségrégation sociale a-t-elle augmenté?" *Société Contemporaine* 62: 69–93.

———. 2009. "La ségrégation ethno-raciale a-t-elle augmenté dans la métropole parisienne?" *Revue Française de Sociologie* 50: 489–519.

Ramnoux, S. 2010. "C'est la consécration pour Paris Métropole." *Le Parisien*. November 8. www.leparisien.fr/paris-75/c-est-la-consecration-pour-paris-metropole-08-11-2010-1140185.php.

République Française. 2010. "LOI n° 2010-597 du 3 juin 2010 relative au Grand Paris." www.legifrance.gouv.fr/affichTexte.do?cidTexte=JORFTEXT000022308227&dateTexte=.

Ronai, S. 2004. "Paris et la banlieue: Je t'aime, moi non plus." *Hérodote* 113: 28–47.

Schmid, C. 2003. "Raum und Regulation. Henri Lefebvre und der Regulationsansatz." In U. Brand and W. Raza, eds., *Fit für den Postfordismus? Theoretisch-politische Perspektiven des Regulationsansatzes* (217–42). Münster: Westfälisches Dampfboot.

Stone, C. 1993. "Urban regimes and the capacity to govern: A political economy approach." *Journal of Urban Affairs* 15(1): 1–28.

Stovall, T. 1990. *The rise of the Paris red belt*. Berkley: University of California Press.

———. 2003. "From red belt to black belt." In S. Peabody and T. Stovall, eds., *The Color of Liberty: Histories of Race in France* (351–69). Durham and London: Duke University Press.

Subra, P. 2004. "Ile-de-France: La fin de la banlieue rouge." *Hérodote* 113: 14–27.

———. 2009a. "Le *Grand Paris*: stratégies urbaines et rivalités géopolitiques." *Hérodote* 135: 49–79.

———. 2009b. *Le Grand Paris*. Paris: Armand Colin.

———. 2012. *Le Grand Paris: Le géopolitique d'une ville mondiale*. Paris: Armand Colin.

———. 2013. "Pourquoi la région a perdu la gouvernance du Grand Paris." *Le Monde*. March 14. www.lemonde.fr/idees/article/2013/03/14/pourquoi-la -region-a-perdu-la-gouvernance-du-grand-paris_1847398_3232.html.

Tissot, S. 2007. *L'État et les quartiers*. Paris: Seuil.

Urbanisme. 2012. Special Issue. "Les gares du Grand Paris Express." 382: 43–72.

Veltz, P. 2009. *Mondialisation, Villes et Territoires: L'Économie d'Archipel*. Paris: Presses Universitaires de France.

Vincendon, S. 2013a. "Grand Paris Express: ça coute cher ... mais ça apporte gros." *Libération*. March 1. http://grandparis.blogs.liberation.fr/vincendon/.

———. 2013b. "La Métropole du Grand Paris est loin d'être achevée." Cited on the website Association Grand Paris at http://associationgrandparis .fr/2013/12/15/la-metropole-du-grand-paris-est-loin-detre-achevee/. Accessed December 18, 2013.

Walters, W. 2004. "Some critical notes on 'governance.'" *Studies in Political Economy* 73: 27–46.

Weber, E. 1979. *Peasants into Frenchmen: The modernization of rural France 1870–1914*. London: Chatto and Windus.

CHAPTER 15

Genealogies of Urban-Regional Governance
Journeys in a Post-Socialist City-Region

Mark Whitehead

Introduction: The City-Region in Time and Space

IT SEEMS TAUTOLOGICAL to observe that city-regions are spatial phenomena. They are, of course, doubly spatial to the extent that they denote a city that escapes the conventional scalar limits of a metropolis, and a region that has been shorn of its bucolic fringe and exhibits all of the agglomerated coherences of the urban. It is, perhaps, the heightened sense of spatiality associated with city-regions—a city defined by its regional extent/a region defined by its urban character—that leads us to marvel at their geographical features and topological uniqueness. While acknowledging the spatial dynamics of the city-region, this chapter seeks to develop a novel perspective on urbanized regions. This perspective is premised upon developing a temporally oriented assessment of the city-region. Although city-regions can appear to stand outside of history: representing an apparent climax to the urbanization process, city-regions are the outcome of complex historical processes and events. Excavating city-regional histories is thus an important step in developing critical perspectives on how they are governed. This temporal perspective supports this volume's broader concern with the development of forms of comparative urban regional research that acknowledge the ways in which cultural, political, and institutional history shape patterns of spatial governance.

This chapter has two primary foci. The first point of focus is the emerging body of scholarship that seeks to apply Foucauldian theories of governmentality to questions of spatial governance (see Huxley 2006; Legg

2007). The second is the city of Katowice (and the associated Silesian Metropolis) in the southwest corner of Poland. This chapter argues that Foucauldian theories of governmentality provide a valuable interpretive framework within which to understand the spatial histories of city-regional governance. In the context of this volume's desire to conceptualize the city-region as a unit for international comparative analysis (Boudreau et al. in this volume), it is claimed that notions of governmentality primarily provide a methodology through which such interpretative work can be achieved. In attempting to construct histories of city-regional government, however, this comparative project involves not only the analysis of co-present city-regions in different parts of the world, but the comparison of contemporary systems of city-regional government with their own historical predecessors. If one of the purposes of comparative city-regional analysis is to reveal the possibility of spatial difference (and contingency) in the form and functioning of urban-regions, governmentality reveals the historical contingency of *in situ* city-regional governance.

The second focus of this chapter is the urban agglomeration of Katowice (and the city-region of the Silesian Metropolis within which it is located). Katowice offers a complex spatial history of city-regional governance in and through which it is possible to explore the application of a Foucauldian methodology. Described by some as a *hybridopolis*, the Katowice urban agglomeration is a collection of fifteen urban centres that have gradually grown and melded together. Interspersed by mixed agrarian land and former sites of mineral extraction, Katowice embodies many of the jurisdictional and functional challenges that are associated with the development of effective forms of governance at a regional scale. Located near the borders between the Czech Republic, Germany, and Slovakia, the case of Katowice also reveals the complicating role of geopolitics in defining and redefining systems of urban and regional governance.

This chapter begins by exploring the ways in which theories of governmentality can be applied to the study of city-regional governance. The remaining three sections provide a *genealogical* study of the historical emergence of systems of spatial governance around Katowice and the Silesian Metropolis. This genealogy incorporates a discussion of the geopolitical struggles over the region that emerged following the First World War, the formation of the *Upper Silesian industrial District* under the Communist regime, and the more recent development of the UN-sponsored rescue bureaucracy that is the *Katowice Agglomeration Project*. These different moments of urban-regional governance are used to reveal not only the changing spatial form of the city-region, but also the contingency of the city-regional present.

A 'Little Experiment' in the Study of City-Regional Governance

Foucault's writing on the history of knowledge and power has had an enduring impact on the ways in which the social sciences understand the nature of government and governance (Foucault [2004] 2007; [2004] 2008). At the heart of Foucault's analysis of the history of governmental thought and practice is a genealogical method. Acting as what Deleuze terms "a new [kind of] archivist," genealogy enabled Foucault to develop novel ways of understanding the history of knowledge and power, and to destabilize universalized interpretations of the knowledge–power axis (1999). According to Rose, "[g]enealogies seek to destabilize a present that has forgotten its contingency, a moment that, thinking itself timeless, has forgotten the time-bound questions that gave rise to its beliefs and practices" (as cited in Foucault [2004] 2007: 4–5).

Although the primary focus of Foucault's own reflections on the history of government centres largely on the emergence of national systems of state power, his lectures offer fascinating insights into the entanglements between politics, knowledge, and urban space. In addition to identifying the municipal origins of bio-political power, Foucault argues that the planning systems of towns and cities such as Richelieu, Nantes, and Gothenburg reflect the changing historical rationalities of power (and in particular a gradual shift from sovereign and disciplinary forms of government to more flexible, self-governing processes of governmentality) (Foucault [2004] 2007: 17–23). Scholars keen to understand the changing nature of urban power and governance have built upon Foucault's passing metropolitan musings (see Huxley 2006; Legg 2007; Raco and Imrie 2000). Within this emerging body of work, there is a clear desire to understand urban government and governance as the product of the complex interplay between the changing nature of the city (including inner-city congestion, the spread of disease, air pollution, and suburbanization), and the logics of government, which seeks to harness cities in order to achieve specific political and economic objectives (including social control, economic growth, and the commercialization of land). The purpose of this chapter is to consider what the history of city-regional government can tell us about both the changing nature of modern and late modern metropolises, and the rationalities of power through which they are governed. This is not a history of urban government that is constructing for the sake of history, however. This is a history of the city-region that seeks to explore how the city-region came to be formed in and through specific systems of spatial government, and how seemingly inevitable systems of contemporary city-regional government could be constituted in radically different ways.

In relation to these analytical contexts, it is important to point out that this chapter does not interpret governmentality so much as a *paradigm* of government (exhibiting distinctive bureaucratic forms and a tendency toward diffused forms of self-regulated power) (Foucault [2004] 2007: 108) than as a *methodology* for studying the history of systems of government. This chapter takes its methodological cue from Foucault's own reflection on governmentality. At the very end of his 1978 lecture series on the history of government, he describes his project as "[a] little experiment in method" (ibid., 358). Understood as a method of studying government, as opposed to a theory of its modern formulation, governmentality is perhaps best thought of as the political expression of Foucault's broader genealogical project. According to Foucault, what characterizes this governmental methodology is a desire "[t]o show how starting from the relatively local and microscopic analysis ... it is possible, without paradox or contradiction, to return to the general problems of the state, on the condition precisely that we [do not make] the state [into] a transcendent reality whose history could be undertaken on the basis of itself" (ibid., 358).

As a method devoted to the study of the micro-practices of government, this chapter deploys governmentality as a basis for avoiding the teleological explanation of the nature of city-regional government on the basis of the late modern form of the city-region itself. Governmentality provides a methodology that, while not ignoring the role of states, neoliberalism, and globalization in the emergence of contemporary city-regions, seeks to avoid their explanatory allure (see Jonas and Ward 2007; Harding 2007). This form of methodological perspective appears important if we are to better understand how particular city-regions operate in the ways they do today, and how it may be possible to image and develop alternative city-regional programmes.

Governing the Borderland City: 1918–1945

The city of Katowice is now at the centre of the largest conurbation in Poland, with a population of approximately 2.7 million people. This conurbation is a collection of fifteen adjacent towns and cities that are collectively referred to as the Silesian Metropolis (*Metropolia Silesia*). The city also sits at the centre of a larger urban zone of some fifty urban centres, which has a total population of 5.3 million people (this larger collection of cities is know as the *Silesian Metropolitan Area*). The growth and spatial expansion of both the *Silesian Metropolis* and the *Silesian Metropolitan Area* really began in the nineteenth century with the first large-scale

Figure 15.1   The Silesian Metropolis. *Source*: Wikimedia Commons.

exploitation of the Upper Silesian Coal Basin. Drawing on the readily available brown coal (lignite) provided by the Coal Basin, Katowice, and its adjacent urban areas, became specialist centres of mining and metallurgy. The rapid urbanization of the Upper Silesian Coal Basin appears to explain the emergence of early forms of regional governance in and around Katowice, as metropolitan authorities struggled to cope with the increasing spatial scale and complexity of urban life. More careful historical analysis, however, reveals that the origins of regionalized forms of government in and around Katowice have as much to do with geopolitics as urban politics.

Regional governance around Katowice has, from its earliest days, been defined by the city's location at the intersection of the modern-day states of the Czech Republic, Germany, and Poland. At different times Katowice has found itself under the rule of the Kingdom of Bohemia, the Habsburg Empire, Germany, and Poland. The emergence of modern regional governance around the city, however, can be dated to 1918 and the end of the First World War. At this point, the new Polish state claimed that the high proportion of Polish speakers in Silesia should result in it ceasing to be a part of Germany and instead being incorporated into Poland. This move was resisted by Germany, and following a controversial plebiscite in 1921, 30% of the Silesian territories were ceded to Poland (Bialasiewicz 2002). The resolution of the boundary dispute saw the new national boundary between Germany and Poland running through the modern-day Silesian

Metropolis (with Katowice on the Polish side, but the urban communities of Gliwice and Bytom remaining in Germany) (see Figure 15.2). The division between the German and Polish portions of Upper Silesia has been described as a *soft division* between the two states, with significant trade and cross-cultural exchange occurring across the borderline (ibid., 114). Ultimately, the Geneva Convention became an important regulatory framework for the region, ensuring that the minority ethnic rights of Germans and Poles on each side of the border were preserved and respected (ibid.).

It is important to know something of the geopolitical history of Upper Silesia because its multi-ethnic composition lay at the heart of the emergence of regional government in the area. As early as 1920, the Polish state afforded Upper Silesia a special regional status. In order to reflect its ethnic composition, the Polish state granted Upper Silesia its own Parliament (*Sejm*) and devolved key powers to regions (including the taxation *inter alia*) (ibid., 113). In addition, and in order to reflect the diverse geography of local language use and ethnic affiliation, Poland also granted extensive devolved powers to metropolitan centres in Upper Silesia. Consequently, in addition to Katowice's regional subsidiarity, smaller urban authorities had the ability to determine language policy, educational planning, and control policing in their districts (ibid.). In the context of the unusual levels of governmental autonomy that were devolved to regional and urban governments in Upper Silesia during the 1920s, it is important to note that these were not—as with many of the governmental structures described elsewhere in this volume—primarily devised to address issues related to urbanization. The evolution of urban and regional scaled government in and around Katowice was much more about geopolitical compromise than an attempt to govern cities through regions.

There were three main factors associated with the emergence of urban regional governance around Katowice during the 1920s that have implications for the broader genealogy that is being constructed in this chapter. First of all, the formation of a regional scale of government in and around Katowice established a range of regional traditions and competences that continue to inform governance in the metropolis to this day, and certainly afforded Upper Silesia opportunities for regional development that were not experienced in other areas of Poland (ibid.). Second, however, the unusual level of autonomy that was granted to urban centres in Upper Silesia tended to inhibit the development of pan-urban collaboration in the region. Third, the separation of Katowice from its close urban

Figure 15.2 The 1921 division of Upper Silesia between Germany and Poland, with the provinces of Lublinitz, Tarnowitz, Beuthen, Königsh, Kattowitz, Rybnik, and Pleß allocated to Poland and the remaining areas to Germany. *Source:* Wiki Commons.

neighbours on the German side of the 1921 boundary made the emergence functionally integrated city-regional planning difficult to achieve.

The Socialist Region and the Upper Silesian Industrial District

Following Germany's invasion of Poland in 1939, the entirety of Upper Silesia was incorporated in the Third Reich. The German occupation of Upper Silesia saw the emergence of new forms of German nationalism in the region, as those denizens who were deemed to be "German" were enlisted to fight in the German Army (Bialasiewicz 2002). Following the end of the Second World War, concerted efforts were made to remove Upper Silesia's German ties, and to incorporate the region into the fledgling Polish socialist state. In all, some 3.5 million Germans were expatriated from Silesia following the end of the war. According to Bialasiewicz, the incorporation of Upper Silesia into the socialist governmental apparatus involved a fundamental shift in the rationalities of urban and region government in the area (2002: 118). This rationality shift had two key features: (1) an erosion of Upper Silesia's special status as ethnically mixed, and thus a governmentally unique region within Poland; (2) a system of government that prioritized the economic value of Upper Silesia as a key economic asset. Under the Polish state it was recognized that the natural resources and skilled workforce that resided in Upper Silesia were vital to the formation of a viable Polish socialist state. National policies thus worked to construct a fundamentally economic vision of the city-region and sought to support the economic expansion of the urban-regional economy. These goals were formally pursued through the creation of the *Upper Silesian Industrial District*.

The Upper Silesian Industrial District incorporated the major urban centres of the modern-day Silesian Metropolis (which had been previously been divided following the end of the First World War). In the place of regional ethnic identity, the Polish state promoted an image of urban Silesia as the workshop of Poland and a land of great industrial endeavour. In order to support this vision, and to attract skilled labour to the urban region, the Polish authorities built new workers' housing in the region and even vacation residences for miners and steelworkers (ibid., 118). Investments were also made to support the development of modern mining techniques and large-scale metal production facilities. Essentially, the Polish state endeavoured to construct a new structured coherence in the urban region that was devoted to the maximization of economic output. In narrow economic terms, the Upper Silesian Industrial District was successful. By 1991, the urban agglomeration was home to approximately 4,400 industrial plants (Whitehead 2005). The region was also responsible for all of Poland's hard coal, zinc, and lead output (ibid.). By 1990, the region was responsible for 17.8% of Poland's total GDP (ibid.). Combining as it did a bewildering array of urban industrial districts and economic operations, Katowice and the Silesian Metropolis essentially became a workshop for the Polish nation.

The jaundiced economic perspective that the socialist state had on Katowice did, however, have significant social and environmental consequences. Within the Upper Silesian Industrial District, planning was primarily devoted to the maximization of economic output. In an ironic sense, the Upper Silesian Industrial District involved urban and regional planning for largely unplanned forms of urban development. The relatively unplanned industrialization of Metropolitan Silesia under the Polish socialist state had two major consequences. First was the proliferation of significant forms of environmental degradation and despoliation in the region. In the absence of significant forms of environmental regulation, or the economic incentive to improve the efficiencies of industrial processes (see Whitehead 2010), Katowice became the hub for a concentration of socio-ecological problems. By 1994, the black smoke being emitted from the Katowice agglomeration's numerous power plants and metal works was running at six times the permissible European Union threshold (Whitehead 2005). It was for this reason that Katowice actually lay at the heart of eastern Europe's so-called *black triangle* of air pollution. Partly as a consequence of these high levels of air pollution, during the 1990s the Provincial Epidemiology Station for Upper Silesia reported rates of cancer, respiratory, and cardio-vascular diseases significantly above the national average. Rapid industrialization, and in particular the widespread use of open cast mining, also resulted in the despoliation of approximately 20,000 hectares of land in and around Katowice (ibid.).

The second consequence of unplanned urbanization in Katowice was the emergence of a metropolis with only limited levels of integrated infrastructure provision. In part, the poorly integrated road, open space, and waste management systems that have become associated with Metropolitan Silesia were a product of the rapid growth of the city. The lack of investment in infrastructure was, however, partly the consequences of the high levels of autonomy that had been granted to the different urban districts in Upper Silesia during the 1920s. The construction of relatively small-scale, autonomous metropolitan authorities led to a lack of pan-urban integrated planning, and also limited the amount of resources that were available for large-scale infrastructure projects.

The gulf that emerged between the socialist state's promise of a workers' Eldorado in Upper Silesia and the reality of urban decline and ecological catastrophe resulted in significant expressions of civil unrest in Katowice during the 1970s and 1980s. Working-class struggles in Upper Silesia focused on the activities of the Solidarity Movement in the region, and ultimately resulted in the declaration of martial law at the *Wujek Mine* (Bialasiewicz 2002: 118). In 1987, Katowice also saw the birth of one of socialist Poland's first and most influential green groups: the *Silesia Ecology Movement* (Whitehead 2005). Through various scientific projects and political events, the Silesia Ecology Movement sought to draw attention to the environmental consequences of unfettered socialist industrialization in and around Katowice.

Rescue Bureaucracies and Post-Socialist City-Region

The collapse of European socialism in the late 1980s and early 90s provided a new set of opportunities to address the socio-ecological problems associated with the Silesian Metropolis. As part of the broader transition into a post-socialist society, politicians, activists and policy-makers recognized the chance to construct a new form of urban-regional apparatus in and around Katowice (for a broader discussion of the impacts of post-socialist transitions on regional governance in Poland, see Bafoil 2002 and Lackowska-Madurowicz and Swianiewicz 2013). The construction of a post-socialist city-region really began in 1994 with the initiation of the *Katowice Agglomeration Project*. The *Katowice Agglomeration Project* was funded through the United Nations Habitat programme. This new agglomeration project sought to build a new city-region that was framed by the principles of sustainable development. It is best to conceive of the

Katowice Agglomeration Project as a response both to the disjointed systems of urban/regional planning that had taken hold around Katowice in the 1920s, and the overtly economic visions of regional development that were promoted within the *Upper Silesia Industrial District.*

The Katowice Agglomeration Project drew together the fourteen urban districts, which centre on Katowice, in an attempt to construct an integrated framework for urban and regional planning (this definition of the city-region corresponds to the Silesian Metropolis depicted in Figure 15.1). Many city-regions are formed in order to consolidate the power and influence of a given city over its regional hinterland, or to enable a city that has escaped its traditional urban limits to be better regulated. In the case of Katowice, however, the new city-region was a response to the disjointed and environmentally damaging effects of different urban centres growing into each other. In the words of Klaas van der Molen, "The map of Silesia gives a smashed picture of living, economic activities and recreational activities. Instead of having a central idea of a city with its neighbouring landscape we can better speak about an urban field. Moreover the process of fractionation has got its entirely own dynamics, with itself a strengthening character." Although van Der Molen's reflections on Urban Silesia appear to reflect the forms of the in-between city outlined by Sieverts (2003), the Silesian Metropolis has a distinct set of in-between qualities. While Sieverts described the emerge of a patchwork of urban sprawl and rural spaces on the edge of cities, in and around Katowice the in-between city spaces are marked by industrial decline, despoiled land, and a lack of integrated infrastructure (see Perogordo 2010). These are spaces that exist within the fledgling city-region and, at the same time, define the spatial extent of region and prevent it from functioning as a workable socio-economic and environmental space.

Centring on the Silesian Metropolis, the Katowice Agglomeration Project initially prioritized two key areas of policy development: land and water resources. Land-use and reclamation policies focused on trying to address the problems generated by land degradation and contamination in the city-region. At one level, these policies had an ecological focus, and sought to improve soil quality and broader habitat conditions in order to support environmental restoration. However, these policies also had a social justice dimension, as United Nations monies were used to construct a network of parks and green spaces that local residents—long starved of access to well-maintained open spaces—could enjoy. It is important to note that given that many of these spaces of dereliction and despoliation cut across different municipal areas, it was important to create a regional mechanism in and through which action could be taken to develop the consolidated restoration of these areas.

City-regional water policy primarily focused on the development of a modern and integrated municipal sewage system. In the context of the fragmented systems of urban planning that characterized urban Silesia during much of the twentieth century, no integrated sewage system had been developed in the region. With significant levels of unevenness in the quality of waste water between the different municipal districts constituting the Katowice agglomeration, significant amounts of sewage had been entering local rivers and streams. With polluted water affecting all urban districts in the region, there was also limited incentive for more progressive municipalities to invest, unilaterally, in modern waste-water treatment facilities. It was hoped that by bringing the different urban waste-water collection and treatment authorities together, it would be possible to coordinate and fund a more effective waste-water treatment infrastructure.

It is important to note at this point the particular material conditions that appear to have given rise to city-regional government in Silesia during the early 1990s. In keeping with the genealogical method set out above, it is clear that the emergence of a city-region in Silesia cannot be read as an inevitable response to the dynamics of urban expansion or the logics of neo-liberal globalization. In the case of Katowice, late modern urban regionalism appears to have emerged out of the urban-environmental malaise that was produced by socialist era regional policy. In this context we find polluted rivers, poorly maintained sewage networks, and despoiled land, all contributing to the formation of a city-regional capacity-to-act. Moreover, it is also clear to see that in the case of the Katowice Agglomeration Project the formation of an urban-region in Silesia was not an assertion of economic strength, but more an attempt to build a rescue bureaucracy in and through which metropolitan life could be made more bearable.

The Katowice Agglomeration Project provided a template for regionalized urban government that has continued to influence Upper Silesia. Initially, the urban areas involved in the Katowice Agglomeration project came together to form a more permanent and broader ranging regional alliance. This alliance was initially called the *Metropolitan Association of Silesia*. In 2006, participating urban areas signed a new voluntary agreement that formed the Silesian Metropolis. The Polish Republic formally recognized this new "metropolitan municipality" in 2007. In many ways the formation of Silesian Metropolis reflects both the long history of city-regional government in the area, and a continuing desire to develop a form of transformative, insurgent regionalism, which both recognizes local culture, but also attempts to secure sustainable forms of development in the region. In reality, however, the consolidation of this new city-regional apparatus appears to have a much more narrow set of associated intentions. With a strong emphasis being placed on "job creation," "innovative economic development strategies," "road building," and the securing of European Union development funding, it appears that the Silesia Metropolis may reflect the rise of a distinctly New Regionalism in southern Poland. In many respects, it appears that city-regionalism in Silesia reflects the broader tensions associated with transitional societies, such as Poland. While the transition away from socialism offers new opportunities for the development of more sustainable, inclusive, and egalitarian forms of society, the emergence of more entrepreneurial and growth-oriented orthodoxies can threaten these desired goals.

Coda: Reflections on a City-Regional Methodology

It may seem disappointing given all of the talk about radical, non-deterministic city-regional methodologies at the outset of this chapter that we should have arrived at the Silesia Metropolis, replete with all of the expected tropes of the neo-liberal city-regional economy. But, although governmentality offers a method for developing a genealogy of the city-regional present, it cannot, on its own at least, lead us to an alternate present. What a genealogy of city-regional government does do, however, is to reveal the multitude of political and economic rationalities, and material conditions, that have given rise to the emergence of different systems of city-regional government, and how it may be possible to image alternative city-regional systems of government in the future.

Through the case of city-regional government in Katowice we have been able to compare the contemporary post-socialist city-region, devoted as it is to the pursuit of economic innovation and competitive integration into the global economy, with its historical predecessors. These were city-regions that were marked by ethnic sensibilities, the desire to generate cosmopolitan regional spaces, socialist ideologies, and international relief efforts. These are, of course, rationalities from the past that continue to inform the spatial form and functioning of the modern city-region. They are logics of city-regionalism, which have been sedimented into the contemporary region and can be used to contest its contemporary form. As forms of buried city-regional epistemologies, these spatial logics can be used to challenge the assumption that city-regions inevitably have to be about the creation of collective capacities to act within the global market place. They can help to remind us that city-regions can also be about

Figure 15.3   The Silesia City Centre Mall. Opened in 2005, this mall is in many ways an emblem of the city-region's turn toward a more consumerist, post-socialist vision of development.

solving the practical ethnic, economic, environmental, and administrative challenges that confront us within ever-changing regional spaces. The question, however, remains as to whether genealogies of the city-regional present can help to inspire the maps that can shape city-regional futures.

References

Bafoil, F. 2002. "Post-communist borders and territories: Conflicts, learning and rule-building in Poland." *International Journal of Urban and Regional Research* 23: 567–82.

Bialasiewicz, L. 2002. "Upper Silesia: Rebirth of a regional identity in Poland." *Regional and Federal Studies* 12: 111–32.

Deleuze, G. 1999. *Foucault*. London: Continuum.

Foucault, M. (2004) 2008. *The birth of biopolitics – Lectures at the Collège de France 1978–79*. Basingstoke: Palgrave Macmillan.

Foucault, M. and K. R. Cox. (2004) 2007. *Security, territory and population – Lectures at the Collège de France 1977–78*. Basingstoke: Palgrave Macmillan.

Huxley, M. 2006. "Spatial rationalities: Order, environment, evolution and government." *Social and Cultural Geography* 7: 771–87.

Lackowska-Madurowicz, M. and P. Swianiewicz. 2013. "Structures, procedures and social capital: The implementation of EU cohesion policies by subnational governments in Poland." *International Journal of Urban and Regional Research* 37: 1396–418.

Legg, S. 2007. *Spaces of colonialism: Delhi's urban governmentalities*. Oxford: Blackwell.

Perogordo, J. D. 2010. *The Silesia megapolis*. Saarbrücken: Lap Lambert Academic.

Raco, M., and R. Imrie. 2000. "Governmentality and rights and responsibilities in urban policy." *Environment and Planning A* 32: 2187–204.

Sieverts, T. 2003. *Cities without cities: An interpretation of the Zwischenstadt: Between place and world, space and time, town and country.* London: Routledge.

Whitehead, M. 2005. "Between the marvellous and the mundane: Everyday life in the socialist city and the politics of the environment." *Environment and Planning D: Society and Space* 23(2): 273–94.

———. 2010. "Hollow sustainabilities: Perspective on sustainable development in the post-socialist world." *Geography Compass* 4(11): 1618–34.

CHAPTER 16

Building Narratives of City-Regions
The Case of Barcelona

Mariona Tomàs

Introduction

THE DEBATE ON metropolitan governance can be interpreted as a tension between the functional and political definitions of city-regions. On one hand, the regional scale is increasingly considered as a "functional space" for economic planning and political governance (Keating 1998). This conception tends to consider city-region formation as a "by-product of macro-restructuring" (Jonas and Ward 2007: 175)—that is, to think of city-regions in terms of economic agency. The concept of city-region fails to integrate the role of politics and the mechanisms through which the agents attempt to influence change (Harding 2007). For instance, European territorial development policy discussions and plans, such as the Europe 2020 strategy, focus mainly on the issue of economic competitiveness of urban regions. Nevertheless, city-regions are more than territorial or statistical units for planning; they are living territories where political struggles take place around the issues of economic development, social cohesion, sustainability, etc. City-regional narratives are part of the social process of city-region building, where different actors have their own definition of the city-region: ideas on nature, landscape, the built environment, culture/ethnicity, dialects, economic success/recession, periphery/centre relations, stereotypic images of a people/community, etc. (Paasi 2003: 477).

The analysis of how narratives are constructed is inevitably linked to the power relations existing within a city-region. There might be a dominant narrative or competing narratives, depending on the configuration of local actors. The comparison between metropolitan governance in Toronto and Montreal done by Boudreau, Hamel, Jouve, and Keil (2006, 2007a, 2007b) can be read in this way. According to the authors, in Toronto a coalition formed by business groups and political elites (the Toronto City Summit Alliance, now Civic Action) built a shared narrative on the city-region with a globally oriented agenda of local economic development. Differently, in Montreal the existence of competing narratives supported by diverse actors (politicians, chambers of commerce, community groups) makes impossible the construction of a common vision of Greater Montreal. Indeed, there exist disparate ideas of the goals to be achieved (equality, democracy, efficiency, and economic competitiveness), the suitable scale for their achievement (the territorial limits of city-region), and the appropriateness of city-regional cooperation and its form (compulsory or voluntary, number of municipalities involved, etc.) (Tomàs 2012).

Narratives become the symbolic resource for actors pushing for the creation of city-regions to serve their own ambitions, i.e., keeping local autonomy, pursuing economic competitiveness or fiscal equity. However, the political and social strength of the competing narratives on city-regions is not equal: it depends on the power of different groups and their capacity to pass their own conceptions on city-regions. These are filtered by the intergovernmental system and the institutional context (Pierre 1999; Mossberger and Stoker 2001; Sellers 2002), which legitimates some actors and their narratives at the expense of others. Narratives and practices are connected to the inherited institutional milieu and dominant political culture (DiGaetano and Strom 2003). As authors embracing neo-institutionalism have shown, there is an interrelation between ideas, actors, and the institutional context where they operate (Hall 1993; Lowndes 2005).

This chapter analyzes the construction of narratives on city-regions through the case of Barcelona.[1] First, I show that there exists an elastic definition of the city-region, that is, a plurality of definitions of what is considered the Barcelona urban region; each of them corresponds to a different conception of the territory. Second, I examine which actors (economic, political, etc.) are behind these narratives on city-region and for what political purpose. Finally, I study how inherited political cultures and institutional milieux shape the institutionalization and articulation of metropolitan governance structures and processes.

Barcelona City-Region: An Elastic Definition

When analyzing metropolitan governance in Barcelona, the first thing that needs to be stressed is the use of the "regional." In this case, the "region" refers to one of the seventeen decentralized territorial units of the Spanish State (Autonomous Communities) as established by the Constitution of 1978. By "regional government" we refer to the government of Catalonia (called *Generalitat*), with significant legislative and executive powers over a wide range of areas—housing, urban and regional planning, agriculture, transport, health, education, social welfare, and culture—according to the terms of its autonomy statute. The Autonomous Community has a Parliament formed by 135 deputies directly elected every four years. Catalonia has 7.5 million inhabitants living mainly in urban but also rural areas, in a larger territory than the city-region of Barcelona. Thus, as it happens in the European context (Tomàs 2015), we cannot identify the "regional" with the "city-regional" or the "metropolitan" (differently, for instance, from other cases discussed in the present book).

Contrary to Canada or the United States, there is a lack of statistical classification of urban areas both at the state and regional level. It is only very recently that the Spanish census has provided consistent data on links between municipalities based on mobility. Nevertheless, this step has not been complemented by an effort to establish the limits of each of the approximately twenty-five metropolitan areas above 200,000 inhabitants likely to exist in Spain. As a result, there is no official and shared definition of the "urban" and the "metropolitan." In Barcelona up to three definitions of the urban region are used: city-region, metropolitan region, and metropolitan area. Each one refers to a different territory and is formed by different institutions (see Table 16.1).

The Barcelona city-region is taken to be the spatial extent of the Barcelona province, one of four within Catalonia. The provincial division was imposed by the central government in 1833; during the Franco dictatorship, its chief, the *governador civil*, was the delegate of the central power in Catalonia. This radically changed following democracy with the creation of the Autonomous Communities. Provinces are recognized in the Spanish Constitution as a second level of local government, with responsibilities in assisting the municipalities, and are ruled by an indirectly elected board and assembly. The province of Barcelona represents almost 75% of the Catalan population and is formed by 311 municipalities and eleven counties (which are supra-municipal authorities created by the Catalan Parliament in 1987). Over 50% of the population of the city-region (5.5 million) lies within seven municipalities with populations

Table 16.1 Definitions of the city-region of Barcelona

Definition	Population 2012	% of total population	Surface (km²)	Density (hab/km²)	Institutions	Political Representation
Region of Catalonia	7,570,908	100	32,113	236	4 provinces 41 counties 947 municipalities	Direct
City-region	5,552,050	73.3	7,728	718	1 province 11 counties 311 municipalities	Indirect
Metropolitan region	4,798,143	63.4	3,239	1,481	7 counties 164 municipalities	No Representation
Metropolitan area	3,239,337	42.8	634	5,111	1 metropolitan authority 4 counties 36 municipalities	Indirect
Barcelona	1,620,943	21.4	99	16,340	1 municipality	Direct

Source: Author's elaboration with data from the Catalan Institute of Statistics.

of more than 100,000 inhabitants. By contrast, just over 20% of the population resides in 161 municipalities of less than 20,000 inhabitants. Therefore, the urban structure of the city-region is that of a significantly high proportion of the overall population concentrated within a few small towns and cities, with a correspondingly small proportion of the population spread out widely across the city-region.

In Barcelona, the province has been very active in promoting the cooperation of municipalities through local networks and programs. However, for some geographers and a majority of the Catalan political parties, the provincial division is an old-fashioned administrative level that does not correspond to the territorial reality, which would be better adapted through seven territorial districts (*vegueries*), one of them being the metropolitan *vegueria* (see below). The province of Barcelona includes dense urban centres with small rural municipalities; this is why it is seen as a "too large" administration for the metropolitan reality. In this sense, the province is not identified with a city-region but with an administrative division. The European Union has enhanced the province as an urban territorial space through such initiatives as the European Spatial Planning Observation Network (ESPON Programme 2006). The EU uses a hierarchical system for dividing up the economic territory into regions called the NUTS classification (Nomenclature of Territorial Units for Statistics). ESPON projects consider that city-regions correspond to NUTS 3, which is, in our case, the province of Barcelona. However, NUTS 3 in Barcelona does not correspond to continuous built-up areas or functional areas in terms of economic and employment integration (Harding et al. 2010). To summarize, the city-region does not have a bottom-up narrative: it is seen as an artificial division created by the Spanish government, on one hand, and used for statistical purposes by the EU on the other. Moreover, it does not have directly elected representatives and its functions are not well understood by citizens.

Inside the boundaries of the province, the metropolitan region of Barcelona comprises 164 municipalities and seven counties. This territory has higher densities than the city-region and is considered the second ring of the Barcelona agglomeration. Similarly to that of the city-region, the narrative on the metropolitan region is weak. The metropolitan region has been considered the functional area of Barcelona by urban planners, geographers, and architects since the 1960s. On several occasions, metropolitan plans were written taking this scale into account. However, a smaller conception of the metropolitan reality—the metropolitan area—was always adopted. The idea of the metropolitan region as the adequate functional space for planning was finally assumed at the end of the 1990s with the creation of the Metropolitan Authority of Transport. This consortium formed by different levels of administrations is responsible for the cooperation, coordination, planning, and financing of public transit services and infrastructures. It has been essential for enabling citizen mobility across a large part of the city-region's territory thanks to the integration of public transit systems.

Only in April 2010 was a Metropolitan Territorial Plan approved that took into account the 164 municipalities. This plan is a general framework that has to be developed in smaller plans, one of them corresponding to the metropolitan area of Barcelona. The metropolitan region has also been considered as an alternative to the province of Barcelona by some geographers and political parties. In fact, the metropolitan region is formally a level of decentralization of the Catalan Government, the *vegueria*, as stated by the Law of Territorial Organization approved in July 2010. However, this new administrative division has not been implemented for two main reasons. First of all, because the coalition of political parties that approved the law creating the *vegueries* is no longer in power. The new government decided that in the context of economic crises and fiscal deficit, the creation of a new level of administration was not a top government priority. Secondly, provinces are constitutionally recognized. Any reform affecting them requires the approval of the Spanish Parliament, which is very unlikely to happen. Hence the metropolitan region seems to be condemned to be a functional space.

The metropolitan area of Barcelona is the urban core of the city-region and accounts for almost 60% of its population. It has 3.2 million inhabitants and thirty-six municipalities; most of them are immediately contiguous and some cities are physically adjacent to Barcelona and connected by subway. Traditionally, debates on metropolitan governance have been centred on this territory. Indeed, the City of Barcelona and the inner ring have shared the same institutional organization, regional plan, and management of services for the last forty years (for a history of metropolitan governance in Barcelona, see Tomàs 2010). Briefly, from 1974 to 1987, it was ruled by a metropolitan government, which was abolished and replaced by two special districts (public transport and environment) and a voluntary association of inter-municipal cooperation. The law on the Metropolitan Area of Barcelona (MAB), passed in July 2010, put an end to the institutional fragmentation with the creation of a new metropolitan body. Officially constituted after the local elections of May 2011, the Metropolitan Area of Barcelona gathers the political representatives of the thirty-six municipalities and assumes the previous responsibilities in public transport and environment, as well as new powers in economic development and urban planning.

In this case, there is a collective narrative that has been built in the last forty years and strengthened since 2003, with the approval of the first Strategic Metropolitan Plan. This was revised in 2007 and a second Strategic Metropolitan Plan was approved in 2010. The City of Barcelona has a long tradition in strategic planning (three strategic plans were approved in 1990, 1994, and 1999), conceived as the instrument to integrate a collective vision and to design the main guidelines of the city's development. Indeed, the members of the original strategic plan were the City of Barcelona and other actors such as employer's organizations, trade unions, chambers of commerce, Fair of Barcelona, Port and Airport of Barcelona, University of Barcelona, and other administrations. The Strategic Metropolitan Plan includes the participation of representatives from thirty-six municipalities and has served to identify and promote strategies for the economic and social development of the metropolitan area. In addition to the strategic plan, the municipalities of the metropolitan area decided voluntarily in 2009 to create the Consortium of the Metropolitan Area of Barcelona, which joined together the three existing metropolitan entities so as to prepare the institutional transition to the Metropolitan Area of Barcelona. To sum up, there is a consensus coming from local elites that the institutional fragmentation is harmful to the interests of the metropolitan municipalities and that it is better to have a single metropolitan authority. Indeed, all political parties voted for its creation in 2010.

The mayor of Barcelona is the president of the new metropolitan body. The municipality is ruled and administered by the council, formed by directly elected councillors and the mayor, elected by the councillors. After accelerated growth during the 1960s and 70s, the 1980s and 90s were characterized by a steady loss of population that moved out of the city to the surrounding municipalities. The negative trend has changed over the last ten years, with the arrival of foreign immigrants, and the population has held steady around 1.6 million inhabitants. In spite of the loss of the demographic weight, the City of Barcelona has not ceased to be the economic and political centre of Catalonia. The city has a long history and its boundaries have not changed since 1921. In the popular imaginary, Barcelona is identified with the "urban," meaning both the positive and negative aspects of it (cosmopolitism and innovation but also pollution and insecurity). Moreover, the city has traditionally represented the "metropolitan" because of its political leadership among other municipalities (see below). Indeed, the narrative on the metropolitan area is sometimes merged with that of the central city, showing the elasticity of the conceptions of territory.

The contemporary narrative of Barcelona is inevitably linked to the venue of the 1992 Olympic Games: the city created an international image based on a unique model of urban planning that enabled both economic development and social cohesion. However, at the local level, the so-called "Barcelona model" has been put into question in the last decade by community groups and academics calling for solidarity (Capel 2005; Delgado 2007). They argue that the city's policies are increasingly oriented toward economic competitiveness and especially toward the tourist sector, resulting in the transformation of the city into a brand. Other issues, such as the celebration of a new global event called Universal Forum of Cultures in 2004 and the approval of a restrictive normative on the use of public spaces, have also been polemic (Iglesias et al. 2011).

In May 2011 there was a change in the city council with the victory of centre-right nationalist party *Convergència i Unió*, putting an end to thirty-two years of non-stop socialist mayors. Nevertheless, the lack of an absolute majority has required the support of the Socialist Party and the Conservative Party in the approval of the local budget and main projects. In general, the narrative continues to be focused on the need to balance economic development and social cohesion. However, the accent has been put on a new dimension of this dialectic: local sustainability. Indeed, the new mayor endorsed the smart city discourse. Since 2012, the city council has been signing different agreements with powerful companies (IBM, Indra, Cisco, Abertis Telecom, and Schneider Electric) to develop "smart" policies and city protocols based on new technologies. Moreover, the city is using the smart city narrative as a way to contribute to the internationalization of the city. For instance, the city hosts the annual Smart City Expo World Congress and has become an active member of international networks related to this issue.

The process of *brandification* of the city has culminated in the registration of the collective "Barcelona" trademark by the city council. From now on, the use of "Barcelona" in all products is reserved for the city and any exploitation of it is regulated locally: "The regulations are intended to protect the trademark from being used in such a way as to lose its symbolic value and also to put it at the service of economic recovery, with the aim of attracting investment to the city and raising its international profile.... Nor may the city's brand be used for products or services that are of low quality, that take unfair advantage of Barcelona's prestige or which aim to discredit the city council, its metropolitan area of influence or its citizens."[2] Barcelona is the first Spanish city to consider itself officially a trademark.

This overview shows that there is no single definition of the Barcelona city-region. It is an elastic concept that is appropriated by local and regional actors with different conceptions of the territory and seeking different goals. Table 16.2 illustrates this plurality of narratives.

The case of Barcelona reflects the tension between functional and political definitions of city-regions. As Jones and MacLeod (2004: 435) have described, we can distinguish between "regional spaces" and "spaces of regionalism." The first is meant to denote the economic or functional dimension while the second denotes the political attempts to construct regionalism. Regional spaces are said to be the heart of the new globalized economy and the spaces of regionalism are the expression of claims for political and citizenship rights linked to a socially constructed territory. In the case of Barcelona, the city-region and the metropolitan region appear clearly as regional spaces. Differently, the metropolitan area would appear at first glance to be a space of regionalism, since a shared narrative has been built at this scale. However, as we will see in the next section, the construction of the metropolitan scale as a collective actor is influenced by the institutional context, which confines this space to its functional dimension.

Table 16.2   Narratives on Barcelona city-region

Scale	Actor leading the Narrative	Other actors	Goal
City-region	Central government/ European union	Regional and local governments	Urban planning Economic policies Assistance to municipalities
Metropolitan region	Experts	Coalition of political parties in power (2010) at the regional government	Transportation Urban planning
Metropolitan area	Municipalities members of MAB	Members of strategic plan	Public transport Environment Economic development Urban planning
Barcelona	City of Barcelona	Private companies Community groups	Economic development Sustainability Social cohesion

Source: Author's elaboration.

The Emergence of e City-Region as a Collective Actor

One of the questions at the heart of this comparative project is the capacity of city-regions to emerge as a collective actor. Is there a city-regional political space? Is the city-region a suitable scale for social mobilization and political claims? The existence of a shared narrative, that is, the consensus between different actors on the needs and priorities of the city-region, would be a sign of the capacity of this scale to emerge as a collective actor. Nevertheless, we should examine the degree of openness of local governance networks to prove to what extent this new tier of governance brings a political opportunity to actors of the civil society. For instance, initiatives such as strategic plans tend to focus on organized groups and leave aside critical voices (Heinelt and Kübler 2005).

In the case of Barcelona, we have seen that the elasticity of the city-region results in the coexistence of diverse narratives at different scales (city-region, metropolitan region, metropolitan area, and City of Barcelona). At the supra-municipal level, the metropolitan area appears as the scale with greater potential to emerge as a collective actor, for two reasons. In the first place, a shared narrative between regional and local politicians as well as members of the Strategic Metropolitan Plan has been built around this scale. In spite of political conflicts during the last decades, a common idea seems to prevail that supra-municipal cooperation is necessary. In the second place, this shared narrative is supported by a new metropolitan institution created by regional law. A major degree of institutionalization should enable the continuity of the common vision and major citizen participation, according to reformist authors (Sharpe 1995).

The creation of the Metropolitan Area of Barcelona is very recent, but in this period we cannot find any sign of a strengthening of its political dimension. The institutional shape has changed (from three bodies to one) but the role played by its representatives continues to be marginal in the whole political system. The MAB keeps the previous responsibilities in hard policies, such as public transport and environment; the services (public transport, water supply, sewage) are provided by public and private companies. However, some important changes have occurred in the internal organization of the provision of services, especially the privatization of the complete cycle of water management. The majority of councillors of the MAB approved in 2012 the merger of the existing public company of water treatment with a private company—Aguas de Barcelona (AGBAR)—which has been supplying water to the citizens of Barcelona since 1867 and now belongs to the corporation GDF Suez. As a result, AGBAR owns 85% of the new company, spreading its influence over the municipalities of the MAB (the company is the principal supplier of water in the area). The metropolitan politicians argue that AGBAR will be able to manage the water cycle more efficiently, but so far there has been a substantial rise in water bills in a territory with an average of 24% of unemployment. Moreover, prices of public transport, approved by the Metropolitan Authority of Transport, have also increased above the average annual increase. The MAB then influences the quality of life of citizens by approving the rise of taxes linked to water, sewage and public transit services. Nevertheless, the majority of citizens are not aware of this power and the institution has limited accountability.

New metropolitan powers in urban planning and economic development have not yet been developed, mainly for three reasons. First, since the 1980s, municipalities belonging to the metropolitan area have taken an active role in creating and participating in voluntary mechanisms of inter-municipal cooperation (consortiums, plans, projects, etc.). In recent years, they have been especially active in promoting strategies for enhancing economic development, together with other levels of government and private actors. Second, the economic crisis has postponed the implementation of new projects, since the majority of the municipalities (which partially finance the metropolitan institution) have financial problems. Third, the design of metropolitan economic strategies has traditionally been made by the Strategic Metropolitan Plan; this continues to exist in spite of the creation of the MAB, which has its own department of strategic planning.

The integration of a metropolitan dimension by social and economic actors has not increased since the creation of the MAB. Indeed, the transition from the strategic plan of the City of Barcelona to the Strategic Metropolitan Plan meant the entrance of thirty-five new mayors that altered the previous balance of the association between political representatives and social and economic actors. Non-institutional actors have lost representation and the association has been increasingly politicized, becoming less appealing for economic and social agents. In Barcelona, representatives from private companies have created a lobby called *Barcelona Global* that works directly with the mayor. In fact, City Hall has given this organization the responsibility to manage the "Barcelona Brand," that is, to monitor the use of "Barcelona" as a trademark. Therefore, the most powerful companies have built their own space of influence: they no longer need the Strategic Metropolitan Plan as a platform.

Another reason that explains the weakness of appropriation of a metropolitan narrative by social and economic actors is linked to their territorial location. Indeed, most of these actors are physically rooted in the

City of Barcelona, which has not been well accepted by councillors coming from metropolitan municipalities. There are no relevant actors (chamber of commerce, trade unions, NGOs, universities) with a metropolitan basis. Social movements also lack a metropolitan dimension: they are rooted in neighbourhoods and cities, or have a wider regional scope (e.g., the Autonomous Community of Catalonia).

The recent case of *Eurovegas* illustrates this idea. Briefly, during 2012 there was a public debate about establishing a new resort of the Las Vegas Sands Corporation called *Eurovegas*. The chosen site for the resort was in the rural lands of two municipalities that were close to Barcelona and members of the MAB. However, the metropolitan authority—as the institutional collective actor—was absent from the debate. The negotiations with Sheldon Adelson were directed by the Territory Catalan Minister, who ignored local mayors' opinions. Simultaneously, various organizations opposed to the project assembled under the name of "Stop Eurovegas." This comprised a variety of actors, ranging from environmental groups at the local and regional level to neighbourhood associations. This group advocated for the preservation of rural spaces and criticized the kind of development proposed (building casinos and tall buildings) and the activities associated with the project (gambling, prostitution, etc.), but did not bring a metropolitan perspective to the discourse. Even if the project were located physically in the metropolitan area, the debate around *Eurovegas* was considered neither by politicians nor by citizens as a metropolitan issue. Finally, Adelson chose not to build the resort and "Stop Eurovegas" has transformed into an association for the protection of the ecological systems surrounding Barcelona.

Political culture and the institutional milieu explain the lack of political relevance of the metropolitan area. The Barcelona city-region is embedded in a multilevel governance system, formed by local, regional, and national levels. The relationships between the Catalan government and the Spanish government, the Catalan government and the City of Barcelona, and the City of Barcelona and suburban municipalities, all affect metropolitan governance and explain why the metropolitan area has not emerged as a collective actor.

In this complex institutional framework, the national government has powers in local government by general laws that affect their responsibilities and financing system. The Catalan Parliament—respecting the constitutional principles regarding local government—decides the number of municipalities, the existence of other levels of government, and the creation of metropolitan areas. For thirty-five years of democratic rule in Spain, there have not been incentives to promote the consolidation of metropolitan areas as institutional arrangements to deal with complex urban issues. Because of the specific features of the Spanish political system—and specifically those features that refer to its territorial structure—the consolidation of Autonomous Communities has been the priority. Indeed, the development of other forms of local autonomy, which could potentially challenge the power of the new and emerging political actors, has been systematically postponed to a later stage. Metropolitan governance has not been a prominent issue on the political agenda, neither at the national level, nor at the individual level of each Autonomous Community. In Catalonia, claims for more autonomy and regular negotiations with the Spanish government have guided the agenda of the Catalan government during the last thirty-five years at the expense of other issues such as urban affairs.

Moreover, Barcelona is the political and economic centre of Catalonia. As in other metropolises, the relationships between the two levels are complicated because of the distribution of powers (Heinelt and Kübler 2005). For instance, the MAB has powers in hard policies, but they are shared with local and regional governments. These two levels retain responsibility in soft policies, such as social housing, education, and culture. Moreover, the new metropolitan authority applies to thirty-six municipalities. This is a limited conception of the metropolitan reality, which spreads to the 164 municipalities of the metropolitan region or even to the 311 municipalities of the city-region. Limiting the new metropolitan authority to 3.2 million inhabitants instead of almost five million (the metropolitan region) or even 5.5 million (the city-region) is undoubtedly a political choice (keeping the metropolis "under control" in a region of 7.5 million inhabitants). Political factors such as differences in political majorities also influence metropolitan governance. The party-political divergence between the Catalan government and the Council of Barcelona explains in part the abolition of the metropolitan government in 1987. This political decision illustrates the cleavage between conservative Catalan nationalist support in the inner territory and the political dominance of left-wing parties in Barcelona and its metropolitan area. However, party-political congruence between 2003 and 2010 did not lead immediately to a specific recognition of metropolitan reality: this was achieved at the end of the legislature after an intense debate about the Catalan Autonomy Statute. The political convergence between the Catalan government and the Council of Barcelona that existed between 2011 and 2015 has not meant any significant change in the relationship between the two institutions. This is another example of the supremacy of scalar conflicts over political parties' cleavages.

Finally, the metropolitan area has difficulties in emerging as a collective actor because of the resistance of the municipalities themselves. First of all, municipalities provide the basic services for the day-to-day life of citizens and are their closest level of political representation. In the Spanish context, this is especially relevant in urban areas. During the 1980s, local governments had to supply the lack of basic infrastructures and services inherited from the Franco dictatorship, with scarce resources. In Barcelona, this period of adjustment coincided with the existence of the Metropolitan Corporation, which was seen by suburban municipalities as an instrument of domination of the pre-Olympic city. Twenty-five years later, the neo-regionalist thinking of sharing a common vision of the metropolitan challenges has been strengthened. However, the perception that the City of Barcelona tends to dominate the metropolitan area has not faded away.

To summarize, the metropolitan area of Barcelona has not emerged as a political actor but remains a functional level for the provision of services. The parallel processes of decentralization of the Spanish state on one hand and the process of municipalization of urban affairs on the other have left no political space for the metropolitan area. Similarly to Canada, having a strong metropolitan level is likely one level too many (Sancton 2001: 547).

Conclusion: A City-Region for Whom?

Based on the case of Barcelona, this chapter has examined the process of political construction of city-regions. We argue that this is an elastic concept: it includes alternative conceptions of the metropolitan reality conveyed by local and regional politicians, central and European institutions, geographers, urban planners, and architects. These narratives refer to different territories and are supported by diverse actors with specific purposes. In the case of Barcelona, narratives refer to the city-region, the metropolitan region, the metropolitan area, and the City of Barcelona. The institutional context, including both formal structures and political culture, explains why some narratives appear more legitimate than others.

One hypothesis is that the emergence of a collective actor at the city-regional scale depends on the degree of consensus in each city-region on two diverging goals: economic competitiveness on one hand and social coherence on the other. In the metropolitan area of Barcelona, a shared narrative has been built thanks to strategic planning and inter-municipal cooperation. However, this consensus has not lead to a reinforcement of its political dimension, mainly for two reasons. First, the metropolitan area is embedded in a complex system of multilevel governance; in such a system, there is no room for a strong metropolitan political power. Second, citizens are far from integrating this scale in their strategies of collective action: the process of constructing the metropolitan area is dominated by political and economical elites.

Due to the economic crisis that began in 2008, the opportunity for the metropolitan area of Barcelona to become a new space of solidarity and citizenship is at stake. In this context, traditional businesses (such as the construction sector) are no longer lucrative for private companies. On the other hand, services and urban utilities based on new technologies linked to the smart city discourse are a booming market, and not only in the City of Barcelona: they have spread to the metropolitan area and the city-region. At the same time, the privatization of the processes linked to water management has been approved by a majority of local politicians sitting on the Metropolitan Area of Barcelona, leading to a rise in water bills for citizens. Prices of public transport have also increased beyond the average annual increase.

The results of municipal elections held in May 2015 are an expression of citizen discontent. New parties have emerged as an alternative to traditional parties and, in some cases, as a response to austerity policies. In Barcelona, as in Madrid, a coalition of several left-wing parties has won the elections with the promise of changing current policies and politics. For the first time, two women, with no previous experience in formal politics, are the mayors of the most important Spanish cities. In the case of Barcelona, it will be interesting to see if the leadership of Ada Colau will represent a change in the current narratives of city-regional and metropolitan scales.

Notes

1 Part of these findings come from the research carried out in the context of "The case for Agglomeration Economies in Europe" Targeted Analysis, accomplished within the framework of the ESPON 2013 Programme (see Harding et al. 2010). This includes documentary analysis and interviews with leading city-regional stakeholders in selected policy areas conducted in 2010. Further secondary analysis and additional interviews were done in 2012 and 2014.
2 City of Barcelona's website: http://w3.bcn.cat/V01/Serveis/Noticies/V01Noticies LlistatNoticiesCtl/0,2138,1653_1800_3_1814010758,00.html?accio=detall& home=, 8 January 2013.

References

Boudreau, J.-A., P. Hamel, B. Jouve, and R. Keil. 2006. "Comparing metropolitan governance: The cases of Montreal and Toronto." *Progress in Planning* 66: 7–59.

———. 2007a. "Constructing metropolitan political spaces: Montreal and Toronto." In J.-P. Collin and M. Robertson, eds., *Governing metropolises: Profiles of issues and experiments on four continents*. Québec: Presses de l'Université Laval.

———. 2007b. "New state spaces in Canada: Metropolitanization in Montreal and Toronto compared." *Urban Geography* 28: 30–53.

Capel, H. 2005. *El modelo Barcelona: un examen crítico*. Barcelona: Ediciones del Serbal.

Delgado, M. 2007. *La Ciudad Mentirosa. Fraude y Miseria del "modelo Barcelona."* Madrid: Los Libros de la Catarata.

Digaetano, A. and E. Strom. 2003. "Comparative urban governance: An integrated approach." *Urban Affairs Review* 38: 356–95.

Hall, P. A. 1993. "Policy paradigms, social learning, and the state: The case of economic policymaking in Britain." *Comparative Politics* 25: 275–96.

Harding, A. 2007. "Taking city regions seriously? Response to debate on 'city-regions: New geographies of governance, democracy and social reproduction." *International Journal of Urban and Regional Research* 31(2): 443–58.

Harding, A. et al. 2010. *The case for agglomeration economies in Europe*. www .espon.eu/export/sites/default/Documents/Projects/TargetedAnalyses/CAEE/ CAEE_Final_report.pdf.

Heinelt, H. and D. Kübler, eds. 2005. *Metropolitan governance: Capacity, democracy and the dynamics of place*. London: Routledge.

Iglesias, M., M. Martí-Costa, J. Subirats, and M. Tomàs, eds. 2011. *Políticas Urbanas en España. Grandes Ciudades, Actores y Gobiernos Locales*. Barcelona: Icària.

Jonas, A. E. G., and K. Ward. 2007. "Introduction to a debate on city-regions: New geographies of governance, democracy and social reproduction." *International Journal of Urban and Regional Research* 31(1): 169–78.

Jones, M. and G. MacLeod. 2004. "Regional spaces, spaces of regionalism: Territory, insurgent politics and the English question." *Transactions of the Institute of British Geographers* 29(4): 433–52.

Keating, M. 1998. *The new regionalism in western Europe: Territorial restructuring and political change*. Cheltenham: Edward Elgar.

Lowndes, V. 2005. "Something old, something new, something borrowed ... how institutions change (and stay the same) in local governance." *Policy Studies* 26: 291–309.

Mossberger, K. and G. Stoker. 2001. "The evolution of urban regime theory: The challenge of conceptualization." *Urban Affairs Review* 36: 810–35.

Paasi, A. 2003. "Region and place: Regional identity in question." *Progress in Human Geography* 27: 475–85.

Pierre, J. 1999. "Models of urban governance: The institutional dimension of urban politics." *Urban Affairs Review* 34(3): 372–96.

Sancton, A. 2001. "Canadian cities and the new regionalism." *Journal of Urban Affairs* 23(5): 543–55.

Sellers, J. M. 2002. "The nation-state and urban governance: Toward multilevel analysis." *Urban Affairs Review* 37: 611–41.

Sharpe, L. J. 1995. *The government of world cities: The future of the metro model.* London: John Wiley.

Tomàs, M. 2010. "Gobernabilidad Metropolitana, Democracia y Eficiencia. Una Comparación Barcelona-Montreal." *Revista Española de Ciencia Política* 23: 127–50.

———. 2012. "Exploring the metropolitan trap: The case of Montreal." *International Journal of Urban and Regional Research* 36(3): 554–67.

———. 2015. "If urban regions are the answer, what is the question? Thoughts on the European experience." *International Journal of Urban and Regional Research.* DOI: 10.1111/1468-2427.12177.

CHAPTER 17

The Resistible Rise of Italy's Metropolitan Regions
The Politics of Sub-National Government Reform in Postwar Italy

Simon Parker

Introduction

MUCH OF THE LITERATURE of the 1990s and 2000s on urban and regional governance was dominated by the themes of globalization and state rescaling, which were identified as the twin drivers of a re territori-alization of governance at the metropolitan-regional scale (Cox 1993; Cox 1997; Swyngedouw and Cox 1997; Brenner 1998a; Brenner 1998b; MacLeod and Goodwin 1999; MacLeod 2001; Swyngedouw and Baeten 2001; Brenner 2002; Keil 2003; Brenner 2004). A review of the actual "on the ground" transformation of cities and regions into strong state actors with considerable powers of political and economic sovereignty reveals a much more complicated picture, however. Indeed because of its essentially normative and pluralist conceptualization it is hard to identify where "new regionalism" really has emerged even in the European Union, where for a time Jacques Delors's enthusiastic vision of "a Europe of the Regions" offered the promise of a new era of politically and economically assertive sub-national governments (Scott 2009).

A surge of research articles and reports in the 1990s pointed to what can only be described as "the return of the region" as a territorial scale of key importance to students of economic geography, political science and public administration, urban and regional sociology, planning, inter-national relations, and related disciplines (Harrison 2008a, 2008b). The reasons for this upsurge in interest differed across the disciplinary fields, however. For economic geographers the key work of Michael Storper, Ed

Soja, and Allen Scott (Scott and Soja 1996; Scott, Agnew et al. 2001; Scott and Storper 2003; Scott 2011; Soja 2014) on regions as centres of economic production built on that of writers such as Ash Amin and Nigel Thrift on Post-Fordist agglomeration economies (Amin 1990, Amin and Thrift 1992). Distinctive sub-national patterns of industrial production, innovation, and design with clear geographical "clustering" had been identified by Bagnasco (1977), Sabel and Piore (1984), and Sabel and Amin (1994), notably in the so-called "Third Italy" but with similar industrial district features in Bavaria and Baden-Wurttemberg in Germany (Lechner and Dowling 1999, Semlinger 1993) and Catalonia and Euskadia (the Basque Country) in Spain (Santisteban 2006).

However, as Gordon, Harding, and Harloe argue in this volume, the tendency to attach primacy to the forces of globalization as the main agent of the rescaling of territorial governance in a metropolitan direction provides "an insufficient basis for understanding how and why metropolitan governance is clearly emerging in some places, but not in others; how its form varies between places; how it succeeds *and* how it fails—and so on." In the context of Italy, strongly integrated export-led regional economies and highly territorialized political subcultures are important factors in the contestation around regionalism and metropolitan government. Thus, despite the appearance of significant reterritorializing reforms in the 1970s and more recently in the 1990s and 2000s, the rescaling of government in Italy has been more defined by endogenous concerns surrounding the relative advantage to be gained by entrenched political and economic interests than an exogenous "post-Fordist" adaptation to the new state spaces that might potentially result from the reconfiguration of global capital's spatial fix in an Italian economy, which, despite its membership of the Eurozone, remains remarkably "sheltered" by international comparison (Rodríguez-Pose and Fratesi 2007).

Centre and Periphery in Italy: A Brief History

Since the foundation of the modern Italian state in 1861, the one issue that has traditionally united nearly all the political factions has been that "the rule of the parties" (in Italian, the *partitocrazia*) should supersede "the reason of state," and this is why it is so crucial to understand the primacy of politics in any discussion of the reform of the apparatus of government in Italy. For most of its history, "regional Italy," to quote Metternich, existed as a geographical expression, while the ancient form of territorial government, the commune (*comune*), and to a lesser extent the province (*provincia*), was the main point of political reference and source of collective identity. Although a regional dimension did exist prior to unification, this was generally a matter of imperial and ecclesiastical convenience rather than a genuine territorial expression of a distinct culture or "ethnos." The delineation of regions in Italy in the nineteenth century was, as Pacini and Bramanti have termed it, "decided hurriedly and certainly not on the basis of criteria such as efficient governability and the economic and social needs of the territory" (Pacini and Bramanti 1992). The latter part of this statement might equally well describe the much-delayed implementation of the "ordinary regions" in 1970, conceded by a reluctant Christian Democrat party in return for the coalition support of the Italian Socialist Party.

While many in northern Italy in recent decades have shown dissatisfaction with their *national* political space, this does not necessarily imply that the *region* provokes stronger feelings of political and cultural identification than other institutions, or that it represents an area of internal social, economic, and political homogeneity. Nor is it necessarily true that the performance of administrators and politicians at the regional level was any better than that of those at the national level. Given that the fifteen "ordinary" regions only began to assume greater importance in the 1970s, by which time the *partitocrazia* was firmly entrenched, the regions became not so much the harbingers of a new way of doing politics or a force for subsidiarity, but rather, as Gianfranco Miglio put it, "the most conservative part of the old and corrupt unitary state" (Miglio 1999: 65). Therefore, as Murphy advocates, it is important to reflect both on how regions are perceived and understood by their inhabitants and "how and why that understanding has changed over time" (Murphy 1991: 24).

Although dissatisfaction with all levels of government in Italy is higher than the European average, opinion surveys consistently find a lower level of dissatisfaction with sub-national government. But this needs to be seen in the context of a generally low opinion of local and national government among Italians and much higher levels of support for the EU, public education, the system of justice, the Catholic Church, the police and the armed forces, and the President of the Republic.[1] However, because space does not allow an extensive discussion of the historical development of "autonomous" territorial government in Italy, I propose to confine my analysis to the rise of "ethno-regionalist" autonomism in the late 1980s and 1990s; the impact of the local government reforms of the 1990s and the centre-left constitutional reforms (1999–2001); the implementation of limited regional devolution under the centre right Bossi-Berlusconi administration in the 2000s; the increasing importance of regional economic space in the reconfiguration of territorial government; and the most recent creation of new metropolitan authorities under the centre-left government of Matteo Renzi. In concluding, I try to situate the Italian experience of regional and metropolitan government reform within a broader discussion of state rescaling by insisting on the continued importance of organized politics in any reconfiguration of territorial governance in the Italian case.

"Fear of Falling": Territorial Identity and the Demand for Local Autonomy

On the face of it, the Italian experience seems to support the contention that the restructuring of sub-national levels of governance represents one of the key responses made by a national government to the managerial and economic problems thrown up by processes of globalization. Here we have a case in which there has been substantial devolution and decentralization of powers and resources to the regional and metropolitan scales at a pace that has quickened since the 1970s and led to significant growth in sub-national economic development and related functions, particularly at the regional level (Parker 2006).

Toward the end of the 1980s, the newly rich of the northern industrial districts began to suffer from what Tambini refers to as "a fear of falling" or "an insecurity born of economic uncertainty in the globalizing economy" (Tambini, 2004: 30). Neglected by its dominant party, Democrazia Cristiana (Christian Democracy, or DC), in favour of the large industries of the northwest and the south, the provincial north became an area that felt "economically central and politically peripheral" (Diamanti, 2001: 296). Over the course of the 1980s, regional leagues demanding greater autonomy sprang up across northern Italy, with particular points of strength in provincial Veneto and Lombardy, i.e., "the North of small businesses and Catholic political traditions" (Diamanti, 1996: 125). Following the first seat gains in national elections of the Liga Veneta in 1983 and the Lega Lombarda in 1987, the leagues were to enjoy a swift rise that would see the result of their fusion, the Lega Nord, become the second party in Lombardy, the Veneto, and Piedmont, and the third in Liguria, at the parliamentary elections of 1992.

As Cento Bull and Gilbert assert, any understanding of the Lega Nord must be based on recognition of the nexus between the industrial districts of the provincial north of Italy and the emergence of the federalist Leagues. They argue that the Lega "took on the representation of the interests of a local model of economic development" when the DC was no longer able to do so effectively (Cento Bull and Gilbert, 2001: 102). Although derided by the established "system" parties, the Lega was expressing (albeit in populist terms) the needs of a specific territorial socio-economic constituency and many of the issues raised first by the Lega—such as the need for federal and fiscal reform—have since been embraced by those who originally bristled at the very word "federalism," most notably the dominant political figure of the Second Italian Republic—Silvio Berlusconi.

The Lega Nord, as a vocal opponent of the "Roman state" and its southern clientalist electoral base, succeeded in pushing the question of greater subnational autonomy up the political agenda. At the same time, the dramatic collapse of the major parties amidst the corruption scandals of the *Tangentopoli* period helped create the conditions by which changes at the subnational level would also become expedient for the governing class (Gundle and Parker 1996). The early 1990s would see a number of important reforms in this area, the most important being Law 81/1993 that allowed for the direct election of the mayor over two rounds of voting and, through a "bonus" for the winning coalition, a guarantee of an absolute majority. The mayor was also given the power to appoint the members of the council executive and this, while still leaving the mayor with the task of keeping the different parties in the victorious coalition happy, has helped to promote a greater degree of efficiency and account-ability. The enhancement of the powers and autonomy of city mayors under these reforms has even led one commentator to refer to the new municipal polity as "semi-presidentialist" (Fabbrini, 2001).

While the level of political interest and contestation increased with the introduction of the direct election of city mayors and the reorganization of communal administration (Law 142/1990), later incorporated into the so-called Bassanini II law 127/1997, the boost to the institutional legiti-macy of larger city authorities which reformers hoped would result has failed to materialize. Law 142/1990 certainly constituted a re-territorial-ization of government in that it gave elected local authorities the right to devise their own statutes, to initiate inter-authority cooperation, and to directly elect the head of the political executive—all of which were subse-quently adopted by Constitutional Law 1/1999 with respect to regional government. As a result of these reforms the commune was re-established as the basic unit of local government, having responsibility for all the functions and services relating to the population of its territory other than those explicitly attributed to other authorities (Vandelli 2000: 98). In addition, nine new metropolitan authorities were created, including Turin, Milan, Venice, Bologna, Florence, Rome, Bari, Naples, and Cagliari. A further Constitutional Law, passed in October 2001, gave formal recog-nition to the metropolitan cities as an autonomous level of government under Title V of the Italian Constitution—the first time a new tier of government has been constitutionally recognized since the birth of the Republic in 1948. However, it was not until the law on fiscal federalism was passed in 2009 (Law 42/2009) that metropolitan government was provided with the necessary finance to assume the range of responsibilities that its expanded powers and territories would require. In the same year, Reggio Calabria was instituted as a metropolitan city by the Berlusconi government, taking the number of officially designated "city-regions" to ten.

Under the original legislation, the implementation of the new metropolitan authorities required the *voluntary* agreement of the provincial capital, the province, and the surrounding (generally smaller) communes that would eventually form part of the *città metropolitana* (metropolitan city). L.265/99 disposed with the requirement for the metropolitan city and the province in which it is based to reach an accord, but neither was the establishment of a metropolitan authority to be mandatory. Instead, the host region, the major city commune and its surrounding local authorities, had the power to define a "wide area" metropolitan government boundary through mutual agreement.

One of the last acts of the centre-left government led by Massimo D'Alema was to pass a constitutional law in March 2001 (by all of four votes) which, because it altered the provisions of the Constitution without a two-thirds majority from each Chamber, had to be subject to a popular referendum in order for the Act to be brought into force. In essence, the legislation, which was approved after the success of the referendum held on October 7, 2001, consolidated and gave constitutional status to the reforms of local and regional government that had been introduced since 1990. The most important constitutional and jurisdictional innovation was the establishment of the principle of subsidiarity as a basis of the framework of government, which brought to an end a great deal of the supervisory powers of central government and the courts on sub-national administration.

However, the reform also represented a hurried measure by the government in the run-up to the May 2001 elections in order to show the electorate of the north, which had voted the Northern League and its allies in Berlusconi's Forza Italia into power in a majority of regional governments, that it was doing something about delivering federal reform. Perhaps reflecting the haste in which it was pushed through, the constitutional reform lacked, as Anna Cento Bull observed, a "clear-cut division of tasks and responsibilities" and seemed likely to give rise to "conflict between the different levels of government" (Cento Bull, 2002: 188).

With the passing of Constitutional Law 1/1999 and Constitutional Law 3/2001, together with ordinary laws 59/1997 and decree law 56/2000, the institutional architecture of sub-national government in Italy was significantly refashioned. Legislation passed in 1999 established the direct election of the regional president (or rather it granted regional councils the powers to choose this form of election), and the 2001 constitutional law gave regions default responsibility for policy areas (either exclusively or concurrently) with central government other than those specifically excluded in the Act (such as defence, immigration, public order, etc.). Article 118 of Constitutional Law 3/2001 also applied the principle of subsidiarity to municipalities, giving them responsibility for functions other than those directly attributed to the state, regions or provinces (Clarich and Pisaneschi 2001: 365).

The reforms of the centre-left Ulivo (Olive Tree) government could be defined as a period of "permissive decentralization" in that it was left to the regions and sub-regional authorities to decide how far and how fast they wished to use the new powers granted them by the ordinary and constitutional reforms. The legislation also gave regions more control over the distribution of decentralized funding under legislative decree 112/1998, and an early analysis of regional spending found that the regions were very reluctant to embrace fiscal federalism in their own jurisdiction with on average three-quarters of funding being held by the region, 22% being devolved to provincial governments and only 1.2% to the communes (Santori 2000).

La Devolution

The emergence, for the first time since the Second World War, of "alternation" in Italian national government has made for a febrile atmosphere in the context of sub-national governance reform. Italy's rapidly re-modelled party system produced a centre-right government in 1993 under Silvio Berlusconi, followed by a centre-left government in 1996 initially under Romano Prodi, the return of a Berlusconi-led coalition in 2001, and a narrow victory of the centre-left in 2006 which led to premature elections and the return of Berlusconi in 2008 until his forced exit in November 2011. Within the centre-right coalition, long-standing ideological differences between the ethno-nationalist Lega Nord is in stark contrast to the ultra-nationalism of the now disbanded "post-fascist" Alleanza Nazionale party, for whom the unity of Italy and a hostility to local and regional autonomy have long been a sine qua non of Gianfranco Fini's political strategy. Fini's opposition to federalism of a North American or even German stamp explains in large measure the fairly modest transfer of central government policy responsibilities to the regions under the 2001–6 Berlusconi government, despite the fact that Umberto Bossi was nominally in charge of institutional reform and "la devolution." Health care responsibilities had been transferred to regional governments as far back as 1976, and the 2001 reform really represented a completion of this process. The inclusion of community policing and vocational training as the second and third planks of the reform could hardly be compared even to the devolution reforms of Tony Blair's government that saw the creation of a Scottish Parliament and a Welsh Assembly at the end of the 1990s.

With the election of the Casa delle Libertà (House of Freedom) coalition in May 2001, the new minister for Institutional Reform and leader of the Lega Nord, Umberto Bossi, made it clear that in exchange for his party's support, he wished to see the question of "devolution" resolved in two ways. First, he intended to make the newly strengthened regional authorities the sole vehicle for the "Decalogue of devolution reforms" his government intended to pilot through parliament. Second, Bossi intended to overcome power-sharing disputes by decentralizing the entire responsibility for certain policy areas to the regions. What Bossi's reforms deliberately lacked were enhanced powers and funding for the larger metropolitan authorities, which, even in the northern regions, were prone to electing centre-left governments and thus challenging the authority of incumbent centre-right regional governors over matters such as health services, transport infrastructure, and economic development.

Instead, Bossi's constitutional reform proposals were aimed at strengthening the "region at large" where Italy's more conservative voters were concentrated in the smaller communes and less densely populated provinces. These included measures to provide a new organization for the Constitutional Court that "takes account of regional realties," the extension of parliamentary immunity to regional councillors and presidents, the reform of administrative justice, and the institution of a "Chamber of Autonomies," which would be similar to the German Bundesrat and in effect replace the existing Senate. In addition, there would be five "ordinary bills" related to the financing of local government, the limitation of substitutive powers on the part of the national government in relation to local authorities, the participation of the regions in European Union deliberations, international agreements, and the functions of the parliamentary commission for the regions.

The specific responsibilities for which the regions were to be granted exclusive legislative competence included traditional policy areas such as health services, but also school provision and vocational training (although a national curriculum and a national examination system were to be retained), together with local policing. "Our federalism," stated Bossi in his speech to the Senate at the launch of the Bill, "is founded on the principles of subsidiarity and autonomy," which was a far cry from his demand for an "Independent Padania" during the Lega's secessionist phase. It represented a return to the party's federalist stance, on which the Northern League had built its early successes in the late 1980s and early 1990s (Diamanti) and from which it had shied away in the latter half of the decade following the (at least superficial) adoption of pro-federalist positions by most of the other parties on both left and right.

With the passing of the devolution bill as part of the Berlusconi-led House of Freedom coalition's constitutional package in the Senate on March 23, 2005, the Northern League was on the brink of achieving a significant degree of autonomy for the regions, including, crucially, the ability to retain a large proportion of tax receipts at the local level. However, Italy's voters rejected the constitutional bill in the referendum held in June 2006. The degree of opposition or support for the Northern League's "devolution max" proposals reflected the perceptions of those who stood to gain or lose most through fiscal federalism. Northern regions that are net contributors to the national budget, such as the Veneto, voted in favour by a margin of 55.3%, whereas in the southern region of Calabria, which relies on substantial subsidies from Rome, 82% of voters opposed the measure. The so-called "fiscal federalism" reforms of the 2009–11 period were meant to implement Article 119 of the constitution, but, as Massetti and Sandri write, although the reforms "enhanced the fiscal powers of the regions," the paradoxical change of the Berlusconi government's intervention was to "[compress] their overall financial capacity" (Massetti and Sandri 2012: 6). Indeed from 2008 onward there has been a move to provide "standard cost of program delivery" financing for services such as health and education based on the expenditures of the most efficient regions. This tends to penalise the less efficient regional and municipal governments of the south, which is why the government was forced to implement a five-year transition arrangement in order to soften the blow of sharply reduced financial support to these regions.

Regional Economic Spaces and Territorial Governance

Traditionally, national governments had been content to deal directly with the major national employers when discussing economic strategy and support for industry, but from the 1970s the SME sector of "the Third Italy" (the centre-north and northeast) became increasingly important for the country's export-led growth. Smaller firms are traditionally more reliant on locally provided services and infrastructure than large multinational conglomerates, but in many cases regional and local governments lacked the expertise and resources to support their burgeoning industrial districts adequately. Although in the case of Emilia-Romagna, the left-controlled regional government had proved very capable at providing collective services for small industries, the same could not be said of the Christian Democrats and their governing partners in regions of the "white" subculture such as the Veneto (Cooke and Morgan 1998). At the same time, as the welfare state functions of local authorities continued to develop, there was a growing consensus in the 1980s that relations between local authorities and other public authorities and voluntary agencies needed to be better coordinated and professionalized at subnational level. The creation of "Territorial Pacts" between the various economic actors and public authorities operating at the local and regional level represented a concrete expression of the national government's response to these demands, although the results were uneven across Italy as a whole (De Rita and Bonomi 1998).

Some commentators have seen regional government in Italy as an endogenous institutional fix for policy failure at the national level, often taking at face value the existence of "institutionally thick" regional governments and strong regional economies, as if the two are necessarily and causally related (Putnam 1993). But the impressive takeoff of the small and medium firm sector in the "Third Italy" regions of Marche, Umbria, Tuscany, Emilia-Romagna, Veneto, and Friuli-Venezia Giulia took place at a time in the 1970s when regional government was barely functional. Thus Rodríguez-Pose's claim that the granting of autonomy to the (ordinary) regions in 1970 led to "the setting up of regional institutions and policies which are at the base of the success of some of the local systems of governance" (2001: 30) fails to recognize that with the possible exception of Emilia-Romagna and Tuscany, regional administrations have been far less important than trade associations and municipal authorities in stimulating economic growth and enterprise in the Third Italy. For example, the Veneto region, which has enjoyed some of the highest regional growth rates in Italy and which is home to some of the world's most successful companies (such as Benetton and Luxottica), had not even offi-cially defined its industrial districts by the end of the 1990s.

There is also no evidence, in the case of Italy at least, that organized business interests have a clear notion of what the best spatial fix for enter-prise should be in the context of the devolution reform process. Large-scale Italian capital has until very recently been able mostly to ignore local and regional government, since key policy decisions regarding wages and employment, corporate taxation, competition policy, interest rates, credit, and overseas trade are decided in Rome or Brussels. Up until recently the main employers' organization, Confindustria, has therefore adopted an essentially agnostic stance on the subject of federalism and devolution, preferring to respond only to reform proposals that are seen to be inimical to its specific interests. However, Italian business leaders are increasingly waking up to the fact that fiscal federalism threatens their special relation-ship with Rome as the national government begins to lose its monopoly over key policy areas, while Italy's weakened position in the Eurozone following the fiscal crisis of 2008 and the country's growing debt problem has undermined the capacity of Italy's banks and major companies to dictate terms to economic policy-makers. Indeed the former head of Con-findustria and President of Ferrari, Luca Cordero di Montezemolo, pub-licly criticized the Berlusconi-Bossi devolution process as a costly "mess" that would create more needless bureaucracy and increase costs to busi-ness (L'Espresso 2005).

The Birth of the Metropolitan City

Since the decentralization reforms of the 1990s and 2000s, metropolitan mayors have enjoyed increased public profiles and lengthier tenures. Before the system was reformed, the average Italian mayor remained in office for a mere thirteen months. In 1997, by contrast, all those elected four years previously in the larger Italian cities were still in power. If we consider that during the same period, Italy had four different governments, this appears to indicate a break with the pattern of instability that for decades had linked local and national levels of government in Italy. The meteoric rise of Matteo Renzi, the youthful former mayor of Florence, to the head of Italy's centre-left coalition national government in 2014, has refocused attention on the importance of city-regions as power bases for ambitious political leaders. Greater regional autonomy and a more exec-utive-style mayorality in Italy's larger cities have created new incentives and opportunities for local political actors who realize the importance of territorial affinity and the potential for achieving significant reforms at the institutional and policy levels in a more devolved, sub-national polity.

It was therefore no surprise that soon into Renzi's tenure as premier, the Italian parliament approved a law named after its ministerial sponsor and former mayor of Reggio Emilia, Graziano Delrio, which brought into being for the first time ten new metropolitan cities—Turin, Milan, Venice, Genoa, Bologna, Florence, Bari, Naples, and Reggio Calabria. As the national capital, Rome is provided with its own institutional arrangements that differ from the other metropolitan cities. Reggio Calabria's metropolitan authority will not be instituted until 2016, when the provincial council ends its mandate. The previously existing provinces which once provided the equivalent to county government are incorporated territorially and administratively within these new metropolitan authorities. Rather than being directly elected by the residents of the province, under the new reform the president of the province and the provincial executive are elected by the mayors and councillors of the constituent provinces. The existing mayor of the largest city authority automatically becomes "mayor of the metropolitan city"—a type of super-mayor who is expected to work with a metropolitan council directly elected by the mayors and councillors of the component municipal authorities. The mayors of the existing provincial municipalities also constitute a "metropolitan conference," but seemingly with advisory powers only.

Having been initiated by the "Spending Review" Law 135 of 2012 aimed at curbing Italy's budget deficit in line with its European Union Stability Pact obligations, Renzi's local government reforms are intended to produce a more efficient integration of services, transport, and infrastructure while professionalising the public administration by, for example, removing political appointees from departmental executive roles and winding up agencies and local bodies that no longer serve a useful function. An explicit aim of the reform is to allow Italy's major cities to develop more effective institutional arrangements with other European cities and city-regions.[2] The act also transformed Italy's provinces from directly elected bodies to "wide area territorial authorities" (*enti territoriali di area vasta*) with the president of the province now elected by the mayors and the councillors of the component municipalities.[3]

This metropolitanization of the provinces with major urban centres has not been without its controversies or conflicts, however. For example, a number of local authorities surrounding the pre-existing commune of Venice tried unsuccessfully to escape incorporation into the new metropolitan authority which has been criticized for failing to align with the de facto PaTreVe (Padua-Treviso-Venezia) city-region and for a lack of strategic thinking (Messina 2013). Other experiences have been more positive, such as in the case of the "Milano Città Metropolitana" initiative launched by the existing Milan city authority in the run up to the official creation of the metropolitan authorities. This consultation involved an integrated series of projects and public events involving local stakeholders from the city's universities to the provincial authority and local citizens' groups looking at issues such as the judicial and administrative features of the new statute, land-use planning, local economic development, and the re-organization of public services.[4] Bologna, the capital of the Emilia-Romagna, which historically has pioneered pro-citizen local government reform and decentralization (Parker 1992) has been at the forefront of public participation initiatives surrounding the introduction of the new metropolitan statute in January 2014. The component authorities in the province of Bologna organized a series of virtual and conventional "Town Meetings" with the support of the regional government and twenty local authority and civil society organizations facilitated by "Laboratorio Urbano" (Urban Laboratory) in line with a regional law requiring the direct participation of citizens and civic associations. As a result of this unprecedented consultation with civic groups, third sector organizations, business associations, and key local government bodies, the city council of Bologna agreed to suspend its deliberations on the new metropolitan statute until the final document from the public consultation process has been published.[5]

As well as technical and functional requirements that every metropolitan statute must feature (such as how the authority will be organized, what powers will its different bodies enjoy, what coordination mechanisms will be in place to deliver services across the territory, etc.) the Delrio law provides for "facultative content" including the fundamental principles on which the new metropolitan authority bases its governing practice, such as, for example, in the case of Bologna, "solidarity, simplification, impartiality, tolerance, integration," which allows each metropolitan city to constitutionalize to a degree its civic ethos and its relationship to the region, to the nation, and to the European Union.

Conclusion

The absent guests in many discussions of the rescaling of the state are often the political actors who are charged with giving some coherence and vision to the institutional, social, and economic challenges that their cities and regions face in an increasingly uncertain world. Paolo Perulli acknowledges this aspect of regionalism when he writes that "the regional dimension ... appears ... as a response to a problem of legitimacy and

representation and not only in functional terms as one of economic structure" (Perulli 1998: 34). This view is echoed by Alan Pred, who argues
that the "historical unfolding of local civil society has a certain degree of
autonomy," due to the "locally singular combination of presences and
absences, the locally peculiar sedimentation of practical and discursive
knowledge, of commonsense, of behavioural dispositions and coping
mechanisms" (Pred 1989: 218 in Amin and Thrift 1994: 7).

Neil Brenner also acknowledges the role of political actors, but essentially as reactive agents of "global spatial restructuring" (1999), ascribing
variety in the response to globalization at the city or regional level substantially to "the territorial structure of state power" in each respective
country (Brenner 1997). This vaunting of the "spatial fix" (Harvey 1982)
or "spatio-temporal fix" (Jessop 2000, 2001) in terms of the logic of
capitalist accumulation—what might be called "the re-scaling for capital
thesis"—underplays the socio-cultural motifs of territorial identities and
what Gramsci termed the hegemonic repertoires of "the historic bloc" in
establishing, maintaining, and defending political legitimation (Gramsci,
1971). Crucially, it also overplays and over-generalizes the "steering
capacity" of governance under capitalism, ascribing to sub-national state
bodies the ability and the will to offer local level Keynesian solutions to
the supply-side problems engendered by the withdrawal of the (ubiquitous) neo-liberal nation state from direct economic intervention (Jessop
2000: 335).

Andrew Jonas endorses Kevin Cox's suggestion "that more work needs
to be done on showing how territorial politics are constitutive of state
restructuring and rescaling rather than the other way round." In his own
study of New Regionalism in California with Pincetl (2006), Jonas also
argues that "the rescaling of the state and governance around regions
could be as much a strategic bottom-up outcome of organized business
interests as it is a solution which is pursued in a unidirectional top-down
fashion by (central) state interests" (Jonas 2012: 269). The same holds
true for the halting and partial nature of devolution in Italy after 1948,
where despite the arrival of populist ethno-regionalist parties such as the
Lega Nord in the 1990s, a nationally territorialized and orientated party
system has successfully guarded its monopoly of power against the decen-
tralising demands of a weakly organized metropolitan-regional polity.

With the election of the coalition led by Silvio Berlusconi in 2001 and
its intention to introduce "la devolution," the institutional reform process
appeared to be leading Italy toward a quasi-federalist system at the
regional level. A stance in keeping with a broadly neo-liberal approach

that favours greater sub-national self-determination and less reliance upon redistribution from "strong" to "weak" localities and regions. However, as I hope to have shown, the re-territorialization of government in Italy has been, and continues to be, more powerfully shaped by factors internal to its rigidly tribal politics than by external economic and political imperatives such as globalization and the exigencies of the European Union integration process. The Italian case of state restructuring is more consistent with a crisis of legitimacy of the governing class and the party system than the rescaling imperatives of neo-liberalism, and as such needs to be understood in its historical and political context.

As with other movements for local and regional autonomy in Europe and North America, regionalist and autonomist support increasingly highlights cross-party *resistance* to the depoliticizing and centralizing operations of international government-finance coalitions such as the EU/IMF's austerity-imposing Troika. A case in point is Italian comedian Beppe Grillo's highly successful anti-big-capital/big-government Five Star citizen's movement, which won a quarter of the popular vote in the Italian parliamentary elections in February 2013, and which has identified radical plans for the overhaul of territorial government, including the abolition of the provinces and the amalgamation of communes under 5,000 inhabitants. Ironically, so-called anti-establishment political movements such as the Lega Nord and Five Star achieved their initial success at the head of city administrations, which had enjoyed greatly increased powers and financial autonomy due to the reforms of the mainstream parties.

The rescaling of governance in Italy does engage, albeit largely rhetorically, with new public management and new institutionalist arguments around the more efficient management of cities and regions as distinct economic spaces, but in the absence of strong backing from regional and national economic elites, such policy-driven new regionalist arguments have never carried much sway. Thus while the "spending review" law allowing for the introduction of city-regions and the reduction in the number of provinces draws on the language of modernization and the control of public expenditure, in reality the long resisted rise of metropolitan government (like that of the regions before them) is a sign of the continuing sclerosis of the Italian political system.

In so far as Italy's territorial government reforms represent a further attempt at territorial rescaling, it is certainly being generated less from the logic circuits of global capital and more from globalization's populist antinomies in civil society that are seeking to control and "re-humanize" state-capital power ensembles in a more localist, and according to critics,

chauvinist-populist, direction.[6] Thus, in the context of Italy, regionalization and metropolitanization can be seen as essentially political struggles
that invoke the chimeras of globalization and Europeanization in the name
of what remains a fundamentally partisan contest for all scales of governance in Italy.

Notes

I am grateful to Duncan McDonnell for contributing to an earlier unpublished paper
on which this chapter partially draws.

1 A Demopolis poll for the Catholic periodical *Famiglia Cristiana* conducted in
   November 2011 found that only 19% of voters had faith in the Berlusconi government and 33% in the mayor of their city. Support for the President of the
   Republic Giorgio Napolitano ran at 82%, for the police 67%, for the Church
   60%, for magistrates 54%, for schools and universities 51% and for the European
   Union 42%. A survey for the newspaper 'Sole 24 Ore' conducted in 2008 found
   that support for the mayor of Italy's principal cities averaged 55% with 91 mayors
   doing better than 50% satisfaction (Burroni et al., 2009: 1).
2 'Città metropolitane, province, unione di comuni: in vigore la legge Delrio' at
   www.governo.it/governoinforma/dossier/legge_province/.
3 The Renzi government claims to have saved over €100 million from abandoning
   direct elections to the provincial authorities.
4 Urbanistica Informazioni, 245–46, 2012, p. 36.
5 *Lo statuto della città metropolitana di bologna per la convivenza e la democrazia
   deliberativa*, Bologna, 2014. www.bolognametropolitana.org/.
6 Wu Ming Foundation, "Grillismo: Yet another right-wing cult coming from Italy,"
   March 8, 2013. www.wumingfoundation.com/english/wumingblog/?p=1950.
   Accessed August 4, 2013.

References

Amin, A. 1990. *Post-Fordism. A Reader.* Oxford: Blackwell.
Amin, A. and N. Thrift. 1992. "Neo-Marshallian nodes on global networks."
International Journal of Urban and Regional Research 16(4): 571–87.
Brenner, N. 1998a. "Global cities, glocal states: Global city formation and state
territorial restructuring in contemporary Europe." *Review of International
Political Economy* 5(1): 1–37.
———. 1998b. "Globalisation and reterritorialisation: The re-scaling of urban
governance in the European Union." *Urban Studies* 26(3): 431–51.
———. 2002. "Decoding the newest 'metropolitan regionalism' in the USA:
A Critical Overview." *Cities* 19(1): 3–21.
———. 2004. *New state spaces: Urban governance and the rescaling of statehood.*
Oxford: Oxford University Press.
Burroni, L. et al. 2009. *Città metropolitane e politiche urbane.* Florence: Firenze
University Press.
Cento Bull, A. 2002. "Towards a federal state? Competing proposals for constitutional revision." In P. Bellucci and M. Bull, eds., *Italian politics: The return
of Berlusconi* (185–202). New York and Oxford: Berghahn.

Cento Bull, A. and M. Gilbert. 2001. *The Lega Nord and the northern question in Italian politics*. London: Palgrave.

Clarich, M. and A. Pisaneschi. 2001. "Old and new regionalism in Italy." *Review of Economic Conditions in Italy* 3: 353–68.

Cox, K. R. 1993. "The local and the global in the new urban politics: A critical review." *Environment and Planning D* 11: 433–48.

———. 1997. *Spaces of globalization: Reasserting the power of the local*. New York and London: Guilford Press.

Gramsci, A. 1971. *Selections from The Prison Notebooks*. London: Lawrence and Wishart.

Gundle, S. and S. Parker. 1996. *The new Italian republic: From the fall of the Berlin Wall to Berlusconi*. London and New York: Routledge.

Harrison, J. 2008a. "The region in political economy." *Geography Compass* 2(3): 814–30.

———. 2008b. "Stating the production of scales: Centrally orchestrated regionalism and regionally orchestrated centralism." *International Journal of Urban and Regional Research* 32(4): 922–41.

Keil, R. 2003. "Globalization makes states: Perspectives on local governance in the age of the world city." In N. Brenner, B. Jessop, M. Jones, and G. Macleod, eds., *State/space: A reader* (278–95). Oxford: Blackwell.

Lechner, C. and M. Dowling. 1999. "The evolution of industrial districts and regional networks: The case of the biotechnology region Munich/Martinsried." *Journal of Management and Governance* 3(4): 309–38.

MacLeod, G. 2001. "New regionalism reconsidered: Globalization and the remaking of political economic space." *International Journal of Urban and Regional Research* 25(4): 804–29.

MacLeod, G. and M. Goodwin. 1999. "Space, scale and state strategy: Rethinking urban and regional governance." *Progress in Human Geography* 23(4): 503–27.

Massetti, E. and G. Sandri. 2012. "The regionalization of regional elections in Italy." Rome: Paper presented at the XXVI Convegno SISP, September 13–15.

Messina, P. 2013 "Città o area metropolitana? Il caso del Veneto nel contesto europeo." *Economia e Società Regionale* 1(1): 46–63.

Miglio, G. 1999. *L'asino di Buridano: Gli italiani alle prese con l'ultima occasione di cambiare il loro destino*. Vicenza: Neri Pozza.

Murphy, A. 1991. "Regions as social constructs: The gap between theory and practice." *Progress in Human Geography* 11(1): 22–35.

Pacini, M. and A. Bramanti, ed. 1992. *La Padania: Una regione italiana in Europa*. Turin, Edizione della fondazione G. Agnelli.

Parker, S. 1992. *Local government and social movements in Bologna since 1945*. Cambridge: University of Cambridge, Ph.D. thesis.

———. 2006. "Managing the political field: Italian regions and the territorialisation of politics in the Second Republic." *Journal of Southern Europe and the Balkans* 8(2): 235–53.

Rodríguez-Pose, A. and U. G. O. Fratesi. 2007. "Regional business cycles and the emergence of sheltered economies in the southern periphery of Europe." *Growth and Change* 38(4): 621–48.

Sabel, C. and M. Piore. 1984. *The second industrial divide: Possibilities for prosperity.* New York: Basic Books.

Sabel, C. and A. Amin. 1994. "Flexible specialisation and the re-emergence of regional economies." In *Post-Fordism: A reader* (101–56). Oxford: Blackwell.

Santisteban, M. A. 2006. "Business systems and cluster policies in the Basque Country and Catalonia (1990–2004)." *European Urban and Regional Studies* 13(1): 25–39.

Santori, A. 2000. "Gli impatti devolutivi dei primi DPCM ripartizionali attuativi del d.l.g.s. 112/'98 nelle 15 regioni a statuto ordinario. La distribuzione delle risorse conferite dallo Stato tra Regioni, Province e Comuni." Rome: ANCI.

Scott, A., J. Agnew, et al. 2001. "Global city-regions: An overview." In A. J. Scott, ed., *Global city-regions: Trends, theory, policy.* Oxford: Oxford University Press.

Scott, A. and M. Storper. 2003. "Regions, globalization, development." *Regional studies* 37(6–7): 549–78.

Scott, A. J. 2011. "Emerging cities of the third wave." *City* 15(3-4): 289–321.

Scott, A. J. and E. W. Soja.1996. *The city: Los Angeles and urban theory at the end of the twentieth century.* Berkeley: University of California Press.

Scott, J. W. 2009. *De-coding new regionalism: shifting socio-political contexts in Central Europe and Latin America.* Surrey, UK, and Burlington, VT: Ashgate.

Semlinger, K. 1993. "Economic development and industrial policy in Baden—Württemberg: Small firms in a benevolent environment." *European Planning Studies* 1(4): 435–63.

Soja, E. W. 2014. "Accentuate the regional." *International Journal of Urban and Regional Research* 39(2): 372–81.

Swyngedouw, E. and G. Baeten. 2001. "Scaling the city: The political economy of 'glocal' development – Brussels' conundrum." *European Planning Studies* 9(7): 827–49.

Swyngedouw, E. and K. Cox. 1997. "Neither global nor local: 'Glocalization' and the politics of scale." In *Spaces of globalization* (167–76). London: Edward Arnold.

Tambini, D. 2004. *Nationalism in Italian politics: The stories of the Northern League, 1980–2000.* London: Routledge.

Vandelli, L. 2000. *Il governo locale.* Bologna: Il Mulino.

CHAPTER 18

The Uncertain Development of Metropolitan Governance
Comparing England's First and Second City-Regions

Ian Gordon, Michael Harloe, and Alan Harding

Introduction

THE ISSUE OF metropolitan governance[1] is of particular salience in these times. The consequences for large and interconnected urban regions of the dual trends toward decentralization *and* globalization are promoting what Brenner (2004) characterizes as the "rescaling of statehood" and, in these regions, the emergence of "new state spaces" with evolving arrangements for their governance. But governance is (by definition) not simply a matter of the *state*'s role or configuration; it also involves those of *commercial interests*, together with an *institutional dimension*, encompassing networks, habits of co-operation/antagonism and issues of legitimacy—which we see as crucial factors in the (uncertain) reshaping of metropolitan governance.

Metropolitan city-regions are territories that pose particular challenges for governance, because of their combination of two contradictory features. The first is a complex array of spatial interactions, interdependences, and externalities of all sorts of scale and geometry. Managing these adequately defies the capacity of either the neatest multi-level regulatory structure, or a sophisticated market-based system incentivizing co-operation—let alone simple reliance on voluntaristic agreement. The second is their high degree of spatial differentiation (made possible by scale plus internal integration)—of functions, land uses, and populations with distinctive values and interests—leading to a strong potential for (organized) conflict across those axes in which functionality requires collaboration and concertation.

This chapter focuses on comparing and contrasting how the governance arrangements to respond to these challenges are being constructed in London and Manchester, the two metropoles in the UK in which they are currently most advanced. But the case of London should remind us that the issue of how large and interconnected urban areas—with their interdependencies and externalities, their fragmented polities and communities, and complex economies—are to be governed has a long history, at least in a place that was already a world city a century or more ago.

Indeed H. G. Wells in 1903 proposed a new Greater London Authority, a "mammoth municipality" that would govern a functionally extended London region, which he recognized as emerging in the wake of the revolution in mass transport and communication in late Victorian London.[2] This represented one side of what became a recurring conflict in the annals of metropolitan governance, between rational arrangements constructed on the logic of a closely interconnected space economy and real-world "solutions" confined within politically, administratively and/or communally defined boundaries. The continuing salience of this issue reflects the distributional significance of different forms of urban governance, from each of which some interests can expect to gain while others feel threatened. Within Greater London (now just the core of a further expanded region), the classic illustration was a failed effort to secure integrated metropolitan housing policies between 1964 and 1975 (Young and Kramer 1978). Over the wider metropolitan territory, latent conflicts around this issue remain central to the uncertain institutionalization of legitimate and effective arrangements for metropolitan governance.

In this chapter, we first discuss the role and construction of urban governance and the types of issue that have made metropolitan regions a particular focus for efforts to self-consciously reshape governance processes over the past twenty or so years. We then pursue a comparative analysis of developments in these processes in the two leading English city-regions, through a series of case studies focused on whether and how their regional systems have responded to some of (what we see as) the generic challenges of metropolitan governance. Specifically we look at those of strategic economic development, metropolitan-scale traffic congestion, and housing provision for the regional workforce. A concluding section draws some tentative lessons from their varying experiences for the overall project of developing governance capacities in metropolitan regions, highlighting the non-trivial ways in which issues of agency interfere with those of functionality, and a strong suggestion of path-dependency in how those have developed in these two classic cases of capitalist urbanization.

Constructing Urban Governance

The language of "governance" is explicitly (and in recent times pointedly) functional, referring to the regulation of social and spatial systems—such as those of the metro areas on which this book focuses—though not necessarily (just) by state-based "governments." In truth, such governance has always and everywhere involved an amalgam of goal-oriented *bureaucratic structures* with some redistributive potential; *markets*, involving diverse sets of interactions between a plurality of self-interested agents; and *informal institutions*, including networks, norms, cooperative habits, and expectations (Gordon 2006). The last of these components is less commonly highlighted than the others, partly because its elements (co-)evolve relatively slowly, and are path-dependent (the product of agency past and present)—but it has pervasive and necessary, facilitating *and* constraining, effects.[3]

As we see it, governance in these terms only becomes an open "issue" when this set of regulatory processes becomes notably non-functional for some key interests, who then seek some renegotiation of the established governance arrangements for the relevant activities in their field of concern. This process entails changes in the division of labour between geographical areas, sectors (public, private, and civil society), formal versus informal arrangements, differing organizational silos, and their institutional supports. Re-forming governance across these dimensions is a fundamentally political matter, with outcomes that will not be simply and consistently determined by functional considerations. Rather, they can be expected to be (in varying degrees) problematic and/or uncertain in their effects, especially if dependent on collective action to establish new arrangements. Characteristic gaps and imbalances in commitments to pursuing such action by those potentially affected are always liable to produce some dysfunctional biases in the arrangements that emerge—shaped by path-dependent influences on available *agency* in particular cases, as much as by structural inequalities in power. Gaps in the functionality actually achieved are liable to be covered by appeals to symbolic, "placatory" activity, or to have their significance denied.

This means that, while governance is all about functionality, and its reconstruction can properly be evaluated in functional/dysfunctional (as well as distributional) terms, any functionalist interpretation of manifest (or latent) changes in the system is likely to be inadequate—and potentially misleading—as well as over-determinist. Thus we would want to give a substantially greater role to personal and corporate agency than has been allowed recently by those among Brenner's (2004) disciples who view the emergence of stronger metropolitan governance simply in terms of the impersonal agency of global capitalism. Such accounts provide an insufficient basis for understanding how and why metropolitan governance is clearly emerging in some places, but not in others, how its form varies between places, how it succeeds *and* how it fails, and so on. These are not second order issues, matters of local variation in a globally pervasive process whose character we can take for granted; rather, they always codetermine, along with global forces, how far actual changes correspond to functionalist expectations—and how functional new governance systems actually are in practice.

From this perspective, it is critical to look closely at differing, local manifestations of re-formed governance, attending to how agency processes, as well as structural forces, have shaped what did and didn't happen in particular cases—with a view to their implications for understanding the overall profile of change. Comparing different cases in this way reduces the possibility both of misplaced generalizations from particular instances, and/or of relating each to a taken-for-granted (functional) norm. Since key influences on agency are liable to be both qualitative and path-dependent, such comparisons need to start from in-depth, longitudinal analyses of a kind that is only feasible if focused on a very restricted number of individually significant cases—as we attempt in the research summarily reported here—though specific hypotheses can and should be subsequently tested across larger groups of representative cases. Using either methodology, our approach would involve focusing the comparison on a set of common "issue fields," identified generically on a functionalist basis, in terms of where (in the context of a globalized economy) metropolitan regions might be expected to present a new or heightened set of governance issues—rather than pursuing simply those issues which had generated interesting innovations in a particular place. Comparison of this kind can also counter some of the advocacy of "solutions" to metropolitan governance (for example, elected mayors) that are widely advanced on the basis (at most) of particular cases (cities, regimes, and issues) where such solutions seem to have had some success.

This is the motive for our focus in this chapter (and the wider project from which it is drawn) on a set of specific policy areas where a priori functional arguments suggest important metropolitan governance issues, in a pair of British cities (London and Manchester). Though they followed quite different economic and institutional paths over the last two centuries, each faced the same governance shock in the mid-1980s when the UK government abolished their metropolitan authorities. Concentrating on the last fifteen years (of New Labour and then Coalition government nationally), there are some obvious and broad differences in how their governance capacities have been re-formed—notably in London through the *top-down* creation of a directly elected metropolitan mayor (the first in the UK), and in Manchester more incrementally through *bottom-up* processes, culminating recently in a compact (or "Deal" in the current parlance) with central government, including recognition of an integrated authority. But our interest goes beyond a description of these changes, to try and understand both the processes underlying these developments, and also where functionally appropriate responses have not (so far) been forthcoming (at all, or in the expected form).

Challenges for Metropolitan Governance

The governance of metropolitan regions has become a significant current issue in many places for two general reasons. One is that their internal complexity—referred to in the Introduction—has grown substantially as their functional scale has increased, often through the absorption and integration of previously independent centres. This has led to a proliferation of functional linkages and dependencies over a wide range of scales and orientations, not simply along established radial pathways but with an untidier array of orbital/eccentric interactions. The resulting spatial externalities not only cut across the boundaries of established local government areas, but would still do so even with the most rationally re-formed multi-level structure—while their new salience is frequently not widely or fully recognized, even by those most directly engaged. Spatial extension has also tended to increase the degree of social, economic, and political differentiation between areas whose functional integration does not reduce (and may intensify) local residents'—and even businesses'—imagination of them as constituting "communities" to be kept distinct from those of their metropolitan neighbours.[4] Without explicit efforts to build a stronger institutional capacity across the extended metropolitan region, micro-political pressures are more likely to encourage a further fragmentation of governance than the integration that functional considerations require (Cheshire and Gordon 1996).

The second factor that gives especial salience to this metropolitan governance issue is the heightened recognition, over the past twenty years, of the economic dynamism of major city-regions, in relation to national economic performance (as well as, in some cases, to that of lagging regions). More specifically, the point is that the competitive advantage of such agglomerations rests on *well-managed complexity* as the key economic and social asset. This has provided a motive for national (and also trans-national, in the EU case) governments and interest groups to address the metropolitan governance issue—either as a whole or in terms of aspects of strategic importance from their perspective.

Against this background, we have identified a set of policy areas where significant governance issues could reasonably be expected to have emerged, in one form or another, across metropolitan regions. From these we selected six for investigation in this research project—strategic economic development, managing traffic congestion, affordable housing provision, strategic infrastructure projects, human capital development, and intra-regional co-ordination of competitive economic initiatives—the first three of which are reported on in this chapter.

These issue areas represent a set of (potential) policy challenges for actors and institutions in the metropolitan systems. But underlying any responses to these are a further set of political challenges in developing, or re-forming, its governance capacity. In our view, as we have already indicated, this is not going to be simply a matter of designing, empowering, and resourcing a new set of formal administrative or executive bodies—or of rationalizing existing ones so as to free up the market. Rather, we would expect that processes of adaptation would need to be initiated which gave substantial attention to informal institutions and practices, as well as to formal structures and (quasi-)markets.

More specifically, we start with four hypotheses about key factors for development of effective metropolitan governance.[5] First is effective *leadership* (with access to resources), adequate to meet two needs: engendering collective action in ways that serve relatively broad and powerful constellations of interests, and resolving situations where there is a plurality of acceptable options, by being able to privilege one through making a credible resource commitment.[6] The second factor concerns the *legitimacy* of these new metro governance arrangements, measured in terms of the degree of devolved authority they possess and their perceived representativeness, and enhanced by demonstrations of effectiveness in practice. The third factor is the production of an *"imagined metro community"*—to adapt Anderson's (2006) concept[7]—that transcends pre-existing social and political interests and identities across the region. This construction will be a work in progress, being built out of developing habits of cooperation, the awareness of shared threats and opportunities, education and propaganda, and the passage of time. Finally, there is a need to develop a positive *relationship with the central state* and its interests, based on a realistic appreciation of the political and economic stakes involved.

Our approach to intercity comparison has both an analytical and a narrative aspect to it. On one hand, the intention is to derive comparable accounts of governance development in two city-regions in terms of a single set of causal factors. At the same time, we expect to elaborate and amend those ideas in the process, showing in particular how contexts and histories matter and how they may be used to legitimate or thwart change. Given our expectations about the relevance of path dependence to the process of re-forming metropolitan governance in the two cities, and that this will be a source of difference between them, we start by considering (if rather briefly here) their distinctive patterns of political, social, and economic developments from around the mid-nineteenth century onward. Then our prime focus becomes how London and Manchester have each responded over the past fifteen years to the three governance issues listed above, which we expect to be generally salient across metropolitan regions in this era.

The Two Metropolitan Regions and the Path to Metropolitan Governance

Differences between the two cities that have shaped their current contexts and cultures go back at least to the nineteenth century. At this time, Manchester became the first, archetypical city of modern, factory-based industrial capitalism, while London remained the Imperial capital with an economy based on workshops, services, and importing. Socially and politically they contrasted too. Manchester was especially notable for its industrial working class, low-waged and in poverty, poor housing and environmental conditions (as classically described by Engels 1845), but marked by strong collective organization. By comparison, the London economy was based on unstable activities—involving much casual work, unemployment, and a culture of competitive individualism—with substantial disorganization both socially and politically (Stedman Jones 1971). Manchester's more coherent social organization (both working class and among the industrial, commercial and professional bourgeoisie) underpinned the growth of new municipal government in the urban core (the boroughs of Manchester and Salford) from mid-century at a time when London's government remained fragmented, with the historic City successfully obstructing reform, at least until establishment of first the London County Council (LCC) and then a set of metropolitan boroughs, toward the end of the century.

From this background, there emerged in Manchester a clear business-led municipal leadership grounded in the city's role as the industrial and commercial capital of its surrounding region and with a growing role for organized working-class politics within it too. A notable early exercise of such a governing coalition was its ability to generate a cross-class alliance to press successfully for the building of the Manchester Ship Canal to counter economic decline in the city toward the end of the century, and overcome dependence on the port of Liverpool (Harford 1994). Such leadership capacity was lacking in London, whose only significant institutions, until the advent of the LCC, remained the City of London (in the central "square mile" of the trade/financial district), plus a parish-based Metropolitan Board of Works to develop basic infrastructure (notably sewers and associated works) at least (Young and Garside 1982).

The twentieth century saw the Fordist transition—with its increasing orientation to growing consumer markets—shift the national economic focus southwards, favouring London and the South East over Manchester. In the 1960s and 1970s, deindustrialization devastated Manchester's economy and its basis of stable working-class employment, though it retained significant commercial and cultural assets. From the 1980s, deregulation (notably the "Big Bang" in finance and labour market flexibilization) reinforced London's advantages vis-à-vis Manchester (and other provincial industrial centres), while new waves of mass immigration brought a turnaround of its long-term population decline. By contrast it took far longer for a recognizably post-Fordist economy to emerge in Manchester and reversal of population decline has only started since the millennium (Buck et al. 2002; Rees and Harding 2010). Over the whole period we are considering, both cities continued to spread spatially (London more than Manchester), absorbing nearby towns and communities. In London's case this tendency was (unintentionally) intensified after the Second World War by "containment" policies, leading growth to leapfrog an extensive Green Belt. In the current era, both city-regions comprise an urbanized core and a less continuously urbanized, but economically integrated, Metropolitan, or Functional Urban Region (FUR)[8]—plus, in London's case alone, a super FUR/or megacity region (the Greater South East), with economic dynamism and key linkages spread right across it (Hall 2009).

By the middle of the last century this spatial extension brought the realization that, in terms of their government, both cities were considerably under-bounded. Such pressures led, in 1964, to the replacement of the LCC (covering the late-nineteenth-century urban core) by the Greater London Council (GLC) (including all the areas added to that core up to imposition of the Green Belt—but none of the wider FUR). In Manchester a new upper tier metro authority covering almost all of the FUR was formed in 1974. In each case the metropolitan boundaries were effectively set by the area of continuous urbanization (i.e., the morphological rather than the functional urban region, see Figure 18.1) and have survived, despite a continuing extension of the economic region. But the life of the authorities themselves proved short. Under the Thatcher government, from 1979 onward, there was a growing conflict between the radical Left Councils that came to control both and a right-wing national government. Both were consequently abolished in 1986.

Each city-region responded to the evident governance deficit that this created in ways that reflected their distinctive histories. London was left with thirty-three local boroughs, with the City of London as the most potentially powerful, but with an archaic, undemocratic business-based government limiting its legitimacy. Manchester was also fragmented, into ten boroughs, with the City of Manchester at its core potentially able to play a strong leadership role due to its resources and importance. In both city-regions, more informally constituted (i.e., non-statutory) forms of cooperation began to emerge, both to organize and operate some services and to address the increasingly salient agenda of economic development and competitiveness. In London this latter agenda involved various

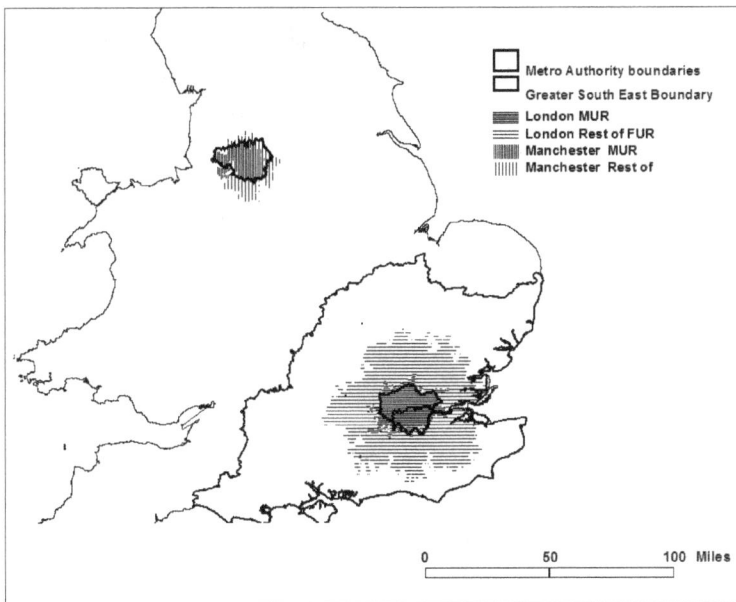

Figure 18.1 Greater London and Manchester Authority boundaries in relation to Functional and Morphological Urban Regions and the Greater South East.

business/City-backed (and nationally endorsed) organizations and alliances, as well as a London Planning Advisory Committee intended to help the national government shape regional spatial strategy (Travers 2004). In Manchester the voluntary Association of Greater Manchester Authorities (AGMA), to which all ten boroughs subscribed, became the vehicle for organization of some key services, as well as the economic agenda. AGMA was characterized by more political coherence and leadership than was available in London, and after a few years its initial Left radicalism faded, to be replaced by a more proactive, capacity-building, and less conflictual interaction with central government (Harding et al. 2010).

Toward the end of the last century, with new encouragement from central government, economic competitiveness became a key leitmotif in both cities. In Manchester the response drew on the strengths of its rich mix of business and professional networks, its comparatively coherent leadership (aided by the historic dominance of the Labour Party in much of the region), and the growing expansion and development of the work of AGMA. London, reflecting its more fragmented political history and relatively weak metropolitan leadership, relied on more narrowly delineated CBD pressure groups promoting a "world city" agenda strongly anchored in the financial and associated services sectors of the metropolitan economy (Thornley et al. 2005).

These developments, underpinned by the post-Fordist transformation of both economies, increased the pressure for a reinvention of metro government in both cities. In London, a top-down solution was established by a new Labour Government in 2000 (reflecting the extent to which London had become a special concern of national government), with an elected Mayor with a primarily strategic role, plus appointing powers for Transport for London, and limited fiscal capacity, subject only to weak scrutiny through an elected Assembly (Travers 2004). In Manchester, change occurred bottom-up, with a protracted period of local and national negotiations leading eventually to the transformation in 2009 of AGMA into a Greater Manchester Combined Authority, consisting of the locally elected leaders of the ten boroughs, to plan and run some key services, and pursue the competitiveness agenda. The new institutional arrangements incorporated considerable involvement of the leading sectors of business and other non-governmental agencies and interests, such as higher education, for example (Harding et al. 2010).

Summary of the Issue Cases

Against this background, our specific analyses focus on developments in the period since 2000. As already noted, we have initially chosen three out of a set of potential issues[9] identified on a functionalist basis as liable to present specific governance issues within the context of contemporary metropolitan regions in advanced economies. These are the development of strategic economic policies for the metropolitan region and key sub-regions; mitigation of traffic congestion in areas where this can be expected to present substantial negative effects across an area beyond the immediate district; and provision for an adequate housing supply to meet the needs of the regional labour force and its potential growth.

In each case we address the following questions: how (if at all) have a particular region's governance arrangements responded to the issue during this period; how this pattern of action or inaction is to be explained; and what the main consequences have been, in relation both to the specific issue, and development of governance processes in the region concerned. Our main findings for each are presented below in a condensed form (given space constraints in this chapter).[10]

Strategic economic development

The functional issues under this heading include establishing some shared visions of feasible economic change and their regional impacts as a basis for prioritizing development activities, integrating related sectoral policies, and restraining wasteful inter-local competition. This has been pursued in different ways in the two places. In London, a central strategy (prioritizing the needs of "global city" in the core) was set authoritatively by the first mayor, during preparation of the initial (spatial) plan—and only moderated in tone by his successor. A modest attempt (by the second mayor) at promoting a set of complementary "super-hubs" foundered, primarily because of lack of borough agreement. In Manchester, on the other hand, the strategy has developed over time, alongside that of a range of economic development institutions, as part of a process of building governance capacity, rather than from a single concerted line. Differences in two other factors relate to this. One is the presence (in London, through City-based business interests) or absence (in Manchester) of a single, strong economic pressure group seeking to shape the policy agenda, on or off stage. The other is the role of central government, which appears an important agent, shaping local strategies in both places, given its continuing control over key resources. But whereas in Manchester this is more or less visible in the way interactions have proceeded and "deals" been negotiated, in

London it has operated much less openly, through the leadership's choice of strategies perceived as in line with national priorities (the global city and Olympics), and thus more likely to unlock infrastructure funding (Harding et al. 2010; Gordon 2004).

Managing transport congestion

The functional issue here arises from the fact that traffic congestion on inter-local routes is a predictable consequence of the growth, spatial extension, and emergent multi-centrism of metropolitan regions, with potentially serious effects on economic competitiveness (as well as quality of life), which cannot be managed locally or by incremental enlargement of route capacities. Very probably it requires demand management, through a combination of (quasi-market) route and space pricing, careful locational planning of new developments, and place-specific restraints on parking, etc. All of these are likely to be unpopular. In both cities, the option of congestion charging was made available to and considered by city leaderships—by a central government unwilling (in the face of opposition from private motorists) to take direct responsibility for its introduction. In both cases, there was a dual motive: in potential for raising revenue in otherwise constrained situations, and the possibility of improving the efficiency of movement in the cities. In each case, the first of these appears to have been very important when leaders (in both cities at different times) decided to pursue this option. There were substantial differences in the coverage of the schemes, possibly accounting for variations in their success. In London, local approval was secured for an (effective) scheme covering only the core central business area, where office/cultural services were predictable net beneficiaries, and their representatives had supported it (Richards 2006). In Manchester, on the other hand, the scheme that failed to gain such approval covered most of the urbanized area. In London, a follow-up scheme for extension of the congestion charge area into a more mixed residential/commercial area was approved by one mayor, but abandoned by his successor in the face of local opposition. Across the wider urban area (specifically Outer London), despite intensifying road congestion, charging cannot even get on the agenda.

Affordable housing provision

The issue here is again one of spatial externalities arising from the tension *between* a functional requirement at metropolitan scale for affordable housing to meet the needs of the labour force that its economy requires *and* local NIMBY resistance to environmental or social change.

This has been less of an issue in Manchester, where the pressure of housing demand and population growth has been less, and more redundant "brownfield" land is available, and it has suited both inner-city and suburban politicians to see most new construction in the core city.

In London, however, it has long been a source of conflict, both openly within Greater London, where the GLC had met some notable failures with its ambitions to place social housing in outer boroughs, and less directly with areas further out in the metropolitan region that have never been under London planning control. The London mayor achieved significant success in imposing affordable housing quotas on new developments. But there has been a retreat from the efforts of the first mayor to impose numerical housing targets on boroughs, while the current government has abandoned the Regional Strategies which were (in principle at least) a vehicle for meeting housing needs via local targets in areas outside the GLA territory. In both cases, there has been a switch toward a more softly-softly approach—including the institution now of financial incentives for communities to accept more new housing, which may be inadequate but in principle represent a significant step toward use of market mechanisms to facilitate collaboration. There is, however, no current mechanism for positively pursuing adequate housing provision at the metropolitan scale. Rather, there is a studied silence from the Mayor about any ramifications of this issue beyond the boundaries of the GLA. The explicit objectives of the London Plan remain ones of meeting the housing needs of its projected population entirely within its own (heavily urbanized) area via a combination of densification of development—with significant resistance in outer London—and opening up less well connected/popular areas to the east. Achievement of a high level of approvals for (largely private) housing within London has, however, not been matched by actual completions, running at less than half the rate over a decade. Analyses across wider housing markets have been avoided in the interest essentially of not provoking opposition to London's economic growth trajectory (Gordon and Travers 2010).

Conclusion. Metropolitan Governance: Ideal and Reality

What does this (summary and rather preliminary) comparative account of the cases of Greater London and Greater Manchester suggest about the importance of the various elements cited earlier as key elements in the emergence of a functioning metropolitan governance? The first point is that, compared to the nation-wide local government reforms that were introduced in the 1970s, the recent experience of metropolitan institutional "emergence" has been much more selective and ad hoc in character. Indeed, London and Manchester are the only places where much attention has been focused—in different ways and by different actors—on the strengthening of metropolitan institutions. Such highly selective metropolitanism might be seen as a favour awarded by national government to specific cities and their metropolitan regions, reflecting their particular salience to its concerns. The recreation (in 2000) of a strategic metropolitan authority and introduction of an elected Mayor for London alone is an obvious case in point. Five years on when the government proposed a strengthening of the Mayor's (originally limited) powers, it made the case in terms of the unique position and requirements of this city, in relation to the economic needs of the nation as a whole (DCLG 2005). This seems a rather double-edged argument, since no reference at all is made to the particular interests or concerns of Londoners. But it is a fact that no such action or statements was offered to any other UK city/metropolitan area.

To the extent that "favours" from government to Manchester/Greater Manchester have been obtained, these have been "won" on the basis of locally generated arguments about *both* the economic successes secured by their authorities through the effective application of local and national resources, *and* the critical role that the metropolitan area/city-region plays in the economic performance of the north of England (see, e.g., MIER 2009). The success of Manchester's "sales pitch" is reflected in an ability to attract discretionary public resources that is unrivalled elsewhere in the provincial UK. But they do not bear comparison with the volume of nominally "place-blind," sector-specific investments—for example in transport, scientific research, cultural institutions, and mega-events, not least the Olympic Games, that have flowed to London and the South East. Indeed, the 2005–10 Labour administration shifted the focus of investment planning away from strategic future provisioning to satisfying bottlenecks, in terms of infrastructure, affordable homes, and labour shortages, in the highest growth areas of London and the South. Manchester's response was to argue that it, too, needed to be able to cope with growth pressures.

In neither London nor Manchester, however, has the recreation of metropolitan governance capacity resulted in strong, institutional capacity that is capable, independently, of generating impacts that rival those that flow from central government's implicit spatial policy.

Drawing on a list, proposed by Le Galès, of the essential building blocks for the emergence of a collective metropolitan actor, we summarize the current condition of each city as follows:

- *A collective decision-making system*: In London this is represented formally (in governmental terms) by the Mayor, his staff, and those of the other organizations under his aegis (notably Transport for London), abetted by their consultees (including the boroughs and sub-regional partnerships). Beyond that, there have been regular but informal relations with a small sub-set of economic interests only—and interaction with central government. In Greater Manchester, there is much less formal concentration of power (or a singular collective actor), but something much more like a regime. This is still led, in practice, if not formally, from the City of Manchester, with links to the other authorities through a set of thematic Commissions (with specific functions) and some engagement with other elements in the city's elite leadership.

- *Common interests—or those perceived as such*: In London, although the Mayor is democratically elected and works to build solidarity as well as support across the city, there has been no effective debate about common interests, nor about the strategic components of mayoral policy-making. In economic terms at least, these have been substantially shaped by representatives of a central London business elite (and central government). London strategies have also contained substantial "social" components, but not ones conflicting with the economic dimension. Greater Manchester institutions are elite-dominated (if not by such a singular group) and also not subject to much public scrutiny. The assertion of a common Greater Manchester collective interest with regard to congestion charging was a fiasco.

- *Integration mechanisms*: In both cities, these largely hinge on symbolic activities allied to traditional communal loyalties and conventional political support-building. In the London region they do not extend beyond the GLA territory in the urban core.

- *Internal and external representation*: In both cases there is a very strong focus on representation at national level, through events and initiatives—notably the (prestigious) Manchester Independent Economic Review. Manchester is particularly adept at using business leaders as emissaries with the government. In the London case, again it does not extend beyond the GLA boundary.

- *Innovation*: In the Manchester case, the uniqueness and breadth of institutions can be seen as innovative (if historically grounded). In the London case, the mayoralty is the main innovation, but sponsorship of a London Living Wage and gestures of support to irregular (as well as regular) migrant communities may also count.

Overall, we must conclude that neither city is yet near to meeting Le Galès's specification of what a metropolitan collective actor would embody. We can also make a provisional comparison of their performance on those underlying dimensions that we initially highlighted, namely leadership, legitimacy, the construction of an imagined metro community, and effective relations with central government. On the first of these, the London mayor and the Manchester CA have both exhibited considerable leadership capacity. But each currently lacks sufficient resources, legitimacy, and power to make major impacts on most of the key issues of metropolitan integration or to override (even when inclined to do so) localist interests. And, specifically, each has lacked the power to engender an imagined community across the functional metro region. However, that does not mean that governance is entirely lacking. Indeed we would argue, on principle (rather than in defence of either city), that an effective governance system for a metropolitan region—meeting the dual needs for legitimacy and leadership—requires a degree of pluralism in its system for aggregating interests and integrating activities. In practice, both cities do display a substantial degree of bargaining around some of those issues we have considered. In both cases, however, central government is (openly or not) a key player, becoming more so with the recent shift from relatively well-funded, centrally designed programs toward centrally mediated, locally competed-for "deals." In this context it seems likely that cities with some emergent form of metropolitan governance are likely to be at an advantage. As the contrasting cases of London and Manchester illustrate, however, being the economic/political capital city makes a substantial difference, with a grant of more formal powers, but also effective constraints (as perhaps in all such places) on the degree to which these can be directed to the priorities of local citizens.

Local agency has clearly been important in the (uncertain) progress of both cities toward a re-formed metropolitan governance capacity, though with big differences between them. In part these evidently reflect structural differences (including the challenges posed by London's greater scale and diversity). But strong echoes of their contrasting institutional development in earlier eras also suggest substantial path-dependence.

Afterword (Summer 2015)

Since the paper on which this chapter is based was completed in early 2013, very little has changed in actual arrangements for government of the London metropolitan region. But in Greater Manchester, there have been further significant developments—which (as noted below) have helped stimulate further thought about London governance, too.

In *Manchester* the dialogue between central government and local civic leadership moved into new territory in mid-2014, with a speech by George

Osborne, the Treasury minister, espousing the idea of a "Northern Powerhouse," with increased investment in science, innovation, and transport to join together the strengths of a set of mutually accessible northern cities (Osborne 2014). He referred specifically to the ten million people within a forty-mile radius of Manchester and plans for improving their connectivity (HM Government/Transport for the North 2015). But he also emphasized the need for strong recognizable leadership (as in London), offering a "serious devolution of powers and budgets for any city that wants to move to a new model of city government—and have an elected Mayor." To a very considerable extent the dialogue with government that has brought about this outcome has been dominated by the civic leaders of Greater Manchester, and Osborne's own awareness (from his nearby parliamentary constituency) of new forms of co-operation across the city's borders.

Following the unexpected election of a majority Conservative government in May 2015, one of its first parliamentary initiatives was to bring forward a bill to enable the devolutionary initiative to be carried forward (Harrison 2015). There may have been some political opportunism in this, given the Labour Party's weakened position, after loss of (almost all) its Scottish seats. But it is also clear that Osborne and the Treasury were persuaded by the case (made by Manchester and other northern cities) that stagnant national productivity levels could be improved through new initiatives to raise those in cities outside London and the South East (not just to divert investment and activity away from these "successful" regions). However, while the new governance arrangements now seem certain to go ahead, delivery on the promise that there would be further substantial infrastructure investment across the northern regions (even though other substantial expenditure cuts were to be made), was very soon brought into question, as the key upgrading scheme for the Manchester–Leeds rail link was "shelved," and release of new cost estimates for the planned high-speed rail link from London northwards added to serious doubts about its affordability.

So far only Greater Manchester has opted for one of the "Big Deals," giving it new powers and resources—for housing, transport, planning, policing, skills and business support, and health—in exchange for introducing a strong (directly elected) mayoral system for the metropolitan authority. In addition, there will be an "earn back" scheme, involving Greater Manchester creating a fund for local investment (through borrowing against revenue) and benefiting from an enhanced share of the additional tax revenues that result (GMCA 2015).

There are similarities between what is emerging in Greater Manchester and what already exists with the London mayor. But there are also novel features, both in relation to the range of powers and financial incentives to be devolved, and in the explicitness of the "Deal." There are significant differences in the formal structure, reflecting the distinctively "bottom-up" route to metro governance in Greater Manchester referred to earlier. Specifically, the Greater Manchester Combined Authority (GMCA) comprising elected leaders of the metro district councils will both act as a Cabinet (chaired by the mayor) and possess powers to veto strategic plans produced by the mayor. In London, by contrast, the Mayor appoints his own Cabinet and is subject only to the rather weak scrutiny powers of a directly elected Assembly.

Although the new arrangements could be adopted elsewhere, in other city-regions there is much less enthusiasm (or consensus) among political and civic elites (Parker, Bounds, and Tighe 2015; BBC 2015). Greater Manchester's (so far) unique determination to move to a new stage of metro governance again reflects both the significance of path-dependent local history and the crucial role of leadership (in the city-region and from central government) in progress along this road. If not yet Le Galès' fully fledged collective metropolitan actor, this city-region continues to put significant foundations in place.

Nothing of such substance has happened in or around *London*, but there has been renewed discussion about the capacity of its (quasi-)metropolitan authority and about engagement with its neighbours. The first has been stimulated by Big Deal activity elsewhere, by the Northern Powerhouse, and a wider debate about English devolution stimulated by the 2014 Scottish independence referendum. In the second case, important factors include a dawning recognition that London is unlikely to meet its own housing targets as large-scale immigration into the city continues, moves by the GLA toward longer term infrastructure planning, and a perception by neighbouring planning authorities that some arrangements for wider co-operation (not just pure localism) are required to fill the vacuum left by the government's abolition of regional agencies and strategies.

One aspect of this new activity has been an attempt to bolster the strategic capacity of the Mayor in relation to development *within* Greater London, to meet the needs of large projected increases in population and jobs, and to promote additional economic growth (in the national interest). To this end a London Finance Commission made a strong case for fiscal devolution, with a freedom to make infrastructure investments being secured through relaxation of borrowing restrictions and transfer of revenue streams including all property taxes (LFC 2013). Borrowing explicitly from the Manchester "Earn Back" arrangement, as well as the government's 2013 business rate reform, their proposals are designed to be fiscally neutral at first, though London would be rewarded for future growth in its tax base. A Parliamentary Select Committee endorsed the LFC principles as generally applicable to English local authorities, while also recommending that the London mayor be more accountable to the Assembly and also seeking a more equitable assignment of future growth in taxable assets. The government has yet to respond to the LFC report, or to a London Enterprise Partnership's submission for a Big Deal—but has firmly rejected giving more power to the Assembly. A first Mayoral Infrastructure Plan, for the period to 2050 (MoL 2014), has, however, been produced, with a comprehensive agenda and explicit discussion of strategic options.

One aspect of the new activity involves relations between the GLA (and London boroughs) and authorities in the rest of London's extended region. Developments are at an early stage, but (beyond responding to statutory obligations to cooperate) have been spurred by the process of revising the London Plan, and references in the Mayoral Infrastructural Plan to relations between radial transport links and residential development beyond the Green Belt, including possible joint development of new garden suburbs. The Inspector's report from the (2014) public examination of the latest amendments to the London Plan urged the Mayor to now "explore options beyond the existing philosophy of the London Plan," suggesting that in the absence of a wider regional strategy this might involve "engaging local planning authorities beyond the Greater London Authority's boundaries in discussions regarding the evolution of our capital city." The government's response warned against this, saying that it had abolished top-down regional strategies that "built up nothing but resentment" and had no intention of resurrecting anything like the former Standing Conference of South East planning authorities (SERPLAN) "from the dead." This may be partly attributable to pre-election nervousness about anything conducive to discussion of options for building in the Green Belt. But an initial Wider Regional Summit meeting has since been held, agreeing to pursue discussions on planning, housing, infrastructure, and economic issues. And the Mayor's Outer London Commission is currently consulting within London about bases for wider South Eastern engagement, ahead of another summit at the end of 2015. Something may at last be moving on this front—if not on the ambitions of the London Assembly's Conservative Group leader for a Thames City super-region to spur on a "southern powerhouse" (Boff 2015).

Notes

1 Le Galès (2002: 15) defines this as "a process of coordinating actors, social groups, and institutions to obtain particular goals, discussed and defined collectively in fragmented, uncertain environments," though we would wish to consider also more pluralistic versions in which multiple sets of goals could be developed (and implemented) via different, overlapping collectives.
2 According to Young and Kramer (1978), who also refer to the long history of waxing and waning campaigns for metropolitan government in North America.
3 These three components (which we see as complementary) have each been the focus of one of the three intellectual traditions—metropolitan reform, public choice, and new regionalism—which in turn have held centre stage within the (very long) debate over how extended functional regions can be regulated (Kubler 2012).
4 See note 7 below.
5 Drawing on a wide range of mainstream literature in the field.
6 As with the Elkins/Stone conception of a regime, this leadership may come from politicians, business people, or professionals (Stone and Sanders 1987)
7 Applied originally to nations, Anderson's idea involved a socially constructed community among people who may never meet face to face but are persuaded that they have a common identity, reflecting shared interests or values. This may be reinforced by circumstances giving credibility to the notion of sharing a common set of risks (Dryzeck and Goodin 1986) or facing a common threat (an imagined enemy perhaps).
8 Defined on a basis comparable to U.S. SMAs by Cheshire and Gornostaeva (in GEMACA 2001).
9 With a further three being covered in the second phase of our research.
10 A more extended version will be published, together with the other three issue cases, in a report on the full study.

References

Anderson, B. 2006. *Imagined Communities*, 2nd ed. London: Verso.
BBC. 2015. "What is the northern powerhouse?" Accessed June 28, 2015 at www .bbc.co.uk /news/magazine-32720462.
Boff. A. 2015. *Southern powerhouse: True devolution for London and the South East*. London: GLA Conservatives.
Brenner, N. 2004. *New state spaces: Urban governance and the rescaling of statehood*. Oxford: Oxford University Press.
Buck, N., I. R. Gordon, P. Hall, M. Harloe, and M. Kleinman. 2002. *Working capital: Life and labour in contemporary London*. London: Routledge.
Cheshire, P. and G. Gornostaeva. 2002. "Cities and regions: Comparable measures require comparable territories." *Cahiers de l'IAURIF* 135: 11–31.
Cheshire, P. and I. R. Gordon. 1996. "Territorial competition and the predictability of collective (in)action." *International Journal of Urban and Regional Research* 20: 383–99.
Department for Communities and Local Government. 2005. *The Greater London Authority: The government's proposals for additional powers and responsibilities for the mayor and assembly*. London: DCLG.

Dryzek, J. and R. E. Goodin. 1986. "Risk sharing and social hustice: The motivational foundations of the postwar welfare state." *British Journal of Political Science* 16: 1–34.

Engels, F. 1845. (Eng. ed. 1892). "The great towns." In *The condition of the working class in England in 1844*. London: Lawrence and Wishart.

GEMACA. 2001. *Les Régions métropoles de l'Europe du nord-ouest: Limites géographiques et structures économiques*. Paris: IAURIF.

GMCA. 2015. "Greater Manchester hails city deal announcement." Accessed June 28, 2015 at www.agma.gov.uk/gmca/city-deal-announcement/.

Gordon, I. R. 2004. "Capital needs, capital growth and global city rhetoric in Mayor Livingstone's London plan." *GaWC Research Bulletin 145*. University of Loughborough.

———. 2006. "Finding institutional leadership for networks: The case of London and the Greater South East." In W. Salet, ed., *Synergy in Urban Networks* (136–60). The Hague: Sdu Uitgevers.

Gordon, I. R. and T. Travers. 2010. "London: Planning the ungovernable city." *City, Culture and Society* 1: 49–55.

Hall, P. G. 1989. *London 2001*. London: Unwin Hyman.

———. 2009. "Looking backward, looking forward: The city region of the mid-21st century." *Regional Studies* 43: 803–17.

Harding, A., M. Harloe, and J. Rees. 2010. "Manchester's bust regime." *International Journal of Urban and Regional Research* 34: 981–91.

Harford, I. 1994. "The ship canal: Raising the standard for popular capitalism." *Manchester Regional History Review* 8: 3–13.

Harrison, B. 2015. "A snapshot of the cities and local government devolution Bill 2015." Centre for Cities: London. Accessed on June 28, 2015 at http://centreforcities.org/blog/a-snapshot-of-the-city-and-local-government-devolution-bill.

HM Government/Transport for the North. 2015. *The northern powerhouse: One agenda, one economy, one north*. London: Department for Transport.

Kubler, D. 2012. "Metropolitanisation and metropolitan governance: Symposium introduction." *European Political Science* 11: 402–8.

Le Galès, P. 2002. *European cities: Social conflict and governance*. Oxford: Oxford University Press.

London Finance Commission. 2013. *Raising the capital: Report of the London finance commission*. London: Greater London Authority.

Mayor of London. 2014. *London infrastructure plan 2050*. London: Greater London Authority.

Osborne, G. 2014. "We need a northern powerhouse." Speech delivered on June 23, 2014, at the Manchester Museum of Science and Industry. Accessed June 28, 2015 at www.gov.uk /government/speeches/chancellor -we-need-a-northern-powerhouse.

Parker, G., Bounds, A. and Tighe, C. 2015 "Osborne offers big cities deal on self-rule." *Financial Times*. May 14, 2015. Accessed June 28, 2015 at www.ft.com/cms/s/0/e141b228-f986-11e4-97b2-00144feab7de.html#axzz3eI16DU9D.

Rees, J. E. and A. Harding. 2010. "Greater Manchester case study." Appendix C2 to *The case for agglomeration economies in Europe*, final report. Luxembourg: ESPON.

Richards, M. G. 2006. *Congestion charging in London: The policy and the politics.* Basingstoke: Palgrave.

Stedman Jones, G. 1971. *Outcast London: A study in the relationship between classes in Victorian society.* Oxford: Clarendon Press.

Stone, C. and H. Sanders, eds. 1987. *The politics of urban development.* Lawrence: University Press of Kansas.

Thornley, A., Y. Rydin, K. Scanlon, and K. West. 2005. "Business privilege and the strategic planning agenda of the Greater London Authority." *Urban Studies* 42: 1947–68.

Travers, T. 2004. *The politics of London: Governing an ungovernable city.* Basingstoke: Palgrave.

Young, K. and J. Kramer. 1978. *Strategy and conflict in metropolitan housing.* London: Heinemann.

Young, K. G. and P. Garside. 1982. *Metropolitan London politics and urban change 1837–1981.* London: Edward Arnold.

North Atlantic Urban and Regional Governance

Julie-Anne Boudreau, Pierre Hamel, Roger Keil, and Stefan Kipfer

THIS BOOK HAS presented a loosely comparative set of conceptual essays and case studies from Canadian and European urban regions. Its declared goal was to highlight and explore the differences in regional governance responses to the structural forces of globalization. We stated our interest in the emergence of regional governance arrangements, what form they take, and who the actors advocating for regional governance are. The results of this endeavour are full of conceptual diversity—new questions asked, new connections made—and, not unexpectedly, a broad spread of real, existing regionalisms in both Canada and Europe (Addie and Keil 2015). We based our guiding framework for the chapters on a broad acceptance of five interconnected departures in urban and regional thinking. Simply put, regions function beyond and despite their borders; this points directly to their political constitution through relations inside but also beyond their territory; the question that follows is whether and how we can or should use a set of terms derived from urban political studies— thinking about regime, growth coalition, growth machine, etc.—for the scale of the region; we assumed, then, that there is some form of regional collective agency; and, finally, that collective agency does not reside in the centre alone: it may be dissipated through the region.

Informed of these broad tendencies, the authors of the individual chapters, particularly those that dealt with specific cases of regional governance in Canada and Europe, engaged more or less explicitly with three sets of questions on the emergence of regional political spaces, on modalities of governance, and on regional identity.

The conceptual essays discuss both opportunity and constraint in an urban-regional environment characterized by globalization and neo-liberalization. We have seen that citizenship and agency are changing rapidly in the new assemblages of state formation that emerge in an urban-regional world (Keil and Addie 2015; Keil and Addie in this volume). As Boudreau and Hamel (in this volume) have emphasized, the presence and continued emergence of new forms of social agency and citizenship have fundamentally changed the political landscapes of urban regionalism. Margit Mayer, for her part, introduces an incipient typology of movements and politics that already react to and alter the rapidly changing urban and regional environments in which they are active (in this volume).

A different set of concerns drive the chapters by Heeg and by Belina and Lehrer (both in this volume). These accounts focus on the institutional and structural powers in urban regions—Heeg on the real estate complex, Belina and Lehrer on municipal politics—to structure and take advantage of a new playing field for urban regional action. As can be expected, the newly enlarged regional terrain for investment and intercommunal competition enables powerful actors to operate effectively on a larger scale that is both more unified and more fragmented, and hence filled with new business and political opportunities. The situation is not as clear for the emerging movements and community actors that attempt to recalibrate their role and test the boundaries of a new arena of citizenship in a less centrally determined environment (Young and Keil 2014).

Moving on to the empirical cases, we can say that they yielded a remarkable breadth of experiences. While all cases have seen dynamic new urban and regional institutions, politics, and actor constellations, they have also shown noticeable internal diversity in approach and execution. They all agree that the regional has emerged as a meaningful political space. But this space varies to the degree that it is produced by different modalities of governance leading to different identities in and of urban regions. Starting with the Canadian cases, we observe that Toronto and Montreal, both subject to metropolitan consolidation in the last twenty years, have now settled into an enlarged frame of reference for urban and regional politics and governance. Rather than fighting against amalgamation or, as in the case of Montreal, fighting for de-amalgamation, actors in these two important Canadian regions have now embraced a spatial frame of operation that includes more than the historical municipal boundaries viewed from the centre on outward. Yet clearly, while some forms of regional appeals now include reference to suburban diversity and immigration in those regions, longstanding grievances sometimes continue to break down along traditional lines such as "urban" or "suburban" identities. This has become particularly virulent in the two areas the case study chapters have highlighted: regional transportation and housing, where modal choice, morphology, tax regimes, sustainability concerns, and other issues continue to divide and define communities and electorates.

The other Canadian chapters provide both support for the Toronto–Montreal-based analysis and diverge from it. Chris Leo shows for the Winnipeg case—a unicity with a sparsely settled regional hinterland—that there is a distinct North American or Canadian regional constellation that forces us to adapt concepts such as the more European *Zwischenstadt*. This can be called Winnipeg's defining political space with a specific regional agency and identity. Moving west to Calgary, we learn from Byron Miller that the seemingly universal struggle between the regional growth machine and the regional political ecology of the land that it seeks to develop—ostensibly establishing a sustainability fix of sorts—shows some distinct and unique characteristics that put Calgary into the double vortex of state rescaling and the dynamics of the oil industry. At the Pacific edge of the Canadian national urban system, in Vancouver, another mode of globalization prevails: trade and globalized real estate. The region's governance, often held up to other regions in the country as exemplary, has addressed convulsive growing pains with a distinct "Vancouverism" at the core and service-based regionalism in the surrounding municipalities, all increasingly held together by a rail-based transportation system that feeds commuters into the core.

In all five Canadian cases illustrated in this book, an intense sense of multi-level interaction prevails. Provinces are the main actors that structure the discourse on regionalism and both define technologically (as they do in Ontario with institutions such as the transportation agency Metrolinx) and redistrict territorially (as they have done in the past in Montreal and Toronto) municipal and regional authority (Addie and Keil 2015). In Vancouver, as it has also been the case in Montreal and Toronto in the past, there is a profound distrust between these political decision-making levels. In Montreal, Toronto, and Vancouver alike, the suburban expansion both along concentric circles from the core and in more post-suburban, independent patterns, is now determined by immigration and ethno-cultural diversity. The governance implications from such a demographic and economic shift are going to be significant as the region's outer rim consolidates into what we have called elsewhere "cities in waiting."

The European cases are even more diverse and multifarious than the Canadian ones, yet they are held together more than the latter by a marked party-political presence at the urban and regional level. While Montreal and Vancouver have municipal parties, the North American tradition of local non-partisanship prevails, as opposed to the more structured partisan landscape in the European region. That said, there are huge differences here, too. The Paris and Frankfurt cases do provide clear alternatives for regional futures along party lines with the traditional bipartisan conservative-social democratic split being largely upheld with a new and often unpredictable presence by the Greens (and other smaller parties). Party politics was also present but not necessarily decisive in Barcelona, Manchester, and London. As we have seen in recent developments in both Spain and the UK more generally, though, local and regional party politics in reaction to and as an outlet of progressive and conservative social movements have gained new significance. In Barcelona in particular, "citizen discontent" led to a new political party geography (Tomàs in this volume). More importantly, though, as is particularly visible in the Italian experience with regionalism, partisan priorities mesh everywhere with regional difference. Various north–south or other regional divides split the range of possibility across nation states—not least overshadowed, as it has been frequently, by regionalist movements of another kind, most recently in Scotland, Catalonia, and the North of Italy.

What remains remarkable about the European cases is the predominance of three interlocking themes of identity, technocracy, and partisanship. In all cases, also, the relationship to central or federal authorities, upper-level governments, remain just as critical as the often-touted "interregional competition." While the latter is visible and "out there" as a policy-driving category, it remains less important in the end than the relationships between individual regions and the nation state. The weight of the relationships between the city-regions and the state in Europe is much heavier than that of their counterparts in Canada, where region-provincial relationships reign supreme.

In both Europe and Canada, intense rearrangements are under way in terms of intra-regional territorial and local-regional conflicts and conversations. Some of those are institutional in nature and rely on formal representations at various levels of government. More often than not, however, they defy given institutional forms and emerge as a rebellious sideshow to formal government. Those intra-regional and local-regional interactions can be about land use, services, development, taxation, the environment, housing, transit and transportation, and other issues. At their core are increasingly unequal socio-economic conditions typical for this period of globalization and neo-liberalization, and increasingly uneven political representation of core and periphery, as well as the "in-between" grey spaces into which the urban region divides itself (Young and Keil 2014; Yiftachel 2008).

What does the book leave us with in the end? We can affirm without doubt that the urban region is a contradictory but real political space in which various modalities of governance (sometimes guided by political difference) vie for relevance in the establishment of collective agency and identity. Territory is important but only when one takes into account the relational modes of its constitution. Institutions make a difference, as does policy. But both institutions and policies need not originate from the territory of the region in order to be effective at that scale. In the Canadian cases, for example, the provinces remain for all intents and purposes the prime regional government. Land-use planning, transportation, housing, waste, and water services are now mostly being viewed in regional, watershed, and commutershed frameworks, and integrative policies will be made by a plethora of actors (while others are more or less systemically excluded). The multi-level state is a visible actor always ready to harness regional agency and to define policy and governance mechanisms. Yet, as expected, top-down regional government is rarely seen in this period of intense roll-with-it neo-liberalization and internalized globalization. While consensus is not always desired or useful to the goals of policy actors, talk of inclusivity has high currency everywhere. Whether that discursive inclusivity is just part of going through the motions of post-political exercises or a meaningful experiment is always an open question (Deas and Headlam 2015).

Beyond this, we believe the chapters in this volume point to two directions for further work. On one hand, there is a clear need to continue the theoretical, conceptual, and methodological debate about how to best capture the unfolding of new forms of "governing cities through regions." While the authors here have approached the key questions asked at the outset with a variety of intellectual tools—from classical political economy to Foucauldian and post-structural approaches—no new paradigmatic thinking has yet emerged. Clearly, the regionally scaled thinking on (sub)urban governance has revealed new assemblages of power and politics otherwise often eclipsed by classical urban-suburban models of centrality and peripherality. But the newly horizontalized and classically hierarchical spaces of politics that rule the urban region in this day and age are not entirely understood, at the same time as new concepts are needed to understand the reconfigured state-citizens relations in such context.

On the other hand, we need more fine grain empirical study of sectoral or spatial cases of regionalized governance such as those provided, for example, by Abbruzzese (on housing) and Addie (on transportation) for the Toronto region, or Belina and Lehrer in comparing Frankfurt and Toronto suburbs. It will be fruitful and necessary to deepen these empirical investigations in order to understand the pathways and trajectories through which regional governance frameworks enter municipal politics.

Building collective agency in Canadian and European metropolitan regions has been an ongoing process in which only some objectives can possibly be fulfilled. From the point of view of creating a structured coherence in line with some majoritarian interests in a particular territory, some initiatives are successful sometimes. In most cases, and especially under the conditions of aggressive neo-liberalization and globalization, this remains, as the Paris chapter concludes, a "pipe dream."

Much future development will depend on how the pendulum swings between different types of regional governance. Various forms of hierarchical and networked governance compete for attention and are supported by various factions of government and business (Deas and Headlam, 2015). While we certainly can say that nothing is predetermined or unilaterally determined by allegedly supra-regional processes such as neo-liberalization and globalization, we can say that being in the confines and parameters of these processes has redefined collective agency significantly. This has created, to quote Deas and Headlam, "uneasy bedfellows: the 'democratic deficit,' post-politics, and the governance of the neo-liberal city" (Deas and Headlam, 2015).

We can safely say on the basis of both the conceptual and empirical chapters in this volume that governing cities is now done at least partly through regions. This is not accomplished in the traditional form of metropolitan government, as was the case for decades in post–World War Two Toronto. Now, government spreads itself between the networked governance and post-political governmentality of neo-liberal forms of rule, where business interests, fragmented class and territorial concerns mix with new ethno-cultural constellations across the urban regions. For the time being, the purportedly rational quest for regional unity and collaboration runs up against the wildly chaotic and often sabotaging effects of various types of competition and political strife.

In a world of real existing regionalism, where the ideological battles over the necessity of more-than-municipal government don't have to be fought anymore, we will see continued lines of contention along territory, talk, and technology (Addie and Keil 2014). In terms of territory, perhaps only Winnipeg stands out due to its isolated location where no neighbour-ing forces interfere with the consolidation and further sprawl of the city. Even in Calgary, with its political culture of free market capitalism, the sprawl now is being restricted in emerging territorial containers and the city will eventually grow in on itself. The existing strong growth manage-ment initiatives in British Columbia and Ontario set the stage to revamp completely the relationships of city-region-province, while in the Montreal region the suburban satellites have begun to develop their own gravita-tional systems that restructure the geological truth of the islands and the rivers as well as the political distribution of power in the region. The talk of the region has now taken hold across the country and serves as a top-down organizing tool for the provinces and a frame of reference for the claims of local actors. Much in these Canadian cities, as Chris Leo has pointed out, does not occur on the same plane of regional service density as we find it does in Europe. But the technological debate on transit, mobility, and transportation (and to a degree modes of housing) has now captured urban and regional polities from coast to coast.

In Europe, regions have long roots, their territories preceding in most cases those of states. Those territories are still under debate, as growth management measures (such as the Frankfurt and London greenbelts) are coming under reevaluation in terms of their potential usefulness for other necessary services, be they "ecosystem services" or housing, recreation, or mobility. But territory is there, it is contested, and it is meaningful, particularly because there are other regional actors one region over that lay competing claims to their neighbours. Discourse in Europe is struc-tured by the European Union and its ability, since the 1990s, to talk up regions as the constitutive particles of the continent. This talk is met by actors at all scales of European multi-level governance, especially in those regions that have felt traditionally alienated from their national states (the English north, the Italian north and south, the Spanish regions, etc.). But it is most effective in real institutional and policy terms in the interface of urban and regional modalities of governance. Lastly, in terms of technol-ogy, European unions enjoy a higher state of mobility and housing choice, and it is more unlikely than in Canada that modal choice alone, for exam-ple, will determine public and technocratic debates.

In the end, the lessons drawn from this book return to the questions raised by Mayer, Boudreau, and Hamel at the outset. What can be the possible democratic claims and processes through which these real existing forms of regionalism remain somewhat responsive to the people who live in them? We remain, as Margit Mayer in particular reminds us in her far-ranging comparative perspective on Europe and North America, in a globally mobilized world of comparable dynamics of large-scale change, while the local—and, we would emphasize, regional—differences remain of central importance in challenging, redefining, and perhaps ultimately changing the territories, talk, and technologies of real existing regionalisms on both sides of the Atlantic. The reconfigurations of state spaces and governance explored in this book are in many ways challenging the European and Canadian long history of state formalization processes. We end this book by turning our attention to the South, where a different history of state (in)formalization processes and a longer experience with flexible spatial and political arrangements may provide us with clues to understanding the current transformation of the transatlantic context.

References

Addie, J.-P. and R. Keil. 2015. "Real existing regionalism: The region between talk, territory and technology." *International Journal of Urban and Regional Research* 39(2), March: 407–17. DOI: 10.1111/1468-2427.12179.

Deas, I. and N. Headlam. 2015. "Boosterism, brokerage and uneasy bedfellows: Networked urban governance and the emergence of post-political orthodoxy." In R. Paddison and T. Hutton, eds., *Cities and economic change: Restructuring and dislocation in the global metropolis.* Thousand Oaks, CA: Sage.

Keil, R. and J.-P. Addie. 2015. "'It's not going to be suburban, it's going to be all urban': Assembling post-suburbia in the Toronto and Chicago regions." *International Journal of Urban and Regional Research* 39(5): 892–911.

Yiftachel, O. 2008. "Theoretical notes on 'gray cities': The coming of urban apartheid?" *Planning Theory* 8(4): 88–100.

Young, D. and R. Keil. 2014. "Locating the urban in-between: Tracking the urban politics of infrastructure in Toronto." *International Journal of Urban and Regional Research* 38(5), September: 1589–1608. DOI: 10.1111/1468-2427.12146.

Notes on Contributors

TERESA ABBRUZZESE is a Sessional Assistant Professor in the Urban Studies program in the Department of Social Science at York University. Her teaching and research interests weave together critical social and urban theory and cultural theory. Her interdisciplinary background has shaped her urban research projects to date, from examining carnival as a site of intersecting and conflicting translocal and transnational mobilities and identities in Southern Italy, to exploring the construction of place and identity in Bruce Springsteen's songwriting, and investigating equity-based regional planning movements in North America.

JEAN-PAUL ADDIE is a Marie Curie Research Fellow in the Department of Geography at University College London. His work interrogates the politics and production of urban infrastructure to address questions of mobility, governance, and social justice in an era of globalized urbanization. He has published research on neo-liberal urban policy, suburbanization, comparative metropolitan governance, and regional transportation, and, as principal investigator for the project "Situating the New Urban University," is currently examining the relationship between universities and city-regional urbanization.

AHMED ALLAHWALA is Associate Professor, Teaching Stream, in the Department of Human Geography at the University of Toronto Scarborough. His research focuses on social policy and social reproduction with a focus on youth, migration, and neighbourhood well-being. Ahmed also engages in pedagogically oriented research on place-based education and participatory action research. He has taught courses on welfare state analysis, city politics, urban planning, migration, and community-based research in both Canada and Germany.

ÈVE ARCAND received her M.Sc. in urban studies from Institut national de la recherche scientifique (Montreal, Canada) in 2013. She worked under the direction of Jean-Pierre Collin on metropolitan land-use public policies. Her interests include metropolitan governance, public administration, transportation, and urban planning. During her master's degree, she completed an internship at the University of Victoria that focused on transportation governance in the Vancouver area. She works for the City of Montreal in transportation planning policy.

BERND BELINA is Professor of Human Geography at the Department of Human Geography at Goethe University Frankfurt, Germany. His research interests include historico-geographical materialism, urban political geography, and critical criminology. He is the author of "Raum," a German-language introduction to Marxist theories of social space from 2013, and in recent years has published academic papers on austerity in Germany, governance of the Frankfurt region, racial profiling, crime mapping, and university architecture.

JULIE-ANNE BOUDREAU is Doctor of Urban Planning from the School of Public Policy and Social Research of the University of California at Los Angeles. Currently Professor at the Institut national de la recherche scientifique, Centre Urbanisation Culture Société (INRS-UCS) in Montreal, she held the Canada Research Chair in urbanity, insecurity, and political action from 2005 to 2015 and was editor of the *International Journal of Urban and Regional Research* from 2010 to 2015. Her most recent book is *Global Urban Politics: Informalisation of the State*, to be published by Polity Press in 2016.

EMMANUEL BRUNET-JAILLY is Jean Monnet Chair in European Urban and Border Region Policy and Director of the European Studies minor and of the European Union Centre for Excellence at the University of Victoria's School of Public Administration. He is a political scientist, specializing in comparative and urban politics. Prior to his appointment at UVic, he worked for the French public sector and was at the University of Western Ontario and at the University of Notre Dame from 2000 to 2001.

IAN GORDON is an Emeritus Professor of Human Geography at the London School of Economics and a member of the LSE London research group. His research interests include urban governance, migration and its impacts, spatial labour markets, agglomeration economies, density and constraint policies in metro regions, the relationship between segregation and inequality, comparative urban analysis, and (most recently) why central London has done so well since the financial crisis. He was a member of the Mayor's Outer London Commission from 2008 to 2016.

PIERRE HAMEL is Professor in the Department of Sociology at the Université de Montréal. He is also affiliated with CÉRIUM, an international studies centre at the same university. His focus as a researcher is on the democratization of urban policies and more generally city-regional development. He has previously published *Suburban Governance: A Global View* (edited with Roger Keil, University of Toronto Press, 2015). He is currently working on issues of suburbanism as a key feature of urban restructuring.

ALAN HARDING is Chief Economic Adviser to the Greater Manchester Combined Authority and a visiting Professor at the Manchester Institute of Innovation Research at the Alliance Business School, University of Manchester. He is responsible for developing and analyzing the evidence that underpins policy decisions on city-regional economic growth, public service reform, and devolution. Previously, he led research institutes and centres specializing in applied research on urban-regional development, policy, and governance at the Universities of Salford, Manchester, and Liverpool.

MICHAEL HARLOE was formerly Professor of Sociology at the University of Essex and then, until his retirement, Vice-Chancellor of the University of Salford. He now has visiting positions at the London School of Economics and Oxford. He was the Founder Editor of the *International Journal of Urban and Regional Research* and has published widely on housing and urban development. He is currently working on metropolitan government (with Ian Gordon) and on the genesis of radical urban research from the 1960s.

SUSANNE HEEG is Professor of Urban Geography at the Goethe-University in Frankfurt/Main. She teaches at the Institute of Human Geography. Her main research interests lie in factors and conditions that influence the production of the built environment in cities. This extends to the examination of the impact on cities of the deregulation of financial and real estate markets. In particular she is interested in calculative practices and the quantification of the built environment in order to transform the built environment into financial assets.

ROGER KEIL is York Research Chair in Global Sub/Urban Studies, Faculty of Environmental Studies, York University in Toronto. A former co-editor of the *International Journal of Urban and Regional Research* (2005–11) and founding Director of York's City Institute (2006–13), he researches global suburbanization, urban political ecology, and regional governance. He is the editor of *Suburban Constellations* (Jovis, 2013) and co-editor (with Pierre Hamel) of *Suburban Governance: A Global View* (University of Toronto Press, 2015).

STEFAN KIPFER teaches urbanization, politics, and planning in the Faculty of Environmental Studies at York University. He has published widely on city and country, space and time in Marxist and counter-colonial traditions, and urban politics in cities like Toronto, Paris, and Zurich. He was co-editor of *Space, Difference, Everyday Life: Reading Henri Lefebvre* (with Kanishka Goonewardena, Christian Schmid, and Richard Milgrom) and *Gramsci: Space, Nature, Politics* (with Mike Ekers, Gillian Hart, and Alex Loftus).

UTE LEHRER is an Associate Professor in the Faculty of Environmental Studies, York University, and a member of the CITY Institute. She has held academic positions at Brock University, SUNY Buffalo, and ETH Zurich, Switzerland. Lehrer is the Principal Investigator of a SSHRC-funded research project on identity constructions of municipalities within global regions, and the co-editor of a book on the suburban land question. She is writing a book on the condominium boom in Toronto.

CHRISTOPHER LEO, who holds a Ph.D. in Political Economy from the University of Toronto, has been researching, teaching, and writing, first about African politics and then urban politics. He has held faculty-level appointments for more than forty years at the University of Winnipeg, where he is currently Professor Emeritus, as well as the University of Manitoba and Queen's University. He is the author of numerous articles and two books. His research-based blog is available at christopherleo .com.

MARGIT MAYER is Senior Fellow at the Center for Metropolitan Studies in Berlin, after having worked as professor for comparative and North American politics at Freie Universität Berlin from 1987 to 2014. Her research focuses on comparative, urban, and social politics as well as social movements. She has published on contemporary urban politics, urban theory, state restructuring, and social movements, and has co-edited the books *Cities for People, Not for Profit, Neoliberal Urbanism and Its Contestations,* and *Urban Uprisings.*

BYRON MILLER's recent work focuses on the spatial constitution of social movements, urban governance and governmentality, and the politics of urban and regional sustainability. He is currently Associate Professor of Geography and Coordinator of the Urban Studies Program at the University of Calgary, where he teaches courses on urbanization and urban planning, urban social geography, urban politics and governance, globalization, and field courses on urban sustainability in Europe.

ANTOINE NOUBOUWO is Doctor in Urban Studies from the National Institute of Scientific Research of the University of Quebec. Currently coordinator of urban development projects in the planning department of the City of Gatineau, he is responsible for the design and implementation of urban development policies such as housing policy, the development of municipal programs, and the assessment of governance structures for project management. He is a member of the research laboratory Ville et espaces politiques (VESPA) of the National Institute of Scientific Research.

SIMON PARKER is Director of the School of Social and Political Sciences, Co-Director of the Centre for Urban Research (CURB), and Senior Lecturer in Politics at the University of York, UK. His research focuses on urban politics and urban political economy and on forcibly displaced persons, refugees, and migrants. Recent books include *Urban Theory and the Urban Experience: Encountering the City*, 2nd ed. (Routledge, 2015), and *Cities, Politics and Power* (Routledge, 2011).

CHRISTOPH SIEGL is a human geographer and urban researcher based in Frankfurt, Germany. He is co-founder and head of research at the independent Open Urban Institute (OUI). His working focus is on the border of academics and culture. Christoph's research interests include public spaces, regional development, urban culture, and most recently spaces of transit/flow and the very special topic of twin towns and sister cities.

MARIONA TOMÀS is an associate professor in Political Science at the University of Barcelona. Her fields of interest are metropolitan governance and urban politics. She has published articles in the *International Journal of Urban and Regional Research*, *Urban Studies*, and the *Journal of Urban Affairs*, among others. She received the Quebec National Assembly 2013 Political Book Prize for her study of metropolitan reforms in Montreal (2013) and the Gold Academic Medal of the General Governor of Canada for her Ph.D. in Urban Studies (2008).

MARK WHITEHEAD is a Professor of Human Geography at Aberyst-wyth University. His early research focused on the changing forms of urban policy under the New Labour government in the UK. His subsequent work has encompassed aspects of political and environmental studies with a particular concern for the changing nature of state power. Mark has written widely on issues of urban sustainability and was an Associate and Managing Editor of the journal *Environmental Values*. His most recent work is an exploration of the nature of neo-liberal-oriented urban adaptation strategies. In 2014 Mark published his latest book, which explored the geographical implications of living in the Anthropocene.

Index

provincial policies, 145, 148; reforming policy regimes, 149–50; Regent Park, 160–62, 161f; repair backlog, 155, 159; sale of housing, 150–51; social mixing, 160–61; socioeconomic inequalities, 157–58; sustainability neglect, 164–65; tower neighbourhoods, 106, 158–63, 166; vulnerable groups, 162–63; wait lists, 154, 157
Toronto, neo-liberalism: about, 147–52; affordable housing, 144–45, 149–52, 154–56, 166–67; approach to governance (four Rs), 145; internalized globalization, 117–18; privatization, 144–45, 152, 166, 167n1; rearranging institutional provisions and jurisdictional powers, 147–48; reconfiguring state and society relations, 147; redefining citizens as consumers, 147, 152; reforming policy regimes, 147, 149–50
Toronto, provincial and federal relations: competition for federal resources, 111; COSGP (Central Ontario Smart Growth Panel), 125–26; history of, 109; lack of housing and transportation strategy, 111, 143–44, 153, 217; levels of government, 101, 110–11; Metrolinx board conflicts, 130–34; province as de facto regional government, 102, 110–11, 117; provincial planning (GTSB), 125–27, 138n1. See also Ontario; Places to Grow plan (Ontario)
Toronto, internalized globalization: about, 101–3, 116–18; data issues, 112; discourse, 107–8, 117; entrenched divisions (416/905 divide), 101–2, 109, 117; global freight transportation, 115, 134; housing, 103, 106, 117–18; institutions as technologies of power, 104, 112–13; neo-liberalism, 117–18; technologies, 112–18; territory, 108–11; transportation, 103, 106, 108–9, 117–18
Toronto, transportation: about, 136–37, 378–79; to airport, 131–32; autos, 116, 117; buses (BRT), 131–32, 135; centre/periphery relations, 116, 135; as conduit of regional governance, 113–14, 131; economic competitiveness, 110, 156–57, 167n7; fare collections,

115, 132–33, 138n5; globalization, 115, 135–36, 135f; internalized globalization, 108–9; light rail transit (LRT), 131; regional integration and scale, 108–9, 115–16; social equity, 137; Toronto Transit Commission (TTC), 49, 115–16, 131–33; transit activism, 49; Transit City plan, 116, 131–32, 135. See also transportation
Toronto, transportation, Metrolinx and GTHA: about, 105, 114, 123–24, 128map, 136–37; to airports, 131–32; Big Move plan, 116, 118, 128–32, 128map, 134, 137; board governance, 114–15, 127, 130–34, 138n3, 138n6; fare collections, 132–33, 138n5; functional "regional spaces" vs. political "spaces of regionalism," 124–28, 136–37; GO Transit, 125–27, 135; Greater Toronto and Hamilton Area (GTHA), 128–30, 128map, 129f, 133, 136–37; history of, 126–30; local conflicts, 116, 130–32; management associations, 134; mandate, 114, 126, 127, 134; mobility hubs, 128–30, 128f, 129f, 134, 138n4; network of existing lines, 116, 134; Places to Grow plan, 126, 128, 138n4; provincial agency, 114–15, 117, 133–37; RTP (regional transportation plan), 129–30, 134; spatial imaginary, 128–30, 129f; TTC services, 115, 133; voluntary coordination, 127–28. See also Places to Grow plan (Ontario)
Tory, John, 116, 144, 150–52, 167n6
transnationalism and theory, 37
transportation: about, 121–24; collective actors on issues, 5–6; as conduit of regional governance, 113–14, 121; congestion charging (UK), 366; functional "regional spaces" vs. political "spaces of regionalism," 5, 124–27, 327, 332; as housing issue, 113, 115, 158, 189; in-between cities, 198–99; internalized globalization, 103, 106, 108–9, 117–18; neo-liberalism, 122–23; protests against expansions, 52; relationality/territoriality dialectic, 123; rescaling of, 122; scholarship on, 121–23. See also Ontario, southern, transportation; Paris, transportation;

www.ingramcontent.com/pod-product-compliance
Lightning Source LLC
Chambersburg PA
CBHW060019030426
42334CB00019B/2108